Economies of Early Modern Drama

Economies of Early Modern Drama

Shakespeare, Jonson, and Middleton

ANNE ENDERWITZ

Great Clarendon Street, Oxford, OX2 6DP,
United Kingdom

Oxford University Press is a department of the University of Oxford.
It furthers the University's objective of excellence in research, scholarship,
and education by publishing worldwide. Oxford is a registered trade mark of
Oxford University Press in the UK and in certain other countries

© Anne Enderwitz 2023

The moral rights of the author have been asserted

All rights reserved. No part of this publication may be reproduced, stored in
a retrieval system, or transmitted, in any form or by any means, without the
prior permission in writing of Oxford University Press, or as expressly permitted
by law, by licence or under terms agreed with the appropriate reprographics
rights organization. Enquiries concerning reproduction outside the scope of the
above should be sent to the Rights Department, Oxford University Press, at the
address above

You must not circulate this work in any other form
and you must impose this same condition on any acquirer

Published in the United States of America by Oxford University Press
198 Madison Avenue, New York, NY 10016, United States of America

British Library Cataloguing in Publication Data
Data available

Library of Congress Control Number: 2023931423

ISBN 978-0-19-286681-3

DOI: 10.1093/oso/9780192866813.001.0001

Printed and bound in the UK by
Clays Ltd, Elcograf S.p.A.

Links to third party websites are provided by Oxford in good faith and
for information only. Oxford disclaims any responsibility for the materials
contained in any third party website referenced in this work.

Contents

Acknowledgements vii
A Note on Transcription ix

Introduction 1
  Early Modern Commercial Theatre 2
  Theatre and Economics 6
  Oeconomy and Commerce 8
  The Revaluation of Interest 12
  'Wisdom of Business', or the Transformation of Prudence 16
  Generic Cross-Pollination 20
  The Book 22

1. Household Management and Commerce in Early Modern England 24
  Introduction 24
  The Household in Classical and Early Modern Writings 27
    Xenophon's *Oeconomicus* 31
    The Aristotelian *Oikos* 34
    The Early Modern *Oikos* 36
    Tropical Exchanges and the Family as 'First Society' 37
    The Power Axis of Household Government: Marriage 42
    Household Guardian or 'Perpetuall Enemie' 44
  Early Modern Commerce 47
    Mercantile Writings 53
    Unnatural Acquisition: Aristotle and Trade 57
    Justice in Exchange 59
    Trade as Godly Calling and the Limits of Sufficiency 61
    Legitimate Profit 66
    Mercantilist and Bullionist Writers 69
    Culture of Credit 73
  Conclusion 77

2. Oeconomy in *A Chaste Maid in Cheapside* and *Macbeth* 79
  Introduction 79
  A Chaste Maid in Cheapside: The *Oikos* in a Marketplace of Desires 83
    Liminal Domestic Spaces 85
    Sexuality as Commodity 89
    The Logic of the Marketplace 96
  Household Politics and Private Interests in *Macbeth* 98
    The Household as Dramatic Subject 101

       Household Space   103
       The Female Body and Household Space   109
       From Ethics to Efficiency in the Service of Private Interest   113
       Private Interests and the Motivating Force of Passion   116
       The Politics of Exchange   119
  Conclusion   123

3. Mercantile Agency and Service in *Othello* and *The Alchemist*   128
  Introduction   128
  The Household as 'Venture Tripartite': 'Wisdom of Business'
    in *The Alchemist*   132
       The Prudent Captain   136
       Persuasion through Amplification   143
       The Alchemical Trope   147
  'Shows of Service' and Mercantile Agency in *Othello*   151
       Transnational Travel and Social Mobility   155
       'Wisdom of Business': Skills and Strategies   159
       Debasement: Credit and Value   162
       Jealousy and Envy as Affective Coordinates of a Mobile
         Society   169
  Conclusion   173

4. Asynchronous Exchanges in *Volpone* and *Timon of Athens*   176
  Introduction   176
  Asynchronous Exchange and Accumulation in *Volpone*   179
       The Temporality of the Gift   181
       Strategic Delay: The Temporality and Intentionality of the
         Promise   183
       Delay as Pleasure Principle   188
       Mastery and Self-Aggrandizement   191
       Delay and Dilation: Principles of Credit and Plot   196
  Timon of Athens: Competing Paradigms of Exchange   201
       The Gift as Investment   202
       The Moral Economy of the Gift   206
       Futurity and the Failure of the Promise   212
       Friendship and Fortune   215
       Exploring the Interval: Delay and Dilation as Plot Devices   219
  Conclusion   222

Conclusion   226
  Oeconomy and Commerce   228
  The Discontents of Social Mobility   232
  The 'Architecture of Fortune' and the Future   234

Works Cited   238
Index   261

Acknowledgements

The first draft of this book came into the world as an habilitation thesis, written on a postdoctoral scholarship awarded by the Freie Universität Berlin (FU Berlin) and funded by the Excellence Initiative of the German Research Foundation. Some of the ideas that shaped this book were also discussed in the following German-language papers that I wrote between 2017 and 2020: 'Humanistische Bildung und ökonomisches Kalkül in Middleton's *A Chaste Maid in Cheapside*', 'Ökonomie und politisches Kalkül: *Macbeth* und die Reformation', 'Eifersucht und Oeconomia im englischen Theater der Frühen Neuzeit', and '"So good that he is good for nothing": Francis Bacons Umwertung der Werte'.

During the years in which this book took shape, the Friedrich Schlegel Graduate School provided me with an intellectual home, and the school's board and administration supported my research with great professionalism and friendliness. Since the first draft, the book has changed shape multiple times, but its central interests and arguments have remained intact, as has the debt of gratitude that I owe to the institutions that supported my work and the many readers who offered their insights.

I am very grateful to Claudia Olk, who supported this project from the start, helped me to secure the time and money that I needed to write it, and guided me through the intricate and highly formalized process of the habilitation. Her trust in my abilities helped me to find my way in academia. I also want to thank the other reviewers and members of the habilitation committee, among them Jean Howard, Michael Gamper, Joachim Küpper, Sabine Schülting, and Roland Weidle, as well as Chanah Kempin and Jonas Cantarella.

I am particularly grateful to Jean Howard, who generously invited me to Columbia University as a guest researcher and from whose knowledge of early modern theatre and socio-economic relations I benefitted tremendously. This book has profited more than I can say from Jean's intellectual guidance and encouragement. My thanks go also to Julie Crawford and Alan Stewart, who took the time to read and offer feedback on an early draft of the *Othello* chapter that I presented at Columbia's early modern research seminar. I deeply appreciate the continued support of Sabine Schülting, André Otto, and Andreas Mahler, who are always available to discuss questions and problems that come up in the course of my research. I also want to thank my friends and former colleagues Leonie Achtnich, Marlene Dirschauer, Heike Winkel, and Marlies Zwickl. Thanks to them, working and teaching at the Peter Szondi-Institut of comparative literature at the Freie Universität was just so much fun.

Ellie Collins and Karen Raith at OUP were kind enough to accept this manuscript, and their encouraging words, patience, and reliability ensured a smooth and rewarding editorial process. My profound gratitude also goes to my readers at OUP. Their feedback was very encouraging and helped me to gain a deeper understanding of what this book wants to achieve. A very special thanks goes to Madeleine LaRue, who read more drafts of this manuscript than anyone else. The book gained immensely from her insightful comments and subtle corrections. I also want to thank my student assistants, Anna Schober and Zoe Steinbrenner, for double-checking the many quotations that feature in this book, and my colleague Markus Asper for explaining the philological intricacies of ancient Greek terms to me. Any mistakes are, of course, my own.

A big thank you goes to my lifelong friends who never doubted that I could write this book: Jule, Kruse, Simone, and Ralf. And the biggest thank you goes to my family: to Jan for having my back in all these years and for countless conversations about life, economics, academic politics, and the future—I wouldn't have wanted to do this without you; to Simon and Jakob for being themselves and for giving me so much joy; to my sisters for being there; and to my parents for raising me to stand on my own two feet.

A Note on Transcription

In citing early modern handbooks and treatises, I opt for what Sarah Werner calls a 'semi-diplomatic transcription' (82) that preserves the appearance of early modern spelling without reproducing it perfectly. It does not attempt to reproduce the 'long s', for instance, but it does retain the alternate graphic forms 'u' and 'v' and 'i' and 'j'. Rather than attempting to reproduce superscript letters, I use italics to indicate abbreviations in the original. I have standardized the capitalization of early modern titles and rendered them in italics throughout. This compromise—reproducing some features while dismissing others—is not unproblematic, but it ensures legibility while affording a sense of early modern spelling practices. Even more importantly, it is a reminder of the historical difference of early modern writing.

Introduction

This book explores how early modern theatre experimented with and made sense of the nascent commercial society in England. Its focus is on socio-economic praxis: on how plays stage the uses and limits of practical rationality in household management and commerce. Early modern plays appear decidedly less interested in ethical behaviour than in efficient and effective action: they explore the ambiguous status of private interest as a key motive of socio-economic action and examine the emergence of a practical expertise that enables entrepreneurial characters to make their fortune. Allied to Machiavellian *virtù*, 'the skill and courage by which men are enabled to dominate events and fortune' (Pocock 92), this 'wisdom of business', as Francis Bacon would say, plays out in the changeable field of socio-economic interactions and transactions.[1]

In the theatre, the household serves as the main setting for staging economic motives and transactions. This is no coincidence: economy comes from the ancient Greek *oikonomia*, 'household management'. Classical works on the agrarian household, which prioritized production and use over exchange, constituted an important point of reference for the early modern writers who discussed household management as *oeconomy* or *oeconomie*.[2] Yet their own husbandry manuals and sermons subtly altered ancient ideas of the household and its management, adapting them to the emergent commercial society and the interests of the 'middling sort'.[3] At the same time as oeconomy experienced renewed interest as a potentially profitable occupation, mercantile writers sought to establish the legitimacy of trade and of material profit. My book traces socio-economic action on the early modern stage in the context of such oeconomic and mercantile writings. Around 1600, the revaluation of profit and practical wisdom was in full swing,

---

[1] In Victoria Kahn's terms, Machiavellian *virtù* describes the 'faculty of practical reasoning and action that is not constrained by ethical norms' (9). Bacon's notion of 'Wisedom of Businesse' (*The Advancement of Learning*, 157) is discussed in greater detail below.

[2] In the following, 'oeconomy' and 'oeconomic' will be used specifically to address those practices and relations that form part of household management, including questions of succession and inheritance, the production and acquisition of goods, domestic service, and family life. In contrast, 'economic' will be used to refer more broadly to those economic practices, objects, and theories that relate to actions and transactions in both household and marketplace and that extend to trade, credit, and different forms of labour.

[3] Wendy Wall describes '*oeconomia*' as 'newly popular with the "middling sort" of the population' (5). See Hillary Eklund, 100–101, on the moral economy of husbandry and the discourse of improvement in agriculture. For the broader picture, see also Joan Thirsk, *The Agrarian History of England and Wales*, and Andrew McRae, *God Speed the Plough*.

with theatre playing a starring role in exploring the incompatibility of a calculus of profit maximization with the existing moral economy centred on subsistence, moderation, and the common good.

Early Modern Commercial Theatre

As a medium that emerged in the late sixteenth century together with the first English global trading companies, and right in the middle of the vibrant trade metropolis London, commercial theatre was singularly poised to explore changing economic practices and values. Andrew Gurr identifies 1567, the year the Red Lion playhouse was built, as a 'watershed' for the 'market for popular plays' (*Playgoing* 10). In 1576, the Theatre was built, followed in quick succession by the Curtain (1577), the Rose (1587), the Swan (1595), the Globe (1599), the Fortune (1600), and a few others.[4] Erected in a vibrant commercial environment and built exclusively for the purpose of playacting, theatres were part and parcel of the larger commercial transformation of English society.[5] Actors' troupes sought patronage, but supported themselves by selling their products to an audience who paid to be entertained. Playhouses were financed on bonds (Bailey 4), and the companies were organized around 'a core of shareholders and decision-makers' with 'a periphery of hired hands' (Gurr, *The Shakespearean Stage* 40). They were frequently backed 'by a theatre- and property-owning impresario who supplied ready cash in return for a share of the takings' (Gurr, *The Shakespearean Stage* 40).[6] Jean Howard suggests that the need to interest and entertain a paying audience encouraged theatre companies to explore a new range of themes that were relevant to their audiences.[7] As she puts it, 'the commercial theatre depended on a public to approve its craft and buy its products' (*Theater of a City* 2). In a similar vein, Gurr describes the commercialization of theatre in distinct playhouses as 'massive stimulus to the production of new plays' (*Playgoing* 11). That many of these new plays

---

[4] The new century saw the building of the Boar's Head (1601), the Red Bull (1604), and the Hope (1614) (Gurr, *Playgoing*, chapter 1).

[5] According to Gurr, only the Hope 'was designed from the start as a dual-purpose arena for playing and for bull- and bear-baiting, with a stage that could be removed when the bears needed the yard' (*The Shakespearean Stage* 149).

[6] The entrepreneurial character of theatre as a commercial organization becomes even more obvious when we consider that certain actors—among them Shakespeare himself—held not just a share in the company, but acquired 'housekeeper share[s]' as well, and thus cofinanced the building of the Globe (Gurr, *The Shakespearean Stage* 63). Gurr points out that this proved to be Shakespeare's 'most profitable investment' (63).

[7] Howard emphasizes the topicality of early modern theatre: 'At the theater Londoners encountered fictions that directly addressed the conditions of social change and dislocation occurring around them ... this is true, I would suggest, for each of the popular stage genres that flourished over this vibrant sixty-year period' (*Theater of a City* 2). For a detailed discussion of the social composition of the audience, see Gurr, *Playgoing* 50–80. The audience at the public playhouses included nobles, gentry, citizens and citizens' wives, apprentices and artisans, Inns of Court students, foreign visitors and ambassadors, cutpurses, and whores.

focused on the desire for material wealth and social advancement is hardly an accident. The newly-built playhouses were situated in London, where the effects of global trade were visible in the ostentatious display of wealth and exotic goods, and where the dream of commercial success and of rising in the world must have been a pervasive social fantasy. Furthermore, the new commercial theatre was intimately acquainted with the need to create saleable fictions. By erecting new buildings and organizing playing companies as shareholding companies, theatre participated in credit networks and used a commercial form of organization.[8] It was ideally positioned to materialize and mediate socio-economic actions and the hopes and fears that accompany them.

Theatre was not only a commercial institution, but also an accessible medium with popular appeal. Despite their peripheral locations just outside the city's jurisdiction, the sheer number of playhouses must have ensured that they were very present in the public imagination. If one includes the hall playhouses, '[t]here was a playhouse of some kind within two miles of nearly every Londoner' (Gurr, *Playgoing* 35).[9] Janet Hill points out that the Theatre and Curtain on their own drew 'enough people to make Philip Stubbes complain in 1583 that Londoners went to "Theatres and curtains" while "the church of God shall be bare and empty"' (110). Stubbes's complaint was, of course, highly polemical, but by the turn of the seventeenth century, the number of seats available throughout London was impressively high. Scholars estimate that the Globe alone may have accommodated about 3,000 people on any given night, and a similar calculation exists for the Swan (Gurr, *Playgoing* 21–22).[10] Even if these numbers may be somewhat exaggerated, theatre was certainly the leading popular forum for representing socio-economic concerns to a diverse audience with varying degrees of literacy. Its broad popular appeal derived from a combination of verbal art and, as Evelyn Tribble recently highlighted, physical skills involving dancing and 'athletic leaps and capers' (182), 'clowning' (183), and 'sword-and-buckler fights' (181). In an ecology of various forms of popular entertainment, theatre competed with 'fencing matches, acrobatic displays, fireworks, [and] bear-baiting' (Hunter 249). Theatre's investment in these skills surely helped to broaden its reach.

The historical significance of theatre as a popular medium is proffered by its structural function. According to Bruno Latour, theatre is one of the means by which a community can 'represent itself publicly to the public, to render visible

---

[8] David J. Baker sketches the theatrical enterprise of Shakespeare and his acting company in his preface to *On Demand: Writing for the Market in Early Modern England* xiii–xiv.
[9] See Steven Mullaney: 'By the turn of the century, when the Fortune completed the scene, the city was ringed with playhouses posted strategically just outside its jurisdiction' (*The Place of the Stage* 27; see also Janet Hill, *Stages and Playgoers* 110).
[10] See also John Orrell, *The Quest for Shakespeare's Globe* 137, and Hill, *Stages and Playgoers* 111. Gurr also draws attention to the sheer quantity of playhouse visits: 'Over the years between the 1560s, when the first purpose-built playhouses were established, and 1642, when all playhouses were closed, well over fifty million visits were made to playhouses' (*Playgoing* 4).

what it is and what it wants' (244).[11] This is due to its medial structure, which implies not just impersonation or performance, but an audience that observes and reflects on theatre's doubling of culture.[12] By putting socio-economic actions and relations on display, early modern theatre allowed playgoers to relate to 'the conditions of social change and dislocations occurring around them' (Howard, *Theater of a City* 2). This is not to say that its cultural work consisted simply in mimetic representation: if theatre held up a mirror to Elizabethan and Jacobean society, it was, as Laura Kolb writes, 'something of a funhouse mirror—showing hyperbolic, amplified, extreme versions of persons and relationships that practical texts treat as utterly mundane' (20). She suggests that 'dramatic hyperbole operates as an analytic tool', defamiliarizing 'the artifice of everyday life' (20). Theatrical exaggeration also expands the limits of what appears possible, as Howard points out: by testing and toying with what might be, plays broadened the scope of what was socially conceivable.[13] Jean-Christophe Agnew aptly describes early modern theatre as 'an experimental medium' (11), and even 'a laboratory of and for the new social relations of agricultural and commercial capitalism' (xi).[14] In his view, theatre was 'constitutive' in that it did not simply 'reflect relations occurring elsewhere [but] modeled and in important respects materialized those relations' (xi).

Early modern theatre's ability to question certainties, to presciently explore emergent values and paradigms, and to model social relations extends to economic processes.[15] Long before Adam Smith's milestone work *The Wealth of Nations* (first published in 1776) appeared, early modern theatre's preoccupation with social climbers and entrepreneurial characters suggests the pervasive status of private interest as the driving force of economic enterprise. At the same time, theatre's heightened attention to instrumental reason and the parameters of economic success suggests a Machiavellian turn in the sphere of business transactions: a decentring of ethics and an investment in efficient and effective action.

---

[11] See also Bradley D. Ryner's discussion of Latour (6).

[12] Eric Bentley famously defined theatre as follows: 'The theatrical situation, reduced to a minimum, is that A impersonates B while C looks on' (150). Tom Stern points out that 'impersonation' may not be a strict requirement. He contrasts Bentley's definition with Peter Brook's: 'I can take any empty space and call it a bare stage. A man walks across this empty space whilst someone else is watching him, and that is all that is needed for an act of theatre to be engaged' (4). Erika Fischer-Lichte emphasizes that it is through the collective observation of a doubling of cultural signs that theatre emerges as 'act of cultural self-representation and self-reflection' (19, my translation).

[13] In *Theater of a City*, Howard suggests that theatre 'expand[s] social subjects' imaginative parameters' (114).

[14] Judith Weil also emphasizes the experimental angle of theatre when she maintains that 'Aristotle's emphasis on constructing unpredictable plots' gave playwrights license 'to play seriously with customs and cultures, testing them through situations which could indeed occur' (15).

[15] Robert Weimann underlined the social significance of Elizabethan theatre as a space in which certainties and hierarchies could be questioned, even if 'the ideas of the new age (such as individualism and profit-orientation) were not yet perceived as a necessary alternative' (*Shakespeare und die Macht der Mimesis* 173, my translation).

To argue that early modern theatre broadened the scope of social possibility is to accord it a complex cultural role that is not reducible to a simple critique of commercialization. In *Theater of a City*, Howard reflects on the socio-cultural labour which theatre 'unconsciously but robustly and imaginatively performed in accommodating Londoners of all stripes to the somewhat bewildering world in which they were living' (14). Agnew makes a similar point about theatre's work of 'sociocultural accommodation'.[16] 'Accommodation' expresses a process of habituation to a new order, even if this new order is still uncertain and lacks coherence (Mahler, 'Welt Modell Theater' 3). In my readings of individual plays, critique and accommodation coincide to create ambiguous representations of socio-economic actions and transactions. City comedies are a case in point. Ever since Brian Gibbons identified a critical impetus in city comedy's proto-realist mode, it has become a commonplace that city comedies expose city vices.[17] Although not wrong, this commonplace falls short of capturing the ambiguity and indeterminacy of many comedies. The pervasive preoccupation with private interest is not intrinsically censorious; it has a normalizing effect that confirms Howard's and Agnew's point about the cultural work of accommodation:[18] if theatre represents a social world in which everyone pursues wealth for their own benefit, this may just be what humans do. City comedy's fascination with strategic and self-interested action recognizes a new commercial reality and confronts early modern playgoers with a changing socio-economic landscape that rewards efficient and timely action and professional skills, while also demanding an adjustment of values. By linking extreme forms of self-interested action with skilled and strategic behaviour, early modern plays combine in uneasy duality a critique of excessive accumulation with the naturalizing work of accommodation to a world which thrived on profit and in which men could rise and make their fortune through their wits and skills. On the London stages, prudence loses its ethical content and emerges as a pragmatic and even instrumental faculty that allows people to shape their fortune in the face of contingent events.

---

[16] Agnew describes theatre in terms of forging 'a broader sociocultural accommodation with an expansive system of capital formation and commodity exchange' (xi). Jill Phillips Ingram stresses the Puritan contribution to 'speed[ing] the accommodation of self-interest as a virtue rather than as vice' (3).

[17] As Gibbons puts it: 'the critical realist writer is primarily concerned to shape character and incident in order to bring alive the underlying social and moral issues *through* the specific and local experience' (17).

[18] I use 'normalizing' here in the modern quantifiable sense of the normal as the average. In a recent essay, Elizabeth Hanson points out that 'normal' had a prescriptive meaning in early modern England: 'a "normall patterne" is one that *should be* followed, not one that usually is' ('Normal School' 69). It is only in the nineteenth century that 'normal' became prescriptive and acquired a quantitative meaning. Hanson perceives a 'proleptic' dimension in Shakespearean comedy, an 'apprehension of normalcy in a more modern, quantitatively informed sense' (72).

Theatre and Economics

Given that early modern literary and cultural studies have been shaped by various historicizing movements, it appears evident that our readings of plays become richer when we understand the economic problems and values that they negotiate. The claim that the study of drama, in its turn, illuminates social structures or even everyday life may be slightly more contentious.[19] Yet early modern plays certainly help us to understand how socio-economic changes were imagined, how contemporaries made sense of them, and what they perceived as problematic. To my mind, theatre complements and enriches our understanding of early modern economics considerably. First, the astonishingly diverse material offered by early modern plays complicates the picture that emerges from oeconomic and mercantile writings. Practical writings of the time, whether concerned with the household or the market, come in a prescriptive and moralizing form that maps ideal behaviour and offers only limited insight into actual practices. Theatrical representations of socio-economic actions provide a necessary corrective to the virtuous behaviour depicted in advice and conduct literature, not because plays are more committed to an accurate representation of social reality, but because theatre derives dramatic tension from the very conflicts, problems, and contradictions that prescriptive literature attempts to circumvent or smooth over.[20] While the latter depicts ideal behaviour, the former tests the outer limits of socio-economic action and materializes emergent social possibilities. To borrow a phrase from Bradley D. Ryner, in their different ways, 'both plays and treatises are equally able to intelligently illuminate socio-economic conditions' (2).

Furthermore, drama provides a valuable resource for exploring the forms, logics, and limits of socio-economic practices and their affective impact at a time when economic theorizing was still rare. By articulating 'human hopes and fears' (Leinwand, *The City Staged* 3), it enriches historical facts with an affective and experiential dimension. With its interest in extreme actions and the passions that motivate them, theatre offers a complex picture of socio-economic experience. If social historians measure increased social mobility in numbers, drama enacts the affective framework that comes with new possibilities of social advancement. And while the risks of entrepreneurial projects can be calculated, drama gives us an idea of the thrills and exhilaration that were associated with commercial enterprise. Theatre's interest in insubstantial promises and hopes, in risk management, acquisition, and fear of dispossession reveals circulation as a risky

---

[19] Weil lays out reasons for historians' 'professional caution' in using creative literature as a source (14).
[20] See also Kolb, who makes a similar argument about credit in practical literature and dramatic works: in contrast to practical works that 'present credit culture as navigable', 'dramatic works zoom in on credit culture's conflicting demands, making its impasses and contradictions the ground for tragic and comic actions' (20).

and exhilarating process, driven by futile, never-to-be satisfied desires. Through different characters and their actions, superimposed layers of meaning and unresolvable ambiguities, drama articulates conflicting value systems and logics of economic action.[21] A combined reading of oeconomic and mercantile writings and plays offers a fuller, albeit more contradictory picture that illuminates a society in transition and allows for studying concrete practices, scenes, and discourses without having to subsume all social action under a totalizing economic metaphor.[22]

Oeconomic and mercantile discourses share with theatre a keen interest in how to manage particular circumstances and events. Advice literature is largely concerned with action: with what should or should not be done, when to do it, and how: what to plant in May, how to write a business letter, how not to waste money, how to chastise negligent servants, how to appear an honest man, and whom to trust. Whether oeconomic or mercantile, homiletic or practical, early modern advice literature seeks to teach men (and sometimes women) how to navigate the risks and opportunities of a changeable world of socio-economic actions and transactions. Early modern plays focus similarly on actions and interactions in a shifting field of contingent circumstances. But action is not just at the centre of practical oeconomic and mercantile literature; poetologically speaking, it is also constitutive of drama. According to Aristotle, theatre is foremost concerned with 'actions' and 'agents' (*Poetics* 2, 1448a1).[23] It is through the performance of concrete actions that early modern plays reflect on the desire for social advancement and material gain, and showcase the skills that are needed to make one's fortune in an unpredictable world 'in which men pursue their own ends without regard to any structure of law' (Pocock 165). There is, however, an important difference between practical advice literature and early modern plays. The practical literature of the time performs a balancing act: both mercantile works and husbandry manuals promote efficient and profitable action while relying heavily on a rhetoric of virtue. As noted earlier, theatre is less invested in reconciliation,

---

[21] Margot Heinemann emphasizes the contradictions and ambiguities that characterize theatrical representation in the early modern age as a transition period: 'If we understand this as a period "between two worlds", we shall be less concerned to see all the plays as coherent embodiments of dominant attitudes in the society, or alternatively of subversive ones. We shall rather note the "doubleness", the irreducible contradictions within outlooks and codes, which fascinated dramatists and audiences the more because they were problematic, newsworthy, and not easily resolved' ('Political Drama' 162).
[22] Christopher Pye points out that 'economic description seems to lend itself to a generalized metaphorics of speculation and exchange', which then offers a totalizing account of social relations that maps all social life in economic coordinates ('The Theater' 502). He is, of course, commenting on New Historicism and Stephen Greenblatt's use of economic metaphors as in the well-known phrase of the 'circulation of social energy' (Greenblatt, *Shakespearean Negotiations: The Circulation of Social Energy*). Theodore B. Leinwand remarks in a similar vein: 'words like "exchange," "commodity," "circulation"—especially "market"—function largely as metaphors in such arguments. They serve as tacit markers of structures and practices that we acknowledge but that we can neither feel nor locate with much precision' (*Theatre* 5). I share Pye's and Leinwand's reservations about a totalizing account of the social in economic terms.
[23] See also Weil, who reminds her readers that 'Dramas "imitate men doing"' (15).

instead drawing attention to the tensions and contradictions that arise from competing economic models.

In *Performing Economic Thought*, Ryner argues persuasively that theatre contributed to the production of economic knowledge: 'the stage offered a space for conceptualising different economic models while fully acknowledging—even emphasising—that these models were fictional constructions' (5).[24] He also contends that playwrights 'invited audiences to actively interrogate conflicting models of their common world' (6). It is precisely in exploring conflicting models and the tensions between them that plays open up different ways of understanding socio-economic action. Diverse representations have a denaturalizing effect, because the very possibility of difference highlights the constructedness of each individual model. Consequently, Ryner argues that by representing competing economic models, theatre challenges the status of 'utility maximisation' as an anthropological constant.[25] Part of this book's interest lies in historicizing profit maximization as a rational motive. Discourses and plays around 1600 afford a glimpse of the emergence of private interest as a pervasive and half-legitimate motive that is often coequal with material gain.[26] More radically than the practical literature, theatre represents this emergence in conflictual terms, as a clash with and decentring of the classical model of oeconomy with its emphasis on use, sufficiency, and the common good.

Oeconomy and Commerce

In order to do justice to the diverse ways in which plays examine economic actions and assumptions, this book interrogates dramatic explorations of economic problems from within an early modern discursive framework. Rather than focusing on either the household or the market, it approaches oeconomy and commerce as the intersecting concerns they are both on the stage and in discourses of the time. Its interest lies in where and how commercial principles and family matters intersect,

---

[24] Ryner quotes Michel Serres to make the point that 'literature itself is already able to theorise the world' (3).

[25] Ryner uses Latour to argue that if there is no sense that facts are made and models constructed, 'a *natural* determinism' is inscribed into the 'heart of the *social* system': 'When *homo economicus* is accepted as an objective description of the human, rather than as a necessarily reductive model applicable only to specific historico-cultural situations, the social relations that encourage self-interested profit-seeking take on an aura of immutability' (Ryner 5). Agnew discusses the naturalizing work of political economy, which obscures a historical scene of emergence 'by implanting a trucking and bartering instinct in the individual' (4–5). It thereby rationalizes and naturalizes a socio-economic transformation that constituted in fact 'a radical disruption and restructuration of needs and their mode of gratification via the market' (Agnew 5). Adam Smith famously described 'a certain propensity in human nature', namely 'the propensity to truck, barter, and exchange one thing for another' (25).

[26] See Ingram's preface to her book *Idioms of Self-Interest* for an analysis of 'competing vocabularies' of interest that either condemned 'purely personal gain' (2) or 'defended self-interest in the name of commercial growth' (3).

how monetary value becomes a model for assessing personal worth, how mercantile agency changes ideas of domestic service, and where credit intersects with friendship and the household with the market.[27]

Around 1600, the term 'economy' was still used in its classical sense, which derives from ancient Greek *oikos* ('house') and *nomos* ('managing'): *oikonomia* is the art of estate or household management.[28] Marc Shell enriches the meaning of oeconomy further by distinguishing the aspect of 'conventions (*nomoi*)', and the task of 'distribution (*nemesis*)' (89). By including the meaning of distribution in his etymological account, Shell highlights the difference between Aristotelian household management and profit-orientated chrematistics: where the former distributes—that is, uses and stores—what it has produced and acquires only necessaries, the latter is orientated towards acquisition for the sake of wealth. In the *Politics*, Aristotle defined *oikonomikē* as the art of using 'household stores' in a proper way, while *khrēmatistikē*, in contrast, is 'the art of getting wealth' (*Pol.* I.8, 1256a10–12). Aristotle distinguishes the two explicitly: 'the art of household management is not identical with the art of getting wealth, for the one uses the material which the other provides' (*Pol.* I.8, 1256a10–12). Chrematistics is ethically problematic if it is not subordinate to household management—i.e., limited by the household's needs—but pursues wealth for its own sake. In this case, instead of being a means to a higher end, money becomes an end in itself (Shell 91–92), prompting a desire for unending accumulation. Oeconomy, in contrast, is naturally aligned with ethics. Its interest in wealth is limited by the needs of the household, by sufficiency, and its success depends on virtues such as thrift and moderation. Furthermore, oeconomy serves not just the members of the household, but the entire community: Agnew describes *oikonomia* succinctly as 'a means to the civic ideal of full participation in the life of the *polis*' (19).

In early modern times, classical writings on oeconomy still provided a model for guiding socio-economic action, but *oikonomia*'s ethical orientation was coming under pressure. Hillary Eklund demonstrates this in her book *Literature and Moral Economy in the Early Modern Atlantic* (2015), where she analyses 'how standards of economic sufficiency moved from strict regulations against excess

---

[27] It is impossible to acknowledge all my intellectual debts here, but I want to stress that for my discussion of the transformation of oeconomy in the nascent capitalist society around 1600 the works of literary critics such as Catherine Belsey, Frances Dolan, Michelle M. Dowd, Katherine Gillen, Natasha Korda, Lorna Hutson, Karen Newman, Lena Cowen Orlin, Catherine Richardson, and Wendy Wall proved invaluable. Their work informs my discussion of the household, gender economy, and domesticity throughout the book. Dolan summarizes perfectly how these scholars have contributed to a better understanding of the household: 'Various scholars have demonstrated that the early modern household was a node in networks of global trade, experimental science, and knowledge transmission, rather than a bounded and "private" space, and that women's domestic labor entailed power, skill, knowledge—and violence' ('Afterword' 280).

[28] See *The Oxford Dictionary of English Etymology* 300. Marc Shell points out that classical and early modern oeconomy include both goods and people within the household: 'Domestic economy concerns production and distribution in the household, and relations between master and slave, husband and wife, and father and son' (89).

toward the increasing pursuit of plenty through plunder, trade, and plantation' (xiii). Although Eklund concentrates primarily on the idea of sufficiency, she skirts a question that guides this book as well, namely how profit emerged as a legitimate end.[29] My own research, however, addresses not just the revaluation of profit, but also the changed understanding of prudence that accompanies it. When private interest competes with the common good as the ultimate end of action, the function of practical wisdom changes: from an ethical intellectual virtue that determines the right action to a calculating and instrumental faculty in the service of private gain.

The sixteenth century witnessed an unprecedented increase in new works, as well as translations of old works, on household management and the family. The humanist interest in Greek and Roman texts and their ensuing translations played a crucial role in recovering classical works, but it can only partially account for, for instance, the immense popularity of Xenophon's *Oeconomicus*. Translated by Gentian Hervet in 1532, it appeared as *Xenophon's Treatise of Householde* in at least seven editions before the end of the century (Newman, *Fashioning Femininity* 17; Richards 36). In her article 'Making a Fresh Start: Sixteenth-Century Agriculture and the Classical Inspiration', Joan Thirsk associates the revival of classical oeconomies with the commercialization of agriculture and the motive of profit.[30] She links 'a mounting bookish interest in classical agriculture' ('Making a Fresh Start' 17) with the economic reality of rising food prices (16) that prompted landowners to try their hands at agricultural improvement—and even at writing husbandry manuals of their own. Building on Thirsk and others, Eklund writes that 'gentleman farmers like John Fitzherbert and Thomas Tusser ... conferred unprecedented dignity on the work of husbandry', transferring 'the edifying element of work ... to the accumulation of individual wealth' and helping to create 'values of thrift and profit' (101). The interest in humanist translations of classical oeconomies and early modern husbandry manuals coincided with the re-conceptualization of household and family in the wake of the Reformation, which also led to a surge of new works, among them Robert Cleaver's *A Godlie Forme of Householde Gouernment* (first published in 1598) and William Perkins's *Christian Oeconomie* (1609). These homiletic treatises specify a binary, hierarchical order and promote a gendered division of labour that strengthens the emergent distinction between domesticity and the market. They also establish

---

[29] Eklund wants to tell 'the story of profit's moral victory over subsistence' (xiii).

[30] See also McRae's analysis of the 'improvement' discourse, which served 'to challenge traditional conceptions of socio-economic order' ('Husbandry Manuals and the Language of Agrarian Improvement' 35). 'Improvement' came to denote a legitimate profit-motive in agrarian enterprises (36–37). McRae concludes from a discussion of the different meanings of the term that it 'can thus be seen to emerge as a concept which conflates qualitative changes in land-use with increases in the financial returns of the landlord' (37).

the well-ordered household as a pillar of the community.[31] Practical household works, such as Fitzherbert's *Booke of Husbandrie*, which was first published in 1523 and appeared in numerous editions throughout the sixteenth century, and Tusser's *Fiue Hundreth Points of Good Husbandry* (first published in 1573), which was republished regularly between the sixteenth and nineteenth centuries, readily reiterate commonplaces on diligence, thrift, and the order of family and estate.

At the same time, mercantilists and bullionists made their first attempts at conceptualizing commerce, and specifically the flow of money and commodities across national borders. Notable writers in this tradition include John Wheeler, Gerard de Malynes, Thomas Milles, Thomas Mun, and Edward Misselden. Protestant writers like Perkins reflected on commerce as a divine 'calling', for instance in *Treatise of the Vocations* (first published in 1603). Practical mercantile works, such as John Browne's *The Marchants Avizo* (1589) and William Scott's *Essay of Drapery* (1635), sought to publicize the know-how required for successful trade. The variegated field of socio-economic practices and concerns that early modern oeconomies, mercantile handbooks, and mercantilist and bullionist tracts delineate suggests that the meaning, form, and content of economic practices, motives, and considerations is indeed historical, just as Agnew and others have argued.[32] Around 1600, the field of socio-economic praxis included traditional problems of household management, marriage and childrearing, chrematistic practices and monetary instruments, as well as mercantilist and bullionist concerns with the value of currency and the balance of trade.

Reading plays in the context of a diverse practical literature allows us to identify recurrent concerns, but also to perceive tensions between competing and conflicting ideological positions. These competing positions do not simply mark divisions between texts or types of texts; rather, they often emerge as internal tensions or paradoxical demands within one single text. Thus, an affirmation of classical, humanist ethics often exists side by side with an attempt to make allowances for private interest, and the rejection of deceitful actions goes hand in hand with the appreciation of dissimulation as a legitimate social strategy. This paradoxical quality is at least in part facilitated by the dialectical structure of 'the humanists' deliberative rhetoric' (Victoria Kahn ix). Commenting on Machiavellian rhetoric, Victoria Kahn suggests that 'the humanist technique of argument on both sides of the question becomes a mode of dialectical thinking, in which

---

[31] See Newman, *Fashioning Femininity*, esp. chapter 2: 'The Crown Conjugal: Marriage in Early Modern England'.

[32] Agnew claims that political economy 'takes as absolute and eternal a particular grammar of motives—the hedonistic calculus—that should rather be seen historically as one of many efforts to render intelligible, acceptable, and controllable the socially and culturally subversive implications of the "free" market' (5). He emphasizes the historicity of the concept of self-interest when he remarks just a little later: 'economists treat social exchange as a matter of buyers and sellers (or their surrogates) engaging in the pursuit of their self-interests, though evidence again indicates that the very concepts of selves and their interests are historically conditioned ideas' (5).

positive terms are logically implicated in and give rise to their opposites': 'faithful imitation inevitably involves the possibility of feigning; what appears to be virtue may in practice turn out to be vice' (19). This dialectical structure provided a form for articulating and debating contradictory social possibilities in a society in transition, in which people were acutely conscious of the indeterminacy of social behaviour, and in which an ethics derived from classical ideas of household management had to be reconciled with the reality of global commerce.

The Revaluation of Interest

On the early modern stage, households are radically shaped by the drive for profit and by an instrumental and amoral use of prudence. Mercantilist writings suggest that, in the early seventeenth century, the pervasive force of private gain as an economic motive is largely accepted as a given. Even in a work that is not predominantly economic in nature, such as Robert Burton's *Anatomy of Melancholy* (first published in 1621), private gain is represented as an inescapable social reality: 'In a word, every man for his owne ends. Our *summum bonum* is commodity, and the Goddesse we adore *Dea Moneta*, Queene mony, to whom we daily offer sacrifice, which steeres our hearts, hands, affections, all' ('Democritus Junior to the Reader' 51; vol. 1). The social implications of this powerful motive remained contested, but *that* it constituted a powerful motive seemed evident. Gain was ambiguously represented, partly as a dangerous motive that fuelled excessive passion and needed to be controlled, and partly as a productive force that ensured increase, not just for individuals, but also for the commonwealth.[33]

The ambiguous status of profit as a rational motive and object of irrational passion resembles the status of 'interest' in the seventeenth century. Indeed, the fact that both profit and 'interest' are similarly ambiguously placed between reason and passion foreshadows the later identification of 'interest' with 'economic advantage' (32). Long before Adam Smith identified self-love as an anthropological constant, the force and meaning of interest, as well as its relation to ethics, were widely discussed.[34] Critics such as Albert O. Hirschman (*The Passions and the Interests*)

---

[33] Joyce Oldham Appleby's discussion of Malynes's and Misselden's works provides an excellent example for these diverging views. Both authors characterize gain as a driving force of commerce. Malynes, however, identifies it as a potential threat to the commonwealth, whereas Misselden sees it simply as the motor which keeps trade going. While both Malynes and Misselden recognize profit as a powerful and pervasive motivation, their interpretations of it are wildly different: 'Where Malynes had found a crime in the merchant's making a profit through the exchange of money, Misselden discovered an advantage' (45).

[34] Famously, Smith wrote: 'man has almost constant occasion for the help of his brethren, and it is in vain for him to expect it from their benevolence only. He will be more likely to prevail if he can interest their self-love in his favour, and shew them that it is for their own advantage to do for him what he requires of them. ... It is not from the benevolence of the butcher, the brewer, or the baker, that we expect our dinner, but from their regard to their own interest. We address ourselves, not to their humanity but to their self-love, and never talk to them of our own necessities but of their advantages' (26–27).

and Pierre Force (*Self-Interest before Adam Smith*) have explored the remarkable career of private interest in detail. As a concept, it developed from an ethically dubious motivation in medieval and early modern writings into a legitimate one in the eighteenth century, when interest 'came to be centered on economic advantage as its core meaning' (Hirschman 32).[35] In the late sixteenth century, as Hirschman points out, 'its meaning was by no means limited to the material aspects of a person's welfare; rather, it comprised the totality of human aspirations, but denoted an element of reflection and calculation with respect to the manner in which these aspirations were to be pursued' (32). Force emphasizes that interest and the passions were often treated as one and the same, although reason-of-state philosophers described the two as antithetical. The identification with passion applied especially to the interests of individuals: 'Following Montaigne, Hobbes and Locke mention private interest as a destructive force because the content of private interest is defined by private passions' (141). On the early modern stage, the pursuit of private interest is staged as both excessive *and* rational, as driven by acquisitive desire but following a rational calculus. The 'element of calculation and reflection' that Hirschman identifies tends to supplant ethical considerations and thus transforms the very nature of practical decision-making. Significantly, the skills and strategies needed to build one's fortune are not merely unethical, but also constitute a highly effective form of knowledge that empowers the self.

The rising recognition of profit as a legitimate motive is felt not only in the new self-confidence that mercantile texts articulate, but also in oeconomic works, even if both the homiletic literature and practical husbandry manuals are reluctant to engage with commercial matters. Andrew McRae explains in *God Speed the Plough* that sixteenth-century husbandry manuals are orientated towards 'the conservative ideal of an estate in which the landlord's aim is the achievement of no more than a modest surplus' (140).[36] And yet, as McRae demonstrates and as Thirsk's point about the appropriation of classical literature for agrarian improvement suggests, households were also caught up in a commercial dynamic, and husbandry manuals testify to this.[37] With their insistence on diligence and thrift, they prepare

---

[35] Don E. Wayne sums up Hirschman's insight as follows: 'In place of the old connotation of avarice, a new conception arose of *interest* as the one human passion that had positive value' (122).

[36] This echoes Thirsk's comments on the household of German 'Hausväterliteratur', 'whose members strove not for the large profits of a modern enterprise, but aimed to achieve efficient estate- and house-keeping that would result in a modest surplus' ('Making a Fresh Start' 20).

[37] This is in tune with Appleby's account of commercialization: 'The steady commercialization of grain growing, grazing, fishing, and mining and the increase in cloth making, metal-working, and shipbuilding opened up gainful enterprise to farmers, artisans, clothiers and landlords. New networks of buyers and sellers replaced the isolated economies of local consumption' (Appleby 3). Appleby contrasts this dynamic with the regulations of food production under the Tudors. These negated 'the food producer's freedom to manipulate the market for personal gain' (27–28): 'Grain was not seen as a commodity to be moved through the countryside in search of the best price, nor was it ever absolutely possessed by the producer. The farmer who grew it—be he tenant or landlord—did not really own the corn; he attended it during its passage from the field to the market' (28). See also R. H. Tawney on 'The Rise of the Gentry' (4) and Julie Solomon, who quotes Tawney to confirm that, 'During the sixteenth

the ground for the householder as businessman who seeks to increase his wealth. In the first chapter of the 1598 edition of Fitzherbert's *Booke of Husbandrie*, the picture of the man who 'layeth his hand to the plough and lookes backward' provides a trope for a lack of diligence that is directly linked to a loss in profit: 'as small shall he finde his profit, as his wills industrie' (2). If the instrumental relation of means and ends in pursuit of private interest and the quasi-Machiavellian separation of 'the humanist equation of *honestas* and *utilitas*' (Victoria Kahn 22) is thrown more sharply into relief in mercantile writings, works on estate management and the order of the family are caught up in the same process of commercialization and rationalization.

Famously, the Weber-Tawney thesis associates post-Reformation writings, above all those of Puritan and specifically Calvinist origin, with 'the emerging spirit of modern capitalism' (Nielsen 54).[38] The suggestive force of this thesis lies in the realization that Protestant ethics did not represent an impediment to successful enterprise, but actually helped to overcome 'obstacles which the more rigid institutions and ceremonies of catholicism imposed' (Christopher Hill 36). That the identification of economic success with virtue, as well as the sense of a 'close personal relationship with God' (Hill 18), played a role in the growing self-confidence and the social and material aspirations of the middling sort is a highly persuasive argument. And yet, any assumption of an unequivocal code of values cannot fully do justice to the copious and ambiguous works that appeared around 1600.[39] These texts harbour competing or even contradictory demands

---

century, English "agricultural, commercial and industrial interests [became] inextricably intertwined." Landowners devoted themselves to industry, trade, mining, and land improvement. English nobles took economic advantage of the growth of the English wool trade to enclose commons and did not need merchants to show them how to do it' (66).

[38] Max Weber described the 'peculiar ethic' (17) derived from the worldly asceticism of Calvinists and Puritans and other forms of ascetic Protestantism: 'The earning of money within the modern economic order is, so long as it is done legally, the result and the expression of virtue and proficiency in a calling' (Weber 19). Similarly to Weber, Tawney perceived the ideological work which Puritanism performed in justifying commerce and profit: 'Discarding the suspicion of economic motives, which had been as characteristic of the reformers as of medieval theologians, Puritanism in its later phases added a halo of ethical sanctification to the appeal of economic expediency, and offered a moral creed, in which the duties of religion and the calls of business ended their long estrangement in an unanticipated reconciliation ... It insisted, in short, that money-making, if not free from spiritual dangers, was not a danger and nothing else, but that it could be, and ought to be, carried on for the greater glory of God' (*Religion and the Rise of Capitalism* 238).

[39] Laura Caroline Stevenson points out that 'Tawney's thesis dealt mainly with the "later phases" of Puritanism—the post-Restoration theology of Richard Baxter and his contemporaries' (131). Regarding the novelty of this ethics, Stevenson claims that values such as diligence and thrift may look proto-bourgeois, but are in fact only two of many virtues derived from an aristocratic and classical tradition. She suggests that it was only in the Restoration period that 'godly diligence' (155) emerged as entrepreneurial ideal, with writers such as Sir Richard Steele and Daniel Defoe: 'The elite and the bourgeoisie have different value systems in the early eighteenth century; in the sixteenth century they did not' (156). It is also questionable whether the distinct class which was supposed to emerge together with these values did exist in the early seventeenth century. Appleby suggests that, 'If a middle class did in fact emerge and improve its social standing, it coalesced with, rather than displaced, the existing ruling class' (11).

and prescriptions that signal shifting paradigms and ideologies. In the sixteenth and seventeenth centuries, the priority of the common good was still a rhetorical staple feature in political, oeconomic, and mercantile texts, even if the question of how to act profitably and efficiently played an ever-greater role. While pragmatic and frequently casuistic handbooks made allowances for dissimulation and promoted shrewd sales strategies in the service of profitable enterprise, all kinds of writers warned against excessive acquisition and miserliness. Any writer who attempted to legitimize gain in the sixteenth and early seventeenth centuries was very careful to dissociate deserved gain from coveted profit. Rather than absolutely corresponding with or diverging from an emerging 'spirit of capitalism', these texts are a bit of everything: traditionalist and highly invested in a classical and aristocratic ethics, but, at the same time, keen to square the Aristotelian circle and to establish gain as a legitimate end of commerce rather than as a mere ethical risk.

The plays that this book discusses find their subject in this same revaluation of private interest and practical wisdom. They stage its social impact in the form of a radical reconfiguration of households and thus generate a trope for the demise of classical oeconomy as a framework for socio-economic behaviour, but also as a stable paradigm of order. Self-love, as Adam Smith will later call it, the anthropological constant which ensures predictability and calculability, is here represented as a force of madness and chaos. And yet not wholly so: on the stage and in the practical literature, agents count successfully on the self-interested behaviour of others, while a universal desire for gain and social advancement structures and shapes urban life in city comedies and tragedies alike. In commercial society, the profit motive is at once the new normal and a disruptive force. The revaluation of private interest and practical wisdom in the commercial arena went hand in hand with heightened attention to the relations between individual enterprises and the commonwealth. Mercantilist writers such as Mun and Misselden paved the way for the emergence of political economy when they 'joined the discrete acts of buying and selling to a single commercial process' (Appleby 48). On the one hand, they thereby established the balance of trade as an abstract market mechanism, but, on the other hand, asserted that the economic rationality of merchants and other economic agents played a decisive role in the financial wellbeing of the commonwealth.[40] Misselden asks rhetorically: 'What else makes a Common-wealth, but the private-wealth, if I may so say, of the members thereof in the exercise of Commerce amongst themselues, and with forraine Nations?' (Misselden, *The Circle of*

---

[40] See also Lars Magnusson, who explains that 'To relate private and public interests was a problem which haunted discussions on politics and economics back to the sixteenth century' (5). He traces this problem explicitly to the discussion between Malynes, Mun, and Misselden in the early 1620s. If Adam Smith's 'self-equilibrating economic system monitored by an invisible hand' (2) appears to resolve this problem, Magnusson demonstrates that it does not entirely disappear. An 'uneasiness' about the possibility that 'private vices ... might lead to a policy grounded on special interests and corruption' persists in Smith's writings (Magnusson 4).

Commerce 17; also qtd. in Appleby 45–46). In a similar vein, Mun used the 'estates of priuate persons' (*A Discourse of Trade* 1) and metaphors of prudential household management to exemplify how the prosperity of a kingdom is to be attained: 'industry to increase, and frugalitie to maintaine, are the true watchmen of a kingdomes treasury' (2; also qtd. in Appleby 40). These authors linked the success of national commerce to the merchant's prudential pursuit of private gain and the householder's careful spending practices.

'Wisdom of Business', or the Transformation of Prudence

Prudential behaviour is at the heart of early modern oeconomic and mercantile advice literature. Although the rhetoric of the common good remains pervasive, the pronounced practical preoccupation of this literature and its interest in legitimate profit implies a focus on individual socio-economic success and the skills and strategies that it requires. Theatre performs a similar shift via its highly efficient and versatile tricksters and villains, but it also explores acquisitive desires and social ambitions through gulls who overestimate their own practical intelligence. The quasi-Machiavellian transformation of prudence in matters of oeconomy and business that this book seeks to delineate is formulated with great clarity in Bacon's writings. Bacon's notion of 'wisdom of business' provides theatrical performances of economic rationality with a conceptual counterpart that establishes socio-economic action and success as a form of practical expertise. He introduces his discussion of 'wisdom of business' in *The Advancement of Learning* (first published in 1605) with three proverbs that highlight human agency in making one's fortune. The three precepts, 'A Man is maker of his own fortune', 'The wise man will command the stars', and 'No way is impossible to virtue' all drive home the same point: with skill and courage, one may become the architect of one's own fate.[41]

Aristotle had identified prudence as the intellectual moral virtue of making the right choices in particular cases. For him as, later, for Cicero, prudence referred to an ethically informed practical wisdom that responded to particular and ever-changing circumstances.[42] Early modern writers were eager to understand the kind of behaviour that allowed men to thrive in changing circumstances, but for them, 'prudence did not necessarily direct an individual to do what was

---

[41] See Bacon, *The Advancement of Learning*: 'Faber quisque fortunae suae, sapiens dominabitur astris: Inuia virtutis nulla est via' (164): 'A man is maker of his fortune', 'The wise man will command his stars', 'No way is impossible to virtue', as translated in the notes (345).

[42] As Jon R. Snyder explains: 'Until the early modern era, prudence, or *phronesis*, occupied the most prominent position in philosophical and moral reflection on how to evaluate and adapt to changing circumstances and the shifting winds of fortune' (8). An exacting and complex faculty of deliberating about the right action in a particular situation, 'prudence was a matter of practical conduct and practical reason': in concrete terms, 'Prudence was the exercise of *versatilitas*, involving foresight, preparation, judgment, patience, quickness, perspicacity, maturity, and caution' (8).

most moral ... but what was morally practicable in a given situation' (Vallence 100). Ethics could be adapted—or even sacrificed—to circumstances, and ethical considerations could lose ground to pragmatic ones. David Armitage, Conal Condren, and Andrew Fitzmaurice comment on this shift in their introduction to *Shakespeare and Early Modern Political Thought*:

> As prudence became an increasingly valued skill in the sixteenth century, the virtues it was intended to secure became increasingly obscured. For the citizen or subject, self-interest replaced the *bonus homo*, and the "reasons" or interests of state could be held to compete with the common good as the aims of the government.
>
> (7)[43]

Famously, Machiavelli's *Il Principe* (first published in 1532) presents a transformed version of prudence: 'from the humanists' practical reason, informed by moral considerations, to the calculating, potentially amoral faculty of judgement appropriate to the man of *virtù*' (Victoria Kahn 21). Victoria Kahn explains that 'Machiavellian *virtù* is structurally like the classical and humanist notion of prudence or practical reason' (37): it is 'a faculty of deliberation about particulars' which 'implies practical success but does not guarantee it' (38). In contrast to prudence, however, Machiavellian *virtù* lacks a firm ethical orientation, for 'to be ethical in every case is harmful and impractical' (38). Kahn concludes that Machiavellian *virtù* 'implies nothing whatsoever about the compatibility of the practical wisdom of *virtù* with ethical norms' (38).

Bacon has a keen interest in practical considerations and the ethical compromises that successful business negotiations demand. His *Essays* provide many examples of the casuistic revaluation of traditional virtues.[44] Yet the text that most forcefully illustrates my point about the transformation of prudence in matters of business is a section of the second book of *The Advancement of Learning*. Under the heading of civil knowledge and its subdivision 'wisdom of business', Bacon discusses prudential behaviour in quotidian exchanges.[45] He introduces 'ciuile knowledge' (*The Advancement* 156) as a type of practical knowledge that is distinct from moral philosophy. The difference between civil knowledge and

---

[43] Snyder suggested that the sixteenth and seventeenth centuries saw a semantic shift from self-preservation to self-interest: 'writers on the topic increasingly abandon the motive of self-preservation and turn toward a more instrumental notion of self-interest' (9).
[44] See, for instance, my 2020 article on Bacon's Essay XIII, 'Of Goodnesse *And* Goodness of Nature': '"So good that he is good for nothing": Francis Bacon's Umwertung der Werte'.
[45] He discusses civil knowledge in Book Two, 156–181, and wisdom of business from 158–179. As Brian Vickers suggests, 'the *Advancement* is a critical survey of knowledge designed to expose deficiencies and gaps; it is an "encyclopedia" of work needed, of not yet existing knowledge' ('Francis Bacon' 504). Rather than providing a systematic study of 'civil knowledge', the *Advancement* shares insights, which, sporadic as they may be, point the way to a new type of knowledge that is conducive to business. Bacon's *Essays* also demonstrate his keen interest in what it takes to rise in the world. Essay IV, 'Of Simulation and Dissimulation', and Essay XL, 'Of Fortune', are but two that come to mind.

moral philosophy is telling: 'morrall Philosophye propoundeth to itself the framing of Internall goodnesse: But ciuile knowledge requireth onelye an Externall goodnesse: for that as to societye sufficeth' (*The Advancement* 156). Goodness is not a moral question here, but a matter of appearance, of performative self-display.⁴⁶ In civil intercourse, there is no need to actually *be* good. *Appearing* good is perfectly sufficient. Bacon establishes civil knowledge as a separate discipline that involves strategic self-display, but also versatile adaptation to sudden changes and the ability to negotiate successfully with unpredictable agents. Versatility is key because people change their minds all the time: in contrast to states which 'as great Engines mooue slowly', 'the resolution of particuler persons is more sodainly subverted' (*The Advancement* 156).

The part of civil knowledge that illuminates the transformation of prudence in matters of business and household management is 'wisedom of Businesse', which, according to Bacon, concerns the action of 'Negotiation' (*The Advancement* 157) in socio-economic transactions.⁴⁷ Bacon's example of the ancient Roman senators who offered counsel on the 'Place' exemplifies the great variety of affairs that are subsumed under this heading. He describes how 'the particuler Citizens would resort vnto them [the senators], and consulte with them of the marriage of a daughter, or of the imploying of a sonne, or of a purchase or bargaine, or of an accusation, and euery other occasion incident to mans life' (*The Advancement* 158). As this quotation suggests, 'wisdom of business' concerns all kinds of occasions, such as family matters ('the marriage of a daughter', 'the employing of a son'), commercial endeavours ('a purchase or bargain'), and social incidents that might influence one's reputation ('accusation[s]'). It refers to the kind of practical wisdom that is needed in oeconomy as much as in business and the maintenance of one's reputation or credit. Its orientation towards private interest not only becomes visible in Bacon's separation of business from moral considerations, but also emerges in his division of 'wisdom of business' into two forms: '*sapere*, & *sibi Sapere*' (*The Advancement* 163).⁴⁸ The distinction between the two forms of knowledge lies in their orientation. While the first 'is a wisedome of counsell', benefitting others,

---

⁴⁶ See also Benet Davetian, who discusses the investment in self-display as part of a broader shift. In the sixteenth and seventeenth centuries, how to succeed in public life was not just of interest to courtiers, but also to citizens who sought to gain control over their social credit. Davetian emphasizes the growing interest in publications detailing 'rules of public conduct' which opened the field to a broader audience of aspiring and affluent citizens (76). Amongst the most important publications advocating and reinventing civility are Baldassare Castiglione's *The Book of the Courtier* (*Il Cortegiano*) from 1529 and Giovanni Della Casa's *Il Galateo* from 1558. In 1558, Erasmus's treatise *On Civility of Boys* (*De civilitate morum puerilium*) appeared, which 'radically departed from the format of medieval courtesy literature. Although the book was written for the son of a nobleman it did not pretend to be exclusively addressed to the nobility' (Davetian 77).

⁴⁷ Civil knowledge consists of 'three parts': 'wisedome of the behauiour, wisedom of Businesse; & wisedome of *state*' (157). These correspond to three kinds of social actions: 'Co*n*uersation, Negotiation and Gouernment' (157).

⁴⁸ Meaning 'to be wise' and 'to be wise for oneself', as the Commentary to *The Advancement of Learning* suggests (344).

sibi sapere benefits oneself (163). It is the 'wisedome of pressing a mans owne fortune' (*The Advancement* 163). With a nod to convention, Bacon states that 'no mans fortune can be an end woorthy of his being' (*The Advancement* 165), thus acknowledging at least formally the priority of the common good over private interest. Nonetheless, Bacon's detailed attention to how to promote one's interests in a changeable world establishes private interest as a legitimate end.

Bacon's interest in how to make one's fortune relegates moral concerns to a subordinate status, and his division of 'civil knowledge' from moral philosophy opens the door for a purely instrumental use of practical deliberation. Highly conscious of the unpredictability of success in a socio-economic field that is peopled by inconstant agents who pursue their own interests, Bacon concedes that rising in the world is a difficult enterprise (*The Advancement* 164). Yet his 'wisdom of business' goes some way towards managing contingent events. Bacon's discussion of 'wisdom of business' appropriates Machiavellian *virtù* for the sphere of household management and commercial transactions.[49] In his discussion of the changeable field of 'Negotiation and occasions', Bacon explicitly commends Machiavelli's treatment of 'Gouernmente' by means of '*discourse vpon Histories or Examples*' (*The Advancement* 162). He considers this approach apt because politics is about particulars, and 'knowledge drawne freshly and in our view out of particulers, knoweth the waie best to particulers againe' and is more pertinent to 'practise' (*The Advancement* 162). Business, too, is a matter of practice and must draw on examples. Using Machiavelli as an example, Bacon suggests only a difference in the material used to exemplify particulars: 'as historye of *Tymes* is the best grounde for discourse of Gouernmente, such as *Machyauel* handleth; so Histories of Liues because it is the moste proper for discourse of businesse is more conversante in priuate Actions' (*The Advancement* 163). Theatre, as this book suggests, also provides examples and explorations in this changeable field of private actions and transactions. It imagines and stages how the desire to raise one's fortune plays out in the field—what people are willing to do in pursuit of their own interests and why and how they succeed or fail. While theatre thus participates in accommodating Londoners to a new understanding of economic rationality, it also reflects on the structural limits of self-improvement and traces the point where the wish to raise one's fortune becomes a kind of mania. Last but not least, with its dramatization of extreme actions, theatre illustrates the consequences of severing practical deliberation from ethical concerns.

---

[49] In *The Prince*, the meaning of virtue is not foremost moral, but a question of strength and doing what is necessary under certain circumstances. Moral virtue alone may not get one very far. Machiavelli remarks in chapter 15: 'if one considers everything well, one will find something appears to be virtue, which if pursued would be one's ruin, and something else appears to be vice, which if pursued results in one's security and well-being' (62).

Generic Cross-Pollination

Comparative analyses of city comedies and tragedies in the individual chapters demonstrate that theatre's economic interest is not confined to just one genre. More importantly, reading select comedies by Ben Jonson and Thomas Middleton together with Shakespearean tragedies (one of which, *Timon of Athens*, was likely a collaboration with Middleton) helps to tease out their respective economic preoccupations.

As a genre, city comedy is very much of its moment: it reflects directly on its own socio-economic environment, depicting the 'ordinary worlds of travelers, merchants, immigrants, factors, and exiles' (Warren 63). With its interest in the 'middling sort of people' and their stakes in social mobility, city comedy is itself a symptom of socio-economic transformation.[50] The fact that it appropriates classical traditions detracts nothing from the cultural significance of its emergence around 1600.[51] City comedy's appreciation of the wit which gives birth to a plot of intrigue or an unlikely business venture, its interest in impoverished gentlemen willing to take their fortunes in hand, and its attention to inventive commoners mark a tangible fascination with entrepreneurship, social advancement, and the huge profit and risks of commercial ventures. It also signals a keen interest in the frame of mind and the skills and strategies needed to be successful in business.

In contrast to Shakespeare's comedies (in particular, of course, *The Merchant of Venice*),[52] his tragedies have received comparatively little attention from critics invested in economics. A notable exception is *Timon of Athens*, which is at the centre of Chapter 4. That play's exploration of the interval between gift and repayment and the competing economies of gift and credit warrants closer analysis. The surplus of juxtaposing tragedy with city comedy lies in an adjustment of the tragedies' interpretative frame. City comedy's performance of city life confronts the distant, outdated, or foreign settings of tragedy with the everyday preoccupations and the deictic here-and-now of London: 'Our scene is London', as Ben Jonson affirms emphatically in *The Alchemist*. When read side by side, the proto-realist mode and vibrant topicality of city comedy pulls the tragedies closer to their context of origin,

---

[50] As Howard aptly puts it, it marks 'a moment in early modern culture when urban commoners, those below the rank of gentlemen, could become the protagonists in theatrical fictions' (*Theater of a City* 19). See also Julie Sanders on the 'bustling world' of the 'new urban communities' who populated the stage in city comedies (133).

[51] As Alexander Leggatt explains, 'English Renaissance comedy' draws on Roman 'New Comedy' (2), but is also influenced by Aristophanic 'Old Comedy' (3). New Comedy accounts for some 'recurrent plot features', such as its attention to 'ordinary domestic life' and its confinement to a given 'neighbourhood' (2). The legacy of Aristophanic 'Old Comedy' is palpable in the 'free-wheeling satire' and the 'crazy extravagant scheme' (3), which is staged, for instance, in *Volpone* and *The Alchemist*.

[52] For economic criticism of *The Merchant of Venice* see, for instance, Aaron Kitch, *Political Economy and the States of Literature in Early Modern England*; Peter F. Grav, *Shakespeare and the Economic Imperative*; Stephen R. Mentz, 'The Fiend Gives Friendly Counsel'; Mark Netzloff, 'The Lead Casket'; Eric Spencer, 'Taking Excess, Exceeding Account'; Karen Newman, 'Portia's Ring'; Lars Engle, 'Thrift is Blessing'; and others.

no matter how exotic or historical their subjects and settings may be. The trickster figures of city comedies shed light on Shakespeare's conflicted, driven, and enigmatic tragic heroes and villains (such as the infamous Macbeths, Othello, Iago, and Timon), while the comedies' unapologetic orientation towards money and social advancement helps to place similar preoccupations in the tragedies. City comedy's explicit treatment of commerce teases out the tragedies' investment in economic problems, among them the nature of value, business skills, household management, and the asynchronicity of credit relations.

Furthermore, city comedy's '"extra-territoriality" from traditional morality' (Susan Wells 51), calls attention to the moral ambiguities of the tragedies. The frequently irreverent and off-handed mode in which city comedies address and occasionally dismiss moral matters encourages readers to move beyond a 'reductive, moralistic kind of reading' (Ryan 69) of Shakespeare's tragedies. Borrowing from Kiernan Ryan's description of orthodox criticism, Shakespearean tragedy is neither a timeless depiction of 'flawed human nature' nor a vindication of 'conventional values' (67). Rather, it explores concrete socio-economic actions and their ethical implications in an ambiguous mode that resists closure. Lady Macbeth may be in the wrong from a moral standpoint, but her rhetoric, her powers of reasoning, and her entrepreneurial spirit are still compelling. Malcolm, the future king, poses as a just ruler, but his political strategies have more in common with those of the Macbeths than one might think. Timon is generous, but he is also prodigal; his friends may be on the right side of the law, but they are still wrong to refuse his request for money. In all these plays, morality is bogged down by ambiguity as the plays explore the affective framework of commercial enterprise and trace shifting values in the transition from feudal to early capitalist society.

From the perspective of economic criticism, the juxtaposition of city comedy and tragedy benefits foremost the exploration of tragedy as a genre that has gone comparatively neglected by economic critics. As 'context' for the 'text' of the tragedies, the city comedies encourage attention to the tragedies' interest in social exchanges, calculation, and the manipulation of value. Yet 'context' and 'text' are relative terms, and the discussion of the tragedies also reflects back on the city comedies.[53] At the same time as city comedy helps to render visible a mercantile logic that also animates the tragedies, *Macbeth*, *Othello*, and *Timon of Athens* highlight the role of the household as the object of economic considerations and the site at which economic decisions play out. They suggest that the dissolute and commercially-minded households of city comedy are not to be seen as comic bywork that comes with the setting, but rather as signalling a paradigm change from

---

[53] Howard wrote in 1986: 'Literature is *part* of history, the literary text as much a context for other aspects of cultural and material life as they are for it' ('The New Historicism' 25). In using one type of literary text (city comedy) to illuminate another (tragedy), while reading both against oeconomic and mercantile writings, this project takes seriously the idea of the literary text as prolific 'context'.

an economic logic centred on household management to one based on commercial exchange. The tragedies help to insert the seemingly light and trivial subject matter of city comedy into a bigger narrative of socio-economic transformation. Framed by prescriptive writings and against the backdrop of the dramatic force of tragedy, the peculiarities of this genre assume new meaning. Far from being simply comic or critical of city vices, city comedies tackle the departure from oeconomy as a guiding logic of socio-economic action and explore the new skills and opportunities that commerce affords in entertaining and deeply ambiguous ways. Juxtaposition with Shakespeare's tragedies adjusts readers' expectations of city comedy: it reveals larger patterns in the city comedies and teases out allegorical meanings. The representation of the female body in the case of Mrs Allwit in *A Chaste Maid*, for instance, has allegorical meanings that extend to household and city. They become apparent in conjunction with Lady Macbeth's infinitely more famous bodily transformation, which signals domestic and political disorder. Last but not least, the juxtaposition enables us to see the tragic in the comic. Sir Walter Whorehound, the gentleman suitor in *A Chaste Maid*, turns into a tragic figure when he is ousted from the economy of the play: he exemplifies not only the pattern of the zero-sum game in commercial society, according to which someone's gain is always another's loss, but also the risk of total loss implied in profit-orientated exchange.[54] In juxtaposing, in each chapter, a tragedy with a city comedy, my aim is not simply to mine the 'socio-economic content' of the comedies. They are literary works in their own right, and they are far too fascinating and complex to reduce them to a contextual role. For this reason, approximately half of each chapter will be devoted to the comedies. They enable new perspectives on the tragedies not merely as part of a broader cultural context, but as equal partners in the enterprise of commercial theatre.

The Book

This book discusses how early modern theatre engaged with private gain as a key motor of socio-economic action, and how it explored and represented the uses and limits of practical wisdom in matters of oeconomy and commerce. To render early modern drama's interest in the varied field of socio-economic praxis visible and intelligible, the following chapters discuss select plays in the context of classical philosophical, early modern oeconomic, and mercantile works. In reconstructing a discursive context, my aim is to identify widespread concerns and problems; I

---

[54] *The Merchant of Venice* famously addresses the possibility of total commercial failure. Think of Bassanio's consternation when he reads that all of Antonio's ships are lost: 'But is it true Salerio? / Hath all his ventures failed? What, not one hit, / From Tripoli, from Mexico and England, / From Lisbon, Barbary and India, / And not one vessel scape the dreadful touch / Of merchant-marring rocks?' (*MV* 3.2.265–269).

aim for breadth, not for complete coverage. Nonetheless, I believe that the material is rich and varied enough to prevent easy conclusions from a few illustrative examples. My take on the plays is, in a sense, the reverse. I opt for a limited set of plays—three city comedies and three tragedies—to prevent a reductive and superficial reading of what are in each instance very rich plays. In relating early modern plays to economic problems of the time, my aim is to enrich our understanding of them and not to reduce them to mere manifestations of an economic order that is simply given, independent from its material manifestation on stage.

All four chapters in this book discern a similar dynamic of commercialization that is changing both individual households and the community. The chapters are arranged to illuminate the pursuit of private interest and the uses of practical rationality at the interface of household and market from different perspectives. Chapter 1 lays the groundwork with an analysis of classical and early modern ideas on household and commerce. It reviews ethical, oeconomic, and mercantile discourses to establish a historical context for the economic interests of early modern theatre. Chapter 2 looks at households in the grip of a profit-orientated logic: it discusses oeconomy and family relations in *Macbeth* and *A Chaste Maid*, concentrating particularly on marriage. Chapter 3 shifts the focus from marriage and kinship to subservient surrogates who mediate the relation between household and market. As *The Alchemist* and *Othello* suggest, practical wisdom in servants was both desired and feared by householders who relied on the devolution of agency. With its discussion of *Volpone* and *The Alchemist*, Chapter 4 moves from a spatial paradigm to a temporal one: it highlights the ways in which households are entangled in credit relations and explores how householders and servants handle asynchronous exchanges. Crucially, economic transformation is not only a 'theme' that drama tackles in a spirit of critique, entertainment, or normalization; it also shapes the deep structures of theatre, from both a material culture perspective and a poetological one.[55] From a poetological perspective, the commercial theatre around 1600 affords a whole new world of settings, characters, and plots, and, with city comedy, even a new sub-genre. Therefore, each of the three chapters on individual plays is also designed to pay particular attention to one of these theatrical elements: to the household as setting, to the mercantile agency of individual characters, and to the temporality of plot.

---

[55] The material conditions have been researched quite thoroughly by a number of eminent critics. Not just by Gurr and Howard, who have already been quoted, but also by, for instance, Douglas Bruster (*Drama and the Market in the Age of Shakespeare*), Melissa D. Aaron (*Global Economics: A History of the Theater Business, the Chamberlain's/King's Men, and Their Plays, 1599–1642*), Tiffany Stern (*Documents of Performance in Early Modern England*), and Amanda Bailey (*Of Bondage: Debt, Property, and Personhood in Early Modern England*).

1
Household Management and Commerce in Early Modern England

Introduction

When reading economic histories, one can easily get the impression that there was little reflection on economic matters worth noting in the sixteenth and seventeenth centuries. Yet by the end of the seventeenth century, political economy had as if magically come into its own as a new constellation of knowledge that combined questions of political government with the flow of people and goods and the actions and passions of individuals (see Joseph Vogl 12). As early modern literary and cultural scholars have noted, this new knowledge had a substantial prehistory in the sixteenth and seventeenth centuries. With the Reformation, increasing interest in the organization of family life, an orderly household, and a gendered division of labour ensured a steady flow of sermons and advice books on oeconomy. As explained in the Introduction, 'oeconomy' comes from ancient Greek and refers to the management of a household or estate. This meaning persisted into the early modern age.[1] Here, just as in antiquity, the household constituted the smallest unit of reflection on the production, acquisition, use, and distribution of wealth. At the same time, commerce, money, and credit emerged as objects of serious reflection in mercantile advice books and theological tracts. The turn of the seventeenth century saw the first publications of the early mercantilists and bullionists, and thus also the first attempts at theorizing the market. In various ways, merchants, theologians, and philosophers around 1600 reflected on the distribution of goods and the acquisition of wealth, the nature of value, and the flow of money and commodities between countries.

Enquiring into how Shakespeare and his contemporaries pictured socio-economic praxis further enriches our understanding of early modern socio-economic relations and values. By the time of Adam Smith's *The Wealth of Nations*, profit had been transformed from a highly suspicious source of avaricious temptation into a reasonable anthropological motive. How did this happen? As this book seeks to show, the new commercial theatre of around 1600 played an important

---

[1] David Landreth is one of many critics who pointed out that '"economy"—or, as Elizabethans usually spelled it, "oeconomie"—retained for the Renaissance its Greek meaning, that of the management of a household' (34).

part in the revaluation of economic actions and motives. Contemporaneous with the emergence of joint-stock companies and the first London exchange, commercial theatre evolved into a key medium for making sense of the socio-economic transformations that shaped its own present, such as high-risk ventures, conspicuous consumption, and unprecedented social mobility. It experimented with unconventional business ideas, portrayed the increasing commercialization of individual households, and reviewed the relations between household and community in a commercial environment. Theatre's cultural work is often ambiguous: it combines a critique of profit-seeking practices with the work of accommodation to the new reality of global commerce. By demonstrating the pervasive presence of self-interested and profit-seeking behaviour, and by interrogating the skills and frame of mind necessary to succeed in this new reality, early modern theatre habituates Londoners to a commercial environment in which the pursuit of private interests is a driving force.

To contextualize theatre's role in representing and experimenting with socio-economic change, this chapter offers an introduction to the disparate body of early modern practical writings on how to manage the household and preserve its order, how to acquire and use wealth, and how to safeguard one's credit. The rise of commercial theatre was accompanied by a growing body of newly-written and -translated practical writings. This disparate body of texts demonstrates the breadth of economic concerns around 1600, yet in light of the sheer amount of relevant writings on oeconomic and mercantile topics, my discussion of these discourses can only be radically selective. The selection of themes in this chapter is designed to contextualize the socio-economic actions and conflicts that theatre explores and to underpin the sense of an ethical and socio-economic transformation that early modern plays convey.

Following the classical distinction between oeconomy and commerce, many of the writings discussed in this chapter can be sorted into one of two categories: those that focus on household management (oeconomy) and the order of the family, and those that focus on commercial exchange. Yet this division is by no means absolute. On the contrary, discourses of household management and commerce communicate with and inform one another. Texts on oeconomy establish comparisons with and borrow from the field of commerce to construct elaborate tropes and vice versa.[2] While mercantilist and bullionist authors address England's economy in terms familiar from household management, works on the household establish a gendered division of labour that allows for the emergence of a separate sphere of business. Authors of oeconomies and mercantile texts alike

---

[2] In his sermon *The Merchant Royall*, for instance, which was first published in 1607, Robert Wilkinson, Doctor in Divinity, explored the biblical analogy of the wife as merchant vessel and the householder as seafaring merchant. Merchant John Browne's advice to his servant in *The Marchants Avizo* (first published in 1589) evokes the emphasis on thrift in the advice habitually given to householders: 'Be circumspect and nigh in all your expences' (5).

situate questions of household management and commerce firmly in the context of virtue ethics, but also shift this framework to make space for profitable enterprise. In light of such overlapping interests, concerns, and metaphors, this chapter seeks to establish a better understanding of the changing field of socio-economic praxis by combining an introduction to early modern oeconomy with a sketch of the developments in commerce and mercantile thought at the turn of the seventeenth century. The rise of global commerce in the sixteenth century, the growth of the trade metropolis London and the building of the first Royal Exchange, and the introduction of new monetary instruments and luxury goods from overseas brought about changes to individual households and greater city life alike, and shaped the milieu in which commercial theatre emerged. Keeping one eye on the effects of the expansion of trade and the other on the early modern fashioning of the household as an orderly and hierarchically structured institution that served as model of the commonwealth enables a fuller picture of how early modern writers negotiated the transition from feudal to commercial society.

Together, oeconomic and mercantile writings reflect the economic concerns of the time and the ethical negotiations taking place within both discourses. Influenced by classical philosophers, notably Aristotle and Cicero, early modern writers continually reinscribed the common good as the ultimate end of socio-economic action. Yet despite this rhetorical effort, their often-ambiguous representation of material profit and private interests indicates shifting values and contributes to a revaluation of private interest. Theatre played a special role in staging diverse logics of socio-economic action. While oeconomic and mercantile tracts offered their endorsements of profit only in combination with a rhetoric that sought to contain excess and promote the common good, theatre was able to explore more freely the motivating force of excessive desire and to stage the appeal of, as well as the moral problems with, a pragmatic rather than ethical use of practical wisdom.

The first part of this chapter focuses on the house as a highly symbolic socio-economic space. It discusses the roots of oeconomy in classical antiquity as well as its evolution in early modern prescriptive writings. The discussion concentrates on the household's ties with ethics and politics. It also explores its relation to wealth and the gendered division of authority and labour within the home. The second part focuses on the intensification of commerce in the sixteenth century and on early modern mercantile texts. It begins once more with classical sources: Aristotle's analysis of retail trade and justice (as well as Aquinas's mediation of Aristotle) and Cicero's notion of beneficence. This discussion of the classical and scholastic foundation of early modern ethical thought is followed by an analysis of the tensions between virtue and profit in mercantile writings by John Browne and William Scott, and in clergyman William Perkins's *Treatise of the Vocations* (first published in 1603). Finally, the chapter reviews the main arguments of mercantilist and bullionist writers in the seventeenth century. Besides demonstrating the range of economic thought, the chapter seeks to identify neuralgic points of oeconomy and commerce that inspire dramatic conflicts and tension: gender economy and household politics, the relation between private interest and common good, the balance of trade, and the instability of value. Most importantly, perhaps, the chapter seeks to put a finger on the ethical drift away from an overarching common good towards a legitimate interest in private wealth and the skills to make a profit.

The Household in Classical and Early Modern Writings

In the sixteenth century, 'prescriptive literature' (Fissell 434) on the family and household can be roughly divided into three discursive strands. The first of these consisted of ancient Greek and Roman works on oeconomics, ethics, and politics, which were newly translated, repeatedly reprinted, and commented on in the context of humanism. A second strand was formed of Christian writings on the household, conduct books, and works of household devotion. Written by clergy and theologians, those writings multiplied with the Reformation. The third set of writings was practical in nature, such as John Fitzherbert's popular *Booke of Husbandrie*, the 'first English estate manual' (Wall 29), published in 1523, or Thomas Tusser's *Fiue Hundreth Points of Good Husbandry* (first published in 1573). These distinctions were, however, fluid: Christian writers borrowed from Aristotle or drew on Thomas Aquinas and other scholastics who attempted to reconcile Aristotelian philosophy with Christian beliefs. Practical handbooks mined Christian proverbs and emphasized the importance of Christian stewardship.

Household management poses an array of socio-economic problems, from marriage concerns to housekeeping, from the education of children to the supervision of servants, from production to consumption and exchange.[3] Marriage sermons, domestic conduct books, and works on the art of husbandry positioned the household as a complex and fragile socio-economic structure that demanded careful management. They also inscribed it with a social ordering function that enabled political government.[4] On the London stages, the household's highly charged economic, political, and spiritual functions fuel dramatic tension. Here, the household is not just an innocent setting for the action, but a space that is structured by specific socio-economic relations and ethical imperatives. In both tragedies and comedies, the household takes centre stage to either disintegrate under the

---

[3] In recent decades, these problems have been analysed and discussed by a number of critics, among them Frances Dolan, Michelle M. Dowd, Natasha Korda, Lorna Hutson, Karen Newman, Lena Cowen Orlin, Catherine Richardson, and Wendy Wall. Without their work, this book would hardly have been possible.

[4] As Richardson writes, 'The householder was responsible for the public and private behaviour of those in his care, and that responsibility underpinned communal law and order' ('Domestic Life in Jacobean London' 52).

pressures of commercial society or to adapt to the logic of the market. It is transformed by hopes of social advancement and the often ruthless pursuit of profitable projects, by excessive desire for luxury goods, and by the inescapable forces of circulation that can make or mar individual fortune. In the classical tradition, good household management appeared as the ethical other of commercial exchange (i.e., exchange that is driven by material gain). In the early modern context, staging the ethical erosion of households becomes a means for staging the failure of oeconomy as an overarching paradigm for socio-economic action. As oeconomy is tied to the order of the commonwealth, this failure has both social and political repercussions.

Early modern ideas of the household were modelled on classical conceptions of the *oikos* and its management. The main influences on oeconomy were Xenophon's *Oeconomicus* and Aristotle's practical philosophy, the latter mediated and accentuated by readings of Cicero. Xenophon's *Oeconomicus* was widely read and quoted in early modern England. Though conceived as a dialogue between Socrates and Critobulus, the main part of the text is an embedded conversation between Socrates and Ischomachus, an exemplary citizen and 'husbandman'. It offers advice on various activities of estate management, such as 'administering the domain, supervising the workers, undertaking different kinds of cultivation, applying the right techniques at the right time, and selling or buying as one should and when one should' (Foucault, *The History of Sexuality* 152; vol. 2). The work stands out for its detailed attention to gender relations and roles. As Foucault notes in *The History of Sexuality*, vol. 2: 'Xenophon's *Oeconomicus* contains the most fully developed treatise on married life that classical Greece has left us' (152). It is quite exceptional in the Greek philosophical tradition in that it grants the wife as much self-control as her husband, although only after he has successfully trained her (Xenophon 139).[5]

Aristotle's practical philosophy was hugely influential in shaping the ethical framework and political significance of the early modern household. Aristotle's lasting legacy for early modern intellectual life is well known.[6] The influence of

---

[5] See Sarah B. Pomeroy 33–40 for a discussion of gender roles in the fourth century BC. As Pomeroy explains, Aristotle perceived that 'women's minds have the rational element', but believed that their reason lacked authority: 'Therefore, it is not only natural but also beneficial for women to be ruled by men' (34). According to Pomeroy, 'Aristotle admits of only one situation in which a wife may rule the husband: that is when she is an heiress' (34).

[6] As social historian Keith Wrightson put it, 'The revival of Aristotelianism played a major role in the quickening of English intellectual life in the final quarter of the sixteenth century' ('Sorts of People' 43). Throughout the sixteenth and seventeenth centuries, the *corpus Aristotelicum* 'remained the core of the university curriculum' (Scodel 2), and Aristotle was also an important author of the 'in-house education' of noble boys (Jewell 53). Sir Thomas Elyot's *The Boke, Named the Gouernour* (first published in 1531) 'required the young governor to start learning Greek and Latin at seven ... His youngsters were to read Aesop's Fables, the Select dialogues of Lucian, the comedies of Aristophanes, Homer, Virgil, Silius, Lucanus and Hesiodus, all before they were twelve. Later they studied Xenophon, Aristotle and Plato' (54).

Aristotelianism persisted despite the religious turmoil of the Reformation.[7] Jill Kraye explains: 'With the rise of the universities in the thirteenth century and the availability in Latin of the Aristotelian *Ethics*, *Oeconomics* and *Politics*, the triad of ethics, oeconomics and politics became the normal structure for the moral philosophy curriculum' ('Tripartite Division' 303).[8] This triad was perceived as continuous:

> Not only were both the humanists and scholastics avid students of ethics, but they both saw a natural connection between ethics, oeconomics, and politics. There was a common agreement that these fields—all concerned with the good of man and society—should be studied on the basis of Aristotle's *Nicomachean Ethics* and *Politics* as well as the *Oeconomics* (which was commonly, but falsely, attributed to Aristotle).
>
> (Lines 305)[9]

The Nicomachean Ethics 'was the major university text in ethics' (Scodel 2), even if very few commentaries emerged from English universities.[10] Charles B. Schmitt notes its 'very widespread' appeal, which was 'by no means confined to one social or economic class' ('Aristotle's Ethics' 90). Schmitt writes: 'The "Nicomachean Ethics", perhaps as much as any other work from antiquity, emerged from the Reformation struggles as a keystone of both Catholic and Protestant education' (94).

Cicero's *De Officiis*, which 'was often treated as a more accessible companion to the *Nicomachean Ethics*' (Scodel 2), was taught in grammar schools. A work on practical ethics addressed to Cicero's son, *De Officiis* promoted 'the "mean" ("mediocritas")' and the 'proper "measure" ("modus")' (Scodel 2). As a grammar school text for intermediate and advanced levels, it was known to many people, either directly or through English vernacular writers whose ethical framework had been shaped by the study of Ciceronian letters and essays. Cicero's *De Officiis* was 'the text most often recommended and studied in school' (Green 202), although

---

[7] As C. B. Schmitt suggests, universities remained 'staunchly Aristotelian regardless of confessional affiliation' ('Philosophy and Science in Sixteenth-Century Universities' 491–492). Mark H. Curtis points out that, 'As late as 1636, for instance, the Laudian statutes of Oxford required that determining bachelors of arts argue their propositions in logic, rhetoric, politics, and moral philosophy according to the teachings of Aristotle, "whose authority is paramount"' (229). He quotes from John Griffiths, ed., *Laudian Code of Statutes 1636*, Oxford, 1888, title iv, sec. 2, § 9.

[8] The 'tripartite division' was inherited from the Middle Ages, from commentaries by 'Byzantine philosopher and theologian Eustratius of Nicaea (c.1050–c.1120)', Albertus Magnus, and Thomas Aquinas (Kraye, 'The Tripartite Division' 304). As Kraye writes, in Aquinas's commentary, 'moral philosophy was divided into three parts: *monastica*, which concerned the actions of the individual; *oeconomica*, the actions of the domestic unit; and *politica*, the actions of civil society' (304).

[9] Complete Latin editions of Aristotle's works on ethics and politics were made available in the thirteenth century, with Robert Grosseteste's translation of the *Ethics* in c.1240 and William of Moerbeke's translation of the *Politics* in c.1260 (Sorensen, 'The Reception of the Political Aristotle' 10).

[10] As David A. Lines explains, 'We know of only one prolusion for the fifteenth century and of the commentaries by John Case, William Temple, and Cuthbert Tunstall for the sixteenth' (312).

there may have been a shift in its uses towards the end of the sixteenth century: from helping intermediate students 'compare the rules of grammar and rhetoric they had learnt so far' to 'a guide to essay style and as a bottomless well of quotable quotes for themes and speeches' for older students (Green 204).[11]

Certainly, the classical influences on early modern writers cannot be reduced to Aristotelian or Ciceronian philosophy or Xenophon's *Oeconomicus*. Plato and the Stoics also shaped early modern notions of virtue.[12] Yet Aristotle was omnipresent and the only classical philosopher to be identified with his vocation: he was called 'the philosopher'. Furthermore, his virtue ethics is particularly interesting for a better understanding of socio-economic action because it emphasized not just the excessive edge of the passions, but also their motivational force. Platonists and Stoics believed in the necessity of subjugating the passions and establishing 'reason's rule' (Tilmouth 20) over this destructive and deceptive force, but Aristotle perceived 'passions and desires' not just as 'problems to be negotiated', but as 'positive forces which the soul ... needs to harness for its own good' (21):[13]

> To be morally virtuous, such a man [the would-be virtuous man] must, ultimately, perform good deeds, but he can only do that if he first shapes all his mind's motive powers to support his moral purposes; if, that is, he brings under his command all parts of the desiderative power, passions included.
>
> (Tilmouth 22)

As Christopher Tilmouth suggests, Aristotle gave rise to a tradition of self-government 'which emphasizes the cultivation (rather than suppression) of the passions' (20). Early modern plays stage the excessive tendency and disruptive force of the passions, but they also demonstrate their immense motivational force.[14] Their power to move people, to motivate their actions, is crucial to a seventeenth- and eighteenth-century anthropology of economic man.[15]

---

[11] Ian Green identifies *De Officiis* as likely to have been taught in advanced classes in grammar schools, as well as in the early years of university. *De Officiis* is commonly mentioned in 'English educational treatises, school curricula and university statutes' (196). After 1600, Cicero's letters and essays were entered into the so-called 'English Stock' (197). Students began by studying some of Cicero's letters and then moved on to the essays, most frequently to *De Officiis*, 'the text most often recommended and studied in school' (202). Medieval scholastics, as Green writes, had already 'adopted the four "virtues" of prudence, justice, fortitude and moderation described in *De Officiis* into Christian teaching as the four cardinal virtues, alongside the scripturally based Christian or theological virtues of faith, hope and charity' (196). Green emphasizes the impact of *De Officiis*: 'as the basis of good behaviour', the work 'may have left a deep mark on the views of many of the educated elite, and especially the gentry, in England' (205).

[12] For a lucid account of the Renaissance reception of Stoic philosophy, see Jill Kraye, 'The Revival of Hellenistic Philosophies'.

[13] See also Brian Cummings and Freya Sierhuis's 'Introduction' to *Passions and Subjectivity in Early Modern Culture* for the different treatment of the passions in Plato and the Stoics, on the one hand, and in Aristotle's work on the other (particularly 1–4).

[14] Kevin Sharpe reminds his readers that passion 'signified a suffering or affliction, a *disorder*' (774).

[15] The 'Principle of the Countervailing Passions' (20), which Albert O. Hirschman describes in his famous work *The Passions and the Interests*, builds on this motivating power. Hirschman associates

Xenophon's *Oeconomicus*

With its detailed attention to gender roles and the claim that a well-educated woman may take charge of matters of the house, Xenophon's *Oeconomicus* appealed strongly to post-Reformation writers, who identified woman as a rational creature and promoted a division of labour in the household. Sarah B. Pomeroy, the translator and editor of Xenophon's *Oeconomicus*, suggests that 'the most important reason for the popularity of the *Oeconomicus* is that it provides instruction on marriage' (85). The detailed attention to marital matters, from the choice of a wife to her education and conduct, also characterizes early modern oeconomies. Pomeroy points out that the idea of marriage in the *Oeconomicus* would have appealed to the emerging middle classes because it fitted perfectly into the post-Reformation ideology of diligence in business and partnership in marriage: 'Both husband and wife are thrifty, self-disciplined, impatient of leisure, insatiable when it comes to work, and dedicated to increasing their capital' (84). Ischomachus constitutes a welcome figure for identification at a time when rich citizens shaped their conduct according to the values of the aristocratic elite: he is a 'businessman' 'who manages to remain a thorough gentleman' (Pomeroy 84).

Lorna Hutson also notes the crucial role of the housewife in Xenophon's treatise: the management of the house, which Ischomachus's wife performs, frees *his* attention for activities in the marketplace. This is, in fact, where the dialogue begins: Socrates runs into Ischomachus in 'the *agora* or marketplace' (Hutson 40). Hutson perceives the significance of this setting: 'the discovery of Ischomachus in the text as "being outdoors" signifies a state of apparent leisure which is actually preparedness-for-business, a state of being furnished, or possessed, of the means to speak and act to advantage in the public domain' (40). Discussing Gentian Hervet's sixteenth-century translation, Hutson points out that, 'Hervet's substitution of a "chuche porche" [for the *agora*] would convey to a sixteenth-century reader this sense of a public place for the transacting of business' (40). This scene exemplifies perfectly the utility of a division of labour, for Ischomachus can only be encountered in a public place away from home because his wife takes such good care of domestic matters: 'I certainly do not spend time indoors, for my wife is more than capable of managing everything inside the house, even by herself'

---

this principle with Bacon, who sets '*affection against affection … to master one by another*' (qtd. in Hirschman 22). The full quotation is to be found in *The Advancement of Learning*, Book Two, 150. Here, Bacon insists on the 'speciall vse in Morall and Ciuile matters' (259) of this ability to function as check to each other. By way of analogy he reminds his readers that 'wee vse to hunt beast with beaste, and flye byrde with birde' (150). This principle is a means to control the passions 'by playing one off against the other' (Hirschman 23). Hirschman describes in his monograph how the 'interests' emerged as tamers of passion (31–32). '[E]ventually', he maintains, the concept 'came to be centered on economic advantage as its core meaning' (32). Pierre Force, in his more recent study of self-interest, also perceives Adam Smith as endpoint of this development: 'according to Smith, the desire to become rich is the overriding passion in modern commercial society. All other passions are subsumed into the desire to increase one's wealth' (161).

(Xenophon 139). Hervet translates a little less decidedly, but in a similar vein: 'in dede, good Socr[ates], I do not alwaye byde at home, for my wyfe can order wel inough suche thynges as I have there' (qtd. in Hutson 40).

This capacity to take care of things in the house is the result of Ischomachus's education of his wife, as the ensuing conversation informs us, yet the wife—even at the age of fifteen—had already been trained by her parents in virtues which were recognized as fundamental by early modern writers: she 'had spent her previous years under careful supervision, so that she might see and hear and speak as little as possible ... And besides, she had been very well trained to control her appetites' (Xenophon 139). As Jennifer Richards points out: '*Oeconomicus* can be credited as a source for the division of labour in the household literature of sixteenth- and seventeenth-century England' (36).[16] The ideal of a virtuous wife who was capable of taking care of the house so that the husband was free to conduct business elsewhere was welcomed by early modern writers on household and family. To give but one example: in stanza twenty-one of his 'Good husbandlie lessons', Tusser uses a parallelism to emphasize the equal significance of the husband's and wife's labour while assigning them to different spheres: 'Good husband he trudgeth, to bring in the gaines, / good huswife she drudgeth, refusing no paines: / Though husband at home, be to count ye wot what, / yet huswife, within, is as needfull as that' (21). The husband walks outside and supervises the accounting at home, while the wife drudges within, but both toil equally laboriously and patiently. Tusser assigns the business of casting accounts to the husband, but allots the rest of the domestic work to the wife. This division of labour promotes an emergent distinction of a heterosocial household and a homosocial market.

Another highly influential feature of Xenophon's work was his interest in the relation between oeconomy and politics. In his writings, '[e]mpire and oikos, public and private, are organized according to the same principles' (Pomeroy 241; see also Foucault, *The History of Sexuality* 154; vol. 2) and the *polis* profits from well-managed estates. In his dialogue with Critobulus, Socrates praises the Persian king Cyrus (Xenophon 127) with a dual lesson in mind: Cyrus's attention to estate management establishes oeconomy as an art well worth the attention of a king, but his high valuation of agriculture and his oeconomic skill also provide an indication of Cyrus's virtuous character and—a topos frequently repeated in early modern writings—of his skill in governing. Socrates aligns military and oeconomic excellence in his characterization of Cyrus to conclude: 'if Cyrus had lived, he would, I think, have proved himself an excellent ruler' (127).

---

[16] According to Richards, Cicero 'refers the reader to this text as a source for the ethics of enterprise' (36). She emphasizes 'the important contribution that this text made, along with *De Officiis*, to the defence of profit making as desirable in a period suspicious of usurious activity' (36). Richards refers to a passage from *De Officiis* which discusses 'domestic finances': 'They are maintained by care and thrift, and augmented by these same qualities. Xenophon, the disciple of Socrates, has analysed these topics conveniently in his book *Oeconomicus*, which I translated from Greek into Latin ...' (*Off.* 2.87).

In Xenophon's work, the household strengthens the *polis* by generating wealth, citizens, and soldiers: 'The oikoi constituted the foundation of the polis and served to reproduce the citizen population; therefore strengthening the individual oikoi would result in a more stable and vigorous polis' (Pomeroy 46). There is no indication that estate management establishes a structure of discipline or subjection, as early modern writers suggest. On the contrary, oeconomy has a variety of benefits: exercising the body, leading a pleasurable life, producing first-rate offerings and festivities, being popular with slaves and agreeable to wife and friends.[17] It is the best employment for 'a true gentleman' and hence a noble occupation. Of course, it is also beneficial to the *polis*, but Xenophon does not display the single-mindedness of early modern authors, who pitch the household as a disciplinary institution. For Xenophon, oeconomy was agricultural, a matter of estate rather than household management, and he highlights its multiple benefits:

> This line of work seemed to be very easy to learn and most enjoyable to practise, to make men's bodies most handsome and strong, and to provide their minds with the greatest amount of leisure to devote to their friends and their cities. We thought that farming, to some extent, stimulated those who work at it to be brave, because crops and cattle are raised outside the city walls. Therefore this way of making a living, we thought, enjoys the best reputation among cities; for they believe that it creates citizens who are both extremely brave and most loyal to communities.
>
> (135)

The emphasis is on agriculture's ability to create healthy, brave, loyal, and competent citizens. On the basis of Xenophon's multilayered description of the advantages of estate management, Foucault described the *oikos* as 'a whole sphere of activities', which 'is connected to a lifestyle and an ethical order' (*The History of Sexuality* 153; vol. 2).

To foreshadow the early modern interpretation of the relation between *oikos* and *polis*, we may note that the reader's address to the sixteenth-century translation of Xenophon's treatise indicates a shift in the relation between oeconomy and politics, which is discussed in greater detail below. The reader's address ('To the reder') prefaced the editions of 1532, 1537, 1544, and 1550, which were printed by Thomas Berthelet. It ends with the words: 'whiche boke *for the welthe of*

---

[17] Xenophon lists the benefits of managing an agricultural estate in the form of a series of rhetorical questions: 'And what occupation makes men more suited for running, throwing, and jumping than farming? What occupation provides greater pleasure in return to those who work at it? ... Where is it more comfortable to spend the winter than on a farm with a generous fire and warm baths? Where is it more pleasurable to spend the summer than in the countryside with streams and breezes and shade? What other occupation provides more appropriate first-fruits for the gods or produces festivals with a greater abundance of offerings? What occupation is more popular with slaves, or sweeter to a wife, or more attractive to children, or more agreeable to friends?' (131).

this realme, I deme very p[ro]fitable to redde' (*Xenophons Treatise of Housholde*, my emphasis). This paratext even made its way into a later edition by another printer (1557). In this as in other early modern texts, oeconomy is not merely an end in itself, but serves the commonwealth.[18] The emphasis on '*the welthe of this realme*' ties in with the twist that early modern writers gave the relation between *oikos* and *polis*: household and community were not only run according to the same principles of government and demanded similar skills, but the household became the actual site where political authority and subjection were learned.

The Aristotelian *Oikos*

The Pseudo-Aristotelian *Economics* defines the household cumulatively with Hesiod: 'A house the first, a wife, and ploughing ox' (*Economics* 1343). The basic constellation of material possessions, humans, and beasts persists through antiquity and the early modern age: a household comprises house and land as well as wife, children, servants, beasts, and material possessions. Yet the *Nicomachean Ethics* and *Politics* prove far more fruitful for an understanding of Aristotle's ideas on household management than this brief work. The *Nicomachean Ethics* in particular provides a detailed and lasting ethical framework for individual conduct and the management of the household. Key aspects of Aristotelian and Ciceronian ethics shaped early modern writings on the household, in particular the need for self-government, the doctrine of the golden mean, and the virtues of temperance and justice in matters of consumption and commerce. True to the demands of virtue ethics, the householder observes justice in his commercial dealings, and his actions are governed by the overarching intellectual virtue of prudence (practical wisdom), which guides his choice of means and ends. While the specific good of household management is wealth, this end is limited by the actual needs of the *oikos* and must not be derived from unfair gain. Early modern writers frequently invoked the Aristotelian doctrine of the golden mean to warn against excessive tendencies. Aristotle determines ethical virtue as an 'intermediate between excess and defect' (*EN* II.5, 1106a28–29).[19] This doctrine influenced authors 'of different religious, political, and social commitments and backgrounds', who all affirmed 'the mean as a norm for everyday life' (Scodel 3). The early modern householder had to carefully navigate the extreme poles of deficiency and excess: excessive spending, for instance, was as much to be avoided as niggardly behaviour.

---

[18] See also Christiane Damlos-Kinzel's discussion of Berthelet's address to the reader, 33–34.

[19] As Hallvard Fossheim puts it, virtue is 'a mean between two vices, one of excess and one of deficiency in feelings and in actions' (256). The abbreviation *EN* stands for *Nicomachean Ethics* and will be used throughout the text.

Aristotle distinguishes between moral and intellectual virtues.[20] For reasons of space, the following discusses only two virtues that are essential to oeconomy: temperance and prudence. Aristotle deems temperance the key moral virtue of the good householder. Temperance describes 'a mean with regard to pleasures' (*EN* III.10, 1117b25–26). It refers specifically to the pleasures of 'touch and taste' (*EN* III.10, 1118a26): food, drink, and sexual acts (*EN* III.10, 1118a30–32).[21] Intemperance, the uncontrolled appetite for costly food or sexual favours, constituted a threat both to the moral integrity and the financial stability of the household. In addition to safeguarding the household's wealth, temperance also 'preserves one's practical wisdom' (*EN* VI.5, 1140b12), the intellectual virtue that Aristotle associates explicitly with household management. Practical reason is the ability to calculate and deliberate, but it is virtuous (i.e., wise) only when it is exercised with a view to appropriate means and virtuous ends—in other words, when actions are governed by prudence. The early modern age was still interested in practical reason as the faculty that allowed people to navigate the shifting field of social and economic relations, but theatre suggests that its ethical orientation was weakening: in many plays, private interests take centre stage and, with them, an instrumental form of practical knowledge that cares little for virtue and much for the acquisition of wealth.

The *Politics* clarifies the household's relation to wealth. In the first book, Aristotle discusses the art of acquiring money in order to draw a clear boundary between household management and trade. Wealth is the specific good of household management only insofar as it is a means for the end of a happy life. It is sought not for its own sake, but for its uses in providing 'such things necessary to life, and useful for the community of the family or state' (*Pol.* I.8, 1256b29–30). The orientation towards necessary things naturally limits the amount of wealth required, 'for the amount of property which is needed for a good life is not unlimited' (*Pol.* I.8, 1256b31–32). In oeconomy, wealth is procured, preserved, and spent within an ethical framework that affirms the golden mean and guarantees the careful choice and execution of actions for a good end. Chrematistics, the art of acquiring money through retail trade or usury, on the other hand, is prone to confusing means and end: while money should be a means for the continuing end of a good life, it becomes here an end in itself. As wealth can be increased infinitely, money evolves from a limited means to an unlimited end. For the household, in contrast, money

---

[20] According to John Cooper, the intellectual virtue of practical wisdom and moral virtue can be conceptualized as mutually re-enforcing: Cooper maintains that 'since Aristotle calls the virtues of the non-rationally desiring part of our nature collectively "moral virtue" or "virtue of character" ... this amounts to saying that moral virtue ... presupposes and is dependent upon the virtues of practical reason, the virtues of the mind that he calls collectively "practical wisdom"' (255). At the same time, however, practical wisdom constitutes the result of a virtuous life, of habitually choosing the mean.

[21] As Thomas Hurka puts it, 'the virtue of temperance is a mean with respect to the desire for physical pleasure, a desire the excess of which is self-indulgence and the deficiency of which is insensibility' (13).

remains a means, its use limited to purchasing goods necessary to the household's continued existence.

In the logic of the Aristotelian *oikos*, individual actions and affects are limited by habitual preference for the mean: social intercourse and exchanges are structured by moderation and motivated by needs. In early modern writings on household management, this framework defines individual conduct and social relations. Early modern plays, by contrast, as the following chapters show, explore the disintegration of ethics and oeconomics. They portray the comic and tragic effects of excessive desires and unethical actions that aim at the accumulation of wealth and social advancement.

The Early Modern *Oikos*

In line with the Aristotelian legacy, early modern writers are reluctant to identify the acquisition of wealth as a legitimate end of oeconomy. This reluctance was supported by the Christian characterization of an 'immoderate desire of Gaine' as evil (Bourne 33). Yet gain that is not coveted but given as a reward of diligent work may be enjoyed: thrift and diligence legitimize profit. In 'A Ladder to Thrift', a poem that forms part of his manual, Tusser advises his readers 'To follow profit earnestlie' (16) and warns against excessive consumption: 'prodigall liuers, haue sildome good end' (21). For him, saving one's pennies is a legitimate road to 'individual improvement' (McRae, *God Speed* 148), not just for gentlemen, but for tenant farmers as well. Amplified by Protestant railings against prodigality and pomp, the imperative to save money echoes through the prescriptive literature of the early modern age. David Landreth even describes oeconomy specifically as a 'discipline' that 'coordinated the values of ethics and of thrift' (34).

If the homiletic literature was reluctant to acknowledge gain as a legitimate end, husbandry manuals were a little more open about the desirability and legitimacy of profit. A passage from *Maison Rustique, Or the Countrie Farme*, a sixteenth-century manual translated into English in 1600, exemplifies this. Here, the estate is imagined as 'an other *Pandora*' that so overflows with produce that it attracts people from neighbouring towns to come and spend their coins. The passage deserves to be quoted in full because it illustrates the commercialization of agricultural oeconomy:

> For it is my intent and purpose that this our countrey house should be an other *Pandora*, furnished and flowing with store of all manner of good thinges and commodities, in such sort, as that the neighbour townes might haue recourse and seeke vnto it in cases of their necessities and wants, but without taking or receiuing any thing at their hands but money, as the price and sale of the wares shall amount and come vnto, which it sendeth and furnisheth them withall day

by day. I meane therefore that our farmer should be a baker, panter, worker in pastrie and a brewer when neede shall be: and to be briefe, that he should not be ignorant of any thing which might helpe to keepe, sustaine and inrich his house.

(704)

In this passage, as Andrew McRae points out, the fantasy of 'an unending process of accumulation' displaces 'the ideal of manorial self-sufficiency' (*God Speed* 143): agrarian products become commodities and the husbandman a consummately skilled artisan and tradesman. The aim is not just to maintain the estate, but to increase its wealth by producing all kinds of saleable commodities. The householder must not just 'sustaine' the household, but 'inrich his house'. In order to make a profit, as early modern writers were well aware, one must sell rather than buy. Consequently, Fitzherbert's *Booke of Husbandrie* suggests that the position of someone who needs to buy daily provisions is precarious: he who lacks either 'corne' or 'cattell' 'shall be a buyer, a borrower, or a beggar' (45), with the alliteration emphasizing the downward spiral that buying instigates. In Tusser's *Fiue Hundreth Points*, too, the farmer's aim is to be 'a seller and not a buyer' (McRae, *God Speed* 148). These examples suggest that early modern writers of husbandry manuals considered oeconomy and profit as compatible, even as they were rhetorically invested in an ethics of moderation and sufficiency. With their detailed accounts of how to manage a household or estate, they attempted to provide householders with the practical expertise needed to improve the profitability of their holdings.

The early modern household had, of course, not only an economic function, but also a social and political one. As noted earlier, the often-proclaimed goal of early modern household management was a well-ordered house that would ensure the order and prosperity of the commonwealth. The following discussion examines this in detail via three key aspects: the political significance of oeconomy, the distribution of authority and labour in the house, and the gendering of excessive desires that threaten to upset the household's financial stability as well as the social order. These aspects provide a context for understanding the extent to which theatrical representations of households depart from the ideal and offer insights into the nexus of ethics, oeconomy, and politics.

Tropical Exchanges and the Family as 'First Society'

In a complex tropical exchange, early modern writers represented the household as a miniature realm and the householder as king, as, for instance, in Richard Brathwaite's *The English Gentleman* (first published in 1630): 'As every mans house is his Castle, so is his *family* a private Common-wealth, wherein if due government be not observed, nothing but confusion is to be expected' (155).²² At the same time, authority and political government were rendered intelligible in terms of family relations, as in Alexander Nowell's *Catechism* (first published in 1570): 'all those to whom any authority is given, as magistrates, ministers of the church, schoolmasters ... are contained under the name of fathers' (130; also qtd. in Newman, *Fashioning Femininity* 16). In 1601, Malynes discussed the balance of trade on the grounds of the same pervasive analogy: 'a commonwealth is nothing else but a great houshold or family' with 'the Prince (being as it were the father of the family)' (*A Treatise of the Canker of England's Commonwealth* 2). Patriarchal authority in family and commonwealth was rendered intelligible, but also reinforced, through tropes that figured paternal and political authority as interchangeable: 'Domestic theorists were thus able to clothe fathers with something of the sacred majesty of kingship ... Political theorists, for their part, could link royal authority to a form of government that was familiar to all and accepted as natural' (Capp 5).²³

Tropical substitutions provided the rhetorical frame for pitching the household as a miniature society that prepared its inhabitants for their civic duties within the commonwealth. Early modern writers believed in the key function of the household as a 'schoole', in which authority and subjection were learned. It followed naturally that only a good householder could be a good king or bishop. English cleric Edward Topsell drew on this discursive tradition when he argued in 1609: 'A Housholder is not inferiour to the Gouernour of a Citty, and he that is not wise in Domesticall matters, shall neuer bee trusted in the Common-wealth' ('The Epistle Dedicatorie'). Bernard Capp sums this up as follows: 'No man could be fit to bear public office unless he already knew how to govern his family' (5). This is in line with Foucault's idea of a continuity between ethics, oeconomy, and politics:²⁴

> The art of government ... is essentially concerned with answering the question of how to introduce economy—that is to say, the correct manner of managing individuals, goods and wealth within the family (which a good father is expected to do in relation to his wife, children and servants) and of making the family fortunes prosper—how to introduce this meticulous attention of the father towards his family into the management of the state. ... To govern a state will therefore mean to apply economy, to set up an economy at the level of the entire state, which means exercising towards its inhabitants, and the wealth and behaviour of

---

²² The metaphor of the domestic king and castle is reiterated in many writings of the period. A tract by pastor John Wing from 1620 carries the telling title: *Crown Conjugall or the Spouse Royal* (Newman, *Fashioning Femininity* 15). According to Bernard Capp, William Whately described the husband as 'the prince of the household, the domestical king' (5). See also S. D. Amussen on the king as father and father as king, in 'Gender, Family and the Social Order, 1560-1725', 197.

²³ As Anthony Fletcher put it, '[B]etween the 1590s and the 1640s', Puritan writers played an important role in modelling 'the patriarchal family afresh as the basis of authority and obedience' (204).

²⁴ See also Damlos-Kinzel's discussion of Foucault on 9 and 75.

each and all, a form of surveillance and control as attentive as that of the head of a family over his household and his goods.

(Foucault, 'Governmentality' 92)

Early modern writers relentlessly reiterate the analogy between oeconomic and political government. Christiane Damlos-Kinzel describes the family around 1600 as 'model for political government' (63, my translation), yet the term 'model' tells only half the story. In early modern writings on the household, the family is a pillar of political government, the 'foremost disciplinary site' and 'training ground for political order' (Wall 1). It is here that Christians and political subjects are made. Historian Anthony Fletcher maintains that 'household order was the foundation of effective government' (205). Puritan author Robert Cleaver offered a striking example for this argument in *A Godlie Forme of Householde Gouernment* (first published in 1598), where he praised the political and spiritual significance of a well-governed house: 'A Householde is as it were a little common wealth, by the good gouernment whereof, Gods glorie may be aduaunced [sic], the common wealth whiche standeth of seuerall families, benefited, and al that liue in that familie may receiue much comfort and commoditie' (1). In this description, the family plays a double role as model for, and as actual moral and economic backbone of, the commonweal.[25] Theologian William Perkins positioned the family in his *Christian Oeconomie* (first published in 1609) as 'the first and most ancient' of all the societies and states in the world ('The Epistle Dedicatorie' 2r). From the union of Adam and Eve, 'both Church and Common-weale should spring and grow to their perfection' (2r–2v). The family emerges here as the origin and building ground of communal life, in both a religious and civic sense. Like many early modern theologians, Perkins drew on the classical philosophers to enforce his argument: 'Some of the learned among them, haue called the Familie, *the first societie in nature, and the ground* of all the rest' (2v). According to Perkins, Xenophon compared the family to a 'Bee-hiue' (2v) or a 'Metropolis, or mother Citie, which first traineth vp her natiue inhabitants, and then remoueth some of them to other places of abode, where they may bee framed as members, to liue in obedience to the laws of their Head' (3r). These analogies prepare the reader for the final conclusion: it is the family that constitutes the ground for order and discipline in the commonwealth:

---

[25] Josias Nichols dedicated his little book *An Order of Household Instruction* (first published in 1595) 'to him, who knoweth verie well, how needfull a thing it is in regard of the Commonwealth' ('The Epistle Dedicatorie', B1r). Nichols addressed his work to people who acted as social disseminators: noblemen and gentlemen with large households, tutors in universities and schoolmasters in town and country, and women, especially ladies and gentlewomen, who taught their own children as well as their maids. Elsewhere Nichols warns against the danger that God might withdraw from an 'vnthankfull nation' that fails to heed his word ('To the Reader', B5r). The extension of his concern to the 'nation' identifies the good of the commonweal as the end of his argument.

For this first Societie, is as it were the Schoole, wherein are taught and learned the principles of authoritie and subiection. And look as the Superior that faileth in his priuate charge, will prove vncapable of publike employment; so the Inferiour, who is not framed to a course of Oeconomicall subiection, will hardly undergoe the yoke of ciuill obedience.

(3v)

The order of the commonwealth depends absolutely on a rightfully ordered household: 'For an error in the foundation, puts the body and parts of the whole building in apparent hazard' (4).

The order of the household was strictly hierarchical, defined by poles of authority and subjection. According to Cleaver, there were two sorts of people in every family, to be represented in form of a dichotomous Ramist diagram:[26] '1 The Gouernours' and '2 Those that must be ruled' (15). This dichotomy draws an absolute distinction between those who govern and those who submit to their rule, while a curly bracket identifies them as two parts of a single structure. With this diagram, Cleaver establishes authority and subjection as the defining poles of the household. In *The Artes of Logike and Rethorike* from 1584, Calvinist theologian Dudley Fenner also posited an absolute distinction between governors and governed while using a curly bracket to subsume both into a single order (A1r).[27]

Wendy Wall suggests that the emphasis on the family as disciplinary site created a powerful and enduring ideology:

As scholars have noted, the early seventeenth century witnessed the transformation of what was in effect a 'vaguely articulated societal theory into an intentional political ideology,' one so powerful that the family secured a place of importance in political debates for the next one hundred years.

(7)[28]

---

[26] According to Karen Newman, Ramism classified 'concepts by dichotomies; a subject was defined by division into halves, those halves into halves, and so on, down to the so-called indivisibles or essentials' (*Fashioning Femininity* 21). This dichotomous diagram provided a matrix for 'rigid sexual divisions' (25), which enforced order as the new paradigm of family life: 'By the 1590s and the early decades of the seventeenth century, with the publication of William Perkins' *Christian Oeconomie* (Lat. 1590, tr. 1609), the preoccupation with adultery and whoredom characteristic of the early conduct books, handbooks, and sermons virtually disappears. The traditional biblical origins of marriage ... remain. But the elaborate attacks on adultery and whoredom are increasingly displaced by representations of ordered family life' (25). For a detailed account of Ramism in England: Howell, *Logic and Rhetoric in England 1500–1700*, chapter 4. Brian Cummings discusses the relation between Ramist logic and puritanism in *The Literary Culture of the Renaissance* 252–264.

[27] As Brian Cummings explains, 'In Fenner's *Artes of Logike and Rethorike* a union is declared between Calvinist theology and humanist literary theory, to the mutual discursive advantage of each' (275).

[28] Wall quotes from Gordon J. Schochet, *Patriarchalism in Political Thought: The Authoritarian Family and Political Speculation and Attitudes Especially in Seventeenth-Century England* 55.

In a similar vein, Karen Newman points out that '[t]he continued rehearsal of the microcosm/macrocosm trope represents the construction of an enabling ideology for consolidating sovereign power in the state: masters of families were exhorted to join hands with magistrates to ensure the orderly working of the commonwealth' (*Fashioning Femininity* 17). Within the frame of communicating orders on a micro (*oikos*) and macro level (*polis*), an unravelling of the internal order of the *oikos* threatens the order of the commonweal. As the two systems are similarly structured and communicate, their stability is mutually dependent. Thus the household, in early modern writings, has a curious triple role: first, it constitutes a serious subject for oeconomic reflection; second, it acts as a trope for political government; and, third, it is a causal factor in the commonweal's fate. Early modern drama exploits the household's polyvalent function for dramatic effect. *Macbeth* is a case in point: the household of Macbeth and his 'dark lady' (Lupton 367) is a subject of interest in itself, but Macbeth's failure of government at home also signals a general disorder and restructuring in the political sphere and, finally, plays an active role in triggering a political crisis.

The detailed attention early modern writers pay to household management testifies to the public interest in the *oikos*. Whatever happened inside individual households was of prime importance to the order and well-being of the commonwealth because the household had a key disciplinary function in producing subjects who were governable in a political sense.[29] Early modern authors affirmed the disciplinary function of the family and transformed household management into an art of government that allowed them to frame the household as a paradigm of order and model political government on oeconomy. The matrix of authority and subjection that orders the *oikos* within also enables and constitutes the social order without.

The sheer amount of verbal instructions in the prescriptive literature of the time indicates the household's political significance, but also its lack of transparency and the anxieties this produced. The commonwealth had little actual control over the institution that secured its order and produced its subjects. The contradictory claims on the household meant that it was a particularly interesting dramatic subject: the household constituted the basis of political order, and yet existed apart as its own little kingdom, and while it was supposed to labour for the good of all, it was also encouraged to increase its private wealth. Highly regulated down to the

---

[29] Even in Kyd's translation of Tasso's *The Housholders Philosophie*, which follows the model of antique oeconomies (notably that of Xenophon), the orientation of the *oikos* towards the good of the commonwealth is evident. Damlos-Kinzel points out that the political dimension of the text emerges in the general education prescribed by the commonwealth (67). Education aims at transforming children into valuable members of the commonwealth: 'Thy priuate estate requires that so thou teach and bring vp thy Children, as they may become good members of the Cittie where thy selfe inhabitest, or they shall dwel, good seruitors and subiects to their Prince, which in theyr trades if they be Merchaunts, in good letters if they bee learned, and in wares if they be able, they may shew themselues' (D1v; also qtd. in Damlos-Kinzel 67).

smallest practical details but ultimately a paradoxical, opaque, and self-contained structure, it fed the imagination and gave rise to suspicions and speculations.

The Power Axis of Household Government: Marriage

Post-Reformation works dwell at length on the gendered distribution of authority in the house, and early modern writers were at pains to demonstrate the importance of wives' submission to their husbands (Fissell 442). Yet although the wife's duty is to subject her own will to her husband's government, she is also interpellated as cogovernor. The discourse of government cuts out an ambiguous position for the mistress of the house as both subject to and 'fellow helper' (Cleaver 19; Fenner B2v) of her husband. As 'fellow helper' she governs with her husband: in recognition of this role, both Cleaver and Fenner employ the plural for 'governor' when they divide those who govern from those who are governed (Cleaver 15; Fenner A1r). Perkins also emphasizes her role as a cogovernor, 'a person which yeeldeth helpe and assistance in government to the Master of the familie' (*Christian Oeconomie* 173). She is the master's 'associate, not only in office and authoritie, but also in aduise, and counsell vnto him' (173). As Newman suggests in her chapter on marriage in *Fashioning Femininity*, for post-Reformation writers, the wife is no longer a creature of voracious desire that must be tamed or chastised, as in pre-Reformation literature (20–21). She is interpellated as a subject who submits to rational order *and* helps to maintain it. Newman sees order as the new paradigm of family life that was enforced by the Ramist method of dichotomical representation (21–22). In this order, the wife was ambiguously poised between subjection to the household head and superiority over the rest of the house.[30]

Early modern writers were for the most part keen to acknowledge that subjection in the case of wives meant something different than in the case of servants or children. In his brief anatomy of the householder's power, Perkins, who enjoyed an 'international reputation as a Calvinist divine' (Cummings 258), draws on Aristotle to demonstrate why the husband has no absolute authority over his wife:[31]

> Hereupon the Heathen Philosopher said, *That the master of the familie exerciseth (after a sort) a power Tyrannical ouer his seruants, a power Regall ouer his children; because Kings are fathers of their Common-weales: but in respect of his wife, he exerciseth a power Aristocraticall, not after his owne will, but agreeable to the honor*

---

[30] See also Amussen: 'Theoretically, the husband ruled his wife, and she obeyed him in all things; he provided wise government and the necessities of life. At the same time she was joined with him in the government of the household, and was often responsible for the day-to-day education and supervision of both children and servants' (201).

[31] Perkins is usually categorized as a Calvinist (Cummings 258), but William E. Patterson has recently argued that Perkins 'was not so much an Elizabethan Puritan as he was an apologist, perhaps the chief apologist, for the Church of England as it emerged in the late Elizabethan period' (40).

and dignitie of the married estate; and consequently, that he ought not in modestie to challenge the priuiledge of prescribing and aduertising his wife in al matters domesticall, but in some to leaue her, to her own will and iudgement.

(*Christian Oeconomie* 126)[32]

William Gouge also describes a wife's 'place of inferiority, and subiection' as one that 'is neerest to equality that may be: a place of common equity in many respects, wherein man and wife are after a sort euen fellowes, and partners' (356). As Newman points out, early modern writers 'recognized the special nearness of wives, their knowledge of their husbands' habits and faults, and the possibility they might use that knowledge against them' (*Fashioning Femininity* 17).

Early modern writers differed in their views as to how independently the wife should be allowed to act in the domestic sphere (Anthony Fletcher 205). While Gouge 'explicitly limits the woman's power over the disposal of family goods' (Miller 77), Perkins advised in the quotation above that the mistress should be left to her own judgement and will in some domestic matters (*Christian Oeconomie* 126). The husband should correct her only if he saw her at fault, and then only verbally, not with strokes (127). The anonymous author of *A Glasse for Housholders* advised the husband and master to give 'the gouernaunce of the house ... wholly to youre wyfe' (D4v). As she should not meddle with business and merchandise, he should not busy himself with things of the house (D4v).[33] 'In practice', Anthony Fletcher suggests, 'it was the woman who had to do much of the hour-by-hour direction and decision-making about the conduct and activities of young children and of servants under her charge' (205).

Already in Xenophon's *Oeconomicus*, as his translator Pomeroy points out, the marital relationship 'is viewed as fundamental to the success of an oikos' (33). Early modern writers also identified the relation between husband and wife as a crucial factor in the household's fate. Marriage constituted the neuralgic point of the household: the household's existence was seriously threatened by marital strife and mismanagement, but a couple that worked well together could turn their house into a place of abundance. Tusser addresses both possibilities and

---

[32] See also Wilkinson, *The Merchant Royall*, who suggests that authority over the wife is 'authoritie tempered with equalitie' (37). In 'The Household and the State', Constance Jordan analysed the changing relations between household and state from Aristotle to James I. Aristotle distinguished between the government of wife and children, who are free members of the household, and the government of slaves. Wife and children are again subject to different forms of government, with the former being 'political' and the latter 'monarchical' (Jordan 311). Jordan states that 'The image of the married couple, in which both partners are free and in that respect the same, but one of whom commands while the other does not command, is a near paradox' (311).

[33] In *A Godlie Forme of Household Gouernment*, Cleaver gives discretion in this matter to the husband: 'The husband, as the head and chiefe guide of the familie, must haue the custodie & chiefe gouernment of the goods in the house: yet may he discharge himselfe of the whole, or of part, as himselfe shall think meet and conuenient: yet let him remember, that hee intreat her not as a seruant' (201).

their respective outcomes in stanza six of his 'Good husbandlie lessons': 'Where cooples agree not, is rancor and strife, / where such be togither, is seldome good life: / Where cooples in wedlocke, doo louelie agree, / there foison remaineth, if wisedom there bee' (18). Here, marital harmony coupled with practical wisdom is the key to successful household management. In Robert Wilkinson's sermon *The Royall Marchant* (first published in 1607), the uncertain outcome of marriage is captured by the allegory of a sea-faring venture: 'She is like a Ship indeed, for first whosoeuer marries, ventures, he ventures his estate, hee ventures his peace, he ventures his libertie, yea many men by marriage aduenture their soules too' (8).[34] The implications are evident: marriage is a high-risk enterprise. It can be as risky, but also as profitable, as a commercial venture, with sea-faring commerce bearing both the greatest risks and the greatest profits.

Household Guardian or 'Perpetuall Enemie'

In Protestant and Puritan oeconomic writings, the wife emerges as highly significant factor in the success of the *oikos*. Cleaver described the gracious wife as a prudent spender and skilled supervisor of children and servants. Her main duty consists in saving, not by being 'a slender huswife' (90), but rather a skilful one who observes all household proceedings closely to identify unnecessary expenses: 'She must bee wise, to marke and see, what needles burthens, vnnecessarie expences and losses there doe vpon occasions fall out within doores, and preuent such occasions afterwards' (91). To prevent temptation, the housewife must beware that 'she should not be idle at any time', as the 1598 edition of Fitzherbert's *Booke of Husbandrie* emphasizes (147). Most writings on household and family sing the praise of the thrifty wife who saves what she can without being niggardly. The insistence on saving is omnipresent. It is reinforced by rhetorical alignments of '[f]inancial expenditure and loss of virtue' (Miller 77). This is an extremely interesting point: the wife emerges here as guardian of the household, but she assumes this position against a discursive tradition that associates women with excessive bodily appetites.

In her book *Blood and Home in Early Modern Drama*, Ariane M. Balizet identifies the body as 'governing metaphor of the household ... in early modern domestic guides and treatises' (56). She terms this metaphorical model *'somatic domesticity'* (56). The metaphor of the household as body 'implicates every stratum of household government, from the wise and judicious head (husband); to the fleshly body,

---

[34] The sermon was written for the occasion of 'the Nuptials of the Right Honourable Lord Hay and his Lady'; it is based on Proverbs 31:14: 'She is like a Merchants Ship, she bringeth her foode from a farre'. (1)

heart, and womb (wife); to the labouring hands and feet (household servants) in the animation of a properly functioning household' (56). Identified with the fleshly trunk and vital organs of the household, women were associated with excessive appetites that had to be controlled by a male head. Torquato Tasso's *The Housholders Philosophie*, which was translated by Kyd in 1588, offers a prime example for the gendering of desire and reason that justifies patriarchal authority:

> [I]t often commeth to passe that he [the husband] shal find her [the wife] so exceeding waiward, crabbed and disobedient, that where he thought hee made his choyce of a companion that shold helpe to lighten and exonerat that ponderous & heauie loade which our humanity affordeth, he findes he is nowe matcht and fallen into the handes of a perpetuall enemie, who euermore none otherwise impugneth and resisteth him then our immoderate desires, that in our minds so much oppose themselues to reason: for such is woman in respecte of man, as is desire in comparison of understanding...
>
> (C2r)

In this analogy, the relation between husband and wife corresponds to the relation between reason and desire, who are locked in a struggle of forces.[35] As a woman is prone to excess, she may ruin the household if she is not kept in check by her husband. The 'Renaissance commonplace', according to which 'man is figured as the head, woman as the body' (Newman, *Fashioning Femininity* 16), suggests the female need for rational control and supervision by a father or husband.[36]

Early modern writers did not tire of warning men against rash and imprudent marriage choices. Clergyman Thomas Gataker, for instance, lamented the blindness of men in choosing a wife in a marriage sermon from 1623: 'Many haue good skill in chusing of wares, in valuing of lands, in beating a bargaine, in making a purchase, that are yet but blinde buzzards in the choise of a wife' (10). In Wilkinson's sermon *The Merchant Royall*, the wife is not only a 'perpetuall enemie' but an 'executioner': 'as the saying is, that many men marrie their executors; so is it true likewise, that many men marrie their executioners' (26). Gataker compares the bad wife to 'a rocke or a shelfe to Sea-men in a storme' and, implicitly, likens the good wife to safe 'harbour and shelter' (6). Such utterances demonstrate the

---

[35] Already in the *Politics*, Aristotle links reason and passion with gender: 'And it is clear that the rule of the soul over the body, and the mind and the rational element over the passionate, is natural and expedient; whereas the equality of the two or the rule of the inferior is always hurtful ... Again, the male is by nature superior, and the female inferior; and the one rules, and the other is ruled; this principle, of necessity, extends to all mankind' (*Pol.* I.5, 1254b6–16).

[36] The typical formula can be found in Thomas Gataker's sermon ('A Wife Indeed'): 'A Wife then, say those Apostles, is one, that is subiect and obedient to her Husband, as her Head' (14; part of *A Good Wife Gods Gift*).

double coding of the female as household guardian *and* existential threat.[37] Anxieties about the excessive desires of woman are omnipresent in the insistence of early modern writers on moderation.[38]

Excessive female consumption (Archer 185) was often represented as an immoderate desire for luxurious gowns. For Cleaver, a wife must 'be content with such apparell and outward port, as her husbands estate can allow her' (89). In Middleton's *Women Beware Women*, Leantio asks his mother not to incite his new wife, who has married beneath her social status, so that she may not 'rise with other women in commotion / Against their husbands, for six gowns a year / And so maintain their cause, when they're once up / In all things else that require cost enough' (*Women Beware* 1.1.76–79). In Jonson's *Epicoene*, to give another example, Truewit warns against the excessive spending habits of women: 'she feels not how the land drops away, nor the acres melt, nor foresees the change when the mercer has your woods for her velvets' (*Epicoene* 2.2.95–97). And in John Fletcher's comedy *The Tamer Tamed*, the first two things that Maria demands from Petruchio are 'liberty and clothes' (2.5.137). In a later scene, she tortures Petruchio with her desire for excessively luxurious clothes:

> MARIA. [To servants] I do not like that dressing; 'tis too poor.
>   Let me have six gold laces, broad and massy,
>   And betwixt every lace a rich embroidery;
>   Line the gown through with plush, perfumed, and purfle
>   All the sleaves down with pearls.
>   (3.2.99–103)

The preoccupation with women's desire for luxury goods signals a high level of anxiety around women's excessive desires.[39]

The topos of gossiping is frequently used to exemplify the need for moderation. It has an excessive edge that is thoroughly uneconomic. In the act of gossiping, not only are too many words lost, but also too much time: 'They perceiue not how time runneth, nor how vntowardly their busines goeth forward, while they sit idle' (Cleaver 95). The concern with gossiping is tropically linked with temperance. In sixteenth-century writing, a loose tongue pointed to loose morals: 'disallowed

---

[37] Catherine Belsey comments on the early modern commonplace that men must 'choose wisely when they select a wife' (*Shakespeare and the Loss of Eden* 76) and points out that the biblical model, Eve, is herself an 'anarchic' figure who 'betrayed her husband': 'the good and bad wife are one and the same person' (77).

[38] Jean Howard links female waywardness with consumption. She describes 'the fear ... that woman's desire, stimulated by the availability of foreign luxuries, will lead her out of her domestic space and out of her marriage into adultery' in 'Women, Foreigners, and Urban Space in *Westward Ho*' (155). See also Newman's *Fashioning Femininity* 131–143.

[39] With rhymed advice, the anonymous author of *The Husband's Instructions to his Family* also urges his wife to beware of letting her passions reign.

speech is a sign throughout the period of sexual transgression' (Newman, *Fashioning Femininity* 11). Newman claims that in many writings, 'An open mouth and immodest speech are tantamount to open genitals and immodest acts' (11).[40] Gail Kern Paster discusses a tendency of early modern discourse which 'inscribes women as leaky vessels by isolating one element of the female body's material expressiveness—its production of fluids—as excessive' (*The Body Embarrassed* 25). It 'links this liquid expressiveness to excessive verbal fluency', representing a 'particular kind of uncontrol as a function of gender' (25). Shannon Miller explains: 'Attempts to control Renaissance women consequently idealized a classical, contained body; the traits praised in a woman were a closed mouth, carefully guarded chastity, and limited physical mobility' (76).

The representation of female incontinence in early modern household literature brings into focus key points of household management and government. As women were represented as prone to excessive consumption, they were imagined as having a huge impact on the household's financial stability. At the same time, the order of the commonwealth relied on the patriarchal order of individual households; the female body as the site of excessive desires thus also posed a threat to the social order. For the sake of social order and the economic stability of the household, discipline had to be enforced at the level of oeconomy, and it fell to the master of the house to keep those excessive desires that the female represented in check. Thus, the mistress of the house found herself in a paradoxical position: the wife was a vital factor in managing the household successfully and securing its future by means of reproduction, but her excessive appetites also turned marriage into a high-risk enterprise. Filled with uncontrollable desire, she was ever in danger of succumbing to unethical conduct and excessive spending that threatened disorder and financial ruin. Successful management of the house depended on the careful education of the wife as 'fellow helper'. It relied on a gender economy that regulated the division of labour and the distribution of duties, and exemplified supervision and political government. As the following chapter shows, early modern plays perform, examine, and milk this gender economy for comic and tragic effects and use it as a means to examine both economic and political crises.

Early Modern Commerce

Ethical and political concerns frame not just oeconomic, but also mercantile reflections of the period. Around the turn of the seventeenth century, handbooks and advice literature on how to conduct business were published. They were written by merchants who addressed their sons, apprentices, and fellow merchants.

---

[40] 'The slippage from the whore's thirsty mouth to her insatiable genitals is a commonplace' (Newman, 'City Talk' 184).

Browne's *The Marchants Avizo* (first published in 1589) and Scott's landmark *Essay of Drapery* (1635) are notable examples. They discussed the art of trade, its moral implications, and the education it required, and strove to establish the merchant as a self-confident and worthy citizen. The turn of the century also saw the first attempts to describe and regulate the nation's economy on the part of mercantilist and bullionist writers such as John Wheeler, Gerard de Malynes, Thomas Milles, Edward Misselden, and Thomas Mun. They discussed trade regulations and exchange rates with a reformative impulse and rather polemical rhetoric.[41]

All merchant writers faced the problem of legitimizing gain against an ethical discourse that prioritized the common good. This ethical framework was fed by two sources, one classical, one Christian. Aristotle's virtue ethics, with its golden mean, was the most important classical influence, bolstered by Cicero's insistence on the key virtues of wisdom, justice, courage, and temperance (Walsh xviii).[42] Aristotle's critique of retail trade and its excessive pursuit of wealth set the tone for centuries to come and was reiterated time and again in early modern works. From a Christian standpoint, 'greed became more prominent in the pantheon of sins' with 'the gradual growth of commerce in the later Middle Ages' (Folbre 10). Post-Reformation treatises warned against 'the gathering of wealth and riches' (Perkins, *Treatise of the Vocations* 81) and the many temptations that come with covetousness, the 'root of all evil' (1 Tim. 6:10). Like Thomas Aquinas, the 'theologian-philosopher' who was an important mediator between Aristotle and Christian doctrine, post-Reformation writers rejected disproportionate gain at the expense of another as unjust.[43] In an exchange, all parties involved should benefit. Although it is true that Protestantism 'was kind to merchants' (Folbre 11), because it established commerce as a divine calling and wealth as potentially God-given, suspicion of material wealth was omnipresent in post-Reformation writings of the late sixteenth century.

Mercantile documents offer insights into how merchants argued for the social benefits of trade and commercial ventures, how they negotiated ethical demands and, specifically, how they evaluated the ethical legitimacy of gain as the end of trade. Read together, Puritan treatises and sermons, as well as mercantile texts

---

[41] Mary Poovey highlights the connection between economics and politics in Misselden's and Mun's works: 'both borrowed from and contributed to a theory of politics that had begun to acquire considerable currency throughout northern Europe in the last quarter of the sixteenth century: *ragion di stato, raison d'état*, reason of state' (66).

[42] Cicero introduces the four cardinal virtues in Book One of the *De Officiis* as follows: 'All that is honourable emerges from one or the other of four sources. It is found in the perception and intelligent awareness of what is true; or in safeguarding the community by assigning to each individual his due, and by keeping faith with compacts made; or in the greatness and strength of a lofty and unconquered spirit; or in the order and due measure by which all words and deeds reflect an underlying moderation and self-control' (1.15).

[43] Gert Sorensen explains that it was Aquinas who 'succeeded in incorporating the Greek philosopher into dominant theological thought' (10–11).

of the late sixteenth and early seventeenth centuries suggest a revaluation of self-interest. Where the logic of household management (oeconomy) privileged virtue and the common good and limited the lawful acquisition of wealth with sufficiency, the growth of commerce established gain as a common motor and even legitimate end of action.[44] On a national level, mercantile discourses about England's wealth and competition with other countries facilitated the emerging sense of a national economy.

The audience for mercantile writings may have been significantly smaller than for household homilies, oeconomies, and ballads. Even those who could not read would have had to listen to sermons on marital life in church and been exposed to readings about religious and domestic duties in the circle of the family. Yet the number of readers of mercantile writings was hardly insignificant. According to Laura Caroline Stevenson, literacy levels among tradesmen in London were high.[45] Works on commerce and trade were written by merchants and addressed to their fellow merchants, sons, and apprentices (or even to policy makers such as the king and/or Parliament).[46] Those who were not directly familiar with mercantile writings would have encountered remarks on the ethics of trade, material gain, and the dangers of covetousness in church.

To contextualize the reevaluation of commerce and profit in mercantile writings of the period, I want to briefly illustrate the dynamic of economic change that gripped London in the late sixteenth and early seventeenth centuries. Its status as a commercial centre was not new. Historian Derek Keene pointed out that already in the Middle Ages, London had been 'a center of trade' for finished goods from the mainland ('Material London' 57).[47] Its role as a key hub for the export

---

[44] See Malynes, who identifies gain as the heart of commerce in *The Center of the Circle of Commerce* (first published in 1623): 'All the riuers of *Trade* spring out of this source, and empt themselues againe into this Oceean' (55).

[45] Stevenson builds on statistical data analysed by David Cressy. As she points out, 'already in the 1580s, 72% of them [tradesmen] could sign their names, and by 1603 that figure had risen to 83%' (61–62). She concludes: 'It is safe to say that only the men in the most menial crafts and the least-prosperous members of the poorer trades were likely to be illiterate within the city walls' (62). Stevenson explains the rapid increase in literacy with immigration to London, which brought not just 'many impoverished people', but also 'attracted an increasing number of literate tradesmen during Elizabeth's reign' (62). Furthermore, with the reorientation of the domestic market (with London's growth requiring the importation of more and more wares), the ability to keep records became increasingly important. Meir Kohn points out that the use of bills of exchange by international trading companies also meant that merchants had to be able to write fluently: 'Its legal standing was established by being written entirely in the hand of the taker—a signature was not sufficient' (3–4). For a detailed discussion of the social structure of illiteracy, see Cressy's chapter on 'The Structure of Illiteracy' in *Literacy and the Social Order*, 118–141.

[46] As Andrea Finkelstein writes: 'Following in his father's professional footsteps, Gerard de Malynes the assay master served on a government commission on foreign exchange in 1600. His first book (*A Canker of England's Commonwealth*) may have been, in essence, that commission's report' (26–27).

[47] As Keene explains in 'Material London', 'The dominance of London, in both population and wealth, had for centuries been an established feature of the English scene' (57). Already in 1300, London contained 'the largest and most diversified concentration of manufactures in the kingdom' (57) and already then 'something like a mass market in cheap manufactured goods had ... come into existence in London' (59). London was a focus of national power and expenditures in the late thirteenth

of wool and the import of goods continued in the later sixteenth century, 'when large quantities of relatively cheap manufactured goods were imported to London, both for consumption there and for distribution throughout the country' ('Material London' 60). If London's commercial significance was long-standing, the sixteenth and seventeenth centuries saw an intensification and global expansion of trade. It implied 'ventures in wider European, Atlantic, and Asian markets' (Sacks, 'London's Dominion' 24) and was accompanied by technological innovations.[48] Several joint-stock companies were chartered: the Muscovy Company in 1555, the Levant Company in 1592, and the East India Company in 1600.[49] The Levant Company came into existence as a merger of the Venice Company and the Turkey Company, and many of the members of the Levant Company proceeded to become members of the East India Company. In consequence, 'the first decades of the seventeenth century' saw 'an enormous increase in England's import trade' (Howard, 'Women, Foreigners, and Urban Space' 151).[50] With its port, the city was the main collecting point for outgoing and incoming wares. According to Daniel Vitkus, 'The total amount of London-based shipping trebled its size in tonnage between 1582 and 1629' ('"The Common Market of all the World"' 23). Jean Howard describes the London of the latter half of the sixteenth century as

century, and certainly by 1300, it was a powerful magnet for migrants looking for work (58). Keene notes that 'Londoners of the fifteenth and sixteenth centuries steadily became more directly exposed to, and thereby acquired a taste for, Italian silks, lace, glassware, and paper; German and Low Countries metal goods, including blades, armor, brassware, and engraved instruments for measurement and navigation; the decorated leather of Spain and Brussels; the textiles of Southern Germany; the furniture, furnishings, and miscellaneous consumer goods made in and around Antwerp; and a host of other goods ... By the mid-sixteenth century the "Turkey carpet" was probably a common feature in wealthier English households' (64–65). He explains that 'London paid for its imports with exports of white, unfinished woollen cloths, a trade which expanded rapidly during the first half of the sixteenth century ... and continued to serve as the backbone of the city's overseas trade' (63).

[48] Howard explains this in some detail: 'Technological changes accompanied and enabled this expansion of trade: advances in mapmaking; the development of maritime insurance to protect investors from losses at sea; the increasingly widespread use of bills of exchange and other financial instruments that made it unnecessary to transport large sums of money to distant markets; improved navigational instruments' ('Afterword: Accommodating Change' 265).

[49] Andrea Finkelstein explains the difference between joint-stock companies and regulated companies such as the Merchants Adventurers: 'The East India Company was organized as a joint-stock company: although its active members were merchants, any individual could, and many of the gentry did, buy shares of stock in the firm that yielded them proportionate shares of the profits earned by the Company trading as a whole. The Merchant Adventurers were organized as a "regulated" company: only qualified "Merchants" who had been passed by their peers after serving an apprenticeship and/or paying a suitable "fine" could trade under their protection. Members of regulated companies traded as individuals, keeping their own profits or absorbing their own losses, although bound by the terms of trade set by the company (as on the maximum yardage each member could export annually). Both joint-stock and regulated companies were forms of government-sponsored monopoly: either might have the sole right to trade in a particular commodity in a set region, or the sole right to all trade with that region, or something in between the two' (62). Due to 'the greater capital demands of the longer-distance trades', the joint-stock company was more efficient in intercontinental trade, while trading companies focused on intracontinental trade. However, '[b]y reexporting to Europe whatever East India goods they could not sell in England, they were also competing in the same markets (though not necessarily in the same products) as the older firms' (63).

[50] Howard bases her argument on Robert Brenner, *Merchants and Revolution* 51–91; chapter 2.

'an increasingly cosmopolitan metropolis where products from abroad filled the shops and infiltrated English homes and kitchens' ('Afterword: Accommodating Change' 265).[51]

Andrea Finkelstein measures the scope of change not in terms of commodities, but by the development of new financial instruments in the seventeenth century: 'At the century's dawning, Bills of Exchange were specialized instruments familiar only to a narrow circle of merchants, while at its evening, paper money was common throughout the land' (4). Shareholding and different forms of paper money, such as bills of exchange and debt bonds, are perhaps the most important innovations that facilitated the financing of ventures. The new financial instruments may well have altered people's sense of what constituted value. In the early eighteenth century, Daniel Defoe used the term 'Air-Money' to describe the virtual character of value in an age of paper credit and speculation,[52] yet merchants and playwrights around 1600 were already very much attuned to the instability and insubstantiality of value and its dependence on a volatile market.

With the intensification of commerce, consumption habits and the organization of trade changed. The year 1568 saw the completion of the first stock exchange in London, the Royall Exchange, which was also called Gresham's Bourse after its founder (Howard, *Theater of a City* 29). This was just a few years before James Burbage erected in 1576 the first commercial theatre in Shoreditch, the so-called Theatre (14). The Royal Exchange offered not just a space in which foreign and English merchants could bargain and trade, it also served as England's first shopping mall, with many small shops lining the galleries on the first floor and selling 'all kinds of haberdashery, fancy goods and souvenirs' (Saunders 12).[53] As Howard points out, by the end of the sixteenth century the Royal Exchange was firmly established and featured in several plays: in *Englishmen for My Money* (1598),

---

[51] 'The Levant Company, the East India Company, the Venice Company, and the Muscovy Companies collectively were bringing to England a vast array of sought-after consumer goods from currants to Italian silks to spices to perfumes to sugar' (Howard, 'Women, Foreigners, and Urban Space' 151).

[52] Daniel Defoe used the term 'Air-Money' as a metaphor for virtual monetary value and to underline its imaginary nature, for instance in his *Review of the State of the British Nation* (11 June 1709, VI. 30, 119). Here, he rails against an additional subscription to the Bank of England which, as he suggested, raised 'the Credit of Stocks to an imaginary Value beyond the Intrinsick' (120). Sandra Sherman explains that the term denotes in Defoe's work 'financial instruments floating beyond apprehension' (*Finance and Fictionality in the Early Eighteenth Century: Accounting for Defoe* 1; see also 25). Defoe pinpoints the curious mutability of paper when he writes in the *Tradesman* that credit 'makes paper pass for money, and fills the Exchequer and the Banks with as many millions as it pleases, upon demand' (409).

[53] Before the Royal Exchange was built, 'Men bargained and negotiated in their shops or homes, in guild headquarters and in taverns, or in the open street itself, Lombard Street being the usual meeting-place' (Saunders 1). Kathryn A. Morrison explains that 'Although it housed London's first fashionable shopping promenade, the Royal Exchange was intended primarily as a free public meeting place for merchants who had previously conducted their business in the open air at Lombard Street' (31). At the same time, it housed perhaps as many as 'a hundred' shops (12). Morrison writes that 'The four ranges of the Royal Exchange contained a total of 120 shops or booths, located in the basement and on the upper floors' (31).

Westward Ho (1604), and *A Chaste Maid in Cheapside* (1613) (*Theater of a City* 29–30). An augmented edition of John Stow's *The Annales, Or a Generall Chronicle of England* from 1615 claimed that the Royal Exchange 'is now called the Eye of London' (868). In its ambiguity, this metonymy suggests that the Royal Exchange was a place for both the visual display of luxury goods and for self-display. In 1609, Robert Cecil's New Exchange opened 'on the south side of the Strand' (Howard, *Theater of a City* 165).[54] Another key hub for consumption and one with a long medieval tradition was Cheapside, a vibrant shopping street with multiple shops and trading plots that was synonymous with consumption and costly goods.[55] The wealth of goods to be had in London is addressed in contemporary accounts.[56] As Keene points out, 'observers particularly remarked on the fine clothing of the citizens and their wives; the ostentation, extravagance, and rapidly changing fashions in the dress of the gentry' ('Material London' 59). In discourses around clothing, consumption emerges as an intersecting concern of oeconomy and commerce. As mentioned above, women were suspected of nursing an excessive desire for expensive clothes, which was seen as a drain on household resources. At the same time, clothing formed part of conspicuous consumption: in the context of the increasing availability of luxury goods, the display of wealth in the form of costly apparel emerged as an alternative taxonomy of social rank.[57]

Historian Keene confirms that London grew substantially in the sixteenth and seventeenth centuries, both in terms of people and the turnover of goods:[58] 'There was a strong sense of new commodities, changing fashions, new manufactures,

---

[54] According to Morrison, 'In form, it resembled a single range of the Royal Exchange. It was anticipated that merchants would gather within an arcaded walk ... The interior was arranged as a shopping complex' (32).

[55] More on Cheapside in Chapter 2, 83–84.

[56] Sir Thomas Smith described the change in London commerce in *A Discourse of the Commonweal of this Realme of England* (written in 1549, printed in 1581): 'I have seen within these twenty years when there were of these haberdashers that sell French or Milan caps, glasses, daggers, swords, girdles, and such like, not a dozen in all London. And now, from the Tower to Westminster along, every street is full of them; their shops glitter and shine of glasses, as well looking as drinking, yea, all manner vessels of the same stuff—painted cruses, gay daggers, knives, swords, and girdles that is able to make any temperate man to gaze on them and to buy somewhat though it serve no purpose necessary' (64). See Frederik Duke of Wirtemberg's account of London (qtd. in Howard, *Theater of a City* 1) as well as Ian W. Archer, 'Material Londoners?' 177, and Ann Saunders's account of the impressions of a German traveller, Paul Hentzner, who 'marvelled at the Exchange as a "public ornament ... [for] the convenience of merchants" and did not know whether to admire more "the stateliness of the building, the assemblage of different nations, or the quantities of merchandise"' (14).

[57] Various royal proclamations and sumptuary laws provide evidence for the social significance of dress (Bromley 144). Howard describes 'Dress, as a highly regulated semiotic system', which 'became a primary site, where a struggle over the mutability of the social order was conducted' ('Cross-Dressing' 23). Conspicuous consumption also played a role in other parts of the household. W. Harrison lists in *The Description of England* from 1587 the costly furniture and tapestries displayed in houses of all sorts of people, from noblemen to knights, gentlemen, merchants, and other wealthy citizens and even artificers and farmers (200). See also Jenstad 375 and Chapter 2, 86–89.

[58] According to Keene, '"subsistence migration" by the economically weak made a substantial contribution to the population growth of London, which, as far as we can tell, was probably greatest from about 1570 onward ... At this time the concentration of mercantile and landed wealth and expenditure in London was much greater than in former centuries' ('Material London' 58–59). David Harris Sacks

and of reaching out to new worlds where Englishmen had hardly penetrated before' ('Material London' 68). Although London may still have been 'a city of the past', which looked decidedly old-fashioned compared with 'Antwerp, Venice, or even Paris' (69), Londoners must have felt a keen sense of social change in a fast-growing city nourished by global commerce. As noted in the Introduction, London's theatres were singularly poised to engage with and examine these changes. First, because of their spatial proximity to the city and, second, because they were themselves part of this economic transformation. London's theatre companies took the form of joint-stock companies, and they took out great loans to make and sell a product that had to be profitable.[59] Last but not least, theatre's medial structure of doubling socio-economic actions and transactions for an interested public is singularly suited for reflecting on a society and its economic culture.

Mercantile Writings

Authors who attempted to delineate the merchant's role, to assert 'the dignity of trade' (Stevenson 115) and emphasize its socio-political significance were faced with a long tradition of hostile discourses. Andrea Finkelstein's list of authors who distrusted merchants and doubted the social benefits of commercial ventures stretches from Sir Thomas More to 'anonymous pamphleteers' (15), the clergy, and King James I, who complained in his *Basilikon Doron* from 1599: 'The Merchantes think the whole common-weale ordained for making them up, & (accounting it their lawful gaine & trade, to enrich them-selues vpon the losse of al the rest of the people.)' (59; Finkelstein 16). The most frequent charge levied at merchants and retail traders was that of unfair dealings and of disregarding the common good. Yet Stevenson identifies a shift in the perception of merchants in the sixteenth century, from a negative representation to a 'literature that praised

---

gives an idea of London's growth between 1500–1700: 'London's population stood at perhaps 40,000–50,000 in 1500, 200,000 in 1600, and 500,000–575,000 in 1700. In 1500, ten European cities, excluding Constantinople, had more inhabitants than London and six others had roughly the same population; in 1600, only two European urban places—Naples and Paris—exceeded the English capital in size, and neither by a very large margin' ('London's Dominion' 22). See also Steve Rappaport, *Worlds Within Worlds* 61–62, Roger Finlay, *Population and Metropolis* 6, and David J. Baker, *On Demand* 7.

[59] Amanda Bailey discusses the place of theatre within a culture of credit: 'The theatre was an enterprise shaped by the exigencies of credit, but, more particularly, the business of playing revolved around managers' and players' reliance on the penal debt bond. Bonds enabled the building and leasing of playhouses. Playscripts, costumes and properties were obtained on bonds' (4). Vitkus examines the similarities between trading companies and theatre companies: 'In both cases, investors took a shared risk in hiring others to carry out their ventures, and in both cases large profits were made' ('"The Common Market of all the World"' 20). Yet the scale of economic participation differed in trade and theatre: 'for every profit-taking shareholder in the Globe, there were dozens of wealthy merchants making money in foreign markets' (20).

merchants and craftsmen':[60] 'tales of the heroes of trade went through edition after edition in Elizabeth's reign, and some of them remained popular for years thereafter' (2).[61] Despite this effort to revaluate the merchant's role and despite their wealth, merchants continued to be seen as 'inferior to gentlemen in both status and social worth' (Stevenson 79). They modelled their behaviour on aristocratic notions of conduct and civility and continued to aspire to the ranks of gentle folk.[62] In consequence, formerly 'insular courtly conduct standards' (Davetian 76) were democratized and transformed into 'rules of public conduct' for a broader audience (77).[63] Middleton's play *A Chaste Maid in Cheapside* satirizes such social aspirations and the acquisition of a corresponding habitus.

Mercantile writers laboured hard to establish the political significance and moral worth of their kind. Caught between a commercial reality in which wealth was desirable and a moral paradigm that propagated moderation and the common good, mercantile authors struggled to carve out a dignified place for themselves and their likes. A standard rhetorical move was the denunciation of 'bad' and deceitful merchants in order to affirm the existence of 'good' and honest ones.[64] In order to dissociate themselves from the negative image of the covetous merchant, even authors of practical handbooks, such as Browne, never tired of highlighting the necessity of virtuous behaviour. Browne's *The Marchants Avizo* offered detailed advice concerning foreign currencies and units of measurements 'for ease of our tender wittes' (A2r). It includes exemplary business letters, models that were to be 'employed by merchants abroad' (Newbold 275), bills of exchange, bills of debt,

---

[60] Stevenson writes that 'Before Elizabeth's reign, merchants and craftsmen appeared only in negative literary contexts—in sermons condemning avarice, in estates satires exposing greed and dishonesty, and in chronicles lamenting the fickleness of the commonalty' (2). Diana Wood's account of trade and merchants in medieval texts paints a more varied picture. Although Wood concurs with Stevenson in that '[t]he impression, at least from late medieval England, was that in practice many merchants were guilty of shameful gain' (113), she suggests that a change in attitudes develops already within medieval culture: 'From the twelfth century on, canonists and theologians laboured to justify the activities of the merchant, even to hold out the hope of Heaven to him, and to make trade appear "respectable"' (115). Later she concludes: 'The commercial climate of the late medieval period led to a transformation in views on trade and merchants' (131).

[61] Archer argues similarly: 'Over the course of the Elizabethan and Jacobean decades, more positive evaluations of the merchants emerged and the dissentient voices more frequently expressed' ('Material Londoners?' 180–181).

[62] Stevenson explains that authors who wished 'to assert the dignity of trade' and to raise the social credit of merchants pointed out 'that gentlemen [thought] well enough of merchants to apprentice their sons to them' (115).

[63] Benet Davetian discusses specifically the contributions of Erasmus and Giovanni Della Casa to this process (75–80). For a general account of how conduct and advice literature and other practical works appealed to the middling sort, see also Wright's *Middle-Class Culture in Elizabethan England*, especially chapter 5: 'Handbooks to Improvement', 121–169.

[64] As Archer writes, 'Writers like Nicholas Breton, employing the binary systems of classification which so characterized popular thinking, distinguished between a type of the "good merchant" and a type of the "bad merchant" in his contribution to character literature' ('Material Londoners?' 178). Wilkinson, in *The Merchant Royall*, distinguishes merchants according to what they sell: 'as he is not the best Merchant to the Common-wealth which bringeth in toyes and trifles, but he which bringeth in such things as best may serue necessitie' (28).

and other business documents a merchant had to be able to draft. Browne's practical advice was accompanied with warnings against unjust behaviour: 'Be most faithful & iust in all your accompts with euery man, & defraud no man willingly not the value of a farthing' (5). Browne combined such moral admonitions with an introductory poem ('To the Reader'), which vindicated the merchant's enterprise by emphasizing his crucial role in enriching the commonwealth. The first and the last stanzas of the poem frame a long list of all those professions and people who profit from the merchant's ventures. The first stanza links the fate of the commonwealth to the success of trade:

> When marchants trade proceedes in
>   peace.
>   And labours prosper well:
> Then common weales in wealth increase,
>   As now good proofe can tell.
>
>   (A3r)

The final stanza mobilizes prayers for commercial success:

> Let no man then grudg[e] Marchants state,
>   Nor wishe him any ill:
>   But pray to God our Queene to saue,
> And Marchants state help still.
>
>   (A3v)

The juxtaposition of queen and merchant as equal recipients of good wishes emphasizes the socio-political significance of merchants, who labour in the interest of the commonwealth.[65] Mercantile texts demonstrated at length how valuable the services of merchants were to the state. Wheeler, secretary of the Society of Merchants Adventurers, also described trade as essential to the material and moral well-being of the commonwealth: 'without Merchandise, no ease or commodious liuing continueth long in anie state, or common wealth, no not loyaltie, or equitie it selfe, or vpright dealing' (5–6). He also suggested that merchants were vital to emerging national interests and strategies in other capacities, as spies, explorers, and potential money-lenders: 'either for forreigne intelligence, or exploration, or for the opening of an entrie and passage vnto vnknowen and farre distant partes,

---

[65] A similarly ecstatic commendation of the merchant's role can be found in Wilkinson's *The Merchant Royall*: 'The merchant is of all men the most laborious for his life, the most aduentrous in his labour, the most peacable vpon the sea, the most profitable to the land, yea the Merchant is the combination and vnion of lands and countries' (17). Thomas Churchyard commends 'merchauntes that sails forrain countreyes and bryngves home commodities and after great hazardes abroad do utter their ware with regard of conscience and profite to the publike estate' (qtd. in Archer 180).

or for the furnishing of monie, and other provisions in time of warres, and dearth, or lastly, for the service and honor of the Prince' (5).[66]

Naturally, mercantile writers themselves perceived less of a contrast between private gain and public good than other authors.[67] Where Robert Burton's metaphor of the world as 'a shoppe of knavery ... wherein every man is for himselfe, his private ends, and stands upon his owne guard' ('Democritus Junior to the Reader' 51; vol. 1) emphasizes the egoistic and socially isolating aspects of commerce, Wheeler established exchange as an essentially social anthropological constant:

> [F]or there is nothing in the world so ordinarie, and naturall vnto men, as to contract, truck, merchandise, and trafficque one with an other, so that it is almost vnpossible for three persons to converse together two hours, but they wil fall into talke of one bargaine or another, chopping, changing, or some other kinde of contract ...
>
> (2–3)

Wheeler's description of omnipresent and pervasive commerce, in which anyone exchanges anything, can only be called frenzied, but it constitutes a common activity and thus a social common ground: 'and in a woord, all the world choppeth and chaungeth, runneth and raveth after Martes, Markettes, and Marchandising, so that all things come into Commerce, and passe into Traficque (in a maner) in all times, and in all places' (3).

To fully understand the discursive tensions between self-interest and the common good, it is important to recall Aristotelian teachings on virtue ethics and commerce. As suggested in the first part of this chapter, Elizabethan and Jacobean discourses on oeconomics and commerce were highly indebted to antiquity. In their introduction to *Shakespeare and Early Modern Political Thought*, David Armitage, Conal Condren, and Andrew Fitzmaurice emphasize this legacy with regard to politics:

> Elizabethans and Jacobeans were politically closer to the ancient Greeks and Romans more than one thousand years before them than they were to liberal individualism three hundred years later. They took the *studia humanitatis*, the classical corpus of texts on history, moral philosophy, rhetoric, grammar and poetry as their guide to political life.
>
> (3)

This claim about early modern political life can easily be extended to the ethics of household management and commerce. The persistent association of commerce

---

[66] The page number is obviously a misprint: it should read 8.
[67] See also Jill Phillips Ingram: 'The most vocal contemporary challenge to the negative definitions of self-interest came, predictably, from merchants, tradesmen, adventurers, and others with a vested interest in commerce' (5).

with deceitful and unfair dealings dates back to the virtue ethics that was shaped by Aristotle and Cicero and modified by medieval Christian ethics; it viewed self-interested behaviour and material gain with suspicion.[68] The following section turns to Aristotle's discussion of retail trade as unnatural and unethical in order to delineate the long-standing tradition of perceiving virtue and the self-interested pursuit of profit as irreconcilable opposites.

Unnatural Acquisition: Aristotle and Trade

In Book One of the *Politics*, Aristotle discusses the relation between household management (*oikonomikē*) and 'the art of getting wealth' (*khrēmatistikē*) (*Pol.* I.8, 1256a1–2). As noted earlier, the core concern of household management is how to *use* goods (*Pol.* I.8, 1256a11–12), but as households are not self-sufficient, the 'art of acquisition' in the sense of procuring necessary provisions, is integral to *oikonomikē*:

> Of the art of acquisition then there is one kind which by nature is a part of the management of a household, in so far as the art of household management must either find ready to hand, or itself provide, such things necessary to life, and useful for the community of the family or state, as can be stored.
> (*Pol.* I.8, 1256b26–30)

This form of acquisition serves the household and it is naturally limited by the household's actual use of goods. The question of limits has a crucial place in Aristotle's argument: it allows him to distinguish the 'natural' place of wealth in oeconomy as a means to purchase necessary goods from the 'unnatural' acquisition of wealth by means of retail trade, which aims at wealth for its own sake and knows no bounds.[69] This form of acquisition, Scott Meikle explains, 'he calls *kâpelikê* or *chrêmatistikê* in the bad sense' (163).

Aristotle suggests that although *oikonomikē* and *khrēmatistikē* can be easily distinguished by their different ends, people often conflate them because both acquire wealth, albeit for different reasons:

> The source of the confusion is the near connexion between the two kinds of wealth-getting; in both, the instrument is the same, although the use is different, and so they pass into one another; for each is a use of the same property, but

---

[68] Ian Green notes in his *Humanism and Protestantism in English Education* 'that in early modern England the works of Ovid and Cicero sold far more copies than those of Calvin and Perkins—two of the most frequently republished Protestant authors' (25).

[69] Aristotle writes: 'And there is no bound to the riches which spring from this art of wealth-getting' (*Pol.* I.9, 1257b23–24). And a little later he explains: 'But the art of wealth-getting which consists in household management, on the other hand, has a limit; the unlimited acquisition of wealth is not its business' (*Pol.* I.9, 1257b30–31).

with a difference: accumulation is the end in the one case, but there is a further end in the other.

(*Pol.* I.9, 1257b35–38)

Aristotle explained the function of wealth in terms of 'a number of instruments to be used in a household or in a state' (*Pol.* I.8, 1256b36–37). He argued that 'the instruments of any art are never unlimited, either in number or size' (*Pol.* I.8, 1256b34–36). Retail trade, in contrast, 'suggest[s] that riches and property have no limit' (*Pol.* I.9, 1256b40): 'it is unnatural, and a mode by which men gain from one another' (*Pol.* I.10, 1258b1–2). This categorical difference is needed because 'natural' and 'unnatural' forms of acquisition share the same genealogy: unnatural forms, such as profit-orientated commerce and usury, evolved from money's 'intended' and hence natural use in exchange (*Pol.* I.10, 1258b1–8). In Aristotle's genealogy of the use of coin, people forgot the original function of coinage—easy handling—and pursued money for its own sake because it came to be identified with wealth as such. Since then, 'all getters of wealth [have increased] their hoard of coins without limit' (*Pol.* I.9, 1257b33–34). In early modern writings, the genealogy of money from medium of exchange to value-in-itself closely follows the Aristotelian narrative, which was disseminated by medieval scholastic philosopher Nicholas Oresme in his *De Moneta*.[70] It tells the story of how money starts out as a means to facilitate exchange, and then becomes the end of commercial exchange.[71] From transportable valuation device, which functioned both as 'medium of exchange' and 'repository of value' (Landreth 12) and which made deferred exchanges or purchases possible, money itself emerged as a commodity in the exchange of currencies as well as in usury.

Significantly, Aristotle enriches his historical and functional analysis of trade with a psychological narrative which marks trade as ethically questionable because it is driven by excess:

The origin of this disposition in men is that they are intent upon living only, and not upon living well; and, as their desires are unlimited, they also desire that the means of gratifying them should be without limit. Those who do aim at a good life seek the means of obtaining bodily pleasures; and, since the enjoyment of these appears to depend on property, they are absorbed in getting wealth: and

---

[70] Scholastic philosopher, translator of Aristotle, and man of the church Nicholas Oresme produced the *De Moneta* 'sometime between 1355 and 1360' (Farber 12; Johnson suggests that the work was written sometime before 1370 (x)). Oresme is mainly concerned with intentional alterations of coins on the part of the authority, the prince.

[71] Oresme tells this story in his first chapter: 'Why Money was invented'. After a long period in which barter meant the exchange of things, people invented money: 'as this exchange and transport of commodities gave rise to many inconveniences, men were subtle enough to devise the use of money to be the instrument for exchanging the natural riches which of themselves minister to human need' (4). Originally a 'very useful' instrument, coins then aroused 'the perverse greed of wicked men' (5). For an early modern account, see for instance Misselden, *The Circle of Commerce* 93–94.

so there arises the second species of wealth-getting. For, as their enjoyment is in excess, they seek an art which produces the excess of enjoyment ...
(*Pol.* I.9, 1257b40–1258a8)

This passage identifies excessive desire and a hypertrophic investment in pleasure as the motivational origin of acquisition. Intemperance (the passion concerned with appetite for food, drink, and sex) leads to covetousness (hunger for acquisition). At the origin of profit-orientated exchange, there is an intemperate 'enjoyment ... in excess'. The acquisition of wealth has a usurping side, subjecting both qualities (such as courage) and skills (for instance medical skills) to this end (*Pol.* I.9, 1258a10–12). Thus unlimited desire for wealth is not restricted to trade, but threatens to harness and instrumentalize all skills and qualities. The art of wealth-getting is the unethical doppelgänger of the kind of acquisition that procures necessary provisions for the household. Where the latter has a use-orientated approach to wealth, the former pursues it for its own sake. Early modern writers cling to sufficiency to distinguish ethical from unethical trade, and they ground sufficiency in the merchant's need to provide for his own household. Yet they also perceive gain as a difficult motivational force that tends to muddle the difference between legitimate trade and the avaricious pursuit of wealth.

Justice in Exchange

The virtue that regulates the distribution and exchange of goods is justice. Aristotle deals with justice fairly extensively in the *Nicomachean Ethics*, Book Five, where he distinguishes different forms of particular justice. *Distributive justice* is concerned with the just distribution of wealth according to status and merit: 'It is about having as much as one deserves' (Beever 67). *Rectificatory* or *corrective justice* aims at redressing a past wrong (e.g., a contractual violation or physical injury), and is thus concerned with 'restoring the equality between people when one has wronged the other' (Young 185). *Reciprocity* is the form of justice that regulates '[b]artering of goods and market transactions' (Polansky 164). It 'fits neither distributive nor rectificatory justice' (*EN* V.5, 1132b23–25). In contrast to distributive justice, reciprocity is not concerned with status or merit because in an exchange, both parties have to be seen as equal. Reciprocity shares this insistence on the equality of the parties involved with rectificatory justice.[72] Yet in contrast to rectificatory justice, it is not concerned with past events, but with an imminent exchange. Furthermore, its aim is not simple equality, but 'proportionate requital'

---

[72] Aristotle states: 'For it makes no difference whether a good man has defrauded a bad man or a bad man a good one, nor whether it is a good or a bad man that has committed adultery; the law looks only to the distinctive character of the injury, and treats the parties as equal' (*EN* V.4, 1132a2–5).

(*EN* V.5, 1132b32–33). The problem of reciprocity in exchange, to give the standard Aristotelian example, concerns the right quantity: 'how many shoes are equal to a house' (*EN* V.5, 1133a21–22)? The measure of value of such incommensurable things is money, the 'intermediate' (*EN* V.5, 1133a20) and equalizer of qualitatively different things. Aristotle himself concedes that the commensurability of qualitatively different objects, which is a precondition for equality and hence exchange, lies not in the things themselves. It is established only 'with reference to demand' (*EN* V.5, 1133b20). Describing 'demand' as the basis of commensurability is to affirm the lack of self-sufficiency of individual households as the motivation for exchange: 'demand holds things together as a single unit' (*EN* V.5, 1133b6–7). Yet the exact exchange ratio, as Aristotle argues earlier, is determined by the equation of different kinds of work: of, for instance, 'the shoemaker's work' with 'the farmer's work' (*EN* V.5, 1133a32–3). This dual definition of commensurability via demand on the one hand and labour on the other has led to much debate in the history of reception of Aristotle's work.[73]

In ethical terms, Aristotle distinguishes between a just and an unjust way of determining the ratio of exchange. This becomes evident in his characterization of unjust action at the end of Book Five, Section Five: 'In the unjust act to have too little is to be unjustly treated; to have too much is to act unjustly' (*EN* V.5, 1134a12–13). In exchange, as is true for all other actions, the golden mean between 'excess and defect' (*EN* II.2, 1104a26) must be observed. The unjust man, as Aristotle writes earlier, is 'the grasping and unequal man' (*EN* V.1, 1129a32–33)—someone who wants a greater share of coveted goods (such as wealth and fame) and a smaller share of burdensome things (say, financial losses or responsibility). Although the types of particular justice differ—distributive exchange is subject to status/merit, rectificatory justice redresses involuntary loss or gain, and reciprocity ensures the fairness of voluntary exchange—they are all concerned with the threat of disproportionate gain or loss. Proportionate requital in exchange relations occupies a special place in this scheme, for it helps to preserve the community. In Aristotle's own words: 'For it is by proportionate requital that the city holds together' (*EN* V.5, 1132b33–34).

In *De Officiis*, Cicero also describes exchange and reciprocity as cornerstones of community life. Men are born to be of service to each other: 'Therefore we should follow nature as our guide in this sense of making available shared benefits by exchange of our obligations, by giving and receiving, and in this way binding

---

[73] As is well known, Marx perceives human labour as the basis of commensurability. In his discussion of Aristotle's equation of five beds and one house, Marx asks (and proceeds to answer his own question): 'What is the homogeneous element, i.e. the common substance, which the house represents from the point of view of the bed, in the value expression for the bed? Such a thing, in truth, cannot exist, says Aristotle. But why not? Towards the bed, the house represents something equal, in so far as it represents what is really equal, both in the bed and the house. And that is—human labour' (1:151; Aristotle discusses this example in V.5.1133b23–28 of the *Nichomachean Ethics*).

the community and its individuals closely together by our skills, our efforts, and our talents' (*Off.* 1.22). He warns against greed and applauds beneficence, justice's 'close companion', which he translates as 'kindness or generosity' (*Off.* 1.20). Beneficence comes into play when an action is not subject to contractual obligations. Its social significance is not to be underestimated: it ensures good will and solidarity between the members of a given community. Hence, early modern authors 'who glorified merchants were careful to present their heroes as beneficent men' (Stevenson 116). Conversely, the ruthless pursuit of personal gain at the expense of others was seen as a threat to the community. Middleton's comedy *A Trick to Catch the Old One* is a case in point: in legal terms, the usurious uncle, who tricks his prodigal nephew into contracting his lands for ready cash, may be in the right. Yet his greed threatens familial cohesion and social peace.

Trade as Godly Calling and the Limits of Sufficiency

Mercantile and Protestant authors of the sixteenth and early seventeenth centuries laboured hard to square the Aristotelian circle. Aristotle had marked trade with the aim of wealth-getting as an unethical and unnatural enterprise, so their task at hand was to discursively establish profitable trade as legitimate calling.[74] Perkins's *Treatise of the Vocations* from 1603 provided recognition for the 'middling sort of people', who were able to maintain a household by means of a specialized skill rather than through income based on land.[75] His doctrine of the calling shared the 'Ramist emphasis on the practical utility of knowledge' (Kearney 52) and established wealth as a legitimate end. Perkins makes a point of valorizing skill and

---

[74] 'The doctrine of the calling', as Hugh F. Kearney points out, 'undermined the concept of hereditary social status by demanding that every man should not *inherit* position but *choose* a calling' (52).

[75] For a discussion of this term, see Jonathan Barry and Christopher Brooks, *The Middling Sort of People: Culture, Society and Politics in England, 1550–1800*; especially Jonathan Barry, Christopher Brooks, Peter Earle, and Keith Wrightson in the same volume. Wrightson describes the 'classical social hierarchy' of Elizabethan and Stuart England by distinguishing 'noblemen; gentlemen; yeomen; citizens and burgesses; husbandmen; artisans; labourers' ('Sorts of People' 28). The language of 'sorts' developed in the second quarter of the sixteenth century, providing essentially a dichotomous scheme to differentiate between 'the common sort' (33) and 'those "called to the degree of nobilitie"' (34), between 'the poorer sort' and 'the richer sort' (34). The term 'the middle sort of people' is probably of urban origin, used 'to describe the independent craftsmen and tradesmen who stood between the civic elite and the urban poor' (41). Early modern writers describe the middle sort of people quite literally as occupying a middle place between two extremes: as those who 'neither welter in to much wealth, nor wrastle with to much want' (Mulcaster qtd. in Wrightson, 'Sorts of People' 42) and who are 'neither too rich nor too poor, but do live in the mediocritie' (anonymous author of the *Apologie for the City of London*, qtd. in Wrightson, 'Sorts of People' 42). Wrightson locates the origins of this sociological description in a commercial context, but points out that its sociological usage was rare before the 1640s. See also Theodore B. Leinwand's article 'Shakespeare and the Middling Sort'. Leinwand refuses to give an exact definition, but identifies 'property, income or a voice' as key features: 'We might want to specify self-employment, property, income or a voice in one's community as necessary indicators of membership in the middling sort, but I think that when we attempt to metadefine the middling sort, we can do no more than set as criteria an unspecified amount of property, income, and voice rather than any fixed quantity' (289). After all, he argues, the middling sort is 'a most heterogeneous lot' (292).

labour over landed wealth: 'an Occupation is as good as land, because land may be lost, but skil and labour in good occupation is profitable to the ende, because it wil helpe at a neede when land and all things faile' (11–12). His lesson of diligence and thrift helped to advance and establish a 'gospel of work' (Stevenson 132).[76]

Perkins described '*A vocation or calling*' as a life that was divinely ordained: '*imposed on man by God for the common good*' (*Treatise of the Vocations* 2). He distinguished the general calling of a man to Christian ways from his 'Personall callings' (37). These, again, he divided into two kinds. There are 'Personall callings' that are 'the essence and foundation of any societie' (37). These refer to positions in the family, the commonwealth, and the church (namely, master and servant, husband and wife, parents and children, magistrates and subjects, ministers and people). And there are those callings that serve 'for the good, happie, and quiet estate of a societie': 'some of them seruing for the preseruation of the life of man as the calling of an husbandmen, of a merchant, &c. some seruing for the preservation of health, as the calling of a Physitian' (38). Like the husbandman, the merchant is necessary, even vital, for preserving the 'life of man'. Including the merchant into this category is a recognition of the social significance of commerce. In a sermon printed in 1620, clergyman Immanuel Bourne equally affirmed the legitimacy of this calling, but not without warning seriously against its risks. He notes 'First, that *buying* and *selling* in it [sic] owne nature is a calling lawfull, necessary, and commendable', but then proceeds to state its moral risks: 'Secondly, that it is full of daungers and occasions to sinne' and 'Thirdly, that there are diuerse wayes by which it is made vnlawfull' (25).

Buying and selling emerge as necessary and mutually beneficial practices, in this sermon as in others, because—this is an Aristotelian argument—the many things which are necessary to sustain a household and a commonwealth cannot be produced by everyone individually (Bourne 25–26). This legitimizes commerce and, with it, the profit that derives from trade: 'a fit and conuenient *Gaine*' is 'due vnto euery Trades-man, as a reward of his industry, for the common good' (26). Maintenance of one's household, good works for the poor, and the good of the commonwealth are legitimate motivations of trade (29–30). Yet the risk of unfair pricing and deceit is ever-present. Bourne wrote: 'It is a hard matter between the Commerce of the buyer and seller, that sinne should not enter and spoile the bargaine' (29). If the motivation is an immoderate desire for profit, if 'the principall end of thy *buying* and *selling* be couetousnesse' (Bourne 29), trade is indeed an unethical occupation.

---

[76] See also Christopher Hill, 'Protestantism and the Rise of Capitalism' in *Essays in the Economic and Social History of Tudor and Stuart England*, 15–39. Hill argues that the Protestant appeal to men's hearts (the 'justification by faith' rather than by 'works' (16)) went hand in hand with the conviction that 'industry was a good work, for "the common good", for "the use and profit of mankind"; that negligence in business harms the public state' (31).

Aquinas, the scholastic philosopher and theologian of the thirteenth century, had already laid the ground for the division between deceitful and honest commercial dealings, as well as for legitimizing profit. In the second part of the *Summa Theologiae* (2a2ae), Aquinas discussed commercial deceit, 'fraud committed in the course of buying and selling', under Question 77. In Aquinas's reply to Article Four ('is one entitled to make profits by selling for more than the purchase price?'), the legitimacy of retail trade is at stake. Aquinas reiterates the Aristotelian distinction between 'natural and necessary' exchange and commercial exchange:

> The former sort of exchange is praiseworthy because it supplies natural needs, whereas the second sort is rightly open to criticism since, just in itself, it feeds the acquisitive urge which knows no limit but tends to increase to infinity. It follows that commerce as such, considered in itself, has something shameful about it in so far as it is not intrinsically calculated to fulfil right or necessary requirements.
> (2a2ae.77, 4)

In the next paragraph, however, Aquinas identified profit as 'the point of commerce' (2a2ae.77, 4) and described it in more neutral terms—as neither 'right or necessary' nor 'vicious or contrary to virtue' in itself (77.4). Profit *can be* justified:

> This is exemplified by the man who uses moderate business profits to provide for his household, or to help the poor; or even by the man who conducts his business for the public good in order to ensure that the country does not run short of essential supplies, and who makes a profit as it were to compensate for his work and not for his own sake.
> (2a2ae.77, 4)

It should be added that Aquinas explicitly forbade clerics to engage in profit-orientated commerce, because clerics should 'abstain not merely from things that are bad but from things that look bad' (2a2ae.77, 4). Another reason is 'the likelihood of their falling victim to the vices of business men, as *Sirach* points out, *A merchant can hardly keep from wrongdoing*' (2a2ae.77, 4). In an ethical perspective, Aquinas clearly identifies commerce as a high-risk enterprise. Even if it is not bad in itself, it easily becomes a corruptive influence.

Ethical commerce is based on mutual benefits. A sales transaction, Aquinas argued, is 'introduced for the common benefit of both parties, in so far as each one needs something which the other has, as Aristotle explains' (2a2ae.77, 1). Hence it should be based on an equality of values, which is measured by a given price: 'It follows that the balance of justice is upset if either the price exceeds the value of the goods in question or the thing exceeds the price' (2a2ae.77, 1). The price may only be raised if the seller incurs a significant loss by selling the object (it is not subject to the buyer's need). The truly virtuous man, and here Aquinas refers to an example by Augustine, might pay 'a just price to another, who, out of ignorance, asked for a smaller sum for a certain book' (2a2ae.77, 1).

Following the tradition of distinguishing between necessary exchange and commerce as a self-serving practice, Perkins and other religious and mercantile writers attempted to establish legitimate trade in contrast with its evil twin, a covetous, deceitful, and self-interested occupation. Their discursive strategy is reminiscent of the one which Jon Snyder identifies in the early modern distinction between dissimulation and simulation: 'The early modern discourse on dissimulation was largely organized, for better or for worse, around the assumption that one could separate it from its evil twin' (xviii).[77] Similarly, contrary to his evil money-grubbing twin, the honest merchant pursues wealth only within the limits provided by sufficiency and the common good: 'Here then wee must in general know that he abuseth his calling, whosoeuer he be that against the end therof imploies it for himselfe, seeking wholly his owne and not the common good' (Perkins, *Treatise of the Vocations* 7).[78] To distinguish lawful and virtuous trade from covetousness, Perkins stressed the natural limits of wealth provided by sufficiency:

> As for example, a master of a family, may with good conscience seeke for that measure of wealth, as shal in Christian wisedome be thought meete to maintaine him and his family with conuenient food and raiment: hauing obtained thus much, a pause must be made, and he may not proceede further to inlarge his estate by seeking for that aboundance that may wel serue his owne house, and a second, or many families more.
>
> (*Treatise of the Vocations* 88–89)

'Convenient' suggests that the household was to be maintained according to social status.[79] The measure here is sufficiency, although Perkins acknowledges that it may be hard to tell where sufficiency ends and where acquisitive hunger begins: 'It may be here demanded howe we are to iudge what is sufficient for any man?'

---

[77] Snyder contends that 'there were many [writers] who recognized that dissimulation might, under certain well-defined conditions, possess a specific moral valence distinguishing it from simulation, and at times even justifying its use' (xvii–xviii). Dissimulation refers to an art of secrecy which was widely and controversially discussed in the sixteenth and seventeenth centuries. It referred to controlled self-display which made it impossible to distinguish between authentic self-expression and the wearing of a mask. It served to protect 'the inner space of conscience' (*l'éspace interieur des consciences*) and to keep one's aspirations private (Cavaillé 24). In the 'distinct moral economies' which Snyder identifies (xvii), simulation was associated with lying and deceit and hence clearly despicable, but dissimulation, at least for some writers, was admissible under certain circumstances.

[78] Pursuing self-interested ends is also a sin against God: 'they profane their liues and callings that imploy them to get honours, pleasures, profits, worldly commodities, &c. for thus we liue to another ende then God hath appointed, and thus we serve our selves, and consequently neither God nor man' (Perkins, *Treatise of the Vocations* 33).

[79] See also Cleaver: 'It is not inough to haue a calling though it be neuer so good, but it must be followed, so as it may bring in maintenance for thee, and thine, such as is meete for thy owne estate' (63).

(*Treatise of the Vocations* 89) His answer is that 'our rule must be the common iudgement and practice of the most godly, frugal, & wise men, with whome we liue' (89), a kind of living by example. He also argues that sufficiency is relative. It depends on the 'place and calling' of every man who 'must be measured according to his condition' (89). Yet as vague as it may seem as a criterion for socio-economic action, sufficiency guarantees the existence of a limit that allows for distinguishing the lawful execution of trade from the unlawful and excessive pursuit of wealth. Abundant riches were only admissible if they were a free gift from God—they should not be desired or sought after.[80] It is with such qualifications that the *Treatise of the Vocations* carves out a place for trade as a respectable and godly occupation.

Perkins identified two vices as key problems in the socio-economic field: 'Couetousnes, and Iniustice' (*Treatise of the Vocations* 81). Like Aristotle, Perkins ascribed to covetousness a tendency to hijack any possible 'calling' by turning it towards the end of accumulating wealth: 'Couetousnes is a notorious vice, whereby all men almost applie their callings, and the workes thereof, to the gathering of wealth and riches' (81). In the Christian tradition, covetousness has a special place as 'the root of all evil' (1 Tim. 6:10, also qtd. in Bourne 29). The problem was not 'getting of gaine' as such but 'getting of Gaine vniustly' and 'immoderate desire of Gaine' (Bourne 33). Injustice is a type of behaviour 'whereby men abuse their callings to the hurt and hindrance of others, either publikely or priuately' (Perkins, *Treatise of the Vocations* 96). Perkins addresses injustice specifically in relation to trade when he discusses practices that deceive clients about the real value of commodities:

> In the calling of the Merchant and tradesman, there is false weights, and false measures, diuers weights and diuers measures; ingrossing, mingling, changing, setting a glosse on wares by powdering, starching, blowing, darke shoppes, glozing, smoothing, lying, swearing, and all manner of badde dealing.
>
> (98)

As Perkins summed it up in a treatise from 1606, 'it is a hard thing to become rich without iniustice' (*The Whole Treatise of the Cases of Conscience* 528).

Nonetheless, Perkins establishes the thorough and honest merchant as a role model for Christians. He likens spiritual accounting to the mercantile practices of drawing out 'the bill of our receipts and expences': 'Tradesmen for their temporall estates, keepe in their shoppes bookes of receipts and expences: shall not we then much more doe the like for our spirituall estates?' (*Treatise*

---

[80] As Stevenson explains, 'Readers were encouraged to pray and labour in the confident hope that God would "so prosper [their] endeavours" that "nothing [should] be wanting unto them"; but the divines told them repeatedly that they were not permitted to work for—or even hope and pray for—abundant wealth' (135).

of the Vocations 131) To promote spiritual reflection, Perkins recommends 'a fore-hand reckoning of our selues in the time of this our life' (*Treatise of the Vocations* 130), taking detailed account of the blessings received and the sins committed. This serves as a counterpoint to the negative image of the deceitful merchant. With his exemplary bookkeeping, the tradesman becomes a model of diligence and accuracy that can be transferred to spiritual self-examination: *Robinson Crusoe* (1719) is a prime example of the enduring influence of this idea.

Legitimate Profit

Scott's *An Essay of Drapery* appeared a good thirty years after Perkins's *Treatise of the Vocations*, in 1635. Written by a merchant, it focuses specifically on the trade of cloth. It reiterates the ethical distinctions and reflections offered by Perkins, but shows great interest in the actual practices and strategies of trade. Scott quite confidently defends the pursuit of gain as a legitimate interest. The subtitle of Scott's essay, *Trading Justly Pleasingly Profitably*, denies any essential conflict between justice and profit. In the title, justice comes first and Scott tackles the question of how to avoid injustice head-on: 'It is a happie thing for a man to goe through his affaires without Injustice, which he cannot doe but by bringing his spirit into liberty ... contemplating upon all his actions: so by due consultation, and discreete action, hee may live justly, pleasingly, profitably' (1). Scott's essay establishes trade as a rational occupation, the end of which 'should bee for the good of both parties' (11): 'all contracts must tend *Ad bonum ipsorum contrahentium*, to the good of them which make them. So shall all injustice bee avoyded' (52).

In conformity with the Aristotelian tradition, Scott describes trade as 'good' when it is an exchange of equal values:

> A contract must be made according to the equality of the thing; and that must bee measured by the price that is given. For as time is the masure of businesse, so is price of Wares. If the price exceed the worth of the thing, or the thing exceed the price, the equality of justice is taken away; that both agree is the just rule of trading, against which deceit is opposite ...
>
> (15–16)

Just as trade is contrasted with deceitful dealing, however, Scott extends the meaning of deceit in a way which helps to establish the legitimacy of acting in accordance with one's self-interest: 'taking lesse for them then they are worth, a man deceives himself: to prevent which, my discourse of his living profitably shal endeavour' (16).[81] He insists that 'There is as much injustice in selling commodities too cheap, as too deere' (47) because thus a man hurts himself. Scott acknowledges that 'To deceive others, is worse than to be deceived' (17), but he speaks out against both: 'His rule was peremptory, that said a wise man will not deceive, neither can hee bee deceived' (16). This insistence on safeguarding a merchant's interests is an important step towards establishing the merchant's right to profitable commerce. It is supported by Scott's discussion of cases in which the price may be raised without committing an injustice, for instance in cases of generally increasing prices or of scarcity. The price of commodities may also be raised in the case of retail trade, because of 'the labour and care in selling them thus being the greater' (48–49). In acknowledging that retail trade may justly demand higher prices, Scott acknowledges that trade is a 'profession' that applies labour and care to the product. Last but not least, 'commodities may be sold dearer for time, then ready money' (49). In the case of credit, then, a higher price is admissible.

Scott addresses the question of profit once more, when he discusses socio-economic action as a zero-sum game: 'the folly and fall of one man, is the fortune of an other' (95–96). In order to vindicate the legitimacy of turning a profit, Scott insists on this as a general rule. For him, the zero-sum game constitutes the paradigm case, not just of all human interaction, but of all things:

> for what man almost profiteth, but by the losse of others? Was not Romes rising by the ruine of her neighbour Cities? doe not most Traders thrive by the licentiousnesse of youth? the Husband man by the dearth of Corne: the Architect by the ruine of houses, the Lawyer by contentions betweene men, the Physitians by others sicknesses?
>
> (96)

This is followed by a long argument about how riches are not evil in themselves and how it may become a good man to labour for 'outward blessings' (114). As the final authority on this, Scott refers to Aristotle: 'therefore Aristotle is not to bee taxed for making Riches necessary for some of the Vertues: they are out of all question, *Bonum unde facias bonum*, a good by which thou maist doe good' (115). Scott established '*Sancta avaritia*', 'holy covetousnesse' (143), as the good twin of ordinary covetousness. Apart from performing business in a diligent manner and without seeking abundance, Scott appears to imply with this notion a desire to enrich the mind: 'I would have him thinke, that by every man with whom

---

[81] To prevent deceit, Scott also offers very concrete advice as to the layout of a shop. Here, too, deceit works in two ways, both of which have to be prevented: deceit of the other (commodities that are sold too dear) and of oneself (commodities that are sold too cheap): 'It is to bee lamented, that men have too darke, shops: but more, that they have too darke minds ... A shop may bee too darke, and it may bee too light: therefore it is, or should bee so ordered, that least Commodities bee sold too deare, shops shall not be too darke; and lest they be sold too cheap, they shall not bee too light' (41–42).

he shall trade, he may benefit his mind something' and thus accumulate wisdom (143). Scott also substantiates the usefulness of trade and wealth with a social observation: 'Men are not apt to take so exact notice of those spirituall blessings wherewith the Elect are inwardly adorned ... unlesse temporall blesings bee added to them, therefore labour for them' (115). This link between spiritual and temporal blessings suggests that wealth functions as a visible marker of 'spirituall blessings'. Having thus established wealth as sign of divine approval *and* as a social good, Scott proceeds to declare that there need not be a contradiction between profit and virtue: 'In some cases my Citizen may mingle profit with honesty' (136). The pursuit of self-interest, however, must be reconcilable with the common good: 'My Citizen must then with reason divide betweene selfe-love and society; so walking profitably to himselfe, as hee hinder not the good of the Common-wealth, but further it' (162). As the following chapters show, early modern plays question this easy reconciliation of private interest and common good.

Scott furthermore explains how legitimate profit may be attained by distinguishing legitimate from illegitimate sales strategies. That such strategies constitute a slippery slope of ethical ambiguity emerges in his discussion of dissimulation. Scott condemns 'Flattery, Dissimulation, Lying, &c.' as 'unjust wayes of deceit' (23), but allows for legitimate 'faire speeches' (26).[82] The latter merely offer the customer the treatment he has become accustomed to due to his frequent exposure to flattery. Their use is hence a pragmatic decision, not an immoral one. Just as 'fair speeches' differ from flattery, so dissimulation differs from lying: 'there is no better life then to live according to mans nature, resolving alwaies ... to dip the penne of the Tongue in the Incke of the heart, speaking but what hee thinks; to doe otherwise is impiety, *yet to utter all hee thinks is eminent folly*' (30, my emphasis). While we may not 'lye to save our lives' and 'much less to save or increase our wealth' (33), 'so we need not speake all the truth' (34). Scott explains 'lawful' dissimulation with a domestic analogy:

> Dissimulation is a thing more tollerable [than flattery] with a Citizen; it is with him as with one who hath married a wife, whom hee must use well, pretending affection to her, though hee cannot love her: and indeed Divines hold it in some cases lawfull, to pretend one thing and intend an other.
>
> (27)

Withholding truth in an ethically legitimate manner is a matter of practice: Scott's citizen 'must never turne his back to honesty; yet sometimes goe about and coast it, using an extraordinary skill, which may be better practis'd then exprest' (137). To 'coast' means something akin to circumventing truth without losing sight of it

---

[82] As Leinwand points out, Scott skilfully 'bends the Scripture' to make his case (*The City Staged* 32): 'as the Apostle said; *Be angry but sin not*: So I say, Flatter, but sin not if that be possible ... amiable looks and faire speeches will go farre enough' (Scott 26).

entirely. Clearly, the demands of successful trade require skills of dubious ethical value. When reading Scott, it becomes evident that it may not be always possible to decide where legitimate strategies end and immoral behaviour begins. The ethical ambiguity of dissimulation, for instance, emerges fully when Scott highlights its dangerous proximity to deceit. According to Scott, to dissemble to an ill end is to sin, and 'hee sins thrice that counterfeits himselfe good, to whom he may doe ill' (28).

Mercantilist and Bullionist Writers

Perkins, Browne, and Scott address questions of individual conduct as shaped, on the one hand, by ethical demands and, on the other, by business considerations. Mercantile writers such as Wheeler, Malynes, Milles, Misselden, and Mun, who are today grouped as bullionist and mercantilist, had a broader scope, although they, too, adopted a moralizing tone.[83] They discussed not only individual economic behaviour, but also suggested governmental strategies to preserve and enhance the nation's wealth. Their tracts share the common assumption, as Jonathan Gil Harris writes, 'that the goal of mercantile activity is to increase the nation's wealth, less in the form of productivity or capital assets than of money—that is, gold and silver treasure acquired from abroad' (6). Yet like other mercantile writers, the mercantilists and bullionists of the early seventeenth century were influenced by classical authors and mixed social and political recommendations with ethical reflections. They developed a tentative anthropology of mercantile man, which identified gain as the driving force of behaviour, and they combined such insights with an analysis of depersonalized market mechanisms.

Wheeler and Malynes were contemporaries of Shakespeare, Jonson, and Middleton. Andrea Finkelstein describes Malynes and his opponents Misselden and Mun as 'the best known and most influential of the writers struggling to explain (and find a way out of) an economic crisis that hit England in 1620' (5).[84] For

---

[83] Harris distinguishes '[t]he early "bullionist" mercantilists of the 1590s and 1600s, Malynes and Milles' from '[t]he later "balance-of-trade" mercantilists of the 1620s, Misselden and Mun' (6). Harris understands mercantilism as an unsystematic and frequently incoherent discourse with some '"nation-making" power' (6). Nonetheless, he sees Malynes's association of natural law with mercantile trade in his *Lex Mercatoria* (first published in 1622) as 'part and parcel of the transformation of economics from a subset of ethics to an autonomous, protoscientific discipline' (7). Most cultural critics writing today are suspicious of the notion of mercantilism as a coherent system or unified '"school" with a single theoretical creed' (Magnusson 133; see also Ryner, *Performing Economic Thought* 11, n.4; and Harris 3–6). Julie Solomon argues 'that early modern mercantilist policies developed as governmental strategies to control those facets of commercial culture not comprehended within older and more traditional feudal or customary protocols' (65).

[84] This was 'a major economic depression fueled by wartime international currency manipulation, war, and the ill-advised attempts of Alderman Cockayne ... to grab a greater market share of the wool trade' (54; see also Clay 119). As Lars Magnusson writes, 'The export trade of cloth fell dramatically, many clothiers were brought to the verge of bankruptcy and unemployment was rife. Distress was

her, Malynes—who 'belonged to the generation prior to that of his opponents' (5)—'acts as a baseline for the century as a whole' (5). Malynes published warnings against the undervaluation of English coins as early as 1601. In the 1620s, Malynes and Misselden entered into a prolonged controversy over what should be done to alleviate the trade crisis. Misselden's *Free Trade* (first published in 1622) was countered with Malynes's *The Maintenance of Free Trade* (1622). Misselden met the counter with *The Circle of Commerce* (1623), and Malynes replied once more with *The Center of the Circle of Commerce* (1623).[85] These texts exemplify the pervasive moral framework within which economic thought operated: at least rhetorically, private interests were subjected to common interests, and fair dealings trumped excessive gain. Malynes and Misselden were very learned and highly versed in Aristotelian and scholastic writings on ethics, economics, and politics—and they were proud of their rhetorical achievements.[86] Their controversy offers a useful entry point into the mercantilist and bullionist debate and will furnish most of the material for my discussion in the following. While they differed in their evaluation of how trade should be conducted and regulated, Wheeler and the 'four Ms' generally agreed that trade was necessary and valuable to the commonwealth.

Mercantilist and bullionist authors shared a common concern with the nation's wealth and worried about the state of English trade: 'We all agree', wrote Malynes in a text filled with harsh criticism of his opponent Misselden, 'that there is an ouerballance, which must be remedied by the redresse of the causes' (*The Center of the Circle of Commerce* 60).[87] Yet they had different opinions about *how* this overbalancing should be redressed. Malynes saw the undervaluation of English currency as the main factor in England's negative balance of trade. Misselden, and Mun as well—in his *A Discourse of Trade* (first published in 1621) and the posthumously published *England's Treasure by Forraign Trade*—dismissed Malynes's

---

common throughout England' (62). Monetary manipulations worsened the depression: 'In order to provide money for warfare, princes and kings in Poland, the German empire carried through monetary manipulations by enhancing, debasing and clipping their coins ... Moreover, violent debasement on the continent led to terms of trade turning unfavourable for England as its export wares became increasingly more expensive while simultaneously imports from these parts became cheaper' (64).

[85] Harris describes this as 'one of the most important exchanges of early English mercantilism: the pamphlet war of 1622–1623 between Edward Misselden and Gerard Malynes' (137).

[86] See Andrea Finkelstein 30–31 (on Malynes) and 57 (on Misselden). Ryner writes: 'For Misselden and Malynes, good mercantile writing was good poetry—artfully constructed language that revealed some truth about the material world. Each could seek to discredit the other by revealing his opponent's representations to be fictions, artificial constructs with no necessary correspondence to the real world. However, because all mercantile treatises relied on "poetic" techniques, all mercantile writers were always open to such discrediting attacks' (4).

[87] C. G. A. Clay argues that 'in the later sixteenth century imports from the Levant were regularly worth twice as much as exports' (127). He adds that in the case of the 'East India Trade after 1600, it was often difficult to sell the commodities England had to offer on any terms. In both instances, therefore, trade could only be carried on by the export of large quantities of bullion' (127).

idea of re-establishing a *par pro pari* monetary exchange as ineffective.[88] In their view, England's trade crisis was not primarily a problem of exchange rates, but consisted in an unfavourable balance of trade: money was carried away into foreign lands because imports outweighed exports.

As Harris points out, despite their differences, the above writers agreed on a basic economic principle, derived from oeconomy and articulated over and over again in Protestant economies: 'Malynes, Milles, Misselden, and Mun took it as a rule of thumb that selling native commodities to strangers brings treasure into the nation, while the import of foreign wares stands to lose it' (8). In consequence, they all 'tended to rail against the English consumption of "idle" foreign commodities and luxury goods' (8).[89] And they all argued in favour of a positive balance of trade in which the exports outweighed imported goods. The positive balance of trade was frequently explained in terms of 'good husbandry' (Wheeler 8).[90] A negative balance of trade, which threatened the loss of treasure, was linked to moral degradation.[91] Under the reasons for trade decay, Misselden listed 'people liv[ing] above their callings' (Andrea Finkelstein 72). Discussions of the balance of trade were thus phrased in terms of household management. Mun's clear articulation of the balance of trade is underwritten with a moral argument:

> So doth it come to passe in those Kingdomes, which with great care and wariness doe euer vent out more of their home commodities, then they import and vse of forren wares; for so vndoubtedly the remainder must returne to them in treasure. But where a contrarie course is taken, through wantonnesse and riot; to

---

[88] It must be said, however, that Misselden's argument varies greatly between his *Free Trade or the Meanes to make Trade Flourish* (first published in 1622) and the later *Circle of Commerce* (Magnusson 69). In the first text, he adopts Malynes's idea that undervaluation effected the exportation of English coins and demands 'the raising of the King's coine' (Misselden qtd. in Magnusson 69). In the later essay, 'he was turning his previous analysis upside down', insisting on the plenty or scarcity of commodities and monies as determinant of their prices and rates of exchange (Magnusson 70).

[89] Alan Stewart draws attention to the 'familiar trope' 'of good exports being swapped for bad imports': for 'trinkets' and '"trifles"' (161).

[90] Wheeler explains this as follows: 'Nowe to vent the superfluities of our Countrie, and bring in the Commodities of others, there is no readier, or better meane then by merchandize: and seeing we haue no way to increase our treasure by mynes of golde, and siluer at home, and can haue nothing from abroad without monie, or ware, it followeth necessarilie, that the abouesaid good councell of *Cato* to be sellers and not buyers, is to be followed, yet so, that we carrie not out more in valew ouer the seas then we bring home from thence, or transport thinges hurtefull to the State, for this were no good husbandry, but tendeth to the subversion of the lande, and deminishing of the treasure thereof, whereas by the other wee shall greatlie encrease it' (8).

[91] Misselden explains the positive and negative balance of trade as follows: 'If the Natiue commodities exported doe waigh downe and exceed in value the forraine Commodities imported; it is a rule that neuer faile's, that then the Kingdome growe's rich, and prosper's in estate and stocke: because the ouerplus thereof must needs come in, in treasure. But if the Forraine Commodities imported, doe exceed in value the Natiue commodities exported; it is a manifest signe that then trade decayeth, and the stocke of the Kingdome wasteth apace: because the ouerplus must needs goe out in treasure' (*The Circle of Commerce* 117).

ouerwaste both forren and domestike wares; there must the money of necessitie be exported, as the meanes to helpe to furnish such excesse ...

(Mun, *A Discourse of Trade* 2)

Immoderate spending threatened not just individual households, but also the commonwealth.

For some merchants, there appeared to be no contradiction between private interest and public good. In Wheeler's *A Treatise of Commerce* from 1601, there is no sense that the interests of individual merchants might diverge from those of the commonwealth, or that the Prince's interests might deviate from the common good: there is no conflict between private and public interests. Misselden— originally a Merchant Adventurer's man just like Wheeler—also linked the fate of the commonwealth directly to successful trade: 'For when *Trade flourishes*, the *Kings Revenue is augmented, Lands and Rents improoued, Nauigation is encreased, the poore employed*. But if *Trade* decay, *All these* decline with it' (*Free Trade* 4). Via a handful of rhetorical questions, Misselden pitches private profit quite confidently as the natural end of trade *and* as means for the common good:

And is it not lawfull for Merchants to seeke their *Privatum Commodum* in the exercise of their calling? Is not gaine the end of trade? Is not the publique involved in the private, and the private in the publique? What else makes a Commonwealth, but the private-wealth, if I may so say, of the members thereof in the exercise of *Commerce* amongst themselues, and with forraine Nations?

(*The Circle of Commerce* 17)

Misselden hastens to rank his obligations and interests as a member of the Merchant-Adventurers so that the common good emerges as the highest obligation: 'I am a brother, though vnworthy of that worthie *Society*: and so I am of other Companies also: and so also am I a member, though one of the least, of the great Common-wealth of this kingdom; wherein I haue learnt to preferre, that publique, to all these particular obligations' (*The Circle of Commerce* 65). Yet despite his eagerness to show that he has got his priorities right, there is little sense of a potential conflict between private benefit and common good.

Malynes discussed the same question in his reply to Misselden's treatise, but appears less optimistic about the claim that the pursuit of private advantages has necessarily social benefits: 'It is demanded, whether it be lawfull for Merchants to seeke their *Priuatum commodum* in the exercise of their calling, whether gaine be not the end of Trade, and whether the priuate be not inualued in the publike?' (*The Center of the Circle of Commerce* 45). His answer suggests the potential conflict between private and common interests: 'Albeit the generall is composed of the particular, it may fall out, that the generall shall receiue an intolerable preiudice and losse by the particular benefit of some' (45). Clearly, private interests may go against the common good: 'Merchants ... may procure their priuate gaine, and yet impouerish the Kingdome' (56).

Although Malynes stated in *England's View* that 'there can be no Commonwealth without a priuate wealth' (119; see also Andrea Finkelstein 39) and commends the merchant's role in international relations,[92] he understood that private wealth did not automatically benefit the commonwealth. 'For Malynes', as Finkelstein explains, 'self-interest was quintessentially irrational and dysfunctional: rather than functioning to insure a society's economic survival, it was forever threatening to rip asunder its social (read *moral*) fabric' (40). Despite this understanding of private interest, Malynes perceived gain as the most powerful anthropological motivation: it is the centre of commerce and that 'which beareth the sway in all humane actions' (*Center of the Circle*, 'Dedicatory Epistle'). Whether for good or ill is no longer the question—gain is simply that which drives and determines trade: 'Nothing doth force trade but Gaine' (53). Using a circular metaphor in which gain serves both as motivation and end, Malynes describes commercial activity rather poetically: 'All the riuers of Trade spring out of this source, and empt themselues againe into this Occean' (55).

Culture of Credit

If gain forced trade, as Malynes put it, it was credit that kept it going. Social historian Craig Muldrew famously discussed the 'culture of credit' in early modern England as a moral economy based on trust and the currency of reputation.[93] He argued convincingly that for the 'economy which Malynes, Locke and Smith knew the use of credit was much more important' than the use of cash ('Hard Food for Midas' 83). Considering that '[t]he amount of actual gold and silver currency in circulation was small' and that inflation diminished its value (*Economy of Obligation* 98), it is hardly surprising that these writers saw money as a means for measuring value rather than as medium of exchange ('Hard Food for Midas' 82–83). Coins alone would not have been sufficient to

---

[92] '[T]he State of a Merchant is of great dignitie and to bee cherished; for by them Countreys are discouered, Familiaritie betweene Nations is procured, and politike Experience is attained.' ('The Epistle Dedicatorie' to Lex *Mercatoria*, also qtd. in Andrea Finkelstein 47)

[93] Muldrew identified credit from 'the mid-sixteenth century' (*The Economy of Obligation* 3) onwards as a 'currency of reputation' (3): 'a public means of social communication and circulating judgement about the value of other members of communities' (2). Reputation constituted a currency of trust that determined 'the creditworthiness of households attempting both to cooperate and compete within communities increasingly permeated by market relations' (3). As Muldrew suggests, credit was increasingly used after 1530, when 'consumption expanded' and 'the amount of buying and selling increased', while 'the amounts of gold and silver in circulation' remained limited (3).

sustain the expansion of commercial transactions in the sixteenth and seventeenth centuries.[94] Muldrew estimates that money may have played a role in fewer than ten per cent of exchanges (*Economy of Obligation* 100). No wonder, then, that Tusser rhymed: 'Who liuing but lends? And be lent to they must, / else buieng and selling, might lie in the dust' (21). Commerce was sustained by informal credit, and formal monetary instruments such as bonds and bills of exchange. Coins were only used in certain cases: for instance, for the settling of mutual debts, in exchanges between strangers, or when travelling ('Hard Food for Midas' 84).

Daily exchanges between neighbours and acquaintances were for the most part executed on the basis of informal credit. Such informal acts of lending and borrowing structured social relations to a considerable degree: 'People were constantly involved in tangled webs of economic and social dependency based only on each other's word, or the word of others, which linked them together' (Muldrew, 'Interpreting the Market' 174). Most of these informal agreements were not even set down in writing. Historian Eric Kerridge, who confirms that '[d]omestic commerce ran on credit' (*Trade and Banking* 33), points out that inland bills of exchange often came in oral form.[95] Bills of exchange were a key financial innovation of the late thirteenth century with roots in the late twelfth century. They were an acknowledgment of a sum received and an order to pay a fixed sum of money at a certain date to a specific person or the bearer.[96] Crucially, bills of exchange also facilitated commercial exchange between countries: 'Bills of Exchange were used to move money from country to country without moving coin' (Andrea Finkelstein 44). The bill of exchange, together with goldsmiths' receipts, constitutes an early form of paper money. Contrary to bullion, these slips of paper lacked intrinsic value, a fact which Misselden smoothed over with a quasi-magical explanation of how bills of exchange related to money: 'in a word, it's nothing else but a transmutation of money from place to place without transportation' (*Circle of Commerce* 95). This is an elegant way of obscuring a huge change in the nature of

---

[94] 'From about 1550 the number of transactions on the market increased dramatically, and as a result of the lack of cash this expansion of buying and selling was supported on a web of sales credit' ('Hard Food for Midas' 83).

[95] Kerridge explains that the inland bill of exchange was very informal and that the whole business could be carried out without any written statement whatsoever: 'the whole exchange could be conducted by word of mouth' (*Trade and Banking* 62). In fact, he writes, 'Early bankers preferred to receive orders to pay by word of mouth in person on their premises rather than by written order, for writings could be forged more easily than people could be impersonated' (*Trade and Banking* 62).

[96] Kerridge, *Trade and Banking* 45. Meir Kohn explains that bills of exchange evolved from a promissory note called the 'cambium contract', which was used in the 'trade between the inland cities of Northern Italy and the Fairs of Champagne' (1): 'One merchant acknowledged the receipt from another of payment in local currency and promised to repay him at a specified future time and distant place in the currency of that place' (1). The development of the bill of exchange resulted from a restructuring of long-distance trade in the late thirteenth century, when 'the itinerant merchant was increasingly giving way to the large trading company with permanent branches in the commercial centers' (1). This made it 'easy for them to offer remittance services' (1).

money: from tangible and intrinsically valuable coin to a near-weightless promise of temporally deferred and spatially distant payment.

According to Muldrew, the ubiquity of sales credit meant that 'trust was a central factor in economic exchange' (83). As payment and repayment or product and recompense did not change hands at the same time, the lender or seller had to trust in the borrower's or buyer's ability and readiness to repay their debt at a later time. Consequently, Muldrew argues, 'reputation for honesty became a type of cultural currency which had an enormous value in terms of social estimation' (83). In a recent publication, Alexandra Shepard questions whether an individual's trustworthiness was the exclusive determinant of their creditworthiness.[97] She claims that social appraisal of one's own worth and that of others had also a material basis in a person's belongings (or 'moveable goods'): 'that the concrete evaluation of the material "worth" of households and individuals was critical to the processes whereby credit and wider social standing was assessed ... Notions of "honesty" were rooted as much in estimations of substance as in behavioural norms' (35–36). Shepard concludes that '[t]he consequent processes of estimation involved sophisticated forms of accounting, premissed as much on what people had as on a reputation for honesty in ethical terms' (36). Character and wealth and the extent to which these appeared to be linked were crucial in estimating creditworthiness. In *Fictions of Credit in the Age of Shakespeare*, Laura Kolb highlights the pressure that social appraisal put both on performative self-fashioning and the ability to assess others: 'Advice for borrowers taught them how to dress, speak, and act in such a way that "being lent to" remained a real possibility; advice for lenders reminded them not to take surface appearances at face value' (3).

Where oral agreements were deemed insufficient, the bond provided a written form for lending arrangements. Bonds were written promises to repay a loan (the 'principal') on a certain date, and they could be legally enforced. Rather than charging a sum of money merely for the act of lending—which would have been a usurious act—such bonds merely 'stipulated a penalty to be paid in event of repayment of the principal being delayed beyond a specified, agreed date' (Kerridge, *Usury* 7). In *The Culture of Usury in Renaissance England*, David Hawkes appears to suggest that credit was coextensive with usury, but it is important to understand that the conditions, meanings, and implications of acts of lending and borrowing were diverse.[98] Kerridge discusses the difference between usury and those forms of interest that were legitimate from a Christian point of view in *Usury, Interest*

---

[97] See also Kolb 10.
[98] Hawkes writes, for instance, that 'everyday economic business was normally conducted on the basis of credit, and usury was therefore a practical issue in the quotidian lives of early modern English people' (18). In this as in other passages in *The Culture of Usury*, credit and usury appear to coincide. Although this identification is unnecessarily reductive, Hawkes is of course right when he claims that the ubiquity of credit relations fuelled an 'intensive debate over what exactly constitutes usury' (18).

and the Reformation (7–12).⁹⁹ In principle, usury means to take payment 'over and above the amount lent merely and solely in return for a secured loan' (5). As Kerridge explains, it was seen as 'ungodly, immoral, unproductive and a grave impediment to economic advance' (*Trade and Banking* 34). It described a loan where the lender received more than he was owed and the borrower carried all the risk: 'The usurer lent not merely for gain, but for certain and assured gain; he took no risk' (34).

Interest, in contrast, refers to 'a man's *verum interesse*' (*Usury* 7): to his legitimate interest in a business transaction. Kerridge distinguishes four forms of interest. First, a person had a right to compensation for his loss and forebearance in the case of belated repayment (*poena conventionalis*), but also, second, in the case of expenses, unexpected losses, or when the borrower defaulted (*damnum emergens*) (7–10). Third, the lender was entitled to interest when, 'because he had not been repaid on time, [he] missed an opportunity to profit elsewhere' (*lucrum cessans*) (10). Fourth, in the case of *periculum sortis*, 'the lender or investor shared the risks of the business with the borrower or partner' (10). In consequence, he took a share of the gain as 'lawful interest' (11). Although Kerridge argues that (legitimate) interest was opposed to usury, he also concedes that the distinction was somewhat fluid. The instrument of the bond, for instance, could be used by usurers who counted on the borrower's inability to repay a borrowed sum on time (8). Thus a charitable act of lending might disguise an act of usury, as in Middleton's *A Trick to Catch the Old One*, in which an usurious uncle deprives his nephew of his estate. In his Essay XLI, 'Of Usurie', Francis Bacon introduces 'a Cruell Moneyed Man' who would rather profit from the forfeiture that the bond stipulates than profit from a fixed rate of interest for lending.¹⁰⁰ Perhaps because of this fluidity, early modern Englishmen and -women were not always able to tell the difference between usury and interest.¹⁰¹ It is, however, important to keep in mind that credit took multiple forms that were evaluated in diverse ethical terms—from small and informal acts of helping kin, a friend, or a neighbour in need (Muldrew, *The Economy of Obligation* 113; Wrightson, *English Society 1580–1680* 51–53) to large-scale investments that aimed at profit, from oral agreements to bills and bonds.¹⁰²

The early modern 'culture of credit' and the social functions of reputation and material wealth or solvency will feature prominently in Chapter 4. Here, suffice it to say that many early modern plays—among them *The Alchemist*, *Volpone*, and *Timon of Athens*—examine the instability of value and credit relations. They

---

⁹⁹ For the medieval discourse on this distinction, see Wood's account of usury and interest in chapter 8 of *Medieval Economic Thought*.
¹⁰⁰ Bacon has the 'Cruell Moneyed Man' say: 'The Devill take this *Usury*, it keepes us from Forfeitures, of Mortgages, and Bonds' (Essay XLI, 'Of Usurie' 126).
¹⁰¹ Kerridge quotes 'the alleged victim of a Marlborough usurer' who described this usurer 'as a man "who did usually lend mony for interest"' (*Trade and Banking* 36).
¹⁰² Bruce Carruthers notes in *City of Capital*: 'When discussed by contemporaries, however, credit relations were interpreted through an ethos of neighborliness, and framed by a language of moral obligation' (192).

depict economies that are grounded in insubstantiality and in which—in the end—dreams of wealth, or even just of well-deserved repayment, go up in smoke: 'Till it, and they, and all in fume are gone' (*The Alchemist*). The keen theatrical interest in the instability or even insubstantiality of value, performances of virtue, and cheap promises is surely related to the performative and even fictitious qualities of the culture of credit, in which an adept performance and strategic consumption and display could do much to suggest honesty, solvency, and creditworthiness.

Conclusion

Oeconomy and commerce communicate in multiple ways: together, household and mercantile writings delineate the field of socio-economic action. It is well worth noting the key role of ethics in both sets of discourses. Writers on household and commerce offer an ethical narrative throughout, which borrows heavily from both classical texts and Christian theology. Like the homiletic literature on the household, mercantile discourses insist on the priority of the common good. Most writers strive to emphasize the socio-political significance of household and commerce: in early modern oeconomic and mercantile discourses, the well-ordered household and the merchant's work are praised as pillars of the commonwealth. Anxious concerns with household savings and the monarch's filled coffers can be seen as discursive rationalizations of accumulation, but they coexist with and are tempered by praise of charity, beneficence, and the recurring rejection of greed.[103] At the same time, early modern writers who linked domestic virtue to the realization of 'individual oeconomic interest' (Orlin, *Private Matters* 138) worked in synchrony with mercantile writers who claimed the legitimacy of profit in commerce.[104] Finally, oeconomy, with its investment in moderate purchases, provided a model for conceiving of the nation's trade as a whole in terms of a balance that needed to be tilted in one's favour. Mercantilist and bullionist writers identified a nexus between the behaviour of individual householders and the commonwealth: a householder's excessive consumption or prudent spending shaped the balance of trade as much as his successful management of his wife or his indulgence in her desire for exotic commodities.

The level of detail in early modern texts can be overwhelming. Early modern writings offer exhaustive rules of conduct, as well as detailed practical advice about any number of issues. Practical works on household and estate management

---

[103] Stevenson does not 'believe that Perkins, Greenham, Cleaver, Dent, and the other leaders of Puritanism ... had discarded their suspicion of economic motives', but she also concedes 'that sixteenth-century Puritans did not frown on wealth if it were God's gift, not man's goal' (136).

[104] Orlin develops this argument through a reading of Thomas Heywood's play *A Woman Killed with Kindness*. She suggests 'that the Renaissance concept of domestic virtue which succeeds the moral philosophy of friendship and benefice is one lodged in the realization of its philosophical opposite, individual oeconomic interest' (*Private Matters* 138).

include recipes and month-by-month accounts of when to do what, while mercantile handbooks include templates for commercial documents and offer advice concerning effective sales practices. Despite an overarching rhetorical commitment to ethical behaviour and the common good, the intense attention to how to act in specific circumstances testifies to and helps to realize an increasing interest in practical wisdom as a faculty that appeared instrumental in the pursuit of private gain. The exacting attention to individual aspects of household management and commerce is often rendered through copious speech, enriched with multiple analogies, metaphors, and allegories, along with numerous quotations from the Bible and philosophical works. The abundance of sources, commonplaces, and examples may suggest the difficulty of formulating guidelines for prudent behaviour in a changeable world in which values and virtues had to be adapted to the new commercial reality.

Early modern discourses on socio-economic practices articulate a number of concerns and highlight neuralgic points that also inform the drama of the time: they delineate prudent behaviour, dwell on the imperative of moderation and the restraint of excessive impulses, and emphasize the unruly nature of woman and the risks of excessive consumption. They also outline the political significance of authority and subjection as coordinates of domestic order and discuss the instability and multidimensionality of value as well as the effects of lending and borrowing. Mercantile and oeconomic works ponder the virtuous and the expedient, praise diligence and thrift, outline practical skills, and reevaluate the legitimacy of profit. Mercantilist and bullionist writings negotiate the nature of (monetary) value and seek to protect the balance of trade against the excessive lust for foreign luxury wares. The discussion of individual plays in the following will return to these concerns.

Against the rhetorical dominance of the common good in extra-theatrical discourses, early modern drama stages the pursuit of self-interest in a deeply ambiguous way. The immoral but highly efficient use of practical wisdom emerges as villainous, but *also* as highly attractive. Lady Macbeth and Iago combine a seductive and skilled rhetoric with admirable energy and wit in pursuit of their private interests. While oeconomies and mercantile tracts are written in a prescriptive mode, theatre is explorative and experimental in its take on socio-economic change. The frenzied representation of socio-economic exchanges in city comedies marks a shift in the relations between virtue, self-interest, and the common good. Here, the pursuit of private interests is no longer simply marked as evil, but is also a fascinating entrepreneurial force. Early modern plays thus criticize the ruthless pursuit of private interests, but they also perform important ideological labour in displaying the pervasive presence and motivational power of the acquisitive drive, and in representing the wide range of commercial opportunities that emerge from beyond the constraints of virtue ethics.

2
Oeconomy in *A Chaste Maid in Cheapside* and *Macbeth*

Introduction

The first part of Chapter 1 discussed the social relations that constitute the household, as well as its ethical framework, on the basis of classical oeconomies, Christian sermons, and advice and conduct literature. This chapter turns to the household on the early modern stage to explore a strikingly different picture. Theatrical performances of household management depart in drastic ways from the prescribed norms of conduct literature. Where the latter details ideal behaviour, theatre's preoccupation with the household is explorative and even experimental: both domestic tragedies and city comedies stage households that transgress ethical boundaries and upset the dichotomous order of authority and subjection. The wildly different representations of the household in print and on the stage signal a disparity between prescriptive ideal and social reality. The point is not that the plays are more realistic; they bow to generic demands and are naturally hyperbolic in their tragic and comic effects. Yet theatre's investment in transgression and disorder in the household signals the extent to which oeconomy as an ethical system is under stress. It confirms the suspicion that one might have had all along: that the intense preoccupation with the household and its social roles in the prescriptive literature of the time signals an awareness of socio-economic change that required both reassurance of a continuity of values and accommodation to this change. Homiletic writings and oeconomies preached moderation and praised the common good just as the inhabitants of London were being confronted with a commercial reality of profitable trade and luxury goods from all over the world, as well as unprecedented possibilities of social advancement.[1] Theatre is a leading medium in exploring and acting out the tensions between the ethical framework of oeconomy and a commercial reality of profitable exchange. As early modern plays suggest, negotiating this reality required more than just a reflexive condemnation of profitable commerce. Plays as diverse as *Macbeth* and *Othello*, *A Chaste Maid in Cheapside* and *The Alchemist* or *Volpone* explore new opportunities

---

[1] R. H. Tawney noted 'the divorce between religious theory and economic realities' by 'the end of the sixteenth century' (*Religion and the Rise of Capitalism* 197).

for wealth and social advancement, and they examine the practical expertise that it takes to make one's fortune and manage risks of ethical and economic failure.

As a traditional object of oeconomic reflection, the household constitutes a topos and trope through which playwrights explore the transformative potential of commercial society. It provides a polymorphous setting to enact in various ways the confrontation between the ethical framework of oeconomy and the commercial imperative of profit. The mode of this confrontation may be satirical or tragic, but is rarely harmonious. In fact, the term 'setting' itself is inadequate. It suggests the theatrical function of a mere backdrop to the action, but in many early modern plays, the order and fate of the household is at the very heart of the plot.[2] It is in the changing order, the shifting values, and the social aspirations of households that the sense of a social and economic transformation becomes palpable. This dual role of the household, as setting and focal point of the action, stems from its dual character as both a physical space and a socio-economic constellation. As the latter, it is structured by hierarchical relations, specific social functions, and a gendered division of labour.

This chapter discusses Middleton's *A Chaste Maid in Cheapside* and Shakespeare's *Macbeth* to explore different ways in which the strategic pursuit of profit and social advancement shapes households. City comedies such as *A Chaste Maid* offer sometimes grotesque and always satirical versions of city life, but in painting an exaggerated picture of the commercialization of social relations, they indicate a very real consciousness of change and a keen interest in the anxieties and hopes that attend it. In the context of the dissolute and materialistic households of city comedy, *Macbeth*'s fascination with domestic life and the way in which it interferes with the politics of succession reveals new levels of social meaning. The play's scrutiny of self-interested behaviour, excessive desire, and strategies of instrumental rationality suggests a heightened attention to the logics, limits, and implications of socio-economic action. In and through *Macbeth*'s investment in politics and domesticity emerges a commercial logic which accepts self-interest as a motivational force. With its focus on material and social gain, this logic performs a pragmatic and even instrumental turn towards efficient and effective means, thus emptying prudence of its ethical content.

Traditionally, critics approached *Macbeth* as a play of sovereign power and succession, resulting in two different traditions of reading *Macbeth* as a political play. Some critics argue that the play was designed to flatter King James.[3] According to others, however, the matter is less unequivocal: far from simply flattering the king,

---

[2] See also Ruby Chatterji, who remarked as early as 1965 that in *A Chaste Maid of Cheapside*, 'the family is the nexus of the play's various complications, the basis of its thematic as well as structural unity' (106).

[3] See for instance Henry N. Paul, *The Royal Play of Shakespeare*, and Alvin Kernan, *Shakespeare, the King's Playwright*. Paul suggests that *Macbeth* 'was a royal play specially written for performance before King James' (1).

Macbeth may be said to examine 'conflicting early modern discourses that constituted sovereignty' (Carroll 349).[4] The following discussion sympathizes with the work of critics such as William Carroll, Jonathan Goldberg, Arthur F. Kinney, Bernice W. Kliman, and David Norbrook. Its focus, however, is on the intersection of the domestic and the political. My analysis seeks to enrich and complement political interpretations of the play by taking its focus on oeconomy seriously and by revealing the effects of a chrematistic logic that exerts pressure on the relation between oeconomy and politics. The entrepreneurial energy of Lady Macbeth, the play's concern with marital relations, and its pervasive mercantile rhetoric all exceed a merely political reading of the play. Both *Macbeth* and *A Chaste Maid* stage households in disarray that are symptomatic of a larger shift in the value system that governed socio-economic action in the sixteenth and seventeenth centuries. They give form to an ideological conflict between the demands of virtue ethics on the one hand and, on the other, the imperative of gain and the promise of social advancement as driving forces of commercial society. The crisis of the household is also a crisis of virtue ethics as a touchstone of socio-economic conduct.

Superficially, the plays could hardly be more different: *A Chaste Maid* is an anatomy of urban household life in seventeenth-century London, while *Macbeth* examines a noble household in medieval Scotland. In Middleton's comedy, the crisis of oeconomy is performed by means of shifting domestic spaces, which are reconfigured through commercial relations. In Shakespeare's tragedy, it shapes the fate of a noble household that is disconnected from the community. In the first case, the social space of the household communicates with others to a degree that dissolves the idea of the household as a distinct unit. In the second case, the household isolates itself and erodes from within. Yet it is against the backdrop of such differences that the similarities appear all the more conspicuous. This is hardly surprising: despite *Macbeth*'s anachronistic placing in feudal Scotland, the

---

[4] As early as 1987, Jonathan Goldberg criticizes the 'flattery thesis': 'Shakespeare—so the common line has it—recombines and simplifies his materials to offer a saintly king and his villainous murderer, and thereby makes differences clear-cut' (248). Goldberg counters this simplistic interpretation with a more complex one which notes that, both in the beginning and the end of the play, 'a supposedly saintly king has let another do his dirty work' (249). David Norbrook suggests that the play 'draws on sources whose political vision was in many ways inimical to James's' (80). He also argues that 'Shakespeare could ... have made Banquo a less shadowy and ambiguous figure, and thus made the dynastic compliment more direct' (94). He wonders: 'Is the play really an appropriate compliment to a Scottish king?' (94). Arthur F. Kinney links *Macbeth* both to James's theatricality and to his 'political practices' and to 'subtle and shadowy lexias of his theoretical pronouncements about right rule' (86). In fact, he writes: 'The Macbeths share James's view as they reach for power' (93). Hence, the play exposes absolutism's involvement with tyranny: 'Playgoers in 1606 could argue, then, that the very idea of government as perpetuated by James involved tyranny; insofar as it meant absolute rule, it was potentially a dangerous matter' (96). Bernice W. Kliman sums up the debate (11–13) and concludes: 'The play could be a pattern for action in the face of absolute rule and at the same time an ambivalent portrait of the amalgam of valour and injustice in an absolute prince' (13).

play invites us to look to its own present, the early modern age. Theatre's juxtaposition of fictional settings with the deictic here-and-now of the audience stems from the double referentiality of theatrical space: the real space of the theatre coincides with the fictional setting of the play (Pfister 246).[5] Thus, in the heterotopia of the playhouse, medieval Scotland as fictional setting coincides with early modern London.[6]

Both plays focus on individual households to examine oeconomic disorder and mismanagement, and both explore the demise of oeconomy as an ethical paradigm of socio-economic exchanges. Both plays stage the exploits of practical rationality beyond the limits of virtue ethics, and they contribute to the revaluation of private interest in commercial society. From these shared concerns emerge markedly different positions. In *Macbeth*, the ruthless pursuit of private interests develops a destructive force, which is only contained by the tyrant's death. In *A Chaste Maid*, in contrast, it is fully at home in the city—satirized, to be sure, but also recognized as a new social force. This chapter seeks to identify differences and similarities, but it also wants to muddle comfortable distinctions between the moral ambiguities of comedy and the restorative, conservative impulse of tragedy. Framed by the discussion of *A Chaste Maid*, *Macbeth* emerges as a deeply ambiguous play that explores the ruthless pursuit of private interest without laying its spirit to rest in a conciliatory ending. It performs not just the death of a tyrant, but, with Malcolm, also the rise of a new, potentially self-interested, and efficient type of ruler. Equally, its representation of Lady Macbeth not only signals excessive desire and a household in disarray, but also displays fascination with the character's entrepreneurial energy, practical rationality, and socio-economic ambition.

The first part of the chapter focuses on *A Chaste Maid*. It seeks to tease out the commercial logic that shapes the social space of households in this comedy and to shed light on how the household emerges as the focal point of dramatic action. It analyses the commercialization of domestic space as well as the role of sexuality as an object of exchange and a social binding agent. The pervasive sway of private interest emerges as an ordering force, which creates and structures fluid household spaces and the social network in which they are embedded. The spatial dynamic that derives from this is expansive, in striking contrast to the household of the

---

[5] Manfred Pfister theorizes this as follows: 'The superimposition of an external communication system over an internal system also occurs within the structures of time and space. The actual space taken up by stage and auditorium on the external level corresponds on the internal level to the fictional space in which the story unfolds, whilst the fictional temporal deixis of the story corresponds to the real temporal deixis of the performers and the receivers, though of course the fact that the present tenses on both levels are identical should not tempt us into confusing the real *hic et nunc* of the audience and actors and the fictional *hic et nunc* of the figures' (246). The internal communication system refers to the interaction of the fictional characters in the fictional space in which the plot unfolds.

[6] Foucault writes: 'The heterotopia is capable of juxtaposing in a single real place several spaces, several sites that are in themselves incompatible. Thus it is that the theater brings onto the rectangle of the stage, one after the other, a whole series of places that are foreign to one another' ('Of Other Spaces' 25). It also brings together two categorically different spaces and times, real and fictional.

Macbeths, which is affected by a constrictive dynamic of self-isolation. While the discussion of *A Chaste Maid* in the first part of the chapter concentrates on the relation of oeconomy and commerce, my analysis of *Macbeth* in the second part relates oeconomy to politics. This relation is inflected by a rhetoric of business and shaped by an overarching concern with accumulation. The play's preoccupation with marital conspiracy signals a rising interest in gender roles and the division of labour in the house, in the relation between oeconomy and politics, and in the strained relation between private interest and the common good.

A Chaste Maid in Cheapside: The *Oikos* in a Marketplace of Desires

A Chaste Maid explores a household life that differs notably from that detailed in the prescriptive literature of the time. The play substitutes the house as a governable and stable spatial entity with dynamically constituted multifunctional spaces. Setting the tone for the entire comedy, the first scene is staged in a goldsmith's shop in Cheapside, 'the very street where the City's wealthiest goldsmiths pursued their trade' (Newman, '"Goldsmith's Ware"' 103). This location signals the extent to which the households of city comedy depart from the rural estate described by Xenophon and other classical and early modern writers. The prominent naming of Cheapside in the play's title situates its households right in 'the commercial center of London' (Newman, '"Goldsmith's Ware"' 103). As Manuela Rossini points out, 'even before the first word is spoken', Cheapside functions 'as an emblem of the brave new world of commerce' (91–92).

Cheapside was indeed one of the hotspots of trade in early modern London and the one with the longest tradition. Already in medieval times, 'Cheap' was a key hub for vibrant commercial traffic. Derek Keene estimates that the area had some four hundred shops and four thousand trading plots that employed enough people 'to populate a market town of considerable size' ('Shops and Shopping' 40).[7] Throughout a period ranging from the twelfth to the seventeenth century, Keene maintains, 'Cheapside was without rival as the principal shopping street in London' (29). As Dorothy Davis explains in her *History of Shopping*, 'in Elizabeth's reign, [Cheapside] had been almost monopolized by goldsmiths and silk mercers, the two richest retail trades' (108).[8] The goldsmiths' shops cemented 'Cheapside's role as a place of display' by exhibiting their wares 'in shop frontages

---

[7] The size and number of shops varied in the later medieval and early modern period, with a marked lapse in prices of shops and plots in the second decade of the fourteenth century and the following decades due to economic problems and pestilences. Around 1550, however, 'there was a marked revival in the demand for Cheapside properties and within fifty years land values again equalled their late 13th century levels' (Keene, 'Shops and Shopping' 42).

[8] Not long after, the area changed. Goldsmiths, Row was invaded by the 'meaner trades', as 'a member of King James' court' complained in a letter from 1622 (Davis 109).

of some elaboration and splendour' (Keene, 'Shops and Shopping' 31).[9] Because of its width and its 'fine houses over the richest shops', Cheapside constituted 'the setting for all the great civic gatherings and processions' (Davis 108; see also Harding, 'Cheapside' 77). The play's setting in the heart of commercial London offers an interpretative paradigm centred on exchange, consumption, and profit.

Crucially, due to the multiplot structure of Middleton's comedy, households exist here in the plural.[10] They form a network structure: individual households do not consist of a fixed set of people, but rather fluctuate. The incessant traffic of people and goods between households models the activity in a marketplace; it creates the sense of a dynamic network structure maintained by exchange. It transforms the social space of the household from a seemingly stable container of domestic relations into a fluid space of uncertain extension and duration. Recurring appearances of the same characters in different households strengthen the sense of permeability and interconnectedness. In the first scene of the first act of *A Chaste Maid*, Sir Walter enters the Yellowhammers' shop, in the second scene the Allwits' household. He moves freely from one to the next and dons the roles of suitor and rich lover as the various households demand. Sir Walter is one of a number of 'free radicals', mostly unmarried characters, who set the circulation of people and goods among the individual households in motion. Other shifting characters are the whore who poses as a Welsh gentlewoman; Touchwood Senior, who temporarily dissolves his household; and his brother Touchwood Junior, who finally—after an intrigue in the manner of New Comedy—succeeds in marrying the goldsmith's daughter, Moll.[11] These characters forge new ties and act as binding agents between households.

This dynamic network structure is clearly at odds with the discrete, governable space of prescriptive literature. Yet the comedy's performance of multiple relations of socio-economic proximity suits the overcrowded metropolis, which Lena

---

[9] Keene quotes a traveller who 'certainly had Cheapside in mind' when he wrote around 1500: 'in a single street, called "The Street" (*la strada*) leading to St. Paul's there are fifty-two goldsmiths' shops, so rich and full of silver vessels, great and small, that in all the shops in Milan, Rome, Venice, and Florence together it seems to me that you would not find so many of such magnificence as you would see in London' ('Shops and Shopping' 31). See also T. F. Reddaway, who quotes a Swiss traveller, Thomas Platter, who wrote in 1599 that, 'In one very long street called Cheapside dwell great treasures and vast amount of money may be seen here' (Reddaway 181). According to Reddaway, it was the goldsmiths' section of the street 'which most dazzled foreign visitors' (181).

[10] Richard Levin distinguishes four plots: the main plot, which focuses on Touchwood Junior's attempt to win Moll; the second plot, which links the Allwits with Sir Walter; a third plot that involves the Kixes and Touchwood Senior; and a fourth, somewhat marginal plot, which concerns Tim, his tutor, and the alleged Welsh gentlewoman (15).

[11] According to Alexander Leggatt, New Comedy 'is distinguished by recurring plot features: two lovers get together, overcoming opposition both internal and external. The solution is produced after a period of confusion, including an intrigue managed in Roman comedy by a clever slave, and managed more often in later comedy by the lovers themselves. A generational conflict, young folks outwitting old folks, is frequently involved' (2). The plot of *A Chaste Maid* follows this model by including both a helpful servant and lovers who are clever enough to outsmart Moll's parents.

Cowen Orlin described in *Locating Privacy in Tudor England*.¹² The cohabitation which the comedy performs with the Allwits and Sir Walter on the one hand, and the Kixes and the Touchstones on the other, had a basis in the shared spaces of early modern London: 'Most residents [of London] lived in conditions of structural codependency resulting from the subdivision of space' (Orlin, *Locating Privacy* 163). Middleton's comedy generalizes and radicalizes the sense of shared spaces by staging changing household sets in which identities are constituted by a dynamic relationality.¹³ In *A Chaste Maid*, household member, guest, or stranger are not stable identities; such allocations are relational, situational, and performative. The sense of shifting identities in ongoing exchanges is clearly at odds with the firm distinctions of household literature. Dudley Fenner's Ramist diagram in 'The Order of Housholde' (the third part of his *The Artes of Logike and Rhetorike* from 1584) suggests an absolute distinction between two sets: 'those in the housholde' and 'straungers or guestes comming into the same' (A1v). With the changing positions of individual characters, the inside/outside distinction becomes fluid. Instead of showing concern for the unity and integrity of individual households, householders in *A Chaste Maid* are happy to share home and wife and to sell off their children in marriage in order to better their circumstances. As the moral integrity of the household erodes with increasingly fluid social relations and positions, the comedy wittily explores the obsession of the 'middling sort of people' with 'social ascent and consumption' (Schülting 103).

Liminal Domestic Spaces

A Chaste Maid in Cheapside is set in different households and in the streets that link them. Two of these household spaces are liminal ones in which domestic and commercial concerns converge: the goldsmith's shop and the lying-in room of Mrs Allwit. In itself, the proximity of domestic life and commercial enterprise is hardly remarkable. Referring to Ralph Treswell's survey of London from 1616, Sallie Anglin explains that 'public and domestic life were not spatially distinct; most houses facing the street opened into a shop that was often connected either to a kitchen or a warehouse, while the living rooms were on the second floor' (11; see also Richardson, 'Domestic Life in Jacobean London' 53). Yet *A Chaste Maid* makes the most of this proximity. In the goldsmith's shop in the very first scene, family and customers meet in a 'semi-domestic' setting (Anglin 14) in which quasi-commercial negotiations are part and parcel of domestic concerns. In this setting, 'two conversations about wives and value become entangled' (Richardson,

---

[12] See in particular Orlin, *Locating Privacy in Tudor London* chapter 4, on the boundaries of city households.

[13] See also Andreas Mahler's reflections on space in 'Topologie' 18.

'Domestic Life in Jacobean London' 53). A lover poses as client, a suitor courts the goldsmith's daughter and inspects her family's wealth, and a mother deliberately exposes her daughter to unwanted attentions. Clearly, in this family-run shop, a commercial logic of profitable exchange interacts and clashes with oeconomic principles of moderation, temperance, and prudence. The Yellowhammers run both their household and business on the principle of securing the greatest social and material profit.

The scene's attention is focused on Moll, their daughter, who is to marry Sir Walter Whorehound and become a gentleman's wife. Her appearance in the shop signals her status as an object to be displayed and exchanged. This evokes a curious sales practice that positioned women in a space of public display.[14] It developed in Cheapside, where 'tradesmen's wives [were] sitting in seats "built-a-purpose" at the doors of the shops to engage passers-by in conversation and entice them into making purchases' (Davis 109).[15] This created an ambiguous position for wives of shopkeepers but, as married women, they may have been *qua status* on the safe side of an enticing conversation. The Yellowhammers' display of their unmarried daughter, in contrast, clearly borders on pandering.

The Allwits' lying-in room similarly fuses domesticity with commerce, more precisely with sexual exchange and conspicuous consumption. The lying-in space constitutes the setting of the gossip's feast in Act Three, Scene Two; it occupies 'the structural center of the plot' (Inbody 93). Traditionally, the lying-in room was a decidedly female space, which was open to midwives, 'gossips', and a few selected men.[16] In *A Chaste Maid*, this space is invaded by a crowd of bawdy gossips, Sir Walter as (god)father, Mistress Yellowhammer, Lady Kix, and Tim and his tutor. This ensemble exaggerates the greater accessibility of the conventional lying-in room as opposed to its predecessor, the birthing chamber, which was sealed off radically from the rest of the house during childbirth (Paster, *The Body Embarrassed* 185; see also Pollock 300 and Adrian Wilson 26).[17] The scene derives its comic potential

---

[14] Keene confirms that, 'Women were often to be seen in shop windows or doorways, and this was presumably part of a strategy for drumming up trade' ('Shops and Shopping' 41). Rossini writes: 'If we accept Lefebvre's theory that space is a powerful shaper of gender identity, we can claim that as a "hybrid realm," the shop also produced "hybrid" female subjectivities or bodies: the *chaste* body of the wife or wife-to-be, conceptualized as belonging to one proprietor only, combined with the *chased* body, potentially available to everyone with enough (pur)chasing power. As R. B. Parker informs us in his note to the play's title, "chased" women is a reference to the prostitutes who were "whipped through [Cheapside] at a cart's tail" in a shaming ritual' (93). Samuel Pepys enjoyed flirting with a shopkeeper's wife (Pepys 157, 196–197; vol. 7; see also Keene 41).

[15] See also Archer, 'Material Londoners?' 186.

[16] According to Janelle Day Jenstad, men 'were normally excluded' (376) from the lying-in chamber (see also Gail McMurray Gibson 10–11.) Adrian Wilson disagrees, at least for the later part of the lying-in: '[I]nitially, only men who were the mother's own relatives could visit her, although by the final stage of lying-in this restriction was apparently relaxed, and it may have been easier for a man to pay a visit if he was accompanied by his wife' (27).

[17] Wilson writes: 'The birth was not only contained within a distinct social space, but also physically and symbolically enclosed. Air was excluded by blocking up the keyholes; daylight was shut out by curtains; and the darkness within was illuminated by means of candles, which were therefore standard

from turning a predominantly gendered, semi-private household space into a setting for random visitors and sexualized exchanges: the drunken Puritans all take a turn kissing Tim and his tutor. A visit to the lying-in chamber was also an opportunity to inspect a family's wealth; in this sense, the lying-in chamber was a space in which the domestic and the public converged. Yet Middleton exaggerates this convergence. His lying-in chamber gives the distinct impression of being an open and carnivalesque space akin to the early modern theatres of the Puritan imagination. Although the scene is 'only tenuously connected to the plot' (Richard Levin 14), it underscores the permeability of the household space, the persistent social traffic that shapes it along with loose morals and illicit desires.

The play identifies the social exchanges in the lying-in room as simultaneously oeconomic *and* commercial. In the early modern period, the birth of a child was a genuine concern of household management. It secured the household's lineage and constituted an opportunity for the public display of wealth. In the context of the play, the new-born babe signifies the sexual and financial exchanges between Sir Walter and the Allwits. The financial benefits of their transaction are put on display in the form of comestible commodities:

> ALLWIT. A lady lies not in like her; there's her embossings,
> Embroiderings, spanglings, and I know not what,
> As if she lay with all the gaudy shops
> In Gresham's Burse about her; then her restoratives,
> Able to set up a young 'pothecary,
> And richly stock the foreman of a drugshop;
> Her sugar by whole loaves, her wines by rundlets.
> (*Chaste Maid* 1.2.32–38)

'A lady lies not in like her', is, as Janelle Day Jenstad points out, ambiguous: 'is her lying-in better or worse than that of a lady?' (374). The ambiguous phrase directs attention to a proto-bourgeois desire for social advancement, which seeks to mirror aristocratic practices but is prone to failure. The parody emerges in the exaggerated celebration of quantity, which says nothing about quality: 'Her sugar by whole loaves, her wines by rundlets' (1.2.38).[18] Jenstad describes the lying-in, and especially the gossip's feast after the christening, as events at which social connections and wealth were displayed through material objects, such as hangings

---

requirements for a delivery' (26). Crowded with female attendants, it was 'a place of enclosure' and 'a place of exclusion' of the male members of the household (Reynolds 32). After the birth, this same space became the setting for the 'ensuing month of lying-in' (Adrian Wilson 26), which saw its gradual transformation into a more open space.

[18] See Jenstad 393. Jenstad also comments on the line 'A lady lies not in like her' (1.2.32): 'Does Mrs. Allwit lie in like a countess or not? The joke may well be that the Allwits and their friends cannot distinguish gaudies from luxury goods. But if there is something imitable about the Countess of Salisbury's lying-in, it is the fact that the goods are purchased. Both lying-in displays seem to have mercantile origins' (393).

and other textiles, as well as food and wine. She compares two lying-in events in different noble families to suggest a shift within the material culture of the lying-in from a tradition of reciprocal borrowing from other aristocratic families to the purchase of objects in the service of conspicuous consumption. In the first case, the provenance of the object generated social meaning by demonstrating kinship.[19] In the second case, material objects demonstrated solvency.[20] Jenstad describes this as part of a larger social shift in which social difference came to be increasingly expressed by markers of wealth.[21] In line with this emerging social 'taxonomy' of wealth (Jenstad 375), Allwit's description of his wife's lying-in celebrates the mercantile origin of goods: the association with Gresham's Bourse in the above quotation suggests that they are bought rather than borrowed. Allwit delights in this display and its benefits for his credit: 'I see these things, but like a happy man, / I pay for none at all, yet fools think's mine; / I have the name, and in his gold I shine' (1.2.39–41).

In *A Chaste Maid of Cheapside*, both the Yellowhammer's shop and Mrs Allwit's lying-in room are spaces in which domestic concerns overlap with material interests and conspicuous consumption. It falls mainly to women to insert the household into a market economy, on the one hand as commodities—as displayed and desired objects that forge new social relations through being exchanged—and, on the other, as potentially excessive consumers of costly and luxurious commodities. In early modern drama, representations of female desire slide persistently between overflowing sexuality and excessive commercial consumption. Karen Newman points out that early modern prescriptive literature as well as 'plays, ballads, and jest books ... all conflate the sexual and the economic when representing feminine desire' ('City Talk' 184). Ian Archer links the slippage between excessive lust and excessive consumption to the Christian tradition.[22] Mrs Allwit's lying-in in the midst of material goods exemplifies this slippage. The gossips' loose talk completes the identification of voracious sexuality and immoderate consumption of food and drink with a third type of excessive behaviour: loquaciousness.[23] With

---

[19] Jenstad states: 'Because the rank of the owner attached itself to the object, temporary possession of the object located the borrower in the same social circles as the lender' (382–383).

[20] As Jenstad explains, '[c]onspicuous consumption is predicated upon a public reckoning; the world at large has to recognize the loss, do the math' (389). Big purchases suggest great spending power.

[21] See Catherine Richardson about the role of 'material display' in working out 'the complex relationships between wealth and authority' ('Domestic Life in Jacobean London' 52).

[22] 'Consumption was a moral problem because the desire for goods was linked with sexual desire. The Christian tradition had conflated luxuria and lust: luxury was equated with desire, and desire with disobedience. Contemporary moralists regularly drove home the parallels between prostitution and trade' (Archer, 'Material Londoners?' 186). Christopher Berry also points out that 'In the *OED*, the first meaning of "luxury" is lust or lasciviousness' (87). He adds: 'In French, the connexion is more evident with *luxure* remaining the standard translation of "lechery" or "lewdness"' (87).

[23] This triangle is frequently evoked in early modern writings: 'The talking woman is everywhere equated with a voracious sexuality that in turn abets her avid consumerism: scolds were regularly accused of both extravagance and adultery' (Newman, 'City Talk' 184). Gossips constituted a traditional network that managed and policed the birth of a child (Inbody 103–104; Pollock 297–298). For

the blabbering and incontinent gossips, who literally 'wet the floor beneath their stools' (Paster, *The Body Embarrassed* 23), Middleton's comedy presents a female community of 'excessive economic consumption' (Miller 81) and excessive output (leakage of words and fluids).[24] Even Lady Kix 'wets as she kisses' bachelor Tim (3.2.180). This bawdy scene of carnivalesque and boundless incontinence contrasts sharply with the period of sexual abstinence which the lying-in usually implied (Adrian Wilson 27), and which the play emphasizes by setting events in the time of Lent. The excessive consumption portrayed in this scene implies the dissolution of ethics as the touchstone of oeconomy. It is, however, a form of *calculated* excess with an economic function of its own. As pointed out earlier, consumption in the lying-in chamber was a case of 'conspicuous consumption', and, as such, a rational act 'predicated upon a public reckoning' to support the household's credit in an economic culture that relied on reputation as a currency for credit (Jenstad 389). While the connection between the lying-in and the performance and display of socio-oeconomic exchanges is hardly new, Middleton turns the screw further by reducing marriage to a form of prostitution, both in relation to Moll's intended marriage and in relation to the Allwits' arrangement with Sir Walter. John Twyning describes prostitution as a 'root metaphor' for 'the abstraction of commodity, the labour process, and pure exchange value' and argues that it is 'a resource for the displacement of all kinds of anxieties associated with trade' (14).[25] The conflation of sexual and acquisitive desire is further explored in the following section.

Sexuality as Commodity

A Chaste Maid examines the changing priorities of household management in an increasingly commercial society. For the Yellowhammers, a daughter is a commodity that can secure social and material profit on the (marriage) market.

---

a discussion of the notion of gossip, see Caroline Bicks, *Midwiving Subjects*: 'Gossips had long been associated with female unruliness and mindless chatter—but not always. Literally "god-sib," or godparent, "gossip" originally described a person, whether male or female, with whom one had contracted spiritual affinity by acting as a sponsor at a baptism. The *Middle English Dictionary* also defines "gossip" as a close friend or confidante. Although it had gender-neutral origins, "gossip" became associated with disruptive female speech as early as Chaucer's time ... By the early modern period, the term "gossip" was regularly used for a woman attending a birth' (27). Several critics have argued that gossip scenes such as this one express male anxieties about female networks beyond male control: men appear to have worried about what gossips might say about their husbands (Capp 63-64), and that they might use '"good neighbourliness" as a cover for secret assignations' (64). Magistrates also worried that those female networks posed a 'threat to social order' because they might be used in the interest of petty crime (64).

[24] Gail Kern Paster writes: 'In the play, not surprisingly, bladder incontinence in particular is presented as an attribute of women of all ages, from the new Allwit baby, who is taken offstage in act 2 to get her bum wiped, to the drunken gossips who wet the floor in act 3 and discuss, among other things, a nineteen-year-old daughter who cannot be married because of "a secret fault," that she wets her bed (3.2.96)' (*The Body Embarrassed* 53).

[25] Katherine Gillen remarks that 'Prostitution provides the most obvious analogue to commercial exchange' (*Chaste Value* 8).

Her commoditization is emphasized through her first appearance in her father's shop, and her value is quantified through her dowry.[26] Even if the argument is *ex negativo*, Moll's value is counted in coin. Reminiscing about her own youth and her dancing teacher, Mrs Yellowhammer reproaches her daughter for lacking grace: 'you dance like a plumber's daughter, and deserve two thousand pound in lead to your marriage, and not in goldsmith's ware' (1.1.14–20).[27] In the prescriptive literature of the time and in many plays, a woman's value derives from her chastity as the crowning female virtue. It is all the more indicative of Sir Walter's disinterest in morals that he prices her virginity much lower than her dowry: he counts on 'two thousand pound in gold, / And a sweet maidenhead / Worth forty' (4.2.92–94).[28] Moll's mother is equally disinterested in preserving her daughter's virtue: in her view, Moll's value is not enhanced by virtuous reticence and chastity, but by flirtatious behaviour. With this particular estimation of her daughter's value comes a transformed understanding of the mother's role. In chastising her daughter, Mistress Yellowhammer performs the traditional role of mother and mistress of the house, but only in a parodic mode: instead of warning her daughter against flirtatious behaviour, she admonishes her for not being flirtatious enough. And instead of supervising her education as the future mistress of a Christian household, she supervises her training as a sexual playmate. The goal is to make her 'fit for a knight's bed' (1.1.10). The mother's very first question sets the tone for the double entendre that characterizes Moll's education: 'Have you played over all your old lessons o' the virginals?' (1.1.1). The virginals was a keyboard instrument, whose name in this context suggests lessons for virgins. What these consist of becomes evident when Mistress Yellowhammer rhapsodizes about her dancing teacher in a speech that is full of sexual innuendo: 'When I was of your bord, he missed me not a night, I was kept at it; I took delight to learn, and he to teach me; pretty brown gentleman, he took pleasure in my company …' (1.1.13–15). Her approach to sexuality is instrumental and goal-orientated—sexuality functions as a means to secure a gentleman as a husband—but also frivolous, true to early modern representations of women as creatures in whom reason is easily overtaken by passion and lust.

Moll's marriage to Sir Walter Whorehound is designed to secure the family's social advancement to the ranks of the gentry. It has a calculated benefit which, in the eyes of the parents, outweighs love. The Yellowhammers' son Tim plays a similar part in his parents' oeconomic calculus: through his studies at Cambridge, where he drinks his broth with the other 'gentleman commoners', he takes the male road to social advancement. His father relishes the social rise that the Bachelor of Arts promises:

---

[26] Gillen writes: 'Moll's commodity potential is highlighted by her association with the gold that her father Yellowhammer keeps in his shop' (*Chaste Value* 133).
[27] See also Newman, '"Goldsmith's Ware"' 106.
[28] See also Gillen, *Chaste Value* 133.

YELLOWHAMMER. A poor plain boy, an university man
    Proceeds next Lent to a Bachelor of Art;
    He will be call'd Sir Yellowhammer then
    Over all Cambridge, and that's half a knight.[29]

(1.1.151–155)

The humanist education of a young gentleman is designed to render him eligible for marriage to a gentlewoman. It comes as no surprise that Tim is all too easily caught by Sir Walter's 'landed niece' (1.1.36), an alleged Welsh gentlewoman who is, in fact, a common whore. She has been 'educated' by Sir Walter in the English language and the sexual arts and is brought to London to secure his own match with Moll. Sir Walter remarks: '"[T]was strange that I should lie with thee so often, to leave thee without English—that were unnatural. I bring thee up to turn thee into gold, wench, and make thy fortune shine like your bright trade. A goldsmith's shop sets out a city maid' (1.1.96–100). Tim and his tutor serve as a laughing stock throughout the comedy, but their constant use of Latin underscores their intention to climb the social ladder.[30] The Yellowhammers' interest in securing social advancement through their children's marriages is a parodically pointed concern, but one which would have been familiar to the audiences of Middleton's plays.[31]

In all the households in *A Chaste Maid*, sexuality integrates the domestic with the market and caters to the motive of material and, in the case of the Yellowhammers' children, social profit. Allwit and his family live off Sir Walter Whorehound, who, as the lover of Allwit's wife and biological father of his children, keeps their household. Allwit celebrates his fortunate state: 'I thank him, h'as maintained my house this ten years, / Not only keeps my wife, but a keeps me / And all my family ... / The happiest state that ever man was born to' (1.2.16–22). Free from sexual demands and exempt from the burden of breadwinning labour, he enjoys an idle and happy life. Allwit's existence constitutes a counter-model both to the Puritan emphasis on diligence and a godly calling as well as to the possessive anxiety that tortures Othello. In contrast to Othello, he is remarkably and deliciously free from jealousy: 'These torments stand I freed of, I am as clear / From jealousy of a wife as from the charge. / O two miraculous blessings' (1.2.49–51). Allwit is happy to give

---

[29] See the explanatory note by Brian Loughrey and Neil Taylor in their *Five Plays* edition of *A Chaste Maid*: 'Sir: a rendering of the title "Dominus" accorded to graduates from Oxford and Cambridge. It constituted only "half a knight" because it preceded the surname' (169).

[30] See my article 'Humanistische Bildung und Ökonomisches Kalkül in Middleton's *A Chaste Maid in Cheapside*'.

[31] Theodore B. Leinwand describes in some detail the social dynamic which linked rich merchants and poor gentry. He writes about the merchants: 'Their wealth pulled them in one direction; the fact that it was money that was used as a criterion pulled in the other. The gentry were caught in a similar bind: by birth and sometimes by breeding they were gentlemen, but their capital value might be well below that of a successful shopkeeper' (*The City Staged* 39).

and take without worrying about the corrupting effects of circulation and without being hampered by the fear of loss.

Touchwood Senior and the Kixes come to a similarly pragmatic arrangement.[32] Touchwood Senior is too sexually active and too poor to maintain his ever-growing household. Luckily, his wife is well versed in oeconomics. She understands that 'The feast of marriage is not lust but love, / And care of the estate' (2.1.50–51) and agrees to temporary separation. When Touchwood encounters the rich but childless Kixes, he manages to turn an apparent disadvantage into financial profit. Touchwood finds in the Kixes the perfect partners for an exchange based on complementary needs. He describes their problems in reverse form: 'Some only can get riches and no children, / We only can get children and no riches' (2.1.11–12). This semantic chiasmus suggests the ideal solution: an exchange of the power to beget children versus money to maintain a growing household. And indeed, Touchwood Senior receives one hundred pounds for successfully 'treating' Sir Oliver Kix and his wife: he impregnates the lady in a manner reminiscent of Machiavelli's comedy *La Mandragola*.[33] Quite conveniently, having an heir secures land for the Kixes that would have fallen to Sir Walter Whorehound had they remained childless. Sir Oliver is ready to pay any price for Touchwood's potion (or 'water'), for he stands to gain doubly with his wife's pregnancy:

> SIR OLIVER. There's land to come; put case his water stands me
> In some five hundred pound a pint,
> 'Twill fetch a thousand, and a kersten soul.
>
> (2.1.200–202)

Delighted by his wife's pregnancy, he invites Touchwood and his family to join his own household. Without further ado and with much insinuation, a deal is struck that promises the happy cohabitation of the two families. It reconciles, as Arthur F. Marotti points out, 'Eros and Pecunia' (68), liberating love-making from financial constraints.[34] Henceforth, the Kixes will keep the Touchwoods and all their children. This arrangement implies, of course, that Touchwood continues producing

---

[32] Richard Levin recognized symmetrical patterns in the four plots: 'It is evident that these plots were placed together with a view to exploiting certain symmetrical patterns of character and action' (17). He groups the Moll/Whorehound plot with the Tim/whore plot and perceives a similar pattern in the Allwit/Whorehound and the Touchwood/Kix plots: 'The central situation in each is a triangle that involves a long-married couple and another man who cuckolds the husband and fathers his children' (18). See also Joanne Altieri 176.

[33] Altieri makes this connection and relates both plays to Aristophanic comedy: '*A Chaste Maid*, for one, could not exist without Machiavelli's *Mandragola*, and that is not Frye's New Comedy, but as clearly [an] Aristophanically-motivated comedy as Middleton's own very early *Family of Love*' (174).

[34] In Marotti's reading of *A Chaste Maid* as a comedy which stages the battle between Eros and Thanatos, Touchwood Senior emerges as 'a life-principle in a world threatened by moral and physical

children for the Kixes, too. The exchange is reciprocal: it is based on complementary needs and is therefore satisfying for both parties. It secures and maintains wealth, joins two families, and confuses their genealogies.

From an ethical perspective, the incontinent sexuality depicted in several plot-strands of *A Chaste Maid* suggests the dissolution of domestic order and the lack of control over the female body in an unbounded and shifting space. The pregnant body as the result of sexual activity is particularly suited for figuring illicit traffic. In all three cases of pregnancy in *A Chaste Maid*, 'the mother is the unchaste woman, an unclosed vessel, since all three pregnancies have been conceived through adultery' (Miller 81). The management of sexuality for the sake of lineage is a key requirement of oeconomy: what could be more threatening than women who open their bodies to men other than their husbands? In defiance of patrilineal genealogy, the sexually incontinent female body may alter the bloodline irrevocably. The female body as a site of excess and incontinency constituted a common trope for a disorderly and prodigal household.[35]

This is the case in *A Chaste Maid*. Here, household and female body invite sexual and commercial traffic. Allwit opens his house enthusiastically to Sir Walter's servant: 'In to the maids sweet Davy, and give order his chamber be made ready instantly' (1.2.5–6). The possessive pronoun 'his' establishes Sir Walter as household head. This is followed by the emphatic repetition, 'Go in, in, in Davy' (1.2.11). As Sir Walter, who arrives later in the same scene, takes off his boots and puts on his slippers, the scene is likely placed within the Allwits' house. Hence the repeated preposition 'in' does not invite Davy into the house, but establishes an open path *within* the house, a path that leads presumably straight into the maids' bedchambers—and perhaps even the mistress's chamber. After all, Allwit's invitation also encompasses his wife: 'Thy very sight will hold my wife in pleasure, till the knight come himself. Go in, in, in Davy' (1.2.10–11). This invitation is highly sexualized through the reference to pleasure, which aligns the preposition 'in' with the act of penetration. 'Till the knight come himself' establishes substitution as a valid principle of household positions. Until the knight arrives, Allwit functions as head of the household; when Davy comes, *he* may give the mistress pleasure in Sir Walter's stead. In the Allwits' household, individuals are replaceable; here, the commensurability of different things, which is the precondition of exchange,

---

disease and death' (67): 'Touchwood Sr. exists, in his erotic vitality, as a healthy counterbalance to anti-life activities like fanatical and hypocritical religious asceticism, ruthless social-climbing, and the stubborn pursuit of wealth for its own sake' (68).

[35] Peter Stallybrass argues that, as a property, the wife 'can bring dishonor to the landlord': '"Covert," the wife becomes her husband's symbolic capital; "free," she is the opening through which that capital disappears' (128). There is a 'real' connection between female body and household because woman was associated with spending practices of the household—intemperate behaviour constituted a threat to the household's solvency.

extends to humans. Significantly, being replaceable is Sir Walter's greatest fear: he worries that Allwit might perform his, Sir Walter's, sexual offices in his absence:

> ALLWIT. Of my soul and conscience sir, she's a wife as honest of
>   her body to me as any lord's proud lady can be.
> SIR WALTER. Yet, by your leave, I heard you were once offering to go
>   to bed to her.
>
> (1.2.103–106)

Sir Walter accuses Allwit openly of cuckolding *him*—the irony hardly needs to be spelled out.

Sexuality functions as a trope for the pervasive sway of a commercial logic of exchange and for the dissolution of household boundaries in commercial society.[36] The households of *A Chaste Maid* do not constitute separate spaces with their very own rules, but are structured by the market, by offer and demand, and by the excessive desire for more—costly goods, social advancement, wealth.[37] The case of the Allwits and Touchwoods is paradigmatic for the dissolution of the ethical basis of oeconomy. Both sell sexual services for the sustenance of their households. Allwit compares his living to other 'trades' involved in selling flesh—to butchers and poulters.[38] This suggests how fundamentally chrematistic practices have altered the household, how oeconomy is subsumed to a commercial logic. No longer the domestic other of chrematistics, the early modern household of Middleton's comedy thrives on exchange.[39] While the play relentlessly ridicules social climbers, it fails to punish Allwit's refusal to conform to the Protestant work ethic. Puritan writings of the time argue forcefully against sloth and idleness, and yet, Allwit, the dropout of early modern Puritan labour ideologies, prospers. Even after Sir Walter's downfall, the audience can be sure that the Allwits will get by. Still capitalizing on Sir Walter's funding of their household, they intend to use the furniture he bought to install a brothel at the Strand: 'The Allwit home is their business as it has always been' (Anglin 17). In fact, it is a significant move towards professionalization when the home is transformed into a brothel, a commercial

---

[36] As Altieri explains, 'sex and money can be constant metaphors for one another'; they imply 'equivalent desires' (180).

[37] Sabine Schülting identifies 'inordinate desire for status, possession and consumption' as the constitutive feature of all characters in *A Chaste Maid* (97).

[38] Jean Howard points out that the literature of the time presents prostitution 'as a business parallel to other forms of urban commerce, in many of which women legitimately and regularly participated' (*Theater of a City* 116).

[39] This overlap between household and commerce is very much in tune with the reality of early modern households. Peter Laslett describes the very real union of family and business by means of the example of a baker's household, which accommodated children and various kinds of servants: women-servants, apprentices, and journeymen. The baker was simultaneously the head of this extended family and an entrepreneur (1–2). Laslett also comments on the 'mixed' character of farming households that were not only engaged in husbandry, but also charged with the preparation of wool for the weavers and dyers by a 'middleman' (15).

enterprise. The brothel signifies the radical social transformation of the household in a society structured by commerce.

Clearly—and this is confirmed by Middleton's refusal to punish extra-marital sex—the standpoint of the household is no longer self-evidently a moral one.[40] Sexual activity has no absolute value, but rather one relative to the calculus being employed. In Allwit's amoral perspective, extramarital sex is good if it brings in money. In Touchwood's perspective, sex is bad if it endangers the financial basis of the household, but good if it can provide a living. Sexual incontinence can be a threat to the *oikos* or provide for its income, but whatever its effect, sexual relations produce a radical interrelatedness of households, which correlates with the multi-plot structure of the play. Within the play, it acts as a binding agent for the network of households. It maintains households reproductively as well as financially. To perceive sexual incontinence solely as sign of a lack of government would mean to apply an ethical perspective to a play that hardly makes ethics a priority. Middleton grants ethically doubtful but inventive characters, such as the Allwits and the Touchwoods, a living and thus economic success *despite* their immoral behaviour. Critics tend to single out the Allwits for ethical or even moral criticism.[41] Yet the Allwits lead as happy a life as the Touchwoods, while pursuing a similar strategy for subsistence.[42] Middleton's comedy provides an anatomy of socio-economic behaviour as driven by private interest without the punishing gesture of tragedy or the forced moral restitution of a comedy such as *Volpone*.

The extent to which plots and households are interwoven emerges fully when we take not only main events into account—marriage, childbirth, impregnation, elopement—but also marginal connections: Touchwood Junior is godfather to Sir Walter's/Allwit's child; Mistress Yellowhammer is one of the gossips at the child's birth; and Tim marries the alleged Welsh gentlewoman, a former lover of Sir Walter's. In *A Chaste Maid*, households are not self-contained and distinct unities in which master and mistress of the house exercise firm control over goods

---

[40] When Allwit, who fears for his comfortable arrangement with Sir Walter, attempts to prevent Sir Walter's marriage to Moll by disguising himself and informing Yellowhammer of Sir Walter's love affair, his warnings fall on deaf ears. Yellowhammer has no intention of acting on this information: 'The knight is rich, he shall be my son-in-law' (4.1.278). He cares little for the knight's moral character as long as he is wealthy and a gentleman. In the end, as Newman writes, 'Sir Walter himself is repudiated not for his promiscuous behaviour, but rather because he is revealed to have lost his fortune' ('"Goldsmith's Ware"' 111). Newman writes that 'comfortable moral values and distinctions are in fact undermined repeatedly by the equivalences Middleton sets up among the four plots ... the play contradicts such moralizing judgements' ('"Goldsmith's Ware"' 110).

[41] Altieri associates them with negative character traits such as 'Allwit's characteristic resentment' (179) and refers to Allwit as 'the loathsome Allwit' (178). Marotti describes the Allwit/Whorehound plot as 'brutalizing' in that it 'strikes at the very foundation of marriage and the family' (70).

[42] Furthermore, as Derek B. Alwes suggests, their 'cool brazenness' in the scene in which they evict Sir Walter 'appeals to our sympathies through comic identification' (105).

and people. Instead, they constitute a network of semi-domestic spaces with fluid boundaries that allow for and change with the free circulation of people and goods. Sexuality in this picture of fluid social relations provides a figure for the mutual and highly unregulated interpenetration of households by 'free radicals' that function as agents of exchange. This is a far cry from the household as disciplinary 'Schoole' of oeconomical tracts. Here, the social space is subject to and transformed by the exchanges in which it engages. These exchanges are strategic, i.e., designed to further the material and social interests of private households and individuals. That they involve sexual favours testifies to an amoral turn of practical rationality which transgresses the ethical bounds of oeconomy. The self-interested rationality of characters in *A Chaste Maid* resonates with Francis Bacon's interest in the 'Architecture of fortune' in *The Advancement of Learning* (first published in 1605; 165). Making one's fortune is the subject of a special kind of knowledge about how to advance one's own interests and rise in the world. As noted in the Introduction, Bacon calls this kind of knowledge 'wisdom of business'. It concerns the problem that all characters in *A Chaste Maid* face: the question of how to steer to one's advantage the interactions and transactions in a changing field of contingent events and unpredictable agents.

The Logic of the Marketplace

In *A Chaste Maid*, the *oikos* is governed by chrematistic principles. The whore aims to capture the goldsmith's son, while he seeks a gentlewoman; Sir Walter pursues the goldsmith's money; and Moll's parents aim at social advancement. The economic dynamic of this fluid network of exchanges is nourished by accumulated money which flows from two sources: the goldsmith's wealth and the inheritance pursued by the Kixes and Sir Walter. Wealth is at the root of the Yellowhammers' social ambition and constitutes Sir Walter's object of desire. The potential inheritance, which finally goes to the Kixes, ensures Sir Walter's credit and keeps the Allwits clothed and fed. Later, it helps to maintain the Touchwoods. Money regulates social roles and fuels the play's action. The true love plot enacted by Moll and Touchwood Junior may constitute an exception to this paradigm, but the lovers succeed ultimately through a quantifiable social exchange: the display of the coffins 'makes a hundred weeping eyes' (5.4.22), their union 'a thousand joyful hearts' (5.4.27). The lovers buy their happiness with an affecting performance, offering a spectacle of love, death, and reunion in exchange for pity and joy.

In his panoramic portrait of city households, Middleton replaces the model of balanced exchanges with the contingency of success and loss. In a world in which practical rationality is free from ethical concerns, reciprocity is no longer the guiding principle. Certainly, it *may* still be the happy outcome of complementary needs. The plot involving the Touchwoods and the Kixes is a case of fair exchange with evenly matched needs. Yet it secures an uneven distribution elsewhere, for the obscure inheritance that is subject to the Kixes' successful procreation goes either in full to the Kixes *or* to Sir Walter. The exuberance of wealth in the win-win situation, which the deal with Touchwood creates, contrasts sharply with the former barrenness of the Kixes, which profited Sir Walter. The Kixes and Sir Walter stand in direct competition: Lady Kix remarks bitterly in Act Two, Scene One: "Tis our dry barrenness puffs up Sir Walter— / None gets by your not-getting, but that knight' (2.1.159–160). Sir Walter's final loss exemplifies the proverbial zero-sum hypothesis of commerce: 'One man's loss is another man's gain'.[43] It is true that he is quite evidently the 'grasping man' and his end may appear as a form of final moral judgement. Yet Sir Walter's vices are hardly singular or even special (Newman, "'Goldsmith's Ware'" 111). Yellowhammer kept a whore himself and has a bastard son; Touchwood produces bastards by the dozen. Marotti suggests that Sir Walter functions as a 'scapegoat figure, carrying with him all the moral disgust the audience might feel for any of the play's other vicious characters' (70). Yet I argue that Sir Walter loses out not merely for conventional moral reasons. He also exemplifies the market logic which implies that the gain of Touchwood and the Kixes *has* to be someone else's loss. As a creature of credit, Sir Walter is predestined for failure. Entangled in a web of hopes for the future, he expects an inheritance which never comes, and angles for Moll's dowry. Once his credit is gone, he is left with nothing, especially as he lacks substantial social ties such as family. His repentance in Act Five, Scene One, is countered coolly by the Allwits, who dismiss him from their home, which is suddenly too 'private' to receive him. Allwit says: 'I wonder what he makes here with his consorts? / Cannot our house be private to ourselves, / But we must have such guests? I pray depart sirs' (5.1.145–147). Sir Walter is a satiric, decidedly non-heroic character, but there is something tragic about the way he suffers from a string of events which makes most other characters happy. Only Sir Walter is ruined and isolated from all social bonds, expelled from a social system structured by money. Only he suffers from '[a] total reverse of fortune' (Bradley 4) and is hence as close as the play gets to a tragic figure.[44] As the 'principal link' between the individual plots (Richard Levin 16), Sir Walter is uniquely placed to demonstrate the formative power of exchange relations.[45] Once

---

[43] According to *The Oxford Treasury of Sayings and Quotations*, this proverb dates from the early sixteenth century (79). On a national level, this same hypothesis is implied by the mercantilist balance of trade. Berry points out that 'The very image of a "balance" suggests that a nation can only prosper, be "up", if others are "down"' (103).
[44] A. C. Bradley perceives the idea of a total reverse of fortune as the essence of medieval tragedy and suggests that this idea is, for instance, still implied in Shakespearean tragedy.
[45] See Richard Levin: 'he is actively engaged in plots one, two, and four, and is vitally affected, as a kinsman of the Kixes, by the outcome of plot three, because his inheritance depends upon their remaining childless, and is lost forever when Lady Kix is impregnated by Touchwood Senior' (16).

he has lost his credit, he turns out to be replaceable in all his functions: as suitor, lover, patron, and heir. His failure is economic rather than moral.

Just as the household cedes its sovereignty to the market, the logic of oeconomy gives way to the chrematistic logic of profitable exchange. The perception of a paradigm change is facilitated by the realist mode of city comedy. With its setting in 'present-day' London, as seen from the perspective of a seventeenth-century spectator, the world of Middleton's drama approximates that of his audiences. It targets the commercial life of the present, confronting playgoers with a satirical version of their own lives. The radical force of its vision of city households is striking. The Yellowhammers fail in their attempt to marry their children off to advantage: instead, the Yellowhammers have to make do with a younger son and a whore as their son- and daughter-in-law. Yet the play's use of poetic justice does not undo the commercialization of households. Allwit and his wife change course when Sir Walter is bankrupt and open a brothel. The Touchwoods are united under the roof of the Kixes, who maintain them in exchange for further children. Neither the play nor the market which it represents appear to care much for conduct or virtue. The logic of commerce does not produce disorder that has to be contained by the play's end, but it is itself a new ordering force, transforming social relations instead of destroying them. In the end, everyone but Sir Walter finds his or her niche—be it in a brothel or someone else's household. The survival tactics of the common people are creative and resourceful, even if they demonstrate the extent to which rationality has departed from ethics in a society no longer governed by the model of oeconomy, but by the logic of the market. *A Chaste Maid* celebrates the makeshift pragmatism of 'intelligent realists' (Altieri 184) who approach the market as place of opportunities without pretending to a life of virtue.

Household Politics and Private Interests in *Macbeth*

The action of *Macbeth* is far removed from a commercial context, although its uses of a mercantile rhetoric betray a preoccupation with the logic of the market: with reciprocity, material gain, and social advancement. More obviously, however, the play shares with *A Chaste Maid* the fascination with a household that departs from an ethical logic of management to pursue its own private interests efficiently. Where Middleton's comedy situates households within a community that is bound together through social exchanges, even if each household has its own interests in view, Shakespeare's tragedy stages a conflict between private interest and the common good: here, the advancement of the individual household and the welfare of the community are diametrically opposed. This conflict is announced through the spatial isolation and fortification of the Macbeths' castle and its 'battlements' (*Mac.* 1.5.40). In contrast to the malleable and open spatial structure that city households constitute in *A Chaste Maid*, the household of

Macbeth and his 'dark lady' (Lupton 367) is a separate and isolated unit. While *A Chaste Maid* explores the intersection of oeconomy and commerce, *Macbeth* focuses on the political implications of oeconomy. However, it frames the relation between household and commonwealth with a mercantile language and contains a powerful fable of accumulation, an original investment that insures its own increase. While Macbeth's investment—the killing of King Duncan—remains fruitless without children, Banquo's line of kings in Act Four, Scene One offers an ideal picture of successful accumulation.

In light of the play's attention to the Macbeths and their home, the question that needs to be asked is this: what does it mean that political conspiracy in this play is enacted in domestic terms? Why is the fate of the commonwealth decided at home? To borrow Kiernan Ryan's phrase, in order to move beyond the 'familiar archetypal narrative' (90) of 'a regicidal usurper' (89), we should account for the 'unpredictable specificity' (89) of the play. It seems to me that a crucial part of this specificity lies in the domestic setting and in the portrait of the Macbeths' marriage as a private and intimate relation between husband and wife. Lisa Hopkins discusses the use of simple, domestic words in the play to conclude that the Macbeths are 'in some sense the most domestic of couples' (254).[46] Even the ultimate political act—regicide—is performed in the home of the Macbeths, and its tragic and dramatic force stems from violating both a relation of kinship and the domestic virtue of hospitality.[47]

The dual focus of the action on domesticity and its political effects may have secured the play's appeal both to a courtly audience and to paying Londoners who might not only enjoy the ups and downs of those in power, but could also relate to the domestic scenes between husband and wife, to marital strife and reconciliation, and to the desire to rise in the world. It is possible that *Macbeth* was first performed in 1606 for King James I at court (Kernan, *Shakespeare, the King's Playwright* 72), but the first recorded performance was at the Globe in 1611 (Kliman 13). With its intimate representation of marital relations, the play effectively performs marriage as the proto-bourgeois 'solitarie and secret society' (111),

---

[46] Hopkins discusses the '"low" diction' of the Macbeths (253) and identifies the terms which Dr Johnson famously criticized (words such as knife and blanket) as household words. Macbeth and his lady, as she writes, 'are, for all their egregious brutality, in some sense the most domestic of couples' (254). Even the supernatural element of the play, the weird sisters, strengthens the sense of domesticity: 'their conversation is notably marked by features serving to associate it with the normal concerns of women in the home' and 'their later parodic rituals of food preparation' strengthen this connection (255). Later she suggests: 'What all these instances of plainness do, however, is work to remove the play from the arena of state affairs and situate the concerns of its main characters, at least, insistently within the realm of the domestic' (263).

[47] Naomi Conn Liebler points out that 'Macbeth casts regicide in the language of inhospitable behavior' and claims that this 'signals the weight of that code for Shakespeare's audience' (206). She refers to the following passage: 'He's here in double trust: / First, as I am his kinsman and his subject, / Strong both against the deed; then, as his host, / Who should against his murtherer shut the door, / Not bear the knife myself' (1.7.12–16). Earlier she states that, 'For Aristotle, the essence of tragic action was the violation of kinship and thus of community' (Liebler 196).

which Perkins described in his *Christian Oeconomie* (first published in 1609). This representation may have appealed to the 'middling sort of people', who were a likely audience for Protestant writings on the family. Yet nobles and gentlefolk could also relate to the domestic crisis performed in *Macbeth*. The 'householder culture' (Harding, 'London, Change and Exchange' 132), with its government ideal of patriarchal authority and wifely subjection, developed into the dominant bourgeois ideology of the eighteenth and nineteenth centuries, but in the early seventeenth century its appeal was less specific: the notion of 'an affectionate but hierarchical relationship was the dominant ideal' not just for citizen households, but '[i]n society at large' (Mendelson and Crawford 132).[48]

The play fills the early modern ideological connection between household management and political government with life. By tying the fate of the commonwealth to an individual household and the married couple that constitutes it, the play stages a crisis of political authority in terms of a crisis of oeconomy. This suggests that oeconomy as a functioning paradigm of social order is under pressure. In *Macbeth*, oeconomy's dichotomic structure of authority and subjection is unhinged by the self-authorization of the lady, and its logic of sufficiency and moderation is replaced by the unbridled pursuit of private interests. The disorder of the household signals a destabilization of virtue ethics as the foundation of oeconomy and politics. The play's attention to a household that is driven and destroyed by the single-minded pursuit of private interests, its intimate observation of a married couple that works together in this pursuit, the threat that it poses to political order—all these features communicate with oeconomic discourses of the time of the play's first performances. Despite its medieval setting, it participates in a renegotiation of values that accompanied the intensification of commerce in the late sixteenth and early seventeenth centuries. The use of a language of business that seeps into households and frames social exchanges and the play's investment in accumulation are a reminder of this commercial environment.

As Chapter 1 argued, around this time Protestant writers such as William Perkins and Robert Cleaver, but also mercantile authors such as John Browne and William Scott, broke a lance for the revaluation of commerce and private interest. They defended the legitimacy of gain and the desirability of prudent, efficient, and well-calculated action against the traditional topos of the deceitful trader whose avarice is without limits. These authors suggested that ethics and an aptitude for business could go hand in hand in the figure of the honest merchant-householder, who worked hard for his family and the common good. *Macbeth* also negotiates ethics and efficiency, but it suggests that private interest and the common good may not be so easily reconciled. Superficially, the play distinguishes between two

---

[48] In the sixteenth and early seventeenth centuries, there was hardly an absolute distinction between the values of noble households and those of the middling sort. See also Laura Caroline Stevenson 154–156.

resourceful and efficient rulers, one unethical—a tyrant who is driven by private interests—and one ethical: a legitimate ruler who serves the common good. And yet, as I suggested earlier, Shakespeare questions this difference. After all, the new king, Malcolm, is an ambiguous and calculating figure, and his motivation ultimately remains obscure. Furthermore, the play steers the attention and sympathy of the audience in a way that runs counter to simple moralizing. With the space and dialogue given to the murderous couple, the play invites the audience to side with them and to identify with their desire to become the authors of their fortune. With its representation of the strategic, entrepreneurial, and strong-willed dark lady, the tragedy communicates the attraction of agency and self-authorization. Perhaps most importantly, in its pervasive attention to the desire for material and social advancement, it recognizes this desire as a structuring force of social life.

The Household as Dramatic Subject

The household of the murderous couple is much more than just a setting. Already in the first and certainly in the second act of *Macbeth*, the household takes centre stage. Kliman describes the play's narrow focus on Macbeth and his lady in the following terms: '*Macbeth* is Shakespeare's experiment in unity of focus. In its concentrated interest on the protagonists, this play differs from the other major tragedies, which from beginning to end offer sharp and distinctive portraits of many secondary and minor characters' (xiii). Kliman points out that Macbeth is present in every single scene, either in person or as the subject of others' speeches, while 'Lady Macbeth is present in nine scenes and discussed and mentioned in four more' (2). Their speeches and conversations are the most compelling of the entire play, and their presence on stage draws us into a private space that remains hidden from the eyes and ears of other characters.

The marital conspiracy at the heart of the plot was not Shakespeare's invention; his probable sources, Raphael Holinshed's *Chronicles* and George Buchanan's *History*, had already emphasized the role of the lady in inciting Macbeth to murder. The *Chronicles* contend that Macbeth's wife 'lay sore vpon him to attempt the thing, as she that was verie ambitious, burning in vnquenchable desire to beare the name of queene' (qtd. in Appendix to *Macbeth* 172). Buchanan writes: 'His mind, already sufficiently ardent of itself, was daily excited by the importunities of his wife, who was the confidant of all his designs' (qtd. in Appendix to *Macbeth* 183). A third possible source, John Leslie's *De Origine, Moribus, et Rebus Gestis Scotorum*, also establishes Lady Macbeth's influence in the murder: 'though fearful of the deed, his wife urged him to it with high promises of his happy outcome' (qtd. in Appendix to *Macbeth* 188). Shakespeare's focus on the Macbeths may also have been encouraged by an earlier episode in Scottish history, in which Donwald killed King Duff when he was a guest in his castle. This heinous deed was followed by a series of supernatural events, some of which feature in Shakespeare as well, such as the hearing of voices. Both sources, Holinshed's *Chronicles* and Buchanan's *History*, blame Donwald's wife: she 'inflamed her already incensed husband' (Buchanan, qtd. in Appendix to *Macbeth* 181) and 'shewed him the meanes' to 'make him [the king] awaie' (Holinshed, qtd. in Appendix to *Macbeth* 164).

Yet Shakespeare's intense attention to the marital couple and their conversations is conspicuous, especially as he suppressed other facts that could have motivated Macbeth's murder of Duncan. In his *Chronicles*, Holinshed reports that Banquo and others participated in the deed (Carroll 363).[49] He describes Duncan as a weak ruler and his son Malcolm as 'not of able age' (qtd. in Carroll 361). According to Kenneth Muir, Duncan gives Macbeth a cause for grievance because he, 'by proclaiming his son Prince of Cumberland, went against the laws of succession' (xxxvii).[50] This rendering is consistent with Buchanan's *History of Scotland*. Buchanan's Macbeth is represented as 'a man of penetrating genius', even if he lacks 'moderation' in his 'unbounded ambition' (qtd. in Appendix to *Macbeth* 182). King Duncan, on the other hand, is Macbeth's weak and inactive cousin. Shakespeare focuses on the relation of the Macbeths at the expense of these alternative historical narratives, suppressing also the fact that the historical Macbeth reigned successfully for ten years (Lemon 78). In portraying Duncan as a virtuous king and in having Macbeth act in sole conspiracy with his wife, Shakespeare erases any possible justification for regicide: 'The play, unlike Holinshed's narrative, offers no reason for the rebellion against Duncan' (Drakakis 6).[51] Without a weak king and without including Banquo as co-conspirator, Shakespeare locates the motivation for the crime squarely within the household of the Macbeths. This leaves Macbeth's own ambition and that of his wife as the key motive for the killing of the king.[52] Shakespeare draws attention to wayward female agency by framing the lady's political ambition with the prophecy of the weird sisters.

The historical pretexts may have furnished Shakespeare with his basic plotline, but they cannot fully account for his extreme focus on marital relations. Muir suggests that 'Shakespeare suppresses' Duncan's weakness and the collective

---

[49] Critics have argued that the suppression of Banquo's involvement can be explained by the fact that '*Macbeth* seems to be designed to flatter King James VI of Scotland, who in 1603 succeeded Elizabeth I as King James of England' because, as Laury Magnus writes, 'James did, in fact, descend from the lineage of Shakespeare's Banquo' (59). William C. Carroll disputes this: 'even this genealogy, the founding myth of the Stuart dynasty, was a product of the imagination, not historical fact. Banquo and Fleance were apparently invented by the early Scottish historian, Hector Boece in 1527' (360). Kliman, however, claims that any flattering intent on Shakespeare's part is purely hypothetical; after all, he could have rendered Banquo 'with more definite approbation', and it is doubtful whether James would have liked a play in which 'two kings are dispatched' (12).

[50] See Kernan, *Shakespeare, the King's Playwright* 78, and Carroll 361.

[51] Kliman also points out that 'Shakespeare does not allow his Macbeth any mitigating circumstances to justify his crime' (10).

[52] Bradley points out quite accurately that Macbeth and his lady 'are fired by one and the same passion of ambition' (306).

conspiracy 'for dramatic reasons to accentuate Macbeth's guilt and to minimize any excuses he might have had' (xxxviii). The focus on the Macbeths' household enables Shakespeare to explore both the practical requirements and the ethical limits of social advancement. The figure of the 'dark lady' acts as a conventional trope for women's destructive tendency towards excess, but it also exemplifies an entrepreneurial spirit that seizes the moment and plots its rise in the world in an admirably efficient manner. The agency and ambition of the Macbeths and their private relationship may have also struck a sympathetic chord in the hearts of citizens who could relate to the homely setting, the couple's intimacy, and to their desire to be architects of their fortune.

Household Space

The homely setting in *Macbeth* is constructed around a lone woman with a letter in hand. At the beginning of Act One, Scene Five, the First Folio simply states 'Enter Macbeths Wife alone with a Letter'. Even without an explicitly named location, the presence of a single reading woman strongly suggests the privacy of a domestic setting, while the letter indicates communication with the outer world off-stage (Fitzpatrick 73). In performance, the sense of domesticity would have been strengthened by indoor dress (Dessen, *Recovering Shakespeare's Theatrical Vocabulary* 165).[53] Catherine Richardson confirms that the early modern stage was bare of scenery, but emphasizes the importance of props—from napkins to large pieces of furniture—for representing domestic space ('Early Modern Plays and Domestic Spaces' 271).[54] In the absence of scenery, the particularity of place and the configuration of space are subject to the dynamic movement of characters and props.[55] The lady's domestic clothing and the letter in her hand are enough to indicate that she is at home.[56] The deictic system that her invocation 'Hie thee hither' (1.5.25) establishes, the king's projected arrival, as well as Macbeth's entrance in

---

[53] As Dessen suggests, 'a primary tool was the use of costume ... indoor as distinguished from outdoor dress' (*Recovering Shakespeare's Theatrical Vocabulary* 165).

[54] Everyday objects such as beds, handkerchiefs (*Othello!*), food, and wine were certainly used as props (Schülting 107). As Tim Fitzpatrick explains, moveable properties 'provide a quick and generally uncomplicated means of establishing place' (103–104).

[55] According to Bernard Beckerman, instead of offering a designed stage set, the stage was to provide 'space for the unimpeded flow of scene after scene, for the instantaneous creation of any place in this world or the next' (63). Richardson notes: 'The advantage of such staging is, of course, that it is supremely flexible. What was "inside" a couple of minutes previously becomes "outside" as someone enters from somewhere else. This is a theatre in which space lacks physical stability' ('Early Modern Plays' 272). G. K. Hunter described early modern spatial construction as a function of the character's actions: 'If in modern drama environment is presented as the creator of character, in Elizabethan drama the character, his entry and his movement create, in so far as we are required to assume one, the environment that is appropriate to his deeds' (qtd. in Dessen, *Elizabethan Stage Conventions* 173, n.8; Hunter, 'Flatcaps and Bluecoats' 21–22).

[56] As Alan C. Dessen argues, the 'here' of early modern stage space transforms into an imaginary place through the logic of 'this'. In Dessen's compelling argument, this required 'no more than a gesture from the actor towards the stage floor or perhaps the edge of the stage' (*Elizabethan Stage Conventions*

the same scene, confirm the gravitational pull of the domestic setting: all paths lead towards the castle of the Macbeths. The spatial dynamic of the first act supports this concentric constriction: the focus narrows from public space—the heath, a military camp, a scene of royal counsel—to the confines of domestic life. Despite this narrowing of focus, Lady Macbeth's first speech positions the household on the political scene. It invokes a seething conspiracy, in which political ambition merges explosively with the lady's restricted scope of action. The tragedy of Macbeth is also the tragedy of Lady Macbeth, who cannot move into the open field of the *polis* but must remain within. Confined to domestic space, Lady Macbeth can only engage in politics when guests enter her home. Her political engagement is one of those outrageous and futile attempts at self-realization Andreas Mahler writes about ('Topologie' 26). A serious threat to social order, her ambition is ultimately thwarted by her madness.

Tied to her home and unable to join Macbeth in the field, Lady Macbeth's injunction 'Hie thee hither' comes close to a conjuration, a speech act that establishes her kinship with the weird sisters. In terms of spatial framing, the sisters and Lady Macbeth occupy opposite positions, but they play a similar role. The open place on the heath suggests the precarious social status of the sisters as unhoused women, but it also corresponds to their wide scope of action. Their influence seems unbounded; with their prophecy, they write political history. Confined to the castle, Lady Macbeth's sphere of movement is far more limited, yet she acquires political agency and power when Duncan enters her house. Her murderous move into politics is equated with a move outside accepted limits, a liminal existence for which the weird sisters 'stand as foils' (Liebler 218).[57] Her performance of domesticity in *Macbeth* is uncanny in an even more literal sense of the word than Freud intended because it quite literally concerns the home (the *Heim* in *heimlich*) and not just the familiar.[58] Critics have called Lady Macbeth 'a perfect wife' (Bradley 332) and 'a perfect housewife' (Hopkins 257). This description is accurate in one sense: the dark lady performs domestic duties in a familiar yet perverted way, which significantly changes their content. In this, she has much in common with Mistress Yellowhammer in *A Chaste Maid*, who also retains some aspects of the traditional domestic role (chastising her daughter for neglecting her duties), but changes their content in substantial ways (she chastises her for

---

59). Accompanied by gestures or naming, the use of 'this' asked early modern audiences to imagine concrete locations.

[57] Liebler points out that in the First Folio the term 'weird' of the 'weird sisters' is really 'spelled "weyard" (Acts Three and Four) and "weyward" (Acts I and II)' (218). Liebler interprets this as '"wayward", "by the wayside"' and as meaning 'beyond the social pale; in other words, marginal and liminal' (218). Interestingly, Tasso uses the same term, 'waiward' (C2r), to describe the wife as perpetual enemy (see Chapter 1, 45).

[58] As Freud wrote, 'the uncanny is that class of the frightening which leads back to what is known of old and long familiar' ('The Uncanny', *SE* 17, 220). Hopkins also refers to Freud: the Macbeths' 'customary domesticity and ... its rapid disintegration ... retains that most distinctive quality of what Freudian theory on the uncanny has termed the *unheimlich* by relying for its full horror on the distortion of the traditional comforts of home' (259).

not being flirtatious enough). Both women act in a strategic, goal-orientated way, paying no attention to virtue except for the sake of appearances.

Domestic duties concerned women of all social sorts (Mendelson and Crawford 301), albeit in different ways.[59] Women of the upper ranks supervised the household work and the 'education of their children' (309) and had 'duties of hospitality and sociability' (Mendelson and Crawford 307). When King Duncan arrives, Lady Macbeth does what she is expected to do as mistress of the house, but she twists the imperatives of household management to suit her own agenda: she 'takes care' of her guest the way a mafioso might take care of a 'problem'. Lady Macbeth encourages Macbeth to leave everything to her: 'you shall put / This night's great business into my dispatch' (1.5.67–68). The term 'business' can refer to the commitment to a task or purpose (*OED* 3), but it also frames the political act of regicide with an economic metaphor (*OED* 14) which conveys a sense of venturing and the promise of profit. Lady Macbeth's peculiar interpretation of the content and scope of domestic action plays on the ambiguities of the female position, which is caught between trivial domesticity and cogovernment of the household as a politically significant institution, 'the Schoole, wherein are taught and learned the principles of authorities and subjection' (Perkins 4). The lady extricates herself from the ambiguous demands of subject and cogovernor by evolving her role from a domestic helper to a key political player. It is only later that the contradictory condition of the female as both fellow governor and subordinate in the house catches up with her. In Act Four, her agency is finally curbed by madness, which announces itself for the first time in Act Two, Scene Two with a vision in which the sleeping king resembles her father. The appearance of the patriarchal father figure is enough to restrain her action.

The fortified space over which Lady Macbeth reigns is characterized verbally by the synecdochic substitution of 'castle' or 'home' with 'battlements'. In the absence of scenery, such verbal characterizations carry all the more weight:

> LADY MACBETH. The raven
> himself is hoarse,
> That croaks the fatal entrance of Duncan
> Under my battlements
>
> (1.5.38–40)

The possessive pronoun that goes with this substitution—'Under *my* battlements'—signals the change in power that crossing the border into the *oikos* entails. The adjective 'fatal' constitutes a foreshadowing: it signals the lethal outcome of this border-crossing. With his 'entrance', King Duncan places

---

[59] As Sara Mendelson and Patricia Crawford note, 'the higher a woman's social rank, the less likely she was to engage directly in the manual work of housewifery. The households of the wealthiest were more complex than those further down the social scale, and women's supervisory duties consequently more extensive' (302).

himself under Lady Macbeth's authority as hostess and governor of her very own realm. The preposition 'under' conveys a claustrophobic image of towering walls, anticipating the later transformation of household into narrow grave. In her essay on hospitality in *Macbeth*, Julia Lupton discusses the wider sense in which any guest is at the mercy of his host. The house (or, in this case, castle) constitutes a distinct space that pursues its own interests and follows its own rules. Lady Macbeth's welcoming of the king opens the house in a highly political show of hospitality, only to assimilate him into its own economy of power: 'Commanding the doorway, the hostess will transform her guest into a prisoner by assisting her husband in the murder of sleep' (Lupton 372). As Lupton writes, 'The threshold occupied by Lady Macbeth', who greets the king in the doorway, 'is the *limen* between the oikos and the polis' (372). This division has perhaps less to do with the opposition of private versus public life—Patricia Fumerton coined the lucid phrase 'being private in public' (68) to describe aristocratic households—than with an ideological impasse of the government discourse. If the householder was a domestic king in his own right while the 'real' king ruled over all households as royal father, who, then, ruled at home when the king visited? The Macbeths take the paradigm of household government literally and force it to its logical extreme: as governors of their miniature realm, they assume absolute authority over life and death, subjecting the common good to their own private interest. The Macbeths usurp the place of the king in their own home, where they already are 'the domesticall king' and queen (Whately 244, also qtd. in Capp 5). Their assertion of domestic sovereignty construes the household as a political space with its very own agenda.

The moment of King Duncan's entrance into the *oikos*'s sphere of power is prepared by the king's approach to the Macbeths' castle. Together with Banquo, King Duncan verbally evokes a scenery that is very much at odds with Lady Macbeth's sinister remarks about Duncan's fatal entrance. The king and Banquo praise the castle's pleasant seat. Their outside view forms a stark contrast to the castle as lived space, and the house martin's lofty nests contrast with the battlements. Juxtaposing 'atmospheric openness with claustrophobia' (Lupton 368), the dialogue prepares the fatal act of border crossing and prefigures the sharp discrepancy between pleasant appearance and the grim reality of a claustrophobic space that harbours a self-interested and murderous intent instead of offering hospitable shelter.

The different perspectives on the same space introduce an essential discrepancy between appearance and reality. The impossibility of drawing conclusions about the real state of things from their outward manifestation constitutes a leitmotif in *Macbeth*, articulated in paradoxes like 'Fair is foul, and foul is fair' (1.1.11).[60]

---

[60] Lady Macbeth admonishes her husband to preserve outward appearances at all costs. In her rhetoric, deception becomes an art: 'To beguile the time, / Look like the time; bear welcome in your eye, / Your hand, your tongue: look like th'innocent flower, / But be the serpent under't' (1.5.63–66).

The discrepancy between the pleasant summer vision of a castle surrounded by martlets and the sinister reality of this bleak home underlines the divide between being and seeming and projects it onto the *oikos*. As a separate, walled-off space, it is necessarily opaque to strangers. When it opens its boundaries and reveals its inner life, this takes place in the highly ritualized form of '*social theater*' (Lupton 373). The display of hospitality in *Macbeth* forms a stark contrast to Allwit's familiar and effusive invitation to servant Davy in *A Chaste Maid*. Davy is ushered in as a familiar, an insider, while Lady Macbeth's elaborate show of hospitality welcomes King Duncan as an outsider. Lupton analyses hospitality as 'a way of soliciting and orchestrating forms of appearing that gather humans, objects, and animals, as well as deities and dust bunnies, in a single if self-divided ensemble of encounter, experience, and recognition' (373). Lady Macbeth's 'infamous cry "What, in our house?" (2.3.89)', which follows upon news of Duncan's murder, 'sits perfectly with her public image as "most kind hostess" (2.1.16)' (Hopkins 257). In her conversations with Duncan and the other nobles, Lady Macbeth carefully presents and upholds this image at all times, suggesting an instrumental use of civil behaviour. Her attention to appearances recalls Bacon's discussion of civil knowledge. Bacon includes in this discussion not only 'wisedom of Businesse', but also 'wisedome of the behauiour' which concerns the action of 'Conuersation' (*The Advancement* 157). Bacon describes the style and function of behaviour with an analogy to clothes: as 'a Garment of the Minde', 'it ought to bee made in fashion: it ought not to bee too curious: It ought to bee shaped so, as to sette foorthe anye good making of the minde: and hide any deformity' (*The Advancement* 158). Knowing how to present oneself is a means to get what one wants. Therefore, this wisdom 'hath not onely an honour in it selfe, but an influence also into businesse and gouernement' (*The Advancement* 157). Lady Macbeth controls her appearance and uses 'behaviour' to her advantage.

As a unit that exists *in* but also *apart from* the commonwealth, the household has the power to show strangers only what it wants them to see. Under the skilful government of the lady, it reveals itself in ritualized and highly theatrical social interactions. Theatre is the perfect medium to stage the theatricality of social roles and values because it can reveal the deceptive potential of role-playing by offering the audience antithetic affects, duplicitous actions, and contradictory statements. For the audience who has witnessed Lady Macbeth's dark conjurations, her profuse professions to King Duncan of loving service and honours lately received are a case of dramatic irony, for those honours are but advances on the kingship yet to come. The discrepancy between her behaviour and her true intentions does not just draw attention to a general divide between being and seeming, but also to her sophisticated skills of strategic self-display and civil conversation.

Duncan and Banquo's approach to the castle establishes a focus on the physical boundaries and the intransparency of the *oikos* by offering a view of the castle's walls from outside. Those physical boundaries are called to mind once more, this time not visually but audibly, with the knocking at the gate after Duncan and his guards have been murdered. The knocking at the gate dramatizes the walls of the castle. In his brief but famous essay 'On the Knocking at the Gate in *Macbeth*' (first published in 1823), Thomas De Quincey analysed the peculiar effect of the knocking in temporal terms as ending an interlude in which ordinary human life is suspended.[61] This interpretation emphasizes the suspension of the outside world and the narrowing of focus that takes place with Duncan's entry into the Macbeths' castle, yet this suspension is not foremost temporal—as De Quincey suggests—but spatial. The repeated knocking, which follows on the murder of King Duncan, reminds the audience of the space beyond the *oikos*, of the existence of an outer world. It is an act of 'spatial meaning-making' (Fitzpatrick 24).[62] The knocking against the closed gate establishes an imaginary outside. It suggests that the *oikos* is not self-contained, cannot be shut off from the *polis*; strangers enter and news leaks out. The presence of an early modern audience, whose members would have seen 'from every perspective ... audience members beyond the players' (Kliman 4), might have acted as physical reminder of the presence of the *polis* beyond the imaginary walls of the *oikos*.

The setting of the murder remains an off-stage space, which is, nonetheless, carefully 'placed' and referenced by means of 'the accumulated entrances and exits of a range of characters through the stage door which stands for the door to Duncan's chamber' (Fitzpatrick 70–71). This placing is given imaginary force with the bloody daggers which Macbeth carries from there and which the lady returns 'to the crime scene' (Fitzpatrick 69). The off-stage setting of the murder emphasizes the obscurity at the heart of the household: that which is not visible to public eyes. Orlin reminds us that privacy in sixteenth-century England 'inspired an uneasy mixture of desire and distrust' and that 'society organized itself around the principle of preventing privacy' (*Locating Privacy* 10). It is in line with this principle that the Macbeths' privacy is staged in terms of a conspiracy and threat to the social order.

---

[61] Note De Quincey's unlikely comparison between the knocking at the gate and the first signs of returning life in a female relative who has fainted to emphasize the moment 'when the suspension ceases, and the goings-on of human life are suddenly resumed': 'Now, apply this to the case in *Macbeth* ... The murderers and the murder must be insulated—cut off by an immeasurable gulf from the ordinary tide and succession of human affairs—locked up and sequestered in some deep recess; we must be made sensible that the world of ordinary life is suddenly arrested, laid asleep, tranced, racked into a dread armistice; time must be annihilated, relation to things without abolished; and all must pass self-withdrawn into a deep syncope and suspension of earthly passion. Hence it is that, when ... the knocking at the gate is heard ... the pulses of life are beginning to beat again; and the re-establishment of the goings-on of the world in which we live first makes us profoundly sensible of the awful parenthesis that had suspended them' (393; vol. 10).

[62] Furthermore, as Tim Fitzpatrick establishes in an acute and detailed reading, the changing sound of the knocking—first within some part of the tiring house, then, much closer, against the stage door—indicates a 'spatial shift' (69) within the scene from the antechamber to Duncan's chamber to somewhere close 'to the south entry' (68).

The Female Body and Household Space

Measured against the prescriptive literature of the time, the household of the Macbeths is clearly lacking in government. With a wife who chastises her husband and propels the household towards immoral action, the household order is in disarray. Closed off from the community by castle walls, it becomes the hotbed of a political conspiracy. The play positions a transformation of Lady Macbeth's body prominently at the beginning of the murderous plot; it is at the centre of her crucial monologue in Act One, Scene Five. With the transformation of the female body through limitless ambition, *Macbeth* taps into the topos of excessive female appetites and plays on the frequent analogy between household and body:

> LADY MACBETH. The raven himself is hoarse,
>   That croaks the fatal entrance of Duncan
>   Under my battlements. Come, you Spirits
>   That tend on mortal thoughts, unsex me here,
>   And fill me, from the crown to the toe, top-full
>   Of direst cruelty! make thick my blood,
>   Stop up th'access and passage to remorse;
>   That no compunctious visitings of Nature
>   Shake my fell purpose, nor keep pace between
>   Th'effect and it! Come to my woman's breasts,
>   And take my milk for gall, you murth'ring ministers ...
>   (1.5.38–48)

'[M]y battlements' is followed so closely by the wish for bodily transformation that the battlements themselves turn into a bodily attribute. The proximity of castle and female body in this passage invokes the tropical relation between body and household. The transformation of the female body suspends, along with femininity and remorse, both the reproductive function and the ethical basis of the household. The ingredients of cruelty, thick blood, and gall, indicate a replacement of normal bodily juices and fluids with perverted and evil humours, and establish kinship with the supernatural. Lady Macbeth's desired bodily transformation offers a trope for the unnatural reconfiguration of the internal order of the Macbeths' household and 'reinforce[s] the idea that the inversion of natural sexual roles leads to political disruption' (Norbrook 105). Disorder is figured as corporeal transformation which preserves Lady Macbeth's feminine appearance but drains her—together with the fluids that make her human—of ethical impulses such as remorse.

The conjunction of motherly love with infanticide in another powerful image offers yet another trope for the reconfiguration of 'natural sexual roles':

> LADY MACBETH. I have given suck, and know
>   How tender 'tis to love the babe that milks me:

> I would, while it was smiling in my face,
> Have pluck'd my nipple from his boneless gums,
> And dash'd the brains out, had I so sworn
> As you have done to this.
>
> (1.7.54–59)

This description of infanticide is all the more disturbing because of the Macbeths' childlessness. If Lady Macbeth has nursed a baby—where is it now? The lack of an heir that could continue the bloodline of the Macbeths is a major problem in the play and gives this question some urgency. Stephanie Chamberlain argues that infanticide 'exemplifies cultural fears about maternal agency' (75) and, specifically, the fear 'of an obtrusive, if secretive interference in the process of patrilineal transmission' (76). Yet this image of a mother who looks lovingly down at her smiling child only to, in the next instant, dash its head against the wall also affords an image of the irrepresentable ambiguity of the female position, which is caught between the irreconcilable alternatives of guardian of life and excessive and hence destructive force. It contrasts the steadiness of maternal love and care that nourishes the household with a sudden, rash, and violent action that destroys its future.[63] If this portrait of an unnatural mother represents the extent to which the household of Macbeth and his lady is out of joint, it does so by emphasizing the unruly and potentially uncontainable nature of woman.

In the character of Lady Macbeth, anxieties about the excessive force of women are mingled with fear of unlimited female agency. Maternal agency might not just disrupt patrilineal succession, as Chamberlain suggests, but could even do away with it entirely. The willpower of Lady Macbeth finds expression in Macbeth's compelling conjunction of the female body with masculinity: 'Bring forth men-children only! / For thy undaunted mettle should compose / Nothing but males' (1.7.73–75). This exclamation links motherhood with the formative power that early modern scholars in the Aristotelian tradition attributed to the father: 'For Aristotle, the semen acted directly on the female menstrual clot and, though contributing nothing material to the future embryo, actually was responsible for forming it and for determining its *telos*; the female, by contrast, supplied the matter on which the semen worked to craft the offspring' (Keller 107). The view of the male as 'the primary progenitor' contrasted with Galenic theory, which attributed 'procreative seed' not only to the male but also to the female (107). The Galenic two-seed model went hand in hand with the assumed homology of womb and penis (Keller 73). It implied that 'both men and women produced seed which mingled at conception to create the child' (Evans 57). Both teachings informed medical discourses of the early modern age. The two-seed model preserved male

---

[63] Its 'terrifying ferocity' is, as Hopkins writes, 'accentuated by the rapidity of the change from the emotional range of "tender" to that of "dashed"' (262).

primacy with the assumption that women's seed was inferior to men's: weaker, colder, altogether less potent (Keller 107; Evans 58). As Jennifer Evans points out, 'The weakness of woman's seed secured the male role in generation; it was only the man's contribution that contained the vital heat required to create a new life' (59). Evans suggests that the assertion of the formative power of man's seed was crucial because 'the two-seed model raised anxieties that women would be able to conceive on their own' (59). Discourses on generation provide an enlightening context for Macbeth's admiring characterization of his lady. While contemporaneous medical writers sought to preserve the male status of the 'primary progenitor', Macbeth heralds his lady as sole maker of her future sons. The speculative phrase 'should compose' suggests single-handed generation, solely on the basis of Lady Macbeth's own 'undaunted mettle'. This radical portrait of the woman as formative principle in reproduction suggests unlimited female agency, rooting it in an unnatural body.

As the analogy of the wife as trunk and the husband as head of the household-as-body demonstrates, the problem of an excessive and unnatural female body cannot be separated from the question of who is in control. As argued in Chapter 1, the question of government and authority in the household was of paramount importance in the post-Reformation period. An early modern audience must have been acutely aware of the discrepancy between the ideal householder and Macbeth's failure in the art of self- and household government. Along with his own lack of moderation, his failure to restrain his wife's unbridled passion offers an effective characterization of the man. As Newman points out, the most widely cited verse from Proverbs in early modern prescriptive texts on household management and marriage identifies the wife as an index of her husband's government skills: 'A good wife is the crown of her husband' (*Fashioning Femininity* 15).[64] This metaphor of adornment conceives of the female as 'mark of her husband's achievement ... in educating and moulding his wife to obedience' (15). John Aylmer's defence of Elizabeth's rule—'a woman may rule as a magistrate, yet obey as a wife' (qtd. in *Fashioning Femininity* 16)—points to the pervasive nature of subjection as an ideology which applied to women of all social standings.[65] In practice, some aristocratic women, especially those of great rank and wealth and with good connections to the court, as well as wealthy women of the middle ranks, may have had great influence or even authority over their husbands, but on a general legal and discursive level, the axis of male authority and female subjection was pervasive. In her discussion of the conjugal division of labour, Lorna Hutson follows

---

[64] Of course, other much-cited biblical passages identify the husband with the (governing) head and the wife with the (subjected) body (Newman, *Fashioning Femininity* 16).

[65] Christian writings of all types—'Catholic, early reform, and Puritan works alike'—'continually reiterate the theme of women's subjection' (Newman, *Fashioning Femininity* 19). They addressed not only commoners but also gentlemen and -women as well as the nobility. Perkins' *Christian Oeconomie*, for instance, was dedicated to Robert Lord Rich, Baron of Leeze (2r).

Catherine Belsey in pointing out how little developed the role of the wife was in Robert Cleaver's *A Godlie Forme of Householde Gouernment* (first published in 1598). With the primacy of wifely submission, the 'explicit delineation of spheres of responsibility' 'comes to appear very nearly meaningless: the husband occupies both spheres after all, is both "indoors" and "outdoors" all at once, negotiating in the marketplace, and governing the godly household. The woman, as good wife, is merely the example of his ability to govern' (21). Viewed from this perspective, the authority of the lady signifies Macbeth's incompetence as domestic governor. As the driving force of the action in the first three acts, Lady Macbeth reverses the hierarchical distribution of power within marriage. The authoritative position adopted by the dark lady, and Macbeth's ready submission, create subject positions beyond the comfortable dichotomies of Ramist diagrams. Needless to say, this bodes ill for Macbeth's skills as future ruler. In his treatise, Cleaver linked political government directly to household government:

[H]e is taken for an honest man ... and he is reckoned worthie to rule a commonwealth, that with such wisedom, discretion, and iudgement, doth rule and gouerne his owne house, and that he may easilie conserue and keepe his Citizens in peace and concord, that hath so wel established the same in his owne house and familie. And on the other side, none will thinke or beleeue, that he is able to be ruler, or to keep peace and quietnesse in the towne or Cittie, who cannot liue peaceably in his own house, where hee is not onely a ruler, but a King, and Lord of all.

(178–179)

As noted in Chapter 1, Cleaver draws here on the well-established discursive parallel between household and commonwealth.

In Shakespeare's conception of Macbeth's marriage, the ambiguous position of the wife that emerges in early modern writings—as 'fellow governor' and subject to her husband, excessive force, and household guardian—becomes fully apparent. With Lady Macbeth, Shakespeare creates a subject position that combines authority with the limited possibilities of female agency, links reasoning powers with excessive desire, and combines vigour with madness. '[U]ndaunted mettle' and masculine will-power combine with a habitual residue of submission to male figures of authority. Lady Macbeth tells the audience how close she came to murdering the sleeping king herself, restrained only by the image of her father: 'Had he not resembled / My father as he slept, I had done't' (2.2.12–13). The tropical equation of king and father, which was a cornerstone of patriarchal order, returns here as bodily likeness and makes it impossible to kill the king-father.

From Ethics to Efficiency in the Service of Private Interest

The play positions female passion and agency at the heart of the plot and poses the question of authority in and government of the house. With the dark lady, the play taps into the topos of the excessive female body and its lack of restraint. Yet Lady Macbeth's eye for strategic action resists this conventional gendering of rationality, and her exceptional willpower suggests that the Lady has *virtù*—the strength, courage, and ability to claim and retain power. Her approach to how to claim the crown suggests a transformed understanding of practical rationality which—like Bacon's 'wisdom of business'—is little concerned with ethics. She values efficiency over ethics, instructs Macbeth, and sets the pace for their ambitious project. The following discussion of her appeal to Macbeth analyses their motive for the murder and traces the way in which the lady strips the action of ethical import, reducing it to a question of desire and willpower.

The audience's understanding of Macbeth is determined by the lady's astute description of Macbeth's ambiguous relation to his own desire:

> LADY MACBETH. Yet do I fear thy nature:
> It is too full o'th'milk of human kindness,
> To catch the nearest way. Thou wouldst be great;
> Art not without ambition, but without
> The illness should attend it: what thou wouldst highly,
> That wouldst thou holily; wouldst not play false,
> And yet wouldst wrongly win ...
>
> (1.5.16–22)

Lady Macbeth accuses Macbeth of inefficiency—he is incapable of 'catching the nearest way'. Her speech contains a paradox, which remains unintelligible if one understands the phrase 'wouldst not play false' in moral terms. Contrary to J. Gregory Keller, who identifies Macbeth's fear that the king's virtues 'will plead like angels' as an ethical consideration of 'the worth of the other' (46), I argue that Macbeth hardly cares for King Duncan's virtues, but worries about his own reputation. Macbeth's preoccupation with social judgement becomes apparent in this speech:

> MACBETH. We will proceed no further in this business:
> He hath honour'd me of late; and I have bought
> Golden opinions from all sorts of people,
> Which would be worn now in their newest gloss,
> Not cast aside so soon.
>
> (1.7.31–34)

Not virtue but the 'golden opinions of others' constitute 'the ornament of life' (1.7.42). It is Macbeth's desire for fame that obstructs efficient action and keeps him from reaching for 'the golden round' (1.5.28), not his moral scruples. With his ambition and desire for glory, Macbeth shares in a character fault that affects many great men, as Cicero tells us in Book One of *De Officiis*: 'the ambition for civil office, military command, power and glory is usually nursed by men of the greatest and most outstanding talent' (1.26).

As a character fault, desire for glory is entirely in line with tragedy's focus on noble men. According to Albert O. Hirschman, it functioned as 'touchstone of a man's virtue and greatness' in 'the medieval chivalric ethos' (10), and appealed strongly to Renaissance audiences.[66] However, Cicero had already warned that the pursuit of power and glory made men 'forget the claims of justice' (*Off.* 1.26).[67] Injustice, according to Aristotle, is an immoderate desire for more than is right.[68] Macbeth's desire for glory suggests the same unbounded desire for more and the same disregard for ethical means which characterizes covetousness, only here it is social rather than material gain. Macbeth's uses of the verb 'bought' and the adjective 'golden' frame the acquisition of reputation as a chrematistic operation, suggesting both the give-and-take of social exchanges and the accumulation of social capital. The unspecified source of admiration—'from all sorts of people'—is general enough to suggest limitless desire for fame. In a culture of credit in which economic success hinges on the opinion of others, winning their respect and trust may become a means to an end.

In the end, Macbeth is easily swayed by his lady. Fortified by her pep talk, he asks only one question: 'If we should fail?' This question concerns not ethics, but the efficiency of means and potential consequences. Macbeth's use of deliberation and dialogue as means for identifying the right action is entirely devoid of practical wisdom as the intellectual virtue that identifies the good *as* good and chooses the means that lead to it. The Macbeths pursue private interests at the expense of public welfare. For all their differences, they exercise practical rationality without an ethical frame: they consider means, desired ends, and unintended consequences,

---

[66] In fact, as Hirschman points out, St Augustine had already formulated some 'attenuating circumstances' for the sin of '*libido dominandi* when combined with a strong desire for praise and glory' (10), in contrast to 'lust for money and possessions' and 'sexual lust' (9). He writes: 'Then, during the Renaissance, the striving for honor achieved the status of a dominant ideology as the influence of the Church receded and the advocates of the aristocratic ideal were able to draw on the plentiful Greek and Roman texts celebrating the pursuit of glory. This powerful intellectual current carried over into the seventeenth century' (11). Hirschman proceeds to tell the story of how this ideal was demolished in the seventeenth century.

[67] Aristotle's discussion of ambition is ambiguous: according to him, we call a man ambitious who aims at great honours but who lacks moderation in his aspirations. Yet as we lack a name for the mean in the case of ambition, Aristotle explains, we sometimes praise a man for being ambitious and sometimes for being unambitious (*EN* IV.4, 1125b8–25). Macbeth is clearly a case of too much ambition.

[68] The just man 'will distribute either between himself and another or between two others not so as to give more of what is desirable to himself and less to his neighbour (and conversely with what is harmful), but so as to give what is equal in accordance with proportion' (*EN* V.5, 1134a1–6).

but they never stop to ask about the good. Their use of practical intelligence is prudential not in an ethical sense, but in a pragmatic, tactical one.

The key problem that concerns practical rationality is how to engage with particular and contingent events to achieve certain ends.[69] This is the domain of prudence, the intellectual faculty of deliberating about the means necessary for certain ends to be attained in the future. J. G. A. Pocock analyses the temporality of prudence in his discussion of Aquinas and Cicero. He describes prudence as the faculty that deals with contingent events in the present based on experience and custom, but with a view to the future: 'Prudence ... was the present and future, where custom was the perfect, tense of experience' (25). In order to secure a favourable future, prudence integrates 'memory of the past, understanding of the present and foresight of the future' (25).[70] It thus bridges 'the gap between innovation and memory, statute and custom, present, future and past' (25). In the Macbeths' preoccupation with the prophesy, the relation between present and future is at stake, but the past also plays a role. The prophecy seduces the Macbeths into taking the future into their own hands, realizing their fate rather than waiting patiently for whatever might happen. It invites them to be active rather than submit to fortune.[71] The play uses the prophecy to dramatize the desire to mould one's fortune, to shape the future. For Howard Marchitello, 'The speed of events in *Macbeth*—and the speed of the play itself' (430) exemplify the collapse of temporality into 'functional instantaneity' (433). Yet the murder is also an attempt to control the future, to jump the interval and make it happen *now*.[72] As Lady Macbeth puts it, anticipating the murderous action: 'I feel now / the future in the instant' (1.5.57–58). At the bottom of her action is the belief that the future can be shaped, that it is possible to be the architect of one's own fate. This belief is thwarted: as her vision of Duncan as father figure foreshadows, her role in the murder cannot be integrated with patriarchal custom and leads to madness. Furthermore, the prophecy really indicates that the future will not bend to one's will. Without children, power cannot be secured for the house of Macbeth, and Banquo's issue stands to inherit the throne.

---

[69] Pocock discusses the difference 'between speculative *ratio* which proceeds from principles and practical *ratio* which proceeds towards ends' (24–25).

[70] Pocock quotes here from Aquinas's *Summa Theologica*: 'He [Aquinas] continues by quoting Cicero as mentioning "three other parts of prudence, namely memory of the past, understanding of the present and foresight of the future," and concludes that these "are not virtues distinct from prudence," but "integral parts or components"' (25).

[71] Pocock addresses the conflict between human agency and impersonal fortune when he discusses virtue (or rather *virtus*) and fortune as opposites and describes *virtus* in terms of 'the heroic fortitude that withstood ill fortune [and that] passed into the active capacity that remolded circumstances to the actor's advantage and thence into the charismatic *felicitas* that mysteriously commanded good fortune' (37).

[72] Marchitello himself acknowledges that 'the play's disconcerting speed may be a function of the play's having "come down to us in a version stripped for action"' (431; he quotes from Harry Levin, 'Two Scenes from Macbeth' 48).

Private Interests and the Motivating Force of Passion

Lady Macbeth recognizes immoderate ambition as the source of Macbeth's care for his reputation and uses this knowledge to propel him towards making a play for the crown. She pitches the truth of desire against Macbeth's concern for appearances, and thus establishes subjectivity, a sense of self, as the benchmark of action. The demand to be true to one's desire empowers the passionate subject. The lady demands the internal consistency of desire and action and replaces social recognition with 'thine own esteem':

> LADY MACBETH. Art thou afeard
> To be the same in thine own act and valour,
> As thou art in desire? Would'st thou have that
> which thou esteem'st the ornament of life,
> And live a coward in thine own esteem ...
>
> (1.7.39–43)

Her passionate argument mimics the 'appeal to inner conviction' or 'appeal to the heart' (35) that Christopher Hill identified as Protestantism's 'great contribution to the rise of capitalism' (27).[73] With its murderous couple, the play performs this inward move as a source of self-authorization which justifies even regicide.[74] *Macbeth* stages the emergence of a self that recognizes and owns what it desires even at the expense of ethics, and thus explores the role of the motivating passions in the emergence of subjectivity. The dark lady acts as midwife for this birth of the self as an agent that *makes* its fortune rather than subjecting passively to its fate. In this scenario, the lady is the more active figure—she takes their fate into her own hands when Macbeth is only dimly aware of the possibilities that the king's visit implies.

The lady's rhetorical focus on 'desire' suggests attention to the motivating force of the passions. In the sixteenth and seventeenth centuries, the passions were often framed as destructive impulses, and selfish and disorderly behaviour was frequently characterized in terms of excessive passion: as greediness, gluttony, miserliness, and disproportionate ambition. As noted in the Introduction, the rise of the term 'interest' during the late sixteenth century (Hirschman 32) reflects both the destructive tendency of the passions and their gradual transformation into a motivational element in the rational pursuit of private ends. The principle of the countervailing passions, in which certain passions put a bridle on others, draws

---

[73] As Hill puts it, 'What mattered was that Protestantism appealed ... to artisans and small merchants, whom it helped to trust the dictates of their own hearts as their standard of conduct' (27).

[74] This is indebted to Robert Weimann, who identified in Reformation writing a new, 'precariously intellectual mode of self-authorization' ('History and the Issue of Authority in Representation' 458).

on discourses that identify certain passions as rational and productive tamers of more destructive ones. This principle provides the backstory for the emergence of private interests as a healthy force of commercial growth in the work of Adam Smith.[75] In the sixteenth century, renewed interest in the motivating rather than simply destructive force of the passions may have been supported by the study of Aristotelian writings. As suggested in Chapter 1, Aristotle gave rise to a tradition of self-government 'which emphasizes the cultivation (rather than suppression) of the passions' (Tilmouth 20) and makes use of their motivating force.

The tragedy of *Macbeth* occupies a curious middle ground between calculation and destruction that reflects the shifting status of the passions. Excessive ambition—Macbeth's 'desire'—is a destructive force that wreaks havoc on the entire country, but, at the same time, the lady's plan of action achieves the desired end: King Duncan is killed and Macbeth is crowned. In her dialogues with Macbeth, Lady Macbeth's rhetoric recalls a practical rationality which continually appeals to the household's interest, discusses means and ends, weighs costs and benefits, and encourages Macbeth with the incentive of profit. Yet despite the initial emphasis on calculation and rationality, the idea of the destructive force of the passions gradually gains the upper hand: by Act Four, the lady has become mad, and Macbeth embarks on a killing spree. His own union with his wife seems to have disintegrated together with her reason: after their numerous intense and secretive communications in the first three acts, they do not speak to each other at all in Acts Four and Five. Their claustrophobic intimacy leaves nothing behind when each descends into their own private hell. As if haunted by the fertile growth of other households, and specifically by the vision of Banquo's numerous offspring, Macbeth kills Macduff's wife and children. This act is both terribly concrete and highly symbolic, but it only accentuates Macbeth's own isolation. With the disintegration of the Macbeths' household and the escalation of Macbeth's tyranny, the notion of the excessive and destructive nature of the passions carries the day. Yet the play's close attention to desire prefigures the anthropological interest of seventeenth- and eighteenth-century writers and their detailed examination of the passions as the motivational foundation of self-interested—and perhaps even rational—action.

The destructive force of passion is explicitly discussed in the dialogue between Macduff and Duncan's son Malcolm, and it is here that kingly ambition and avarice come together. Malcolm, who has a strong claim to the Scottish throne, pretends to be governed by excessive passions such as intemperance and avarice. Designed to 'test' Macduff, his confession inserts a fundamental sense of uncertainty as to the new king's character. Norbrook argues that Malcolm dissociates his speech from 'his inner nature' (111), but Malcolm's performance of the future tyrant is a tad

---

[75] See also Chapter 1, 30–31 (note 16). As Hirschman points out, Smith's *The Wealth of Nations* 'was wholly focussed on the passion traditionally known as cupidity or avarice' (18), which he described not as a passion but in 'such bland terms as "advantage" or "interest"' (19).

too perfect to be easily dismissed as mere show—and his use of performance as a legitimate strategy is too politically savvy to suggest an honest, straight-dealing ruler. The dialogue contains a passage on avarice, in which Malcolm 'confesses' that his greed has no bounds: 'And my more-having would be as a sauce / To make me hunger more' (4.3.81–82). Malcolm paints the portrait of a tyrant who uses the wives and daughters of his nobles after his desire, cuts off 'the nobles for their lands' (4.3.79), and picks 'Quarrels unjust against the good and loyal, / Destroying them for wealth' (4.3.83–84), respecting neither private estates nor families. Macduff confirms that avarice is a more dangerous condition than voluptuousness: 'This avarice / Sticks deeper, grows with more pernicious root / Than summer-seeming lust; and it hath been / The sword of our slain kings' (4.3.84–87). This remark associates King Duncan, the one slain king in the play so far, with avarice. As Malcolm's speeches suggest, covetousness threatens the stability of the realm, for it drives a ruler to ruthlessly pursue his advantage at the expense of social peace. The dialogue also draws a parallel between desire for the crown and avarice. The grasping man who reaches for a crown that is not his and the tyrant who takes away his nobles' land and wives are both infected by the same unbounded desire for more. Just as avarice is boundless (there is always more wealth to be gained), the Macbeths' desire for kingship is out of bounds, because it aims for the highest possible position. The rungs of social hierarchy may be finite, yet the power of kingship is not, as Malcolm and Macduff's dialogue on excessive desire and might on the part of the ruler suggests. Both Malcolm and Macbeth appear to confuse means and ends: for them, kingship is not a means to safeguard the common good, but a good in itself. Their desire for kingship is inflected by a limitless chrematistic logic.

After he has described his alleged vices in detail and once Macduff turns from him, Malcolm shows his true colours and 'abjure[s] the taints and blames I laid upon myself' (4.3.124). Now it appears that his character is flawless:

> MALCOLM. I am yet
>   Unknown to woman; never was forsworn;
>   Scarcely have coveted what was mine own;
>   At no time broke my faith: would not betray
>   The Devil to his fellow; and delight
>   No less in truth than life: my first false speaking
>   Was this upon myself.
>
>   (4.3.125–131)

Macduff is rightly confused after being confronted with two completely opposite accounts of Malcolm's character, which are both put forward in equally persuasive terms: 'Such welcome and unwelcome things at once, / 'Tis hard to reconcile'

(4.3.138–139). As Norbrook realizes, Malcolm models 'himself on Macbeth's own strategies of dissimulation' (111) when he aligns his own 'test' of Macduff's loyalty with Macbeth's political practice: 'Devilish Macbeth / By many of these trains hath sought to win me / Into his power' (4.3.117–119).[76] This exchange between Malcolm and Macduff is important in three respects: it shows the new king's capacity for dissimulation and strategic action; it underlines the destructive force of the passions; and it aligns reaching for the crown with an avaricious intent and thereby recognizes avarice as a motivational force. The parallel actions of regicide (Duncan's murder) and tyrannicide (Macbeth's killing) appear to highlight the key importance of character and virtue.[77] Yet Shakespeare establishes moral differences only to muddle them: Malcolm's successful performance as a future tyrant in his dialogue with Macduff leaves the audience doubtful about his true motivation and aims.

The Politics of Exchange

Already in Act One, the question of who gets what shapes social exchanges and determines the household's position in relation to others. Social exchanges buy loyalties, forge alliances, or breed dissatisfaction. Reciprocity is of paramount importance for the Scottish nobility in the play's fictional world. King Duncan promotes Macbeth to Thane of Cawdor for his loyal deeds, Banquo shares a secret with Macbeth under the imperative of mutual trust, and, after the killing of the king, the Scottish nobles are pacified with a festive banquet. From the very beginning, the possibility of asymmetrical exchange, of a failure of reciprocity, poses risks. The dialogue between Macbeth and King Duncan, after Macbeth's victory, explores the question of recompense through a rhetoric of obligation:

> DUNCAN. O worthiest cousin!
> The sin of my ingratitude even now
> was heavy on me. Thou art so far before,
> that swiftest wing of recompense is slow
> To overtake thee: would thou hadst less deserv'd
> That the proportion both of thanks and payment

---

[76] See also Steven Mullaney's article 'Lying like Truth: Riddle, Representation and Treason in Renaissance England' 42, as well as Lukas Lammers's chapter on *Macbeth* in *Shakespearean Temporalities: History on the Early Modern Stage* 179.

[77] The means are the same—killing a king—but the ends differ significantly. Macbeth is motivated by hypertrophic ambition; Malcolm and Macduff's action against Macbeth appears justified by the common good. Shakespeare, as Rebecca Lemon writes, 'differentiates between two types of treason, one committed in the name of the state and the common good, and the other out of personal interest' (74).

> Might have been mine! only I have left to say,
> More is thy due than more than all can pay.
>
> MACBETH. The service and the loyalty I owe,
> In doing it, pays itself. Your Highness' part
> Is to receive our duties: and our duties
> Are to your throne and state, children and servants;
> Which do but what they should, by doing everything
> Safe toward your love and honour.
> (1.4.14–27)

This rhetoric of obligation also characterizes the later exchange between Duncan and his hostess, Lady Macbeth. Duncan's wishful 'would thou hadst less deserved' and his exasperated 'More is thy due than more than all can pay' seem more than mere rhetoric. This suspicion is confirmed when he declares later: 'The love that follows us sometime is our trouble, / Which still we thank as love' (1.6.11–12). Receiving too much is burdensome when one is placed under an obligation to reciprocate. Under the imperative of reciprocity, imbalance breeds resentment on both sides—both fear that they might have to give more than they receive.[78] Despite Macbeth's profession that his effort is its own reward and Lady Macbeth's declaration of willing service, the audience knows that they are not content with the latest honours:

> LADY MACBETH. All our service,
> In every point twice done, and then done double,
> Were poor and single business, to contend
> Against those honours deep and broad, wherewith
> Your Majesty loads our house: for those of old,
> And the late dignities heap'd up to them,
> We rest your hermits.
> (1.6.14–20)

Lady Macbeth's exaggerated numbers game of a double doubling only serves to deepen the dramatic irony. As their plotting shows, the Macbeths feel they have not nearly received enough, but they dissimulate their intentions behind a mask of loyal service and gratitude. Duncan's exaggerated rhetoric is an attempt to repay the Macbeths in words rather than with the kingship that might have been Macbeth's under Scottish custom. Rebecca Lemon writes:

---

[78] Stephen Deng notes, 'Despite the gracious tone, we sense Duncan's resentment about having to repay Macbeth for all he has done ... Duncan feels uncomfortable for all the courtesies and service Macbeth has shown since he can imagine it would only lead to resentment' ('Healing Angels' 172).

> As David Norbrook has most clearly articulated, *Macbeth*'s immediate narrative sources record that the Scottish practice of succession, tanistry, would place Macbeth as Duncan's successor, not Malcolm ... Electing to follow the newer system of primogeniture rather than tanistry, which would favour Macbeth, Duncan nominates his own son as king as part of the postwar spoils, an action that is ill-timed and impolitic given Macbeth's own recent triumph in the war in contrast to Malcolm's captivity.
>
> (76)[79]

Duncan's hyperbolic words are a poor substitute for the crown, leaving the Macbeths with little to appease their ambition. Later, however, Macbeth makes a similar mistake, but one that is inflated in size: he shuts the social exchange of give and take down completely and works instead by oppression. He refuses the basic social tie of reciprocity that holds the community together and, instead of rewarding his friends and nobles, kills them off, one after the other.[80] Cutting off all social ties reenforces the claustrophobic and inward-looking secrecy of the marital union of the Macbeths and emphasizes the extent to which their household withdraws from the community and shrinks into a tight, twisted kernel. With the lady's death, this kernel disintegrates into nothingness, leaving Macbeth with a life that is emptied of meaning—'signifying nothing' (5.5.28).

Steeped in a rhetoric of business, the play underwrites the feudal logic of loyalty and service with a language of mercantile exchange: Lady Macbeth greets the king with talk of 'compt' and 'audit' (1.6.26–27), Macbeth claims to have 'bought' the 'golden' opinions of his peers (1.7.32–33), and Duncan expresses his thanks to Macbeth for a battle won in terms of 'recompense', 'payment', and 'due' (1.4.17, 19, and 21). The need to balance one's books, as well as monitor obligations, points to the pervasive presence of an exchange paradigm that demands reciprocity. Professions of debt and, in the case of Macbeth and his lady, of duty, are thin covers for the desire to walk away from an exchange with more than one had to give. We might argue that the curious constellation of the domestic and the political serves to represent and explore the ramifications of the calculated, self-interested accumulation of status and wealth. Carroll and others have pointed out that the show of kings in Act Four, Scene One, is 'purely Shakespeare's invention' (347). It 'represents Stuart royal genealogy' (347) and thus directs attention to the legitimizing power of succession in a system of primogeniture. Yet it also provides a model for successful accumulation: for an investment which, in contrast to Macbeth's sexual

---

[79] Norbrook remarks on Duncan's nomination of his son as future king and its political implications for the play: 'If Duncan has to nominate his son, presumably the implication is that he could have nominated someone else, that the system is not one of pure primogeniture' (94).

[80] Compare this refusal of reciprocity with Aristotle's dictum: 'For it is by proportionate requital that the city holds together' (*EN* V.5, 1132b33–34).

and murderous actions, proves productive. It breeds and multiplies. Primogeniture is a focal point of the play, featuring both in Duncan's declaration of his son as future heir and in Macbeth's despair over his lack of an heir:

> MACBETH. Upon my head they plac'd a fruitless crown,
>   And put a barren sceptre in my gripe,
>   Thence to be wrench'd with an unlineal hand,
>   No son of mine succeeding. If 't be so,
>   For Banquo's issue have I fil'd my mind ...
>
> (3.1.60–64)

Macbeth is not so much grieved by the murder, but by the fact that it might all come to nothing for lack of an heir, and that the murder might profit someone else's house. This may account for the irrational decision to destroy Macduff's entire family.

Having learned from his father's murder, Malcolm knows that imbalance causes strife and promptly seeks to redress this problem in the final scene by promoting his loyal thanes:

> MALCOLM. We shall not spend a large expense of time,
>   Before we reckon with your several loves,
>   And make us even with you. My Thanes and kinsmen,
>   Henceforth be Earls; the first that ever Scotland
>   In such an honour nam'd.
>
> (5.9.26–30)

Malcolm's introduction of the English peerage system is a smart move. He repays those who already have a title by giving them an inheritable rank: something that can be passed on and become the basis of accumulated fame and wealth. His awareness of the need for swift recompense shows that he has learnt from his father's fate. Malcolm states a few lines later: 'this, and what needful else / ... We will perform in measure, time, and place' (5.9.37–39), demonstrating that he is aware of the imperative of prompt requital. Yet 'the new king's familiarity with deception', which emerges in the dialogue with Macduff as much as in the battle strategy of hiding behind branches of Birnam wood, indeed recalls 'the tactics of Macbeth more than his father Duncan' (Lemon 83). Malcolm is a new and business-savvy type of ruler, one who commands the art of dissimulation and promptly repays loyalty. With his ascent, Shakespeare ends his extended exploration of domestic and political government, of instrumental reason and the pursuit of private interests, leaving the audience free to moralize or marvel as they like, and to pity or applaud whom they will.

Conclusion

With the household at the centre of the action, *Macbeth* addresses the nexus of politics and oeconomy. It paints a picture of a household that destroys not only itself, but threatens the commonwealth in its unbridled pursuit of private interests. In contrast to *A Chaste Maid*, the tragedy approaches the household from the angle of politics rather than the market. Yet it, too, is concerned with oeconomy as an ethically informed set of rules that are no longer functional as the guiding framework of social action. Furthermore, although the tragedy focuses on the inside life of the household and the interface between *oikos* and *polis*, the logic that it examines is closer to a commercial logic than to the norms of oeconomy. The Macbeths privilege private interests over the common good; they conflate means and ends and combine excessive desire with cool calculation. While the Macbeths' motivating passion appears to be ambition rather than avarice, the play explores the contiguity of power and wealth in the dialogue between Malcolm and Macduff and positions both as objects of the same immoderate desire for more. For Macbeth, however, the acquisition of power provides no satisfaction. He lacks an heir, and thus a future in which the power and riches he acquires will be preserved and augmented. The show of kings that parades Banquo's long line in front of Macbeth captures the dominant concern of oeconomy—to preserve a family line—and provides at the same time a graphic image of growth and accumulation. It is excessive enough to honour James I as Banquo's distant ancestor, but it also highlights Macbeth's futile desire for a growing family line and the power and status it can secure.

Like *A Chaste Maid* and in contrast to the prescriptive literature of the time, *Macbeth* suggests fascination with the passions, with self-interest as a moving force, and with entrepreneurial if unethical action. Both plays enact the transformation of the order of the household through a chrematistic logic that privileges appearances over virtue and involves a desire for 'more'—be it money or social status. With the disintegration of ethics and oeconomy, *Macbeth* and *A Chaste Maid* stage the failure of household management as an overarching framework for socio-economic action. This disintegration is fuelled by desire for social and material gain, and it is figured by means of an excessive female corporeality. Despite these similarities, performances of the household as socio-economic and physical space also differ significantly in the two plays. The alliance of household concerns and politics comes quite naturally to the noble households that the tragedy depicts: the question of royal succession involves the political community as a whole (Richardson, 'Tragedy, Family and Household' 24). City comedy is less invested in noble households than in the 'middling sort' of people, the 'tradesmen' of London (Earle 141). Situated in a commercial context, city comedy explores households not in relation to political government and patriarchal authority, but to the market. Despite its noble setting and cast, however, *Macbeth*'s focus on the marital couple, their aims, and their barrenness directs attention to the household as the key unit of oeconomic considerations. In fact, with its interest in the 'solitarie and secret society' (Perkins, *Christian Oeconomie* 111) constituted by marriage, in a gendered division of labour, and in the efficient pursuit of private interests, the play appears to cater to a proto-bourgeois audience that cares about how to make one's fortune and rise in the world.

Macbeth and *A Chaste Maid* represent two extremes of the household as dynamic and dramatic space: one closes itself off from the *polis* in a dynamic of self-isolation, while the other expands and merges with other households to form a network of exchanges. Only *Macbeth* offers, by way of verbal scenery, an outside view of the house (or rather castle) and suggests, through the sound of the knocking, the physical boundaries of household space. It takes the ideology of a miniature realm-within-the-realm to its limits, and establishes the household as a distinct space, detached from the rest of the *polis*, obscure and claustrophobic. Its relation to the community receives dramatic force with the highly ritualized threshold-crossing of King Duncan. The play's action implies a concentric narrowing of focus on the household from the initial scenes on the open heath to the king's approach and entry into the castle; from his formal exchanges of greetings with the hostess to the daily chore of marital negotiations between Macbeth and his lady. This narrowing of focus stops only in the bedchamber of the then-mad Lady Macbeth (Hopkins 257).[81] It is also tangible in the increasing isolation of Macbeth and, finally, in his lone battle against an army.[82] The play's spatial dynamic is that of a tightening circle: a concentric force that binds Macbeth and his dark lady together as companions in crime and fate. The destructive force of excessive self-interest receives emblematic form in the utter destruction of Macduff's household, including the killing of 'Wife, children, servants' (4.3.211).

A Chaste Maid features a decentralized spatial structure in which households not only interact, but fluctuate or even merge. Their forms and fates are subject to commercial and commercialized social exchanges. In the vibrant marketplace constituted by the different households in *A Chaste Maid*, social identities become malleable piecework. No longer an identifiable unit with firm boundaries, the household cannot serve as the disciplinary foundation of society. Instead, the market is the primary fact of social life: it integrates all households within its bounds and dissolves their boundaries. The logic of the household is irreversibly transformed by the logic of the market: under the paradigm of exchange, wives, children, and sexual performance become all subject to bartering. When households form part of an open market, positions are in flux: wives become

---

[81] Hopkins notes, 'We never see Lady Macbeth out of her own house, and her mental collapse narrows even further the world we perceive her to inhabit, as we are shown her bedchamber' (257).

[82] Anthony Brennan discusses in great detail the battle scene and the techniques with which this battle is staged as 'a battle of Macbeth against an army' (*Onstage and Offstage Worlds* 157). He also analyses Macbeth's gradually increasing isolation, 'the way the hero drifts away from his peers to become a pariah' (158).

prostitutes, prostitutes wives; strangers turn into lovers and cuckolds into happy fathers. Far from constituting merely an abstract force, the market forges here concrete social connections, transforms existing ties, and provides new subject positions (wife as breadwinner).[83] Economic behaviour in this open marketplace is directed not by ethically informed prudence, but by pragmatism and profit.

In *A Chaste Maid*, in contrast to *Macbeth*, the topological distinction between outside and inside is not stable. Anglin claims that '[t]he private shop in its various incarnations acts as a threshold between domestic and civic spaces', but her own reading of 'porous boundaries between the street, the market and the home' (17) suggests that this threshold is really a gateway through which the market extends into the household. The performance of the household as an open place that interacts with a network of other spaces (other households, shops, the street) goes hand in hand with a multiplot structure. The many deals struck in the four interwoven plots suggest the busy commercial life of Cheapside, the bustling shops and trading points that crowded its side streets. The shift in focus from distinct households to the vibrant exchanges of the marketplace has a formal equivalent in this multiplot structure. If the open houses of city comedy constitute a marketplace, the multiplot structure models its dynamic, processual character: the promises, successes, thwarted hopes, and newly-forged relations, and the synchronicity of deals and fortunes. In *A Chaste Maid*, the market is omnipresent, but it is displayed in a very concrete way as a network of relations constituted by specific actions. *Macbeth*, in contrast, offers a monolithic mythos organized around the rise and fall of the tragic hero. In contrast to *A Chaste Maid*, in which the restoration of order involves a brothel, marriage to a whore, and institutionalized adultery, the end of *Macbeth* sees the renewal of political order.

At the heart of domestic dysfunction in *Macbeth* is a reversal of the gendered positions of authority and submission. A similar reversal of political order, attempted by the traitors, threatens the stability of Duncan's reign in the beginning of the play. The instability of the vertical axis of social hierarchy affects both household and realm. This vertical instability is also at the heart of *A Chaste Maid*: both plays are dramas of social advancement, even if *Macbeth* locates ambition in feudal Scotland and *A Chaste Maid* in the city of London. *Macbeth* performs excessive desire for social advancement as a cause of domestic and civic disorder, while Middleton's comedy recognizes self-interest as a new ordering force. This is not to say that the comedy affirms the commercialization of social life: after all, in the end, with Moll and Touchwood Junior true love trumps commodification, even if it does so with an ironic wink. Yet it depicts a society in which commerce competes with the model of oeconomy as a structuring force and guiding logic of socio-economic action.

---

[83] See Agnew, who discusses markets as '*situated* phenomena' (18) and traces the 'historical shift in the market's meaning—from a place to a principle to a power' (56).

Macbeth, with its noble households and story of regicide, seems little concerned with the commercialization of early modern society. If chrematistic practices and concerns creep into language and plot, they do so through the back door. Yet the actions of the Macbeths are tied to boundless desire, to deliberations that ignore ethics, to a hypertrophic investment in appearances that privileges extrinsic over intrinsic worth, to the rejection of moderation and sufficiency as guiding principles of the household's commercial activities, and to a self-legitimizing interest in (social) gain. The play presents a household bent on accumulating power for its own sake and not for the good of all. In their dialogic exchanges of rational arguments, the Macbeths are shown to act out of calculated interest, even if the lady's madness and Macbeth's killing spree connect the plot with traditional ethical discourses of excess. On a literal level, this is a tragic plot about a noble warrior whose hypertrophic ambition effects his downfall. Yet reading this play in the context of contemporary London comedies encourages a less classical and more historical reading, which perceives in this tragedy early modern anxieties about—but also fascination with—the extremity of means in the service of private interest. Ambition is easier to reconcile with classical tragedy than avarice; it is also a genre-appropriate trope for the desire for a higher social status and its material benefits. Kingship, as Malcolm reminds us, retains the power to seize land and goods, and thus unites status and fame with the potentially unlimited acquisition of wealth.

Tragedy and city comedy differ in the fate of the households they depict. *A Chaste Maid* ends on a festive note. Although the play punishes crude ambitions for wealth and gentility, it acknowledges private interest as a pervasive social force and refrains from moralizing. Instead, it explores the opportunities that the dissolution of household boundaries creates for enterprising individuals. The dynamic of tragedy allows for the exploration of social possibilities, only to reject them. Hopes for political power, love, or friendship turn sour as the fate of households develops along the lines scripted by conduct literature: as a story of excessive or unbridled passion that ultimately consumes and thus destroys the *oikos*. The final deaths of Macbeth and his lady can be seen as dramatic attempts to lay the unruly spirit of socio-economic change to rest and to restore moderation and balance as key principles of political and household government. Yet Shakespeare's restitution of order in *Macbeth* is little more than a formal gesture to the conventions of tragedy. The tragic and senseless excess of the murder of Macduff's entire household, Macbeth's isolated and utterly futile fight against an army, and a new ruler who is tactically adroit and capable of dissimulation all subvert belief in the restoration of a meaningful and just order. Malcolm represents a new type of king, one who is willing and able to deceive his followers, and who accepts the imminent reward of loyalty as a pragmatic necessity. Furthermore, Shakespeare's representation of Lady Macbeth's ruthless rationality is seductive enough to question the logic of government and moderation that informs the household. The lady has 'virtù' (Norbrook 101)—instead of waiting for Fortune to spill her cornucopia, she takes her and Macbeth's future into her own hands. If Lady Macbeth embodies a modern rationality, which reduces the ethical problem of means and ends to efficiency and utility maximization, the play evokes the spectre of a purely economic rationality, but is only half committed to laying it to rest. Similarly, but more obviously, Middleton's interest in *A Chaste Maid* lies not in consolidating the nexus of oeconomy and ethics, but in exploring how the pursuit of private interest reconfigures life in the social space of the household.

3
Mercantile Agency and Service in *Othello* and *The Alchemist*

Introduction

The previous chapter analysed the households of *A Chaste Maid in Cheapside* and *Macbeth* as socio-economic spaces that register tensions between competing economic rationalities: between the ethical framework of ancient oeconomy and the imperative of profitable commerce. This remains true for *Othello* and *The Alchemist*, yet my discussion of these plays shifts the focus from marriage and reproduction to another part of the household: the relation between masters and servants.[1] By concentrating on subordinates who labour within the household and manage exchanges without, this chapter continues and expands the exploration of a practical rationality that proves highly effective, but cares little for ethics. As self-interested servants who pretend to work for their masters but really pursue their own interests, Shakespeare's Iago and Jonson's trickster Face approach service with the strategic mindset and keen eye for personal advantage that Francis Bacon described as 'wisedom of Businesse' (*The Advancement* 157). With these characters, the chapter focuses on mercantile agency as a force that is located within the household and shapes its fortune, although it may be at odds with its interest.

Various scholars have commented on the 'wide application' (Burnett 2) of the term 'servant' in early modern England. As Michael Neill describes the institution of service, it is at once a 'universal state—a defining condition of social order' and 'a particular social institution subject to disconcerting local and historical pressures' ('Servant Obedience' 138).[2] The term applied to live-in servants and apprentices, but also to 'players, monks, grooms, gentlemen, lords or courtiers, and even kings' (Burnett 2). Mark Thornton Burnett suggests that a contractual obligation and the 'receipt of a wage' (2) or a different kind of recompense might form part of a

---

[1] See, for instance, Peter Laslett, *The World We Have Lost*, for a description of the different parts of the family or household and the various relations that formed different societies within the family: 'There was the society of man and wife, that of parents and children, and that of master and servant' (2). See also Lawrence Stone, who describes the composition of the household or family in *The Family, Sex and Marriage in England 1500–1800* 26–27.

[2] Quoting from Neill's *Putting History to the Question* 22, Michelle M. Dowd comments on the universal meaning of service: 'As a social institution, the feudal model of service pervaded medieval and early modern culture, and the structures of submission that service engendered permeated virtually all types of social interactions, forming an "unbroken chain of service" that led from the peasant to the monarch and included people from all ranks of society' (21).

working definition of service (3). One may add that a firm hierarchical order, as articulated in Edward Leigh's *A Systeme or Body of Divinity* (1654), was essential to the relationship between servants and their superiors: 'Servants are placed in a lower room, in a place of inferiority and subjection, and so are bound to perform obedience, seeing in all places the Superiour must rule, and the inferiour be ruled, or else neither Superiour nor inferiour shall with any comfort enjoy the places allotted unto them by God' (827).[3] It is this hierarchical relation and the threat of its inversion—the danger that the servant might not act on behalf of the master but seek to take his place—that turns the figure of the self-interested servant into a trope for anxieties and hopes provoked by increasing social mobility.[4] Yet the topos of service was also a very concrete point of reference for London audiences. Servants were a ubiquitous presence in early modern England, taking care of domestic and commercial affairs and labouring not only in the house, but also at the interfaces of household and market.[5] Peter Laslett discusses the example of a baker's household that includes various servants, from domestic maid-servants to apprentices and journeymen (1–3). For many people, service was a biographical interlude between childhood and marriage (hence the term 'life-cycle servant'), for others a permanent mode of existence.[6]

The previous chapter suggested that a crisis of authority in marriage could signal not only domestic, but also political disorder. The figure of the insubordinate servant also has broader social implications. The destabilizing potential of both servants and wives is grounded in the pervasive significance of social hierarchies in early modern England, as well as in the early modern analogy of government of house and state. This is not to say that wives and servants were interchangeable; the difference in their status was illustrated, for instance, in the analogy of the household body in which the wife features as trunk and the servants as hands and feet (Balizet 56). By virtue of her proximity to the household head, the wife was interpellated as not merely a subject, but also a cogovernor. Early modern writers insisted that the subordination of wife and servants to the master of the house meant different things. Judith Weil points out that, 'advice manuals often object to husbands who treat their wives like servants' (50). Yet in the end, both wife and servants were subjected to the master's will. Furthermore, just as the household

---

[3] This is also quoted in Don Herzog, *Household Politics: Conflict in Early Modern England* 150.

[4] Burnett contends that 'the ways in which servants are represented in English Renaissance drama and culture articulate some of the period's deepest sensitivities and aspirations, point to attempts to understand and control the changes that were challenging the contemporary order, and disclose fears of political instability, disorder and social frustration and unrest' (5).

[5] Catherine Richardson writes: '[T]he attention given to master-servant relations bears witness also to the ubiquity of servants and the practice of servant-keeping in society in this period. It was also a recognition of the indisputable fact that household servants underpinned the labour-intensive, hierarchical society of early modern England and were vital to its functioning and well-being' (*Household Servants* 127). See also Laslett 73 on the varying percentage of servants in different areas.

[6] Laslett 15. See also Herzog 148: 'Some spent their entire adult lives as servants. Many more worked as servants while teenagers and young adults'.

depended on the wife as a reliable helper and thrifty manager of household affairs, the servant's labour could play a significant part in its success or failure. Especially in the role of dependable surrogate, a servant was a potential asset who could contribute to the wealth of the *oikos*, but might also pose a serious risk as a potentially self-interested agent. The dangerous proximity and combined threat of a treacherous wife and a disloyal servant becomes tangible in *The Arden of Faversham*, which stages their murderous coalition.[7]

Bacon addresses the ambivalent position of the subservient surrogate in his Essay XLVII, 'Of Negociating'. In the very first sentence, he suggests that it is advantageous to use an intermediary in business negotiations: 'It is generally better to deale ... by the Mediation of a Third, then by a Mans Selfe' (145). These 'third men' must be equipped with a temperament and skills to match their tasks: 'Use also, such Persons, as affect the Businesse, wherin they are Employed; For that quickneth much; And such, as are Fit for the Matter; As Bold Men for Expostulation, Faire spoken Men for Perswasion, Craftie Men for Enquiry and Observation, Froward and Absurd Men for Businesse that doth not well beare out it Selfe' (146). Intermediaries must have the necessary qualities, but not be so cunning that they put their own ends before those of their masters. Bacon advises: 'In Choice of *Instruments*, it is better to choose Men of a Plainer Sort, that are like to doe that, that is committed to them, and to report back again faithfully the Successe; Then those that are Cunning to Contrive out of other Mens Businesse, somewhat to grace themselves; And will help the Matter, in Report, for Satisfaction sake' (146). Bacon's use of the term 'Instruments' diminishes the agency of these intermediaries and reminds readers of their main function: representing their masters' interests and facilitating exchanges. The master depends on the servant's loyalty and practical intelligence in managing some of the affairs that he cannot see to himself.[8] Hence, 'Prudence or Discretion' was a much-desired quality in a servant, but in a world in which prudence is aligned with interest rather than with ethics, practical wisdom is a double-edged sword.[9] One needed intelligent intermediaries to manage exchanges, but one wouldn't want them to question their place as subservient helpers. Both the efficacy of the cunning servant and the socio-economic hazard

---

[7] Frances E. Dolan comments on this threat in her book *Dangerous Familiars*: 'The violently rebellious servant was as threatening a figure as the murderous wife; indeed, the two were feared to conspire in petty treason' (59). The first chapter of the book explores in some detail 'the story of the plotting subordinates' (73) in *The Arden of Faversham*.

[8] In her definition of service, Weil associates it with dependency: 'Early modern service seems to have been defined through association with various forms of dependency' (1). Significantly, this formulation does not specify whether the master depends on the servant or the other way round.

[9] In his *A Systeme or Body of Divinity* (first published in 1654), Leigh highlights three qualities that commend a servant: '1. Diligence. 2. Obedience. 3. Prudence and Discretion' (827). And Thomas Tusser highlights the importance of prudence in servants by listing the 'retchlesse seruant' (20) as the first of six obstacles to thrift. The *OED* defines 'wretchless' in relation to people as 'Heedless, careless, imprudent' (1).

that he represents are exemplified by Face in *The Alchemist* and Iago in *Othello*, albeit in very different ways and with very different results.[10]

Jonson's benign comedy and Shakespeare's rather violent tragedy may, at first sight, appear an unlikely pairing. A closer look, however, reveals similar concerns about subordinate surrogates and their practical intelligence. Both *Othello* and *The Alchemist* explore the self-interested use of 'wisdom of business' in relations of service. In *The Alchemist*, the housekeeper Jeremy capitalizes on his master's absence. Iago has a military rank, but he also characterizes his relation to Othello as one of service, acting as his attendant in both domestic and military matters.[11] He enters and leaves Othello's household as he pleases, converses freely with both master and mistress, and is married to Desdemona's chambermaid Emilia. Both plays model their key characters, Iago and Face, on the cunning subordinate who pretends to represent his master's interests only to pursue his own.[12] Both men manipulate others affectively and shape their perceptions of value, whether in the form of hoped-for future wealth or present debasement. Both assume a domestic function, but their roles are inverted: Face helps his master to a new wife, while Iago works towards alienating Othello from his. Their wit and sense of self-empowerment propels them beyond the imaginative and moral bonds of service. For the greatest part of the plays, these self-reliant characters function as playmakers who drive and control the action. Like Lady Macbeth and the characters in Middleton's *A Chaste Maid*, they monopolize the audiences' attention with their ingenuity and wit despite their immoral behaviour.

The first part of this chapter discusses the peculiar constellation of the household in Jonson's *The Alchemist*. It explores the transformation of household into business and the creative energies that accompany this transformation. The housekeeper's usurpation of the place of the householder enables an impressive display of skills that suggests a post-Machiavellian shift: the emergence of a pragmatic, entrepreneurial, and self-interested form of prudence, a kind of 'wisdom of business'. Its mainstays are knowledge, versatile planning, and persuasive rhetoric. Jonson offers in this play an anatomy of mercantile agency that succeeds in selling a highly speculative and improbable product—a fiction of future wealth. With housekeeper Jeremy alias Captain Face, and with the master's house as the site of business transactions, Jonson situates mercantile agency within the *oikos*

---

[10] Hugh Grady notes for *Othello* that 'the dangerous mentality of instrumental rationality is inserted within "the dangerous classes": Iago is clearly of the subaltern class, and he greatly resents that status' (541).

[11] Burnett comments: 'It is striking that Iago, an "ancient" (ensign) and intimate of Othello, should conceive of his relationship according to a master and servant paradigm' (1). However, Neill explains that the early modern understanding of servant and service was broad enough to accommodate Iago in his role as subordinate ('Servant Obedience' 148).

[12] Their family resemblance is underlined by the fact that various critics have identified both figures separately as descendants of the Vice figure in morality plays (David Riggs and Anthony J. Ouellette discuss Face as a Vice figure 172 and 392, while Bernard Spivack, Leah Scragg, Catherine Belsey, and Anthony Brennan approach Iago as Vice, see note 103 in this chapter).

and accords it an ambiguous role. It threatens the stability and integrity of the household, but ultimately profits and enriches the master.

The second part of this chapter explores Iago's manipulations of affect and social credit in a mobile world. Reading *Othello* against *The Alchemist*'s exploration of mercantile agency on the part of a subordinate surrogate teases out the mercantile associations of Iago's actions as cunning servant and self-interested go-between. The chapter discusses his consummate command of an instrumental version of practical wisdom and interrogates his manipulation of social credit in the context of a dynamic society that is shaped by transnational movement and competition. My discussion links the easy manipulability of human worth to the early modern preoccupation with intrinsic and extrinsic dimensions of value and with the changing nature of value in exchange relations. Last but not least, the chapter suggests that jealousy and envy afford a glimpse into the affective condition of social mobility in an age of global trade.[13] In my analysis, *Othello* resonates with oeconomic and commercial concerns: from anxieties about disloyal servants to anxieties about property, value, and transnational traffic, from the affective framework of social mobility to the skills that enable commercial success.

The Household as 'Venture Tripartite': 'Wisdom of Business' in *The Alchemist*

With its very first scene, *The Alchemist* introduces the audience to a household in disarray, an unruly space that is more marketplace than home. Jeremy, the housekeeper, has set up shop in his master's house with a duo he has taken in from the streets of London: Dol Common, a prostitute, and Subtle, a pimp and rogue. This unlikely trio forms not just an unusual household, but a commercial venture in which the house and a generous dose of wit and theatrical talent function as capital. The three receive a series of clients who hope for wealth and social standing, luck at cards, the philosopher's stone, or gentlemanly skills. While the tricksters readily promise imminent satisfaction of all these desires, they defer delivery into a future that never comes. Thus, their business model consists in promising great but entirely fictive future successes in exchange for real coins. Jonson's earlier masterpiece, *Volpone*, presents a similar business scheme, which is discussed in the next chapter.

The starting point for the mercantile transformation of the house is a classical failure in household management. Jonson's acrostic argument identifies the master's desertion of the house as the key event which enables the tricksters' business as well as the ensuing action: 'The sickness hot, a master quit, for fear, / His house in

---

[13] My discussion of these affects profits from Natasha Korda's groundbreaking work on *Othello* in *Shakespeare's Domestic Economies*.

town: and left one servant there' (*Alch.*, 'The Argument' 1–2).¹⁴ As has been noted repeatedly, the plague anchors the play firmly in its historical present.¹⁵ Within the play, it creates a power vacuum which allows Jeremy to take possession of the house. With his master gone, Jeremy casts off his role as subordinate, assumes the identity of Captain Face, and uses the house as his own. The housekeeper, who is to represent his master's interest, has effectively replaced the master. Yet he lacks the master's authority: the 'venture tripartite' (1.1.135) is rooted in 'equality' (1.1.134), and Face has no right to command his new partners. In the quarrel of the first scene, Dol reminds the rogues that they have sworn to hold 'All Things in Common' and 'Without priority' (1.1.135–136).

This first scene showcases both the instability and entrepreneurial energy of a household in which a cunning servant and his cronies reinterpret oeconomy as a shareholding venture.¹⁶ It begins *in medias res* with a quarrel that presents the audience with different accounts of how the tricksters developed their business.¹⁷ The *ménage à trois* of Face, Subtle, and Dol is clearly at odds with the household's often-proclaimed binary order of authority and subjection. Instead of one master we have two rivals—Face and Subtle—with equal claims to the 'mistress' of the house. Dol is part of the estate that is at stake in the quarrel, but she is also a third and equal partner in their common venture. The absence of a higher power results in an unstable social structure that requires constant negotiation. While the 'venture tripartite' proves very successful in financial terms, the tricksters struggle to maintain an equilibrium of power because they are unable to subject their individual interests to a communal aim and strategy. The three parties form coalitions to outsmart one another and fight about 'primacy, in the divisions' (1.1.131). It appears that life within the house requires as much practical wisdom as the acquisition and management of the clients who enter it from outside.

Dol characterizes the community of the tricksters in political rather than oeconomic or mercantile terms. In analogy to the affairs of state, she reminds each of the men of their roles in a common venture. She chides Face like a lady disappointed in a trusted courtier: 'Nay, General, I thought you were civil' (1.1.88). She also paints the spectre of 'civil war' (1.1.82) and addresses Subtle as

---

¹⁴ Both classic and Christian writers advised householders against leaving the house unsupervised for long periods of time. Edward Topsell, preacher and author of *The House-Holder: or, Perfect Man*, urged his readers: 'wee should informe ourselues, of al our possessions, and not onely referre their care to our balyffes and stewards, who many time stake more paines to get our Liveriues & Badges, then to doe vs seruice and deserts' (104–105).

¹⁵ As Ouellette remarks, '"The Argument" is spoken as the plague rages in London' (381). See also Cheryl Lynn Ross, 'The Plague of *The Alchemist*' 439 and David Riggs, *Ben Jonson: A Life* 170–172.

¹⁶ See also Jonathan Haynes 33.

¹⁷ See also Katharine Eisaman Maus's 'Introduction to *The Alchemist*' in *English Renaissance Drama: A Norton Anthology*: '[W]hen hierarchical precedence is blurred and chains of command get tangled, turmoil ensues ... But in *The Alchemist*, disruption and opportunity go hand in hand. With the departure of the city's property-holding class, the group in which power traditionally rested, new social configurations are free to emerge—enterprises and alliances structured not by traditional bonds of kinship and class hierarchy, but by self-interest and the pursuit of profit' (861).

'Sovereign' (1.1.87) while identifying herself as 'your republic' (1.1.110). With these fragments of political discourse, she invokes civility as well as the reason-of-state rationality of political government to emphasize the need for courteous intercourse in pursuit of a common aim. By identifying herself as 'republic', she aligns herself with *res publica*, with connotations that range from the commonwealth as 'a form of association' (Turner, *The Corporate Commonwealth* 3) to the common good and shared property.[18] That the 'common thing' should speak and, moreover, with the voice of reason, has a comic effect.[19] It capitalizes on the absurdities of an oeconomic discourse which establishes the mistress of the house, paradoxically, as agent and object, as cogovernor and part of the estate. In Hesiod's famous description of the household, the wife ranks just before the ox as the second of three possessions that constitute a household: 'First and foremost a house, a woman, and an ox for the plough ...' (quoted in Aristotle, *Economics* 1343a21). Thus, the estate which is at stake in the quarrel entails Dol herself, the carnivalesque mistress of the house: as part of their reconciliation agreement, Face and Subtle decide to draw straws for who shall claim Dol for the night (1.1.178–179). The lack of civility in this scene betrays the low social origins of the tricksters, but Dol's reminders of political expediency in the unlikely setting of a roguish business signals the play's interest in a pragmatic form of prudence. 'Will you undo yourselves, with civil war?' (1.1.82), Dol asks the two men pointedly, and reminds them of their 'reputations' (1.1.109). If this first scene suggests that the tricksters fail where gentlemen might succeed in establishing civil intercourse, the developing action shows plainly that rhetorical and self-fashioning skills cannot be monopolized by a courtly elite.[20] After all, the tricksters' business relies *entirely* on such skills.

Dol Common is an immensely interesting version of the housewife. Not only does she join Lady Macbeth in highlighting the paradoxical demands to which the mistress of the house is subjected as cogovernor, subject, and part of the estate; as a prostitute (a 'doll' that is held in common), she also embodies the household's investment in exchange, its alignment with a commercial, profit-orientated venture. Prostitution contrasts sharply with the oeconomic aim of reproduction,

---

[18] The identification with the 'republic' may also be a nod to a popular theatrical tradition. In Nicholas Udall's *Respublica: An Interlude for Christmas 1553*, *Respublica* is also female and complains of social disorder (Christopher Warley, 'Reforming the Reformers: Robert Crowley and Nicholas Udall', 273–274). Henry S. Turner discusses '*Respublica*' as the philosophical name and concept of More's *Utopia* (*The Corporate Commonwealth* 3) and comments on the 'principle of common property' (7) on which Utopia is founded.

[19] Elizabeth Cook, in the notes to the New Mermaids edition, translates 'republic' as 'common thing' (35).

[20] 'The underclass rogue in many ways inverted the familiar image of the self-fashioned gentleman who has traditionally been the literary focus and exemplar of the age, but the two characters have more in common than courtiers or humanists would have admitted. Both relied on linguistic prowess and social dexterity to manage their careers, whether by exploiting the politics of privilege at court or surviving by their wits on urban streets' (Dionne and Mentz 1).

and the threesome muddles patrilineal genealogy. Dol's body is, however, not her main asset. Her quasi-professional theatrical skills contribute considerably to the success of the joint venture and turn her into an equal partner. At the same time as she functions as common property, Dol assumes authority. In the first scene, she manages the unruly rogues, partly through physical force (she disarms both men) and partly through persuasive speech. Her power is confirmed once more later in the play, when the two men agree to keep their interest in the wealthy young widow Pliant a secret from her. Henceforth, they keep each other in check with a highly effective form of blackmail: the ominous threat that they will tell Dol 'all' if the other refuses to cooperate.

In this 'venture tripartite', cooperation between the three tricksters is key to its success. Against readings that see *The Alchemist* purely as a scene for the emergence of 'the sovereign individual, the agent of capitalism and liberalism', Jennifer R. Rust highlights the play's interest in forms of 'collective life' (107).[21] Even Face, the trickster figure 'who is most capable of controlling the play' (Ouellette 380), is too entangled in various relations to appear as sovereign individual. First, he forms part of his master's household, then cofounds a communal enterprise that requires daily negotiations. Rather than acting alone, he creates strategic affiliations. In the end, he outwits Subtle and Dol not merely because he has the kind of mental quickness and flexibility that Bacon labels *versatile ingenium*, but because he realigns his interests with those of the master.[22] He resumes his place of service to enter into a relation of mutual government with his master, who declares: 'I will be ruled by thee in anything, Jeremy' (5.5.143). Jeremy/Face is independent and versatile enough to change his affiliations if need be and to occupy different places in the competing economies of household and shareholding enterprise. He may not be an entirely independent agent, but, as a versatile strategist with flexible affiliations, he creates room for self-authorized and self-interested action.

Titling himself 'General' and 'Captain', Face embodies the prudential but amoral mindset that aligns the successful businessman with skilled politicians and military men. His role within the trio is aptly summarized by Drugger, one of the clients: 'I pray you, speak for me to master Doctor' (1.3.20). Subtle is the alchemical doctor, but 'Captain' Face is the broker, the go-between, and as such offers a witty performance of that figure's mediating skills. It is Face who accesses the market of desires and brings clients to the house and who acquires useful information

---

[21] Rust's argument is based on the Foucauldian notion of pastoral conduct and forms of counter-conduct. She also sees alchemy in this context, rather than in a proto-capitalist context of the transformation of all things through the market (97): 'Alchemy is an extension of the pastoral art of government. It seeks to intensify and perfect what is inherent in people and things through a variety of tactics and technologies' (102).

[22] I borrow this notion from Bacon, who uses it both in his essays (e.g. Essay XL, 'Of Fortune' 123) and in *The Advancement of Learning* (172) to denote the mental flexibility and adaptability that one needs to succeed in a world of contingency.

in a truly Baconian manner.²³ He manages the outside relations of the roguish household. In the end, he will have fleeced the clients for his master, who returns to take possession of the accumulated wealth. By recognizing mercantile agency and private interest as forces within the individual household, the play suggests its firm integration into the market. If the 'venture tripartite' suggests how easily a household can be exploited by a self-interested subordinate, the ending portrays a master who profits from his servant's mercantile exertions. The master's happy acceptance of the unexpected wealth enriches the household and suspends any clear division between *oikos* and commercial venture. The mercantile transformation of the household has a lasting effect, even after the demise of the trickster's business.

In the following two sections and before turning to the trope of alchemy, I want to highlight aspects that align Face with a pragmatic and profitable form of prudence. Bacon's 'wisdom of business' and a contemporary military model of prudence serve to establish Face's entrepreneurial and business-savvy agency. It is notable that Face styles himself as a captain, since Bacon himself makes use of that figure to explain the particular kind of knowledge that constitutes 'wisdom of business'. As Lorna Hutson demonstrates, in the sixteenth century 'classical military history ... afforded a fund of metaphors for the unfamiliar cerebral processes involved in the definition of prudence and the experience of enterprise' (109). Machiavelli himself, the patron of political prudence, had written *The Art of War* (first published in 1521), a major work on military craft and strategy. The proximity between politics and military strategy is also apparent in *The Prince*.²⁴ Military prudence was thus readily available as a model for practical wisdom in other contexts. The first section below discusses knowledge, distrust, and *versatile ingenium* as key qualities of the prudent captain, while the second part turns to amplification as a rhetorical strategy. My discussion of *The Alchemist* concludes with an investigation into the tropical implications of the alchemical laboratory and returns to the play's coupling of practical wisdom with service.

The Prudent Captain

As part of his transformation from domestic servant to independent businessman, Face assumes a military title and goes out and about in the city, gathering intelligence and identifying gullible clients. As Ken Jacobsen points out, clever

---

²³ Edward B. Partridge points out that Face remains '[t]o the very end ... the business man, giving the monthly report of the companies with whom he has "traded", and keeping a sharp eye on those with whom he will trade in the future' (161).
²⁴ See Machiavelli, chapter 14: 'Thus, a prince should have no other object, nor any other thought, nor take anything else as his art but that of war and its orders and discipline; for that is the only art which is of concern to one who commands' (*The Prince* 58).

reconnaissance is also a military virtue: '*The Art of War* repeatedly emphasises the importance of knowing the enemy intimately' (507). In his discussion of 'wisdom of business', Bacon similarly stresses the importance of information. As worldly success is achieved in negotiations and transactions with others, the first step towards success involves gathering intelligence about one's partners and competitors:

> First therefore the precept which I conceiue to bee most summary, towardes the preuayling in fortune; is ... to procure good informacions of particulars touching persons, their Natures, their desires & ends, their customs and fashions, theyr helpes and aduantages, and wherby they cheefly stand ...
>
> (*The Advancement* 165)

That the concern with knowledge extends both to military and business matters is no coincidence. Like military action, 'wisdom of business' is concerned with the particular rather than with the universal, and relies on information about concrete circumstances. In the absence of a 'windowe' into men's hearts (*The Advancement* 165), as Bacon put it rather poetically, the art of negotiation demands 'good informations' and attentive observation to determine the right course of action. Bacon compares information and observation to the premises of a logical syllogism, suggesting that deductions about others must rest on the firm ground of positive facts.[25] The conscious acquisition and use of information demands a suspicious frame of mind, because the aim is not least to find out what the other might wish to withhold. Hence, 'the Synewes of wisedom, are slownesse of beleefe and distrust' (*The Advancement* 166).

Just like a veritable Baconian and worthy of his military title, Jeremy 'procure[s] good informations' about the tricksters' clients in the open terrain of the city, where he baits men intent on making their fortunes:

> FACE. ... I am at no expense,
> In searching out these veins, then following 'em,
> Then trying 'em out. 'Fore God, my intelligence
> Costs me more money, than my share oft comes to,
> In these rare works.
>
> (1.3.105–109)

The notion of 'veins' hints at the unearthing of precious metals: information, this extended metaphor suggests, can itself be turned into coin. In the case of the

---

[25] 'These Informations of particulars, touching persons and actions, are as the *minor* propositions in euery actiue syllogisme, for no excellencye of obseruacions (which are as the *maior* propositions) can suffice to ground a conclusion, if there be error and mistaking in the minors' (Bacon, *The Advancement* 165).

tobacco seller Drugger, the second client who enters the house in Act One, Scene Three, good information is key in convincing him of Subtle's divinatory powers. Subtle, acting the part of the 'Doctor' who commands the dark arts, convinces Drugger that he is in for great riches by displaying his knowledge of particular facts: 'Y'were born upon a Wednesday?' (1.3.51). He knows that Drugger is waiting for an inborne merchant's vessel and that he nourishes secret ambitions to become 'a great distiller' (1.3.78). All this information has, of course, been acquired by Face prior to Drugger's visit. It is mixed in with a dose of retrospective prophecy and a pinch of false hope: Subtle claims that it was predestined by the stars that Drugger 'should be a merchant, and should trade with balance' (1.3.57). The mixture of particular facts and commonplaces with which the tricksters confront Drugger persuades him that there are even greater riches in store for him than he had hoped for. As Face not merely excels in procuring information about the clients, but is also able to converse easily and learnedly about any topic, he is an ideal middleman: a master of 'effective social knowledge' (Haynes 35) who can manage any negotiation, whether for himself or on behalf of others.

In Bacon's writings, the need for information and necessary distrust in the absence of a window into men's hearts combine to form a hermeneutics of suspicion.[26] In *The Alchemist*, both tricksters and clients are intent on making their fortune, yet only Jonson's tricksters know the value of information and even approach each other with the distrust Bacon commends. The clients, in contrast, lack the sceptical frame of mind necessary for making one's fortune. Incapable of informed decisions and strategic action, and unacquainted with the Baconian imperative of distrust, they are blind to the tricksters' duplicitous intentions. Only Surly, the companion of the gullible Sir Epicure Mammon, is similarly distrustful. Instead of acting as a moral force, however, he is as devious as the tricksters themselves and angles for the rich widow.[27]

A military model of prudence values not only intelligence, but also a sense of initiative and providential planning that can be extended to 'wisdom of business'. This is evident in Bacon's use of a military precept from Demosthenes in *The Advancement of Learning* (first published in 1605): 'And just as it is accepted that a general leads the army, so should wise men lead affairs so that those things are done which they think should be done, and they are not forced to follow events.'[28] Bacon combines this military model of the providential strategist with a passage on versatility, on how one must 'runne with the occasions' (*The Advancement* 173), to arrive at

---

[26] Elizabeth Hanson's work on the Renaissance subject establishes this preoccupation with 'distrust' as a paradigm of discovery that is pervasive enough to amount to 'an epistemic change': 'a redrafting of the terms on which the subject relates to the world in dominant political, religious, and intellectual discourses' (*Discovering the Subject* 2). In Pye's clever account of Hanson's hypothesis, the early modern subject emerges as 'a function of the scene of discovery' (*The Vanishing* 5).

[27] See Peggy Knapp: 'Surly, though undeceived, gets no noble speeches and no comic victory over deceit' ('Ben Jonson' 173).

[28] The Latin quotation is on 173, the translation in the Commentary on 350.

a model of 'wisdom of business' that implies both an ability to plan and an ability to adapt those plans skilfully when needed:

> For if we obserue, we shall find two differing kinds of sufficiency, in managing of businesse: some can make vse of occasions aptly and dexterously, but plot little; some can vrge and pursue their owne plottes well, but cannot accommodate nor take in: either of which is very vnperfite without the other.
>
> (*The Advancement* 173)[29]

Only the *combination* of effective planning and versatile adaptation to changing circumstances promises success 'in managing of businesse'. Bacon describes '*Versatile Ingenium*' in terms of a mind that 'is pliaunt and obedient to occasion' (*The Advancement* 172). His emphasis on versatility mirrors that of Machiavelli in chapter 25 of *The Prince*: 'he is happy who adapts his mode of proceeding to the qualities of the times; and similarly, he is unhappy whose procedure is in disaccord with the times' (99).

In *The Usurer's Daughter*, Hutson discusses the 'figure of the "prudent captain"' (108) to outline the combination of strategy and versatility in military prudence:

> Unlike the knight errant, who simply fights and follows the chivalric code, the captain responsible for soldiers on a military campaign embodies the very imperative that makes prudential activity—that is, the constant and unceasing emplotment of present circumstances to prevent future disaster and ensure good fortune—a habit of the mind.
>
> (108)

Emplotment implies temporal orientation and strategic planning—relating present circumstances to a desired future outcome—but also the ability to adapt a plan to changing circumstances. This resonates with Sir Thomas Elyot's account of prudence in *The Boke, Named the Gouernor*: 'Prudence involves circumspection,

---

[29] Early modern usages of plot suggest a link between spatial modelling and conceptual planning (Bacon's meaning). In early modern usage, plot referred to a piece of ground used for building or gardening (*OED* I.1.a.), but it could also refer to a map or ground plan (II.3.b.), to an outline of a literary work (II.3.a.), a plan of a dramatic work (II.6.), and, last but not least, to a scheme or clever plan (II.4.). Martin Brückner and Kristen Poole have argued that the literary notion of plot emerged with and was influenced by the development of surveying and building practices in early modern England: 'The proliferation of surveying manuals in the 1580s and 1590s fostered a new structural sensibility ... audiences are trained to read, write, and imagine text as a mappable, structured space' (630). Sir Philip Sidney's *An Apology for Poetry* draws on the spatial origins of plot and its use as a model when he describes narration 'as an imaginative ground-plot of a profitable invention' (124). A milestone on the way from the two-dimensional ground plan to the structure of dramatic action was the theatrical plat, which implied a spatial and temporal plan: 'An elaborate chart of dramatic action, including the all important stage entrances and exits ... to provide guidance for actors during a performance' (Brückner and Poole 635). Brückner and Poole also suggest that these plats or plots made their way to the printer, 'perhaps becoming a textual companion to performance' (637). In their account, the narrative plot evolved from the theatrical plat (630).

providence, opportunity, and the ability to "beholde and foresee the successe of our enterpryse"' (Hutson 106; Elyot 71v). Elyot explained circumspection with a spatial analogy to Quintus Fabius Maximus's strategy of moving his soldiers 'along high ground' (Hutson 107). The resulting metaphor of overview is spatial as well as temporal. According to Hutson, Elyot translates this 'into a graphic metaphor for the mental ability to assume a position of pragmatic vantage with regard to any situation' (107): circumspection means 'beholding on euery parte, what is well and sufficient, what lacketh, how, & from whence it may be prouided', but also 'what hath caused profitte or damage in the tyme passed, what is the estate of the time present, what aduantage or peril may succeede, or is imminent' (Elyot 74v).

Besides circumspection and versatility, Hutson highlights another crucial aspect of prudence: rhetoric as the skill that enables the prudent captain to persuade others of a plan or a change of plans. The emplotment of unforeseen events has an important rhetorical dimension which is prefigured in military history, where 'the conceptual organization of resources for action and their probable justification in discourse' (Hutson 107) go hand in hand.[30] Strategic emplotment means to make use *and* sense of unforeseen changes; it is both a matter 'of practical policy (courses of action) and of persuasive arguments to justify that policy (counsel)' (106). In the enterprise of emplotment, dissimulation is a legitimate tool. Machiavelli advised the prudent captain to dissimulate events that might instil fear in his soldiers: 'If in the fight it happens to you that some accident frightens your soldiers, knowing how to dissimulate it and pervert it for good is a very prudent thing' (*Art of War* 91).[31] By way of example, Machiavelli tells the story of Tullus Hostilius (91). In the middle of a fight, some of his soldiers changed over to the enemy's side and his remaining men lost heart, but he reassured them by announcing that these apparent traitors had followed his very own orders. As a result, his men regained courage and carried the day.

In *The Alchemist*, Face as prudent captain oversees the off-stage terrain of the city. At the same time, true to his former role as housekeeper, he controls the on-stage space of the house. The management of the restricted space of the house in relation to time as the dimension of developing events proves particularly demanding. As the plot progresses, the tricksters struggle to maintain spatial, temporal, and conceptual oversight as they have to accommodate different clients in ways that prevent any unwanted encounters.[32] The excessive traffic of clients that turn up unexpectedly underlines the strain that contingent events impose upon a business

---

[30] Jacobsen also identifies this connection: 'Machiavelli argues that "it is necessary that a general should be an orator as well as a soldier," one who addresses his army to change its resolution and "mold it to his purposes" (*War*, 127–28)' (505).

[31] See also Hutson 109.

[32] As Ian Donaldson notes, 'the time-scheme of the play is organized with extraordinary precision, plotted to the very moment. For most of the characters ... time itself is a matter of the deepest consequence, always at the forefront of their consciousness' (*Jonson's Magic Houses* 89). Turner emphasizes the spatial constraints of the play when he points out that 'the *entire* action' takes place 'within the

plan, yet Face always manages to turn potentially harmful events into opportunities. This is a sure sign of *versatile ingenium*. For those who lack this flexibility of mind, an occasion passes all too quickly, as Bacon reminds his readers graphically in Essay XXI, 'Of Delayes': *'Occasion ... turneth a Bald Noddle, after she hath presented her locks in Front, and no hold taken'* (68).

There is, of course, a distinctly theatrical quality to Face's orchestration of his clients' exits and entrances: *his* plot is also a quasi-theatrical plat that maps movements in an accelerating chain of events. In the first three acts of *The Alchemist*, the clients enter the house one by one, but towards the end of the third act, events pick up speed, and succession turns into simultaneity. The space of the house has to accommodate different clients who must not encounter each other: Dapper is stowed away 'I' the privy' (3.5.78), Dol entertains Mammon in 'The garden, or great chamber above' (4.1.172), and Subtle instructs Kastril and his sister Pliant upstairs (4.2.59). Meanwhile, the Spanish Don alias Surly enters the house and is subjected to xenophobic ridicule (4.3). As Act Four progresses, the tricksters' efforts to keep track of their clients' positions and movements reach new heights of sophistication. With the meeting of the Spanish Don and Dame Pliant on the one hand, and, on the other, Mammon, Dol, and Subtle, a plot that threatened to become irredeemably entangled promises to be resolved. This resolution becomes more and more pressing as the future turns into the present and the clients expect delivery of the promised objects. John Shanahan describes the invariable progress of time in *The Alchemist*: 'Time cannot stretch, it will not disappear in dances or masques, and it barely weakens its hold in brief moments of psychological reverie' (40).[33] To borrow from *Timon of Athens*, we might say that in *The Alchemist*, too, 'the future comes apace' (*Tim.* 2.2.148), unfolding in an unstoppable series of events that must be managed.

The convergence of the clients at the house showcases the tricksters' ability to emplot unforeseen events in ways that turn them into real opportunities. Bacon describes the danger of dissimulation as the threat of getting caught in one's own web, and it appears that the same warning applies to plotting (*The Advancement* 173).[34] The risk of entanglement is very real, but by skilful emplotment of unforeseen events, the tricksters manage to keep this danger at bay. Their command of the clients' spatial movements and their versatile adaptation to unforeseen events enable the different subplots to resolve each other. Mammon's amorous pursuit of the learned but mad Lady (impersonated by Dol) serves as pretence to let the

---

"groundplat" of Lovewit's London house' (*The English Renaissance Stage* 265). Although there are actually a few scenes that play out in the street in front of the house, this spatial constraint is remarkable.

[33] R. L. Smallwood points out that the 'constant impression of living on borrowed time is part of the play's theatrical self-consciousness' (151).

[34] The commentary translates the Latin quotation as follows: 'Dissimulation breeds mistakes in which the deceiver himself is caught' (350).

nearly perfected philosopher's stone combust. The Spanish Don lends plausibility to Kastril's conviction that his sister will marry a lord and, later, provides an opportunity to practice his fighting skills. The comic scene involving the Spanish Don thrives on the audience's xenophobic impulses, even if its real target remains ambiguous: the butt of the jokes is not only the 'Spaniard', but also the tricksters themselves, who do not recognize their compatriot Surly behind the masquerade. In the end, Face outwits his two accomplices by convincing them of a change of plans that is necessitated by the master's sudden return. Just a little later, with yet another turn of the screw, he changes the story once more and tells his former associates that he, in fact, had asked his master to return: 'I sent for him, indeed' (5.4.129). Thus, he establishes himself as the prime emplotter of the trio who is still—at least rhetorically—in control of unfolding events.

In the context of military prudence, Jeremy's self-stylization as 'Captain Face' draws attention to his skills: his strategic acquisition of information, his versatile emplotment of contingent events, and his spatial and temporal overview. Face is versatile enough to adapt his plan (or plot) to changing circumstances and persuade others of a changed course of action. The model of the prudent captain allows us to draw a parallel to *Othello*'s Iago. While the figure of Iago clearly borrows from the trope of domestic servant as trickster, Face draws on military contexts.[35] Like Face—though perhaps less surprising in the military setting of *Othello*—Iago sets himself up as military practitioner, whose practical knowledge far surpasses that of the 'great arithmetician' Cassio (*Oth.* 1.1.18),[36] who 'never sat a squadron in the field / Nor the division of a battle knows / More than a Spinster—' (1.1.21–23). Iago here, to quote Neill, 'dismisses Cassio as a mere pen pusher or accountant' (*Othello* 180).[37] James Siemon adds another important level of meaning both to Captain Face and the ensign Iago when he points out that the military was associated with self-made men: it 'provided opportunities for even the meanest born individual to rise "from the cart, to be a sovereign captain" on the basis of merit' (180).[38] Their alignment with the military establishes both Iago and Face as experienced practitioners and prudential agents who seek to rise in the world in defiance of their lowly origins and in tension with the virtues of service.[39]

---

[35] See Burnett on the tradition of the male domestic servant as trickster type, 80–84.
[36] Jodi Coral points out that Iago uses 'the language and calculus of double-entry bookkeeping and the new arithmetic which in the period came to be associated with merchants and global trade' (288). In 'Cassio, Cash, and the "Infidel 0": Arithmetic, Double-entry Bookkeeping, and *Othello*'s Unfaithful Accounts', Patricia Parker argues that '*Othello* goes out of its way to invoke arithmetical "reckoning"' (226) and that the association with 'arithmetic' in this play 'activates within *Othello* the sense of an "infidel" usury ... both monetary and sexual' (227).
[37] The quotation is taken from Neill's annotations of *The Oxford Shakespeare: Othello: The Moor of Venice* 198, n.30.
[38] Siemon discusses here George Whetstone, *The Honourable Reputation of a Soldier*.
[39] Grady addresses Iago's 'characteristic evacuation of values' that culminates in his well-known exclamation: 'Virtue, a fig!' (539–540).

Persuasion through Amplification

As noted above, persuasive rhetoric is an integral part of 'emplotment'. It is key to Jeremy's transformation from servant to salesman and go-between, and it guarantees the tricksters' economic success. The plausibility of their highly speculative product—the alchemical stone, wealth, luck, and social credit—depends exclusively on words. Their use of amplification as a rhetorical strategy deserves special consideration, because it is the main instrument with which they manipulate the clients' desires. Furthermore, it exposes the workings of greed: with its tendency towards hyperbole, amplification is singularly suited to stimulate and intensify acquisitive desire. Although this desire is itself an irrational passion, recognition of its pervasive influence renders the clients and their actions calculable and allows the tricksters to manipulate them. It opens up that window into a man's soul that Bacon misses in *The Advancement of Learning*. As their deliberate use of amplification demonstrates, the tricksters know very well what is going on in the innermost hearts of their clients.

Amplification develops its force on the level of *pathos*. In Book One of the *Rhetoric*, Aristotle described three modes of persuasion (*Rhet.* I.2, 1358a1–4). Persuasion can be achieved by logical argument (*logos*), by means of the speaker's own character (*ethos*), and by inducing an emotion in the listener (*pathos*). In *The Alchemist*, *ethos* is a matter of performative self-display: Subtle, for instance, plays the role of the virtuous Doctor, while the neighbours all agree that 'Jeremy is a very honest fellow' (5.3.37–38). His social credit is remarkable: in the eyes of the neighbours, he must be telling the truth, even when their own sense perceptions contradict his version of events (Haynes 39). Yet the tricksters achieve persuasion mostly through *pathos*: they manipulate the passions of their clients and provoke the excessive streak that ancient and early modern writers ascribed to them. They whet their clients' acquisitive appetite by consistently promising *more* than the clients ask for. According to Thomas Wilson in *The Art of Rhetoric* (first published in 1553), 'Amplification is a figure in rhetoric which consisteth most in augmenting and diminishing of any matter, and that divers ways' (152). It moves the affections or passions, which are 'none other thing but a stirring or forcing of the mind either to desire or else to detest and loathe anything more vehemently than by nature we are commonly wont to do' (160). In the 1593 edition of Henry Peacham's rhetorical handbook *The Garden of Eloquence* (first published in 1577), amplification serves 'to delight and perswade the mindes of men to the purpose and drift of the speaker' (121). Peacham emphasizes the power of amplification to move the affections (121). In *The Alchemist*, it turns moderate ambitions into excessive desires. The tricksters promise plenty of valuable things and describe a glorious future of inconceivably great fortunes as if it were just on the horizon. Of course, rhetorical amplification never materializes into actual gain for the clients; it achieves only an increase in coin for the tricksters. That the clients respond so easily to amplification establishes acquisitive desire as a passion that hijacks reason: the clients will believe anything if it appeals to their appetite for riches and social success.

Dapper, the clerk and the tricksters' first client, exemplifies how the tricksters work the passions with the promise of yet more wealth. Dapper arrives at the house with a fairly modest desire for luck at games: he seeks 'a familiar' (1.2.80) to win at 'cups and horses' (1.2.83). Subtle hesitates visibly in granting his request, letting on to Face (and allowing it to be overheard by Dapper) that Dapper will have far greater success at games than he envisions: 'He'll draw you all the treasure of the realm, / If it be set him' (1.2.102–103). This hyperbolic augmentation of wealth does the trick. When Face—playing Dapper further—explains to Subtle that Dapper only asks for some modest amusement at the end of the workday, Dapper has already internalized the prospect foreseen by Subtle as his heart's own desire. Warming to the idea of easy gain, he concludes that it is time for a career change: 'I do think, now, I shall leave the law' (1.2.91). Initially willing to pay 'Four angels' (1.2.37) for his 'familiar', Dapper is so overcome by the prospect of *unlimited* winnings that he offers the tricksters a share in his future successes. For obvious reasons, this does not satisfy the tricksters. Offering a bet on the future constitutes their very own business model, and their client's future wealth is, after all, only guaranteed by their own false prophecies. In the outrageous climax of this particular scene, the tricksters identify Dapper as nephew of the Fairy Queen, who is impersonated by Dol. Over the moon with his illustrious family ties, Dapper happily pays another angel upfront. For the tricksters, exaggeration translates directly into profit. In a similar vein, they raise the hopes of another client, Drugger. They employ a rhetoric of proportionality, which emphasizes the great quantity of future gain in order to extract more money from their client: 'A crown! And toward such a fortune? Heart, / Thou shalt rather gi' him thy shop. No gold about thee?' (1.3.85–86). This insistence on requital proportionate to 'such a fortune' is comic because more insubstantial promises hardly generate greater wealth—more of zero is still zero.

The tricksters combine the rhetorical accumulation of wealth with a visual mode of representation that portrays a desired future state as if it were already happening. Their grooming of yet another client, Kestril, is particularly revealing. He desires not wealth but a gentlemanly habitus. Yet Face manages to shift Kestril's desire towards credit and conspicuous consumption as markers of social distinction. Face baits the foolish young man with the verbal description of a viewing device that transposes a desired future into a visualized present:

> FACE. He'll show a perspective, where on one side
>   You shall behold the faces, and the persons
>   Of all sufficient young heirs, in town,
>   Whose bonds are current for commodity;

> On th'other side, the merchants' forms, and others,
> That, without help of any second broker,
> (Who would expect a share) will trust such parcels:
> In the third square, the very street, and sign
> Where the commodity dwells, and does but wait
> To be delivered, be it pepper, soap,
> Hops, or tobacco, oatmeal, woad, or cheeses.
> All which you may so handle, to enjoy,
> To your own use, and never stand obliged.
>
> (3.4.87–99)

Face's description translates the dealings between merchants and gentlemen and the vibrant exchange of luxury commodities into the eternal presence of pictorial representation. This is true to Peacham's definition of *descriptio* in *The Garden of Eloquence*, a figure with which 'the Orator ... doth express and set forth a thing so plainely and liuely, that it seemeth rather painted in tables, then declared with words' (134). Detailed and visual description is a means of rhetorical amplification.[40] Thomas Wilson's *Art of Rhetoric* also describes visualizing an event and describing it as if it were presently happening as a figure of amplification which affects and moves people. Wilson terms this ornamental figure 'An Evident, or Plain, Setting-Forth of a Thing as Though It Were Presently Done' (203). Face's description stirs affections just as Wilson advises: 'In moving affections and stirring the judges to be grieved, the weight of the matter must be so set forth as though they saw it plain before their eyes' (161).[41] With his detailed visual description, Face presents 'the entire urban market for consumer goods ... in an instant' (Turner, *The English Renaissance Stage* 267). He begins in the future tense, suggesting that the 'Doctor' *will* show Kestril this 'perspective', but then proceeds to describe this event as if it were happening in the present.

The 'Setting-Forth of a Thing as Though It were Presently Done' is a crucial tool of persuasion in the tricksters' business. The ambiguity of 'presently' is distinctive: by describing something as if it were currently (presently) happening, such setting-forth evokes the sense that it is really just about to happen (presently).[42] To render promised riches as if they were already in sight is to brush over the uncertainty of future wealth. The result, however, is not just a heightening of expectations, but also a heightening of *present* pleasure by means of the verbal accumulation of riches. Mammon, who has been groomed by the tricksters for

---

[40] Peacham distinguishes various figures of amplification: 'Distribution, Description, Comparison, and Collection' (121).

[41] Wilson is here particularly (though by no means exclusively) concerned with judicial oratory (133).

[42] Gail Kern Paster suggests that Jonson satirizes especially the clients' expectation 'that actuality can ever be more than actuality, that a city can be other than the sum of everyday' (*The Idea of the City* 165).

some time, gorges himself on his very own rhetoric. In Act Two, Scene Three, he produces an inventory of imagined riches:

> MAMMON. My meat, shall all come in, in Indian shells,
>   Dishes of agate, set in gold, and studded,
>   With emeralds, sapphires, hyacinths, and rubies.
>   The tongues of carps, dormice, and camels' heels,
>   Boiled i' the spirit of Sol, and dissolved pearl,
>   (Apicius' diet,' gainst the epilepsy)
>   And I will eat these broths, with spoons of amber,
>   Headed with diamant, and carbuncle.
>
> (2.2.72–79)

The possessive pronoun 'my' introduces this acquisitive fantasy. The exotic inventory at once intensifies and indulges desire, ending with a fantasy of costly consumption. It combines 'description' with 'collection' and gives verbal presence to valuable objects. Alvin Kernan draws attention to 'the incredible density of *things* which Jonson rams into his plays' ('Base Metal Into Gold' 165). Language, in his analysis of *The Alchemist*, is the alchemical stone per se—a means to transform 'base matter into gold' (168). In my analysis, language is a means to channel various desires into an overarching acquisitive urge, a transformation that is further discussed in the next section.

With Sir Epicure Mammon, the 'romantic merchant venturer' (Partridge 158) who travels the colonies in his imaginative vision of wealth, and Kastril, the would-be gentleman, Jonson explores the nature of desire as directed towards ever-greater quantities. Desire's particular mode of satisfaction, as Henry S. Turner rightly notes, lies in the infinite multiplication of objects (*The English Renaissance Stage* 268), 'in desire's simple power to invent and thus draw into consciousness an inexhaustible series of satisfactions' (269) that can never appease desire. Mammon's investment in excess may be related to the fact that the tricksters have already been grooming him for a month. Yet even his appetite is whetted afresh with the ludicrous suggestion of a second philosopher's stone (2.3.54–55). This is deliberately excessive, because even one stone—if it existed at all—would generate more wealth than Mammon could ever spend. Yet Mammon's eagerness demonstrates how easily acquisitive desire responds to amplification, to the promise of ever more wealth. It is because such desire is itself excessive, without limits.

In *The Alchemist*, persuasion emerges as a mercantile skill and one that is as needful for business as for politics or warfare. Early modern writers were well aware of the manipulative power of rhetoric. In 1601, John Wheeler addressed the power of words in his frenzied account of commerce:

> this man maketh merchandise of the workes of his owne handes, this man of another mans labour, one selleth woordes, another maketh trafficque of the skins,

and blood of other men, yea there are some sound so subtill and cunning merchantes, that they perswade and induce men to suffer themselues to bee bought and solde, and we haue seene in our time enowe, and too manie, which haue made marchandise of mens soules ...

(3)

In his description, anything can be turned into a commodity. Wheeler lists words as things that can be sold (think, for instance, of commercial playwriting), but, more importantly, he addresses persuasive speech as medium of commercial exchange. Persuasion's investment in rhetoric is indicated by 'subtle sound' and its manipulative aspect by 'cunning merchantes'. Wheeler identifies persuasion with the work of the devil, who buys men's souls and adopts a warning tone—'we have seen ... enowe, and too manie'—that is remarkable because he appears to endorse and applaud commerce in all other aspects. In his *Essay of Drapery* from 1635, William Scott walks a tightrope when he balances the need to be truthful with the use of rhetoric in the service of successful sales. Although Scott argues that 'However the Dresse be, Truth is constantly the same' (90), he promotes an efficient use of rhetoric. A citizen should be eloquent, 'his words should flow from his mouth' as honey (89) and be adapted 'according to the nature of him with whom he commerceth' (91). That persuasive speech has the power to secure a sale is here implied. Thus, in mercantile matters, rhetoric occupies a precarious position between crucial skill and corruptive instrument. In Bacon's discussion of 'wisdom of business', words occupy a similarly ambiguous position: potentially deceptive, but useful in manipulating others and gaining information. The first meaning is well expressed in Bacon's commonplace warning that 'words and discourse aboundeth moste, where there is idleness and want' (*The Advancement* 161). Other commonplaces might be understood as offering advice about language use, for instance: 'flatterye and insinuation' work best when spoken with a 'shewe of nature, libertie, and simplicity' (161). Bacon also commends the effects of words, especially in combination with passion in opening people up and forcing them to speak truth (166–167).

The Alchemical Trope

The Alchemist stages a transformation from household to business that requires neither capital nor a substantial product, but thrives on wit, skill, and fantastic promises. The tricksters' clients are deeply invested in the multifarious epistemologies of medieval and early Renaissance thought, which accommodate such diverse instruments as helpful spirits, the philosopher's stone, and geometric diagrams. Turner reminds us that *The Alchemist* examines 'the many operative and quasi-empirical modes of knowledge that flourished prior to the "new science" of the seventeenth century' (*The English Renaissance Stage* 265). In contrast to the clients, the tricksters deploy these epistemologies strategically and as a form of social knowledge: they know which suggestions will work with each client. As lowly characters, they transgress the confines of social status, adopting different identities and displaying an ingenuity and entrepreneurial energy that far exceeds the 'Renaissance meaning' of subject, which stresses 'the subordination of the governed' (Hanson, *Discovering the Subject* 2). Their creative use of limited resources signals the transformation of prudence from the intellectual virtue that allows people to navigate changing circumstances in morally unimpeachable ways to the inventive and versatile use of facts and fortunate occasions, of rhetoric and dissimulation.

In this play, theatre itself functions as a laboratory. With its parade of clients, the play sets up a series of encounters to showcase how the business-savvy tricksters play on and with desire—even if their use of 'wisdom of business' is itself driven by the desire to make a fortune. Jonson's intellectually versatile and rhetorically persuasive tricksters are not just witty and reckless: their existence as protagonists on the early modern stage suggests a heightened interest in men who take their fate in hand and push beyond the limits of traditional epistemologies, ethical prescriptions, and social structures. At the same time, the alchemical laboratory provides a setting in which the motivational force and excessive nature of private interest can be explored. *The Alchemist*'s serial performance of trickster-client interactions suggests a specific anthropology of desire: it appears that all desires are at bottom directed at unlimited wealth and the possibilities of consumption and social advancement that come with it.[43] Bacon's interest in 'pressing a mans owne fortune' (*The Advancement* 163) emerges as a pervasive rather than isolated preoccupation, as interesting to London audiences as to the statesman and philosopher.

The nature of private interest is symbolized by the alchemical laboratory. The laboratory is a transformational space, but in Subtle's characterization of the alchemical process, it does not create anything new. Rather, it actualizes a potential that is already there. Surly ridicules alchemy by comparing the making of gold to the hatching of chickens, and Subtle counters by suggesting that turning base metals into gold is actually easier than hatching eggs because any metal has the potential to be gold:

> SUBTLE. Why, I think that the greater miracle.
> No egg, but differs from a chicken, more,
> Than metals in themselves.

---

[43] Donaldson suggests that desire for wealth in *The Alchemist* is also a desire for a social 'transmutation' into a person of higher rank (*Ben Jonson* 247). Donaldson writes: 'Jonson brilliantly combines the central premiss and promise of alchemy, that of transmutation, with a major preoccupation of the day, social mobility. Those who call to see the wise man at his house in Blackfriars all wish in some way to be transformed, as the metals themselves are said to be transformed by the alchemical process' (247–248). As he also claims that social transformation is here 'driven entirely by gold' (248), these are hardly distinct desires, but amount to much the same thing.

SURLY. That cannot be.
The egg's ordained by nature, to that end:
And is a chicken in *potentia*.
SUBTLE. The same we say of lead, and other metals,
Which would be gold, if they had time.

(2.3.130–136)

In teasing out the very substance of 'mature' metal, its gold essence, alchemy affords a trope for the clients' desires.[44] The clients' initial desires are diverse enough to render the ultimate reduction of possible ends to the prospect of wealth noteworthy: initially, Dapper cares about cards, Drugger about a thriving business, Mammon about consumption, Kastril about duelling and nobility, and Surly about the truth. Thanks to Face and Subtle, Dapper's and Drugger's desires are redirected towards great riches, while Mammon hopes for unlimited wealth—a fantasy that reconciles consumption with accumulation because unlimited wealth will never be spent. Kastril is baited with unlimited credit, and Surly develops designs on the rich widow. In the end, the differences between individual desires are superficial as the play builds a case for the pervasive sway of material gain as the key motivation behind economic exchanges. This is quite in line with Malynes's formula for gain as a motor of trade in *The Center of the Circle of Commerce* from 1623: 'Nothing doth force Trade but Gaine' (53). As the alchemical process departs from the hypothesis that all metals are gold *in potentia*, *The Alchemist* suggests that all passions are versions of, or at least rely on, an acquisitive desire which is coaxed out in the transformational space of the market.[45] With its persuasive promise of unlimited opportunities of wealth and unlimited possibilities of consumption, the market channels all desires into an acquisitive urge.

With Face, Jonson's play stages the transition of a household subordinate into an agent who serves his own interests. Rather than being driven by greed, however, Face acts rationally enough not to risk everything for the sake of gain. In the end, he reintegrates himself into the traditional social hierarchy and asks for his master's forgiveness. In contrast, those who lack a place in society (Subtle and Dol), end up with nothing. Given that the accumulation of wealth by the tricksters is interrupted by the return of the master, one wonders whether the analogy of egg and chicken, or of gold purportedly latent within all metals, extends to servants and masters as well. Might servants be masters if they had time enough to work for

---

[44] In 1587, William Harrison presented a related notion when he argued that all metal would naturally and ideally be gold: 'All metals receive their beginning of quicksilver and sulphur, which are as mother and father to them. And such is the purpose of Nature in their generations that she tendeth always to the procreation of gold' (364). Knapp explores the idea of potentiality with regard to the clients' weaknesses: 'In a certain sense the alchemy in the play merely reveals venalities the dupes had in them to begin with. There is surprisingly little hard work for the con artist to do' ('Ben Jonson' 173).

[45] Haynes points out that alchemy 'makes a neat metaphor for nascent capitalism': 'it promises infinite wealth and transformative power through operations scarcely more mysterious than the workings of capital' (36). Knapp argues similarly that 'Jonson's alchemical lab is both a metaphor for capitalism and an instance of capitalist structures of feeling' ('The Work of Alchemy' 586).

themselves, to acquire wealth of their own? Perhaps—but the play hardly portrays Face as a representative of possessive individualism. Rather than existing outside of social relations, Jeremy/Face moves within changing social constellations, and his fortune depends not just on his own actions but also on those of others—be it his master's or Subtle and Dol's. Face is independent enough to move tactically within these constellations, to forge transitory alliances and use social relations to rid himself of others. It is in choosing new and old affiliations that Face acquires agency, not in foregoing them entirely.

As Burnett argues, the figure of the male domestic servant has broader tropical meanings, especially in the case of carnivalesque inversion: a servant who assumed his master's place provided an opportunity to explore concerns around 'social mobility' (110). Yet he also offers a chance to reflect on how commercial society transforms the *oikos* and how the work of subordinates may be both a liability and asset to the profit-orientated household. If Jeremy's mercantile agency first transforms the household into an unstable structure that cannot last, the play ends with the reconciliation of oeconomy and commerce. Upon his master's return, Face swiftly dons the role of the canny servant of New Comedy and presents his master with all the wealth the tricksters have accumulated through their alchemical business. On top of this, the master receives a beautiful and rich bride. Jeremy alias Face is now, again, the loyal subordinate: 'The servant has become the landlord's factor, now called to strict account and ready to engross a rich widow for his master' (Leinwand, *Theatre* 135). The master happily accepts the newly accumulated estate, even if it has not been virtuously acquired. Surrogacy has the great advantage that one may profit by the work of others without having to sully one's hands: the mode of acquisition strains the master's 'own candour' but a little (5.5.152). The initial failure of supervision on the master's part emerges now as an almost providential move as the master profits from the exertions of his clever housekeeper. As his name suggests, Lovewit is well acquainted with Jeremy's wit and 'tricks'—'Come sir. No more o' your tricks, good Jeremy', he says (5.3.73)—and little surprised by his actions.

Despite the rather conventional and seemingly restitutive ending of the comedy, something has changed by the final scene: wealth and widow are integrated into the household, and the temporary inversion of authority has a lasting effect. As Jonathan Haynes explains, 'Face's real strength is his ability to participate in a comic settlement which reins in but does not reject the practices of a new social economy, accommodating it to the strength and durability of the status quo' (39). Jeremy's self-authorized business has proved so successful that the master, highly appreciative of his housekeeper's wit and efficiency, declares: 'I will be ruled by thee in anything, Jeremy' (5.5.143). He even leaves the last word to his subordinate: 'Speak for thyself, knave' (5.5.157).[46] In a metatheatrical move

---

[46] See also Don E. Wayne 112.

that establishes this final speech as the epilogue, Face points out that his degradation from captain to housekeeper is merely conventional: 'My part a little fell in this last scene, / Yet 'twas *decorum*' (5.5.159–160). He also redefines the return of the master as the ultimate device that has freed him (Face) from the claims of clients and fellow rogues: 'I am clean / Got off, from Subtle, Surly, Mammon, Dol, / Hot Ananias, Dapper, Drugger, all / With whom I traded' (5.5.159–162). Indeed, caught up in a series of accelerating events that appeared to lead to irresolvable complications, the master's return helps Face to disentangle himself from the spider's web of lies and obligations. The relation of master and servant is here mutually beneficial. While Jeremy's mercantile agency proves profitable for the household, the question of authority, of who rules whom, continues to hang in the balance, creating a sense of an ongoing and open-ended transformation of social relations in a world now governed by private interest and commerce. The two identities of the housekeeper in *The Alchemist* suggests that Jeremy alias Face belongs to two different and mutually incompatible economic constellations, yet the integration of these constellations is finally achieved by the (re-)integration of Face, the ill-begotten wealth, and the wealthy widow into Lovewit's household. This ending indicates that mercantile activity is not alien to the household, but can profit it in unexpected and less-than-virtuous ways. It also suggests that the housekeeper's role changes along with the household in the emergent commercial society.

'Shows of Service' and Mercantile Agency in *Othello*

Like *The Alchemist*, but in a considerably more sinister vein, *Othello* explores the problematic nexus of service and self-interested practical rationality. In contrast to *The Alchemist*, however, the setting of the play is domestic and military rather than domestic and mercantile. Nonetheless, as I argue in the following, Iago is another one of Bacon's 'third' men, a subordinate who pretends to labour on behalf of his master while secretly working for himself, offering but 'shows of service'.[47] Weil explains in detail how, in his self-representation, Iago plays on and 'overturns countless prescriptions for masters and servants' (70). Placed in the position of a trusted servant, Iago acts as a self-interested broker who manipulates value and manages and controls exchanges of money, words, and affects. Iago makes it his business to inform Brabantio of Desdemona's elopement and to characterize it as theft. He pretends to act as intermediary for Roderigo, whose money he pockets without giving anything in return, and he debases Desdemona in front of Othello. Rather than acting as Othello's 'instrument' (Bacon), Iago is his own man: he negotiates relations between various parties, but instead of facilitating

---

[47] See Iago's speech in *Othello*, 1.1.40–64 (specifically line 51).

their exchanges, Iago meddles where he pretends to mediate and divides people instead of bringing them together.[48]

As noted in the introduction to this chapter, Iago frames his relation to Othello in terms of service. Whereas Burnett conceives this relation in 'analogy' (1) to service, Neill perceives domestic and military service as parts of one and the same system: 'Military "place" was not imagined as something *analogous* to domestic "office", but rather (as the use of the term "officer" in both domestic and military contexts suggests) as another aspect of precisely the same system' ('Servant Obedience' 148). In Othello's household, the domestic and the military contexts of the play merge. Neill points out that 'Iago and Cassio are as much part of the general's military "household", as courtiers like Kent and Gloucester are members of the royal household in *Lear*' (149). In a setting in which a wife accompanies her husband to war, there is no absolute divide between military and domestic structures. As if to underline this, Desdemona's chambermaid Emilia is married to Othello's military man Iago. Weil also perceives a merging of domestic and military functions when she describes the duties of the ensign as those of a personal attendant: 'By making Iago his ancient, Othello gives him an office which does in fact require him, whatever its military function as flag-bearer, to fetch women and baggage, carry letters, and act as an intimate personal attendant' (71). The position of the trusted servant allows Iago to manipulate Othello's perception of his wife's virtue and of his own worth.

The household is positioned at the very centre of this tragedy which concludes with Desdemona's and Othello's deaths in the bedroom, the metonymic space of marital relations. The play's action is framed by oeconomic concerns about the distribution of wealth. The main action begins with the threat of dispossession, of the 'domestic theft' (Korda 143) of daughter and bags, as articulated in Iago and Roderigo's hue and cry: 'thieves, thieves, thieves! / Look to your house, your daughter and your bags! / Thieves, thieves! / ... Are your doors locked? ... / Zounds, sir, you're robbed' (*Oth.* 1.1.78–80, 84–85).[49] The loss of household 'goods', expressed through the nonchalant alignment of daughter and (money) bags, echoes at the end of the drama when the question of succession terminates the plot.[50] With the final speech of the play, Lodovico, a noble Venetian, transfers dead Othello's goods to Gratiano: 'Gratiano, keep the house / And seize upon the

---

[48] Interestingly, Brennan points out that Iago does not just bond with the audience and separate characters from each other, but also separates those characters from the audience (*Shakespeare's Dramatic Structures* 148).

[49] See also Korda, who quotes this passage to underline how Desdemona is 'cast as an object of property at the start of *Othello*' (143). A much older essay by Kenneth Burke also discusses Othello's precarious 'ownership' (167) of Desdemona and her identification with treasured property such as a 'pearl' (165) (5.2.348). Burke loosely relates the representation of Desdemona and of love to the 'increased cultural and economic importance of private property' (167).

[50] In fact, as Laura Kolb points out, 'throughout the text, mentions of money and property form a leitmotif, locating the play's action in a society structured by the movement of cash, gifts, land, and other bearers of material value' such as 'Brabantio's "bags"' (57).

fortunes of the Moor / For they succeed to you' (5.2.363–365). Thus, the beginning and end of the play coincide with the dispossession and redistribution of a household's 'estate'. As Desdemona accompanies Othello to Cyprus immediately after their marriage, this redistribution dissolves a household that was never firmly established in the first place, or at least not set up at home in Venice.[51] A homeless household is a fragile construct; lacking the validation and protection of the community, it is vulnerable to manipulation by 'third' men.[52] While Iago's destructive agency is enabled by his privileged role in Othello's service, it is facilitated by the instability of this unhoused household.

Othello explores the interface of oeconomy and commerce through the actions of a self-interested subordinate who combines oeconomic concerns with mercantile agency. While Iago addresses a key oeconomic concern—the behaviour and virtue of a wife—, he uses a form of practical knowledge that is applicable not just in politics, but also in the marketplace: a Baconian 'wisdom of business'. Like Jonson's tricksters, and just as Bacon suggests, Iago prizes appearance over virtue, practices strategic planning, and excels at rhetorical emplotment and affective manipulation. He describes his loyal service to Othello as a matter of seeming, of mere show: 'Though I do hate him as I do hell-pains, / Yet for necessity of present life / I must show out a flag and sign of love, / Which is indeed but sign' (1.1.152–154).[53] A sign without referent, his 'love' for Othello is nothing but a profitable fiction. True to his description of servile others 'Who, trimmed in forms and visages of duty, / Keep yet their hearts attending on themselves' (1.1.49–50), he professes his love and loyalty to Othello, only to secretly pursue his own interests.

Like Jonson's tricksters, Iago exploits the desires of others, notably Roderigo. In his manipulation of Othello, however, Iago nourishes not desire for an object, but the fear of losing it. Othello resembles the gullible Sir Mammon insofar as they both stand in an inverted relation to what they desire. Othello has the desired object, but fears to lose it, while Sir Mammon desperately wants what he does not have. Both characters desire too strongly, are too much bent on absolute possession. In consequence, Iago's work also functions in an inverse relation to that of the tricksters in *The Alchemist*: where they offer, in the form of the alchemical stone, a highly improbable, even impossible gain as certain success, Iago transforms a merely potential loss into a seemingly certain one when he convinces Othello that his wife has had an affair with his lieutenant. Whether they promise gain or loss,

---

[51] In 'Desdemona's Disposition', Lena Cowen Orlin points out that Othello marries without actually having a house (176), although by the end the couple appears to have set up house in Cyprus.

[52] Patricia Akhimie notes, 'In a culture of conduct, behaviour is observed and evaluated by one's immediate community over a long period of time, allowing neighbors to establish one another's reputation and to build mutual trust. Reputations are maintained by communal judgement' (76).

[53] Neill reminds us of the fact that actors were liveried servants to noble lords ('Servant Obedience' 137–138). Actors had to demonstrate their allegiance to a master even if they 'belonged more to the fluid world of urban commerce than to the ostensibly unchanging world of feudal retainers' (137). Thus, these lines could be read as a metatheatrical comment on the relation between actors and their master.

both the trickster trio and Iago sell a mere possibility as a 'surety'. Iago's manipulations of value, however, are more sophisticated than those of the tricksters. While the tricksters simply promise more wealth and better social skills, Iago manipulates the worth of individuals and thus 'the credit market of the play' (Parker, 'Cassio' 238). As Laura Kolb notes, Iago 'teaches Othello to evaluate his wife in a new way, reading her according to a hermeneutic of suspicion more appropriate to commercial credit ... than to marital trust' (37). By suggesting that Desdemona is unfaithful, he diminishes her worth. Significantly, Othello's faulty reappraisal of his wife has repercussions for his sense of his own worth as a cuckolded husband. In the patriarchal household, the wife's unfaithfulness is not just evidence of her lack of virtue, but also suggests the master's inability to keep his house in order. Iago seeks to influence how the actions of others are appraised and evaluated, yet at the same time he is highly preoccupied with how he himself is 'priced'. The play's preoccupation with human worth accounts for the persistent 'strain of economic language that runs throughout *Othello*' (Kolb 57).[54]

The Roderigo subplot highlights the play's concern with value, property, and exchange by adding a mercantile frame. It demonstrates Iago's lack of loyalty to Othello and positions him as a self-interested broker of quasi-mercantile exchanges. Iago obtains money from Roderigo to buy Desdemona's love, but then uses the money to line his own pockets. The very first speech of the play is Roderigo's, and it expresses his regret at having given Iago unrestricted access to his wealth: 'Tush, never tell me, I take it much unkindly / That thou, Iago, who hast had my purse / As if the strings were thine, shouldst know of this' (1.1.1–3). In Act Four, the question of money and abused trust comes up again. Roderigo reproaches Iago: 'I have wasted myself out of my means. The jewels you have had from me to deliver to Desdemona would half have corrupted a votarist' (4.2.189–190). Being able to freely use Roderigo's purse establishes Iago as a trusted friend, but the failed delivery of money and jewels betrays him as a deceitful broker: 'Thus do I ever make my fool my purse' (1.3.382). The Iago-Roderigo subplot does not appear in Shakespeare's main source, 'the seventh *novella* in the third decade of Giraldi Cinthio's *Gli Hecatommithi* (first published in 1565)' ('Appendix 3', *Othello* 375).[55] As a creative and deliberate addition to the story, it provides Iago with a lowly monetary motive and exposes the 'honest' servant as a mercantile agent who profits from an uneven exchange of money and trust. Patricia Parker points out that the tragedy 'is literally filled with the language of "credit", "reputation", "faith"

---

[54] Already in 1953, Robert B. Heilman picked up on the play's preoccupation with economic terms, and specifically with terms of value and dispossession.

[55] As Brennan pointed out: 'One of Shakespeare's most important modifications of Cinthio's novella is the invention of Roderigo.' (*Shakespeare's Dramatic Structures* 146) A translated excerpt of *Gli Hecatommithi* can be found in Geoffrey Bullough's *Narrative and Dramatic Sources to Shakespeare*, vol. VII.

and "trust"' ('Cassio' 237). The disloyal ensign who puts on a show of loving service to exploit his master's trust articulates the discontents of a mobile society in which seeming proves more effective than being.

In a society that is structured around exchange, the acquisition of an estate is one thing; maintaining it through the shifting winds of fortune is quite another. The spectres of an adulterous wife and a manipulative servant testify to an increasing awareness that the household is not entirely separate from the market. On the contrary, theatrical representations of self-interested servants and potentially unfaithful wives suggest that the household is firmly integrated into and even internally divided by relations of exchange and unruly desires.[56] Although the household and its interests were supposedly governed by a master, both *Othello* and *The Alchemist* reveal the extent to which desires *and* agency had been dispersed in early modern homes. This was reenforced by the gendered division of labour in the house and the delegation of duties to subordinate surrogates in the emerging commercial society. Both plays fix upon the figure of the subordinate to explore the dramatic potential of conflicting interests within the household. Evolving from mere 'instruments' to agents, duplicitous servants threatened to undermine the unity of the household from within. The topos of the insubordinate and self-interested servant gestures towards a socially mobile society and to the proliferating private interests and new entrepreneurial alliances it brought, all of which threatened traditional bonds.[57] Before discussing Iago's 'wisdom of business' and the question of value manipulation further, the following section seeks to contextualize the play within a mobile world characterized by horizontal and vertical movement: by transnational travel and social mobility.

Transnational Travel and Social Mobility

Iago's self-interested manipulations destroy a homeless household that is caught up in transnational travels and exchanges. This household is constituted by a foreign mercenary who joins Venetian society and a Venetian who elopes with him. The play accentuates Othello's uncertain status and his dependence on native servants. Variously described as 'an extravagant and wheeling stranger' (1.1.134) and an 'erring Barbarian' (1.3.356), Othello has relied on Cassio to mediate his courtship

---

[56] Confronted with his wife's ostensible infidelity, Othello laments: 'O curse of marriage, / That we can call these delicate creatures ours, / And not their appetites!' (3.3.272-74) Orlin drily comments that the play 'elucidates a key problematic of the patriarchal system as a text; it both asserts possession and finds possession always uncertain' ('Desdemona's Disposition' 185).

[57] Dowd highlights changes in the institution of service that gave a heightened significance to the figure of the self-serving servant: 'Amidst a growing consumer culture, the feudal concept of universal service ... was steadily being replaced by an emerging ideology of service that emphasized ambition, production, and profit. No longer a long-term commitment based on loyalty, the institution of service in seventeenth-century England demanded an economically diverse and geographically mobile work force that could be employed for temporary labor' (23).

of Desdemona: Cassio, as Othello tells Iago, 'went between us very oft' (3.3.100).[58] As a 'broker or clandestine go-between' (Bristol 189), Cassio seems to have abused Othello's trust. Yet instead of distrusting his other servant—Iago—in consequence, Othello relies on him entirely. Othello's position as a master with a business-savvy subordinate is complicated considerably by his status as a racialized stranger and mercenary, because he depends on Iago as a cross-cultural interpreter. Iago is only too happy to explain to Othello the ins and outs of Venetian femininity, claiming to compensate for his master's ignorance, which he in fact exploits.[59] As a mercenary, Othello's worth is subject to the vagaries of the marketplace of military hire and public opinion, as will be discussed below.

Desdemona's love aggravates Othello's strangeness: by following him into the field, she alienates him from a homosocial military context that does not depend on a single home and national belonging. At the same time, Iago works hard to ensure that Othello remains a stranger in the Venetian household that Desdemona embodies. Her own life is, of course, also complicated by Othello's foreignness and military commission. As noted in Chapters 1 and 2, the prescriptive advice for women to keep (at) home was deeply written into the conduct literature of the time: 'The domestic conduct books repeat countless times the rule that "God hath made the man to travail abroad, and the woman to keep home"' (Orlin, *Private Matters* 220).[60] In Edmund Tilney's treatise on marriage, the fictional character Lady Iulia warns against the behaviour practiced by Desdemona: 'As the wife must be thus ware in going abroade: so must she be as carefull what is done at home, on hir part not to sit ydlely, nor to permit any one suspiciously to come vnto hir, speciallye hir husband being not at home' (E3v). In light of this treatise, Desdemona's travels and her private reception of Cassio are conspicuously unconventional. The reason for Lady Iulia's advice is that a woman's good name, which constitutes the measure of her worth, is easily lost:

> The married woman, must be also verie carefull, and circumspect of hir good name. For a good name is the flower of estimation, and the pearle of credit, which is so delicate a thing in a woman, that she must not onely be good, but likewise must apeere so … The chiefest way for a woman to preserue and maintaine this good fame, is to be resident in hir owne house.
>
> (E2v)

---

[58] See also Pye, *The Storm at Sea* 112.

[59] Helen Hackett situates cross-cultural interpretation in the economic sphere: the Latin *interpres* originally meant 'broker, factor, or agent between two parties' (*Early Modern Exchanges* 37, also 244).

[60] Emma Whipday (215) quotes from Henry Smith's *A Preparatiue to Mariage* (1591) to demonstrate the early modern precept that women must stay at home to preserve their chastity: '[W]ee call the Wife, *Huswife*, that is, house wife, not a street wife … to shew that a good wife keepes her house … as though *Home* were Chastities keeper' (Smith 79).

Tilney highlights here the importance of *appearing* good in a society that valued reputation or credit above all else. In clear violation of such precepts, Desdemona moves 'outside the limits of domestic economy' (Korda 115) and into foreign lands, figuratively by marrying Othello and literally by following him to Cyprus. Desdemona's agency first becomes apparent in her 'elopement' with Othello (Orlin, *Private Matters* 217), with which she 'disrupts the tradition of male-controlled exchange' (Logan 362) and 'asserts her autonomy and self-determination' (361). This self-determination is once more asserted when she follows Othello into the field: this 'is the most troubling—and most portentous— instance of her agency' (Orlin, 'Desdemona's Disposition' 178).[61] Puzzled witnesses can only interpret this wayward behaviour in terms of a crisis of patriarchal authority. Lena Cowen Orlin points out that Cassio calls Desdemona 'our great captain's captain' (2.1.74), while Iago remarks sardonically that 'Our general's wife is now the general' (2.3.309–310) ('Introduction' 8). If parts of the dialogue invoke Desdemona as a prized object, a 'jewel' (her father Brabantio, 1.3.196) or 'pearl' (Othello, 5.2.345), these descriptions suggest agency and underline the difficulty of grasping the social position of a wife in the field.

An early modern audience familiar with conduct and advice literature would have recognized both Desdemona's virtues and her shortcomings.[62] If Othello is the base 'Indian'/'Judean' who 'threw a pearl away' (5.2.345) without recognizing its true value, Desdemona disregards 'the pearle of credit' and endangers her 'good name' (Tilney E2v) by her wilful behaviour.[63] Desdemona's woeful exclamation 'Alas the day, I never gave him cause' (3.4.158) insists rightly on her innocence, but is strangely blind to the problem of reputation. It suggests a naïve interpretation of her own worth as subject to intrinsic virtue. In her chapter on *Othello*, Kolb suggests that the tragedy explores various ways of evaluating 'human worth' (38). The problem of how to evaluate others is accentuated by the changing contexts afforded by transnational movement. *Othello* explores how the estimation of people shifts beyond the familiar compass of a domestic existence, how their sense of their own worth and that of others changes in an unfamiliar context. Domestic here has a double meaning: the 'domestic' in this domestic tragedy oscillates visibly between referring to a household affair and to a community that has transactions with strangers.[64] A foreign mercenary is first integrated into, and then ousted from,

---

[61] As Akhimie writes, 'Desdemona's journey is especially taboo, according to the *ars apodemica* treatises of the period, which state unequivocally that women should not travel under any circumstances. Travel does not make women more worldly, or more valuable people. Instead, it is seen as antithetical to chastity, and a woman's travel becomes a black mark on her reputation' (62).

[62] Orlin notes that Desdemona exhibits 'all the warning signals of unchastity' of the time, even if 'those signs are wrong' ('Desdemona's Disposition' 187).

[63] The Quarto text has 'the base Indian', while the Folio text has 'the base Judean' (Korda 112).

[64] As Diana E. Henderson points out, this 'second meaning of *domestic* ... was current in the sixteenth century'; it 'implied opposition to the foreign or strange' (173). Korda recognizes that Desdemona exemplifies this sliding between both meanings when she violates 'the bounds of domestic and

the community of Venetians; a beautiful Venetian is transported hence.[65] With the constellation of an 'extravagant and wheeling stranger' (1.1.134) who 'steals' a Venetian 'pearl' only to then 'underestimate his wife's true worth' (Korda 112), the play taps into xenophobic and racializing discourses emerging from competitive global trade.[66] By the end of the play, political power and material wealth are firmly back in Venetian hands and, of all people, the malicious villain Iago is instrumental in achieving this redistribution of property and power.

With this disloyal subordinate, the play explores not only the effects of transnational travel, but also of social mobility. In the mobile society of the play, with its shifting positions and competitive surrogates, social status is highly unstable. As Siemon sums it up, '*Othello* portrays struggles surrounding attainments, affirmations, and losses of office, rank, and place—military, civil and domestic' (179).[67] Iago is overtaken by Cassio, who scores the lieutenancy; later, Iago succeeds in replacing Cassio as Othello's confidant. As Julia Genster points out, the lieutenant is a subordinate who can 'assume the command' if necessary (796). As the etymology of the word suggests, a lieutenant is a placeholder and lieutenancy is predicated on 'the condition of replaceability' (797). This becomes clear at the end of the play when Othello has to resign from his office as governor and his second-in command Cassio takes his place. Replaceability suggests a world in which people may rise and fall as their social credit suffers or increases. That Iago might have been lieutenant instead of Cassio diminishes his social distance to Othello. Rather than constituting an insurmountable social difference, military rank has the power to bridge it. At least in Iago's own imagination, he was only one step away from being lieutenant and two from acting in Othello's stead: as lieutenant, he would have been first in line to take Othello's place and might have been able to advance from subordinate to master. In the increasingly mobile English society of around 1600, Iago may have been a highly relatable villain. After all, *Othello*'s original audiences 'confronted their own issues of assimilation to rising standards' in this 'age of unprecedented social mobility, economic expansion, globalized trade,

---

familial duty' by eloping with Othello and strays 'outside the limits of domestic economy' 'by sailing to Cyprus' (115).

[65] Imtiaz Habib points out that the marriage between Othello and Desdemona has political implications: 'by marrying the natural born Venetian Desdemona, Othello will gain legal access not only to permanent Venetian residency but also to political power' (148). As Habib puts it, it is through Desdemona that the stranger hopes for 'physical and psychic housing' (149) in Venice.

[66] Korda discusses Othello in the context of travel narratives and the ways in which 'such texts represent Africans' overvaluation of "trifles" and undervaluation of items of "true" worth' (116). At the same time, the loss of domestic coin and goods to foreign nations and the presence of 'alien workers and merchants' were ideologically charged topoi (Howard, *Theater of a City* 9).

[67] And Sandra Logan highlights the systematic nature and affective dimension of these struggles in the emerging capitalist society, which inscribes 'subjects within a myth of merit-based success, and thus within a competitive model that encourages them to see themselves as threatened or displaced by "undeserving" others' (356).

proliferating commodities, and broader-based literacy' (Orlin, 'Introduction' 7).[68] The performance of a dual dynamic of mobility infuses the play with a heightened sense of ambiguity. Londoners might have pitied Othello and detested the social climber Iago—or, indulging their own xenophobic resentments and their own ambitions of rising through the ranks, they may have admired Iago for dispossessing his foreign master in favour of Venetian citizens. *Othello* dramatizes both xenophobic resentment in a world of global traffic and the ambitions and the grudges that accompany the possibility of social advancement.[69]

'Wisdom of Business': Skills and Strategies

How does Iago manipulate Othello beneath a show of service and signs of love? Iago has been described as 'Shakespeare's most accomplished rhetorician' (Jacobson 498), his 'greatest dissimulator' (Vickers, 'Power' 434), and as a veritable 'essayist' who has learned from Montaigne how to appear 'forthright' (Belsey, 'Iago the Essayist' 166). Political theorists recognized rhetoric and dissimulation as necessary and effective instruments.[70] It is worthwhile noting that these skills were also valued in the marketplace, as Scott's essay and Bacon's 'wisdom of business' suggest. In *Othello*, their self-interested deployment in the household questions the ancient division of oeconomy and commerce—especially with a 'servant' who is engaged in manipulating the mistress's credit. As noted in Chapter 1, dissimulation is ethically ambiguous: bordering on deceit, yet allegedly distinct from it. While a person who dissimulated might in principle still act honourably, one who deceived for ill ends could not: 'hee sins thrice that counterfeits himselfe good, to whom he may doe ill' (Scott 28).

Iago exploits the ethical ambiguity of dissimulation by pretending to withhold the truth for virtuous reasons while really practicing deceit. He covers his lies by performing the role of the honourable dissimulator. The subtlety of his performance is considerably greater than that of the tricksters. While the three tricksters perform the roles of Captain Face, the alchemical doctor, and the crazed lady, Iago pretends to be his true self, but in fact puts on a show to conceal his intentions: 'I am not what I am' (1.1.64). Iago's frequent and exaggerated use of aposiopesis creates an impression of *reticentia* (Beier 42; Jacobsen 517; Vickers, *Shakespeare* 82),

---

[68] Later, Orlin puts this even more succinctly in her discussion of Siemon's contribution: 'Siemon shows that *Othello* played out before an audience of Othellos and Iagos, strivers in the status wars of early modern England' ('Introduction' 9).
[69] Of course, this sinister account of social mobility is only one possible version. It contrasts with Thomas Dekker's success story of social advancement, *The Shoemaker's Holiday*, which provides evidence of a very different and far more positive narrative of social mobility.
[70] See Jon R. Snyder, particularly chapter 4. He writes here: 'Reason-of-state theorists ... tended to see "political" dissimulation as a legitimate technique of information-control for princes to practice in the interest of state security and dynastic stability' (107).

a strategy of dissimulation that signals his reluctance to tell the 'truth'. This is entirely in tune with his role as an honest friend who does not want to endanger Cassio or sadden Othello, but who would rather break off a statement than lie.[71] Othello recognizes Iago's use of dissimulation and reacts to it: 'I know, Iago, / Thy honesty and love doth mince this matter / Making it light to Cassio' (2.3.242–244). Iago's self-conscious performance of dissimulation helps to establish his ethos as 'honest Iago', an epithet that underlines his role as trusted servant and friend and persists until his final demise.[72] This honesty is also part and parcel of his military function: Genster suggests that the ensign had to represent the value and virtue of the company (793).

As skilled rhetorician, Iago combines *reticencia* with equivocation to fuel Othello's jealous imagination. Iago's suggestion that Cassio 'lies' evokes a whole set of possible meanings, the sexual implications of which torment Othello (Christofides 10):

> OTHELLO. What hath he said?
> IAGO. Faith, that he did—I know not what. He did—
> OTHELLO. What? What?
> IAGO. Lie.
> OTHELLO. With her?
> IAGO. With her, on her, what you will.
> OTHELLO. Lie with her? lie on her? We say lie on her when they belie her! Lie with her, zounds, that's fulsome!
>
> (4.1.31–37)

Here, Iago combines *recitencia* ('I know not what') with the strategic use of ambiguous speech ('lie'). He goads Othello into visualizing the crime and thus amplifies his affective reaction. In her essay 'Shakespeare and Rhetoric', Parker described Iago's strategy of manipulation as 'movement from a partial tantalizing glimpse to a full disclosure': 'it is, as Erasmus remarks in the *De Copia*, "just like displaying some object for sale first of all through a lattice or inside a wrapping, and then unwrapping it and opening it out and displaying it more fully to the *gaze*"' (64). Such rhetorical 'unfolding' heightens suspense and substitutes for 'ocular proof' (64). Iago unwraps false facts just as others sell precious objects. Disclosing information in a dilatory mode is a strategy of amplification that works on the level of *pathos*.[73] Jonson's tricksters employ this strategy when they reveal to

---

[71] This is an act of what Verena Lobsien has aptly called 'transparent dissimulation' (*Transparency* 130).

[72] Othello uses this phrase four times altogether (1.3.295, 2.3.173, 5.2.71, 5.2.150), Cassio once (2.3.330). After having killed Desdemona, Othello even doubles the attribute to arrive at 'honest, honest Iago', as if to convince himself that he has acted on the firm ground of truth (5.2.150).

[73] See also Jacobsen's discussion of how 'Iago exploits *pathos* in a manner that mirrors both classical rhetorical theory and Machiavellian precept' (508).

Dapper only gradually (and seemingly unwillingly) that he is descended from the Queen of Fairy and sure to win all future games. Just as the tricksters' clients in *The Alchemist* respond eagerly and with an intensification of desire to the rhetorical accumulation of valuable objects and fantastic prophecies, Othello responds passionately to the gradual unfolding of Desdemona's apparent debasement. Like the tricksters, Iago is not just a skilled rhetorician and dissimulator, but also 'a brilliant improviser' (Charney 7) and emplotter. When Emilia presents him with Desdemona's handkerchief, he grabs occasion by the 'forelock' (Bacon), turning it into 'proof' of her infidelity.[74]

Iago's use of dissimulation and dilation amplifies Othello's affective jealousy. At the same time, Iago develops persuasive force with the help of an argumentative strategy that counts on and intensifies Othello's sense of his own foreignness. As Catherine Nicholson has suggested, Iago's arguments 'rest on the relentless accumulation of likelihoods and commonplaces' (77). They enlist the help of two figures that Peacham described in *The Garden of Eloquence*: '*apodixis*, or the maxim, and *martyria*, or testimony' (Nicholson 80). 'Apodixis' or 'in Latine Experientia' draws on 'generall and common experience' (Peacham 86). Peacham emphasized the persuasive force of arguments that are grounded in commonplaces: 'Of all the formes of speech there is not one more apt, or more mighty to confirme or confute then this, which is grounded vpon the strong foundacion of experience, confirmed by al times, allowed of in all places, and subscribed to by all men' (Peacham 87; see also Nicholson 80). Commonplaces are, however, not subscribed to 'by all men', but by humans in a certain part of the world. As Nicholson points out, they are locally defined, tied to a place and community (78, 80). Hence, Iago's use of commonplaces excludes Othello from a knowing in-group and endows Iago himself with the insider's prerogative of interpretation.[75] As a stranger to Venetian customs, Othello proves particularly susceptible to such commonplaces and happily believes Iago's claims about Venetian women.[76] With 'I know our country disposition well' (3.3.204), Iago establishes his authority as cross-cultural interpreter. The exotic attraction of the unfamiliar works in two directions: as Othello wins Desdemona and the senate with his own ornate description of the unfamiliar, he is in turn won over by Iago's commonplaces about customs unfamiliar to himself (Nicholson 79–80). Iago combines commonplaces with concrete observations, with testimony: 'Martyria in Latine Testatio is a forme of speech by which the Orator or Speaker confirmeth some thing by his owne

---

[74] Katherine Gillen analyses the semiotic intricacies of this object and its metonymic relation to Desdemona's chastity in *Chaste Value* 186–187.
[75] Nicholson suggests that 'Iago's commonplaces not only assimilate Desdemona to a debased and generalized image of Venetian womanhood; they continually remind Othello of his exclusion from the community that would recognize "our country disposition" and "her country forms": these are places to which a Moor has no access' (80).
[76] See also Brennan, *Shakespeare's Dramatic Structures* 152.

experience' (Peacham 85; see also Nicholson 80). Its credibility depends on the speaker's 'knowen credit' (Peacham 86). Hence, for the effective use of *martyria*, Iago's ethos as honest and loyal servant is indispensable. Peacham emphasizes the great strength of this figure and warns that it may be 'abused by the untruth of the testimonie' (86). The combination of observations and commonplaces turns conjectures into facts. Early modern rhetoricians were well aware of the dangers of persuasion by likelihood.[77] In *Tell-Trothes New-Yeares Gift*, the anonymous author identified jealousy as a manipulative and divisive strategy of those who seek to 'sette debate betweene true hartes, and to shuffle in suspition amongst those that are free from thought thereof' (B2r).

Debasement: Credit and Value

Iago's method of manipulation consists in dissimulation, persuasion, and the emplotment of contingent events, while credit constitutes his target: he slanders Desdemona's good name and undermines Othello's sense of his own worth, both as cuckolded husband and racialized stranger. As Kolb suggests, the question of how to estimate human worth is at the heart of the tragedy.[78] The following discussion relates the fluctuating worth of Desdemona and Othello to the dominance of exchange value in commercial society as well as to the different dimensions of value in early modern coins. For early modern bullionists and mercantilists, money posed the problem that a single object (the stamped coin) combined differing dimensions of value—extrinsic and intrinsic—that did not always coincide. A reflection on money and human beings in relations of exchange helps to highlight contradictory impulses within the play's take on value. Desdemona's death affirms virtue as the true source of human worth and suggests thereby the primacy of intrinsic value over and against the merely nominal and extrinsic worth of reputation. Othello's death, in contrast, highlights the extent to which human worth is shaped by demand for certain skills and kinds of labour and demonstrates the conventionality and fluctuating nature of value. Furthermore, the changing worth of Othello and Desdemona suggests that value is mediated through gendering and racializing discourses.[79] The following discussion moves from the common

---

[77] Thomas Wilson calls this an 'oration conjectural': 'The oration conjectural is when matters be examined and tried out by suspicions gathered and some likelihood of thing appearing' (125). The doubtful relation to truth of this kind of oration emerges in Wilson's follow-up statement that accuser and accused may pursue the same strategy and employ the same topoi for their orations (128).

[78] Kolb also comments on 'Iago's exploitation of the basic tension between external appraisal and intrinsic quality' (41), which is crucial to my argument in this chapter.

[79] Korda also scrutinizes 'racializing discourses of under- and overvaluation' in the play (112). In *Chaste Value*, Gillen argues similarly that Iago's manipulation of value approaches 'gendered and racialized bodies as commodities' (196).

association of female sexuality with commerce to a reflection on the different dimensions of value of early modern coins and, by means of analogy, of circulating women. It concludes with a discussion of Othello's fluctuating value as mercenary and householder.

Iago's debasement of Desdemona's social credit is facilitated by the topical association of female sexuality with exchange, specifically with commerce and consumption.[80] A comment in *The Arden of Faversham*, parts of which were likely written by Shakespeare,[81] may exemplify how widespread the association of commodification and female sexuality was. When Arden confesses his grief at his wife's lack of chastity, his best friend seeks to reassure him by pointing out that infidelity is a common enough occurrence among women: 'Comfort thyself, sweet friend; it is not strange / That women will be false and wavering' (1.20–21). The resigned note gives little comfort to Arden, but it gives a taste of female infidelity as an early modern commonplace. While prostitution offered a common trope for the commodification of social relations, chastity defined a locus of intrinsic value that had to be defended against consumption and exchange.[82] Of course, many female characters on the early modern stage are quite oblivious of the need to safeguard an intrinsic value that might be corrupted upon contact with the sphere of circulation. Dol's streetwise pragmatism is completely at odds with the notion that female sexuality must resist exchange. In fact, she herself constitutes a form of shared property (*respublica*) and exemplifies only temporary possession in a world governed by exchange. Although associated with shared property, she is hardly more objectified than Desdemona: as a partner in the 'venture tripartite', she has more authority and greater agency. In *Othello*, Desdemona's insistence on virtue is contrasted with Emilia's claim that she would not 'do it' for a petticoat, but certainly in exchange for the whole world. Whereas the tricksters in *The Alchemist* indulge in illegitimately appropriated and shared property and thrive through exchange, Othello stakes his honour and happiness exclusively on individual property, and on safeguarding that property from entering the sphere of circulation.[83]

In a sense, chastity's relation to exchange is fundamentally paradoxical. Chastity signified resistance to exchange, but it had to prove its value on the marriage market and hence in a one-time exchange: women enter the marriage market only to

---

[80] See Jean Howard's chapter on '(W)holesaling: Bawdy Houses and Whore Plots in the Drama's Staging of London' (*Theater of a City* 114–161) and Gillen, *Chaste Value* 8.
[81] See MacDonald P. Jackson's detailed study *Determining the Shakespeare Canon: Arden of Faversham and A Lover's Complaint*.
[82] As Gillen suggests, 'chastity often stands in opposition to prostitution, signifying an inherently valuable entity that resists commoditisation' (*Chaste Value* 9).
[83] Korda links Othello's jealousy to possessive individualism. She writes, 'jealousy is predicated on possessive individualism (a sense of entitlement to and satisfaction in "our owne proper good"), while at the same time being fraught with the anxieties of loss that subtend it' (136).

drop out again of the sphere of circulation.[84] In the beginning of the play, Brabantio frames Desdemona's elopement with Othello with a narrative of interminable circulation, from father to illegitimate lover and from there to (potentially) any number of men: 'Look to her, Moor, if thou hast eyes to see: / She has deceived her father, and may thee' (1.3.293–294). Here, the father assumes the structural position of the betrayed husband; Brabantio's warning suggests that this betrayal bodes ill for Desdemona's constancy. Iago exploits her willful turn from one man to another, when he reminds Othello much later that Desdemona 'did deceive her father, marrying you' (3.3.210).[85] Othello's success in wooing Desdemona becomes 'incontrovertible proof of her unfaithfulness': it 'proves that other men can as easily take her away from himself' (Coral 294). This is a familiar narrative: in *Arden of Faversham*, it is Alice Arden's infidelity with Mosby that nourishes Mosby's own fear that he, too, will one day be cuckolded: 'You have supplanted Arden for my sake / And will extirpen me to plant another' (8.40–41). No matter whether the first man to be betrayed is the father or husband, a woman who gives herself wilfully to another man may continue to do so. A woman who circulated from one man to another would become worthless as the bearer of the household's future: cuckoldry may have been a rich source for comedy on the stage, but it threatened the ultimate loss of all property in an uncertain line of succession. Paradoxically, the fear of women circulating like commodities is tantamount to the fear of female agency: of women following their own desire and intent, of treasured objects that give themselves away.

In pitching Desdemona's reputation against her virtue, *Othello*'s performance of conflicting dimensions of personal worth reproduces a monetary model of value that distinguishes between intrinsic and extrinsic value. In medieval and early modern England, coins were made of bullion—silver and gold—that carried the prince's stamp. Ideally, their value was based on the quantity and finesse of the bullion, but for various reasons the intrinsic value of the bullion and the extrinsic, stamped value could differ. Woman constituted an ideal trope for this duality and the implicit threat of diverging values: in the wife who secretly betrays her husband, apparent virtue and 'real' virtue have drifted apart. Conversely, the woman whose intact reputation was but an outward sign of her virtue constituted an ideal metaphor for the unity of extrinsic and intrinsic value. It must be said, however, that the notion of a direct correspondence between money's extrinsic and intrinsic value has always had a mythical component. Aristotle claimed in the *Politics* that the operation of weighing and pricing was once identical: the function of the 'stamp' was simply 'to save the trouble of weighing and to mark the value' (*Pol.* I.9, 1257a40–41). Yet already Aristotle distanced himself from this simplistic account

---

[84] For this reason, Gillen sees chastity as 'a vexed concept': it combines, rather paradoxically, 'stability and exchange', resulting in the idea 'that virgin purity could persist into marriage' (*Chaste Value* 9).

[85] See also Nicholson 78 and Orlin, 'Desdemona's Disposition' 180.

by invoking people who 'maintain that coined money is a mere sham, a thing not natural, but conventional only' (*Pol.* I.9, 1257b10–11). As a conventional object, the value of money was doubtful and unstable: the price or amount of bullion could vary, while the stamp might not represent its value accurately.

Englishmen and -women of the sixteenth and seventeenth centuries were aware of a possible rift between intrinsic and extrinsic value because they were familiar with narratives of the great debasement under Henry VII. As Landreth explains, Henry 'first cut the silver value of his coins by more than a third, and then continued incrementally to debase the coinage until it was utterly evacuated of silver' (16). Only Elizabeth finally succeeded in restoring the purity of English coins, but this meant that in the early seventeenth century the 'moralized account of the Debasement was fresh in memory and vital to policy' (17). John Stow's 'A Commemoration of Queene Elizabeth' in *The Annales, Or a Generall Chronicle of England* from 1615 actually ends by giving due weight to Elizabeth's achievement in stabilizing the currency: 'She was the first that suppressed all manner of base Moneys, and reduced all the English quoyne into golde and siluer' (815). Yet even beyond state policy, debasement was an ever-present threat of monetary transactions since 'early modern coins would often be clipped, shaved, or debased' (Deng, *Coinage and State Formation* 10). On top of voluntary manipulation, circulation would diminish the value of coins through wear and tear. The shortage of bullion, and hence the rarity of actual gold coins, was notorious in early modern England.[86] Their rarity may have turned gold coins—especially good ones—into prized possessions. Thomas Gresham claimed that the deterioration of coin implied that '"bad" money drives out "good" money': 'a consumer who receives a good quality coin is likely to hoard it for its precious metal content rather than to spend it' (Deng, *Coinage and State Formation* 10). When given the choice, it made sense to hold onto 'good' coins rather than feed them back into circulation. Although money, in the Aristotelian perspective, had its use in circulation,[87] the varying content of precious metals, their differing quality and varying exchange rates would have turned the circulation of coins into a hazardous enterprise. The threat

---

[86] Craig Muldrew explains that 'the supply of actual money' was 'always much smaller than the demand for it in exchanges so that its value was maintained' (*The Economy of Obligation* 99). Yet the relation of supply and demand became even more unbalanced in the course of the sixteenth century (*The Economy of Obligation* 100). Muldrew's study demonstrates the extent to which commercial exchange relied on credit.

[87] This purpose is faithfully reiterated by Oresme, who follows in his first chapter, 'Why Money was Invented', and in chapter 4, 'Of the Form or Shape of Money', the Aristotelian narrative very closely in terms of the function of money (4). He also reiterates Aristotle on the function of a coin's stamp: 'When men first began to trade, or to purchase goods with money, the money had no stamp or image, but a quantity of silver or bronze was exchanged for meat and drink and was measured by weight. And since it was tiresome constantly to resort to the scales and difficult to determine the exact equivalent by weighing, and since the seller could not be certain of the metal offered or of its degree of purity, it was wisely ordained ... that they should be stamped with a design, known to everybody, to indicate the quality and true weight of the coin, so that suspicion should be averted and the value readily recognised' (8–9).

of debasement through circulation, in combination with the duality of feminine value—intrinsic virtue versus reputation—resulted in a modelling of female worth within a monetary paradigm of value. It facilitated tropological exchanges between female sexuality and the circulation of coin. Desdemona exemplifies this: because circulating money was more easily debased than hoarded coin, the seemingly adulterous Desdemona can exemplify 'the contemporary alignment of adultery with adulterated coin' (Parker, 'Cassio' 230).[88]

The notion that Desdemona is debased through entering into sexual exchanges with other men emerges through Iago's speech on reputation and the 'purse'. Although not explicitly aimed at Desdemona, this speech constructs an interpretative frame that shapes Othello's recognition of Desdemona as an object debased through circulation. Iago celebrates 'Good name in man and woman' as 'the immediate jewel of their souls', only to juxtapose the absolute value of reputation with a disdainful description of his circulating 'purse': 'Who steals my purse steals trash— 'tis something—nothing, / 'Twas mine, 'tis his, and has been slave to thousands' (3.3.160–161). Elizabeth Hanson pointed out correctly that 'one of the suggestions loaded into this burdened utterance is that Desdemona could circulate like a purse of money' (*Discovering the Subject* 80).[89] Iago's speech juxtaposes social credit (reputation) with cash (the purse) to reject the materialism of the purse as mere 'trash'. In contrast, the good name is elevated as a jewel, an object that appears intrinsically valuable.[90] The phrase that sees the 'good name' of people as 'immediate jewel of their souls' suggests an insoluble link between reputation and inner virtue, with a good name adorning a virtuous character. Conversely, a damaged reputation suggests a corresponding lack of virtue. Obviously, Iago's analysis of the significance of reputation is entirely strategic. At other times, he rejects the belief in a natural unity of credit and virtue opportunistically by emphasizing the merely nominal value of a 'good name': 'Reputation is an idle and most false imposition, oft got without merit and lost without deserving. You have lost no reputation at all, unless you repute yourself such a loser' (2.3.264–267). In this speech, there is no connection at all between a person's inner virtues and their good name—in fact, character or inner virtues are barely mentioned. Similarly, Iago's disdainful rejection of the material purse contrasts with an earlier speech in Act One, where he attempts to convince Roderigo to invest more money into his pursuit of Desdemona (1.3.335–373). Iago invokes different forms of value strategically, using tropes of credit, money, and valuable objects how and where he sees

---

[88] Neill draws attention to the linguistic association of the Latin *adulter* with debasing or counterfeiting coin. He notes that '[T]he same extended meaning is present in Medieval English *adulter* ("corrupt" or "debase")' (*Putting History to the Question* 135).

[89] As Gillen points out, 'purse' was also 'a slang term for vagina' (*Chaste Value* 185).

[90] See also Kolb, who emphasizes the intact link between inward qualities and outward recognition in the good-name speech: 'good name is the outwardly recognized reflection of the inward qualities that make a person fundamentally himself or herself' (61). She also discusses the various uses of reputation and purse in the play in her exploration of the unstable opposition of 'good name and goods' (64).

fit. Through him, the play explores competing dimensions of value and reflects on their apparent autonomy and interdependence.

The good-name speech highlights not only what Desdemona loses if she circulates from one man to another; it also frames her as a transferrable object, 'a commodity' (Gillen, *Chaste Value* 182) that can be owned by 'thousands' (3.3.161). Here again, the ambiguous status of married women becomes palpable: imagined as inalienable property, the initial 'purchase' (2.3.9.) of a wife, as Othello puts it, submits her to 'the language of commoditisation' (Gillen, *Chaste Value* 185). If plots of cuckoldry articulate anxieties of dispossession as well as of fluctuating value, a truly virtuous wife offered an image of inalterable value: natural, permanent, and reliable rather than conventional, changeable, and mystifying. Desdemona's rehabilitation in death is a restorative effort to salvage the primacy of intrinsic value (virtue) by restricting fluctuations to her apparent or extrinsic value (reputation). In affirming Desdemona's chastity, the play's ending imagines a substantial core of value which cannot be touched by commercial transactions and manipulative agents.[91] Even if Iago's debasement of Desdemona erodes trust in the concept of unitary value in which one's 'name' expresses one's 'soul', the final recognition of her innocence suggests that chastity transcends and outlives external appraisal. *The Alchemist*, in contrast, does not bother with an intrinsic core of value: Dol's value resides precisely in her ability to appear as someone or something she is not—a lady, and even the 'Queen of Fairy' (1.2.126)—and hence in her semi-professional skills as an actress. Marketable skills and nominal labels determine *her* worth—not an intrinsic notion of virtue.

Desdemona's devaluation through Iago's slander dissolves belief in the correspondence between intrinsic and nominal or extrinsic value. Yet Othello's downfall suggests that there may not be a neat distinction at all between outside and inside, between social estimation and intrinsic value. As Othello internalizes Iago's racializing discourse (Adelman 125–126), this distinction emerges as a fiction. Desdemona's posthumous reevaluation upholds the notion that there is an intrinsic value that external estimation cannot alter, and the beginning of the play appears to suggest much the same thing with the figure of the 'noble Moor' (2.3.134). The Duke plays Othello's virtue against his dark-skinned appearance when he tells Brabantio: 'If virtue no delighted beauty lack / Your son-in-law is far more fair than black' (1.3.290–291). The notion of virtue as a stable property that defines the worth of a man intrinsically is, however, counteracted by Othello's internalization of Iago's racializing perspective, which determines how he perceives himself.[92] This results in self-division when Othello introduces his suicide with the story of a 'Turk' who harmed a Venetian. He proceeds to describe

---

[91] In Gillen's words, 'the play's conclusion moves toward removing chastity from the commodity sphere' (*Chaste Value* 195).

[92] See also Kolb on how Othello comes to see himself 'in terms of racial difference', a mode of 'self-evaluation [that] prefigures the internal division between Venetian self and Turkish other' (65).

his reaction: 'I took by th'throat the circumcised dog / And smote him—thus! [He stabs himself]' (5.2.352-353). Narrative switches here to performance as Othello plays two roles at once: 'valiant Othello' (1.3.49) slays his alter ego, the 'turbanned Turk' (5.2.351).[93] If Desdemona upholds the myth of intrinsic value, Othello demonstrates the impossibility of maintaining an autonomous sphere of intrinsic value against social estimations. Benedict S. Robinson points out that such social estimations shift with shifting discourses of 'transnational identity' (78).[94]

Othello's position as mercenary highlights the fact that his value depends fundamentally on how others evaluate his skills and virtues as a general. It also depends on Venice's need for defence. Some decades later, Hobbes succinctly determines a soldier's value in terms of demand:

> The *Value*, or WORTH of a man, is as of all other things, his Price; that is to say, so much as would be given for the use of his Power: and therefore is not absolute; but a thing dependant on the need and judgement of another. An able conductor of Souldiers, is of great Price in time of War present, or imminent; but in Peace not so. ... And as in other things, so in men, not the seller, but the buyer determines the Price. For let a man ... rate themselves at the highest Value they can; yet their true Value is no more than it is esteemed by others.
>
> (Hobbes 50; chapter 10)

The value of Othello as warrior and governor depends on external circumstances and diminishes quickly in times of peace.[95] His value as a soldier becomes questionable at the same time as he experiences debasement as a householder who lacks authority over his wife. Not just on the market, but also in his domestic existence, his value depends on social estimation of his and his wife's conduct.[96]

Siemon points out that even Othello's appointment as general is not just due to his reputation, but also to 'expediency': Othello himself is but a substitute for the absent Marcus Luccicos (188). When Othello is exchanged for Cassio—'Cassio shall have my place' (4.1.261)—he is replaced by the very man who has *already* taken his place (or so he thinks) as his wife's lover.[97] If the character

---

[93] See Vitkus, *Turning Turk* 91, on early modern uses of the words 'Moor' and 'Turk' as interchangeable signifiers.

[94] 'The conflict, in *Othello*, between the assimilative erotic fictions of romance and the language of a racism for which such fictions are perverse, monstrous, signals a wider contradiction between different modes of belonging—that is, finally, between the fictions sustaining a medieval notion of Christendom and those helping to shape an emergent sense of Europeanness' (78).

[95] Logan points out that the Senator's measured response to Brabantio's accusations 'is based on their recognition of Othello's value as servant to the state, not on a tolerance for alterity per se' (360).

[96] See Kolb 60. Dolan points out how Othello's credit suffers when he strikes his wife in public ('Household Chastisements' 215). Lodovico exclaims: 'Is this the noble Moor whom our full senate / Call all in all sufficient? This the nature / Whom passion could not shake?' (4.1.264-266) And Iago capitalizes on this public act by reinforcing the impression that 'He is much changed' (4.1.268).

[97] That the domestic lends itself to fantasies of replacement is also apparent in *A Woman Killed With Kindness*. Here, Wendoll is called upon to 'be a present Frankford in his absence' (6.76). While Anne

of Desdemona, and plots of cuckoldry more generally, articulate anxieties about debasement in circulation, Othello's fate demonstrates the exchangeability of men in a marketplace of commodified social relations in which each and every person is replaceable.[98] As Christopher Pye writes, *Othello* is associated 'with surrogacy generally, a preoccupation that underwrites the entire drama of protective jealousy' (*The Storm at Sea* 109). Being replaceable is inherent to a commercial society in which the primacy of exchange establishes equivalences, between both goods and people.[99]

Jealousy and Envy as Affective Coordinates of a Mobile Society

The following section looks at how the affective framework of *Othello*'s socially mobile society is represented. Dominated by exchange and preoccupied with fluctuating value, it is shaped by jealousy and envy, the two passions that drive Othello and Iago, respectively. Aristotle himself had paired jealousy with the related emotion of envy and discussed both under the name of *phthonos*. While both affects are acted out within 'a triadic relationship' between two agents or competitors and an object of desire (Meskill 17), they concern different parts of this triangle. Jealousy 'focuses on the *desired object*' (17). Envy, by contrast, is less about wanting an object that someone else has than about wanting to dispossess the person who has it: it 'focuses on the *possessor* of the desired object' (17).[100]

With Othello, the play positions jealousy at the centre of the domestic drama. Natasha Korda describes jealousy lucidly as an early modern 'discourse of subjective dispossession' (114) that gives voice to 'covetous desires' and 'anxieties of loss' (132). She quotes from Tilney to highlight such 'anxieties of loss': 'ieolousie is a certaine care of mans minde, least another shoulde possesse the thing, which he alone would enioye' (qtd. in Korda 114; Tilney C7r). Fear of dispossession is a fitting affective condition for an emerging commercial society constantly witnessing the circulation of objects through exchange networks. Once gained, there is no reason why an object of exchange should be permanently possessed. Everything, and—as Emilia suggests—everyone, has a price. Desdemona, who circulates from father to husband and potentially to other men, suggests a key premise of early modern

---

says this quite innocently, it foreshadows the betrayal: Wendoll will also perform Frankford's offices in Anne's bedchamber.

[98] See also Genster's article 'Lieutenancy, Standing In, and *Othello*' (1990).

[99] Gillen suggests that the play invokes a commercial model in which 'racialised "others" do not acquire agency through their subjugation to the economic interests of the state, but are instead assessed as commodities' (*Chaste Value* 173).

[100] Korda, who perceives Iago as 'a man consumed by envy' (134), distinguishes envy from jealousy according to its relation to possession: 'envy is characterized not by the desire to possess ... but rather by the desire to dispossess' (136). In this sense, it is 'the inverse of jealousy' (ibid.): 'envy threatens to undermine the possessive model of personhood altogether by robbing the other while failing to enrich the self' (ibid.).

mercantile thought: that someone's gain is always someone else's loss, and that, over time, gainer may turn into loser. There is an inescapable dynamic to a market in which everything has its price. It becomes tangible in Wheeler's almost manic description of all-encompassing traffic quoted earlier: 'all the world choppeth and chaungeth, runneth and raveth after Martes, Markettes, and Marchandising, so that all things come into Commerce, and passe into Traficque (in a maner) in all times, and in all places' (3). This notion of hypertrophic and omnipresent commerce suggests the impossibility of permanent ownership—nothing and no one appears safe from perpetual trafficking. The incessant circulation of objects renders ownership vulnerable. Iago uses this anxiety to his advantage.

If acquiring and retaining valuable things is, within bounds, a reasonable desire, jealousy points to the limits of reason, where desire for absolute possession becomes a force of madness. Significantly, Tilney describes jealousy as a case of projection. He identifies the cause of jealousy not in the object loved, but in the lover himself. The fear of being dispossessed originates in desire for other people's possessions: 'Two kinde of persons are commonlye sore sicke in this disease, eyther those that are euill themselues, or they, that in their youth haue gone astraye, supposing that as other mens wifes haue done towardes them, so will theirs doe towardes others' (C7r–C7v).[101] Fear of infidelity results from one's own unruly desires.[102] In her discussion of Richard Tofte's translation of Benedetto Varchi's work on jealousy from 1615, *The Blazon of Jealousie*, Korda also links jealousy to a hypertrophic and covetous desire: 'In Varchi's anatomy of jealousy, all paths lead back to the desire for exclusive possession. "Jealousie", he says, "springeth from our owne covetous minde and proper greedinesse"' (137). As an expression of excessive desire, jealousy is not accessible to reason. Emilia explains in *Othello* that jealous souls 'are not ever jealous for the cause, / But jealous for they're jealous. It is a monster / Begot upon itself, born on itself' (3.4.160–162). As 'there can be no ocular proof of innocence' (Orlin, *Private Matters* 226), submitting to jealousy means entering into an unstoppable and self-intensifying affective dynamic. As a trope of covetousness, jealousy casts acquisitive desire as a form of mania.

As is well known, Iago also claims jealousy as a motive for himself: 'I hate the Moor / And it is thought abroad that 'twixt my sheets / He's done my office. I know not if't be true, / But I for mere suspicion in that kind / Will do as if for surety' (1.3.385–389). Iago suggests that only a balancing out of affective states might satisfy him: 'And nothing can or shall content my soul / Till I am evened with him, wife for wife' (2.1.296–297). This statement is full of scandalous sexual innuendo, suggesting a servant who seeks to fill his master's place in bed. Yet Iago's decision to treat the mere suspicion of Emilia's and Othello's adultery as 'surety'

---

[101] Tilney concludes that this mode of reasoning is the 'greatest foolishnesse to speake off' (C7v).

[102] Robert Burton describes jealousy as a variation of love-melancholy, which is an excessive desire and 'burning lust' for a beautiful beloved. When love-melancholy rages after marriage, it constitutes '*Jealousie*' (54; vol. 3), which translates desire for possession into fear of loss.

seems rather contrived. Tellingly, Iago's statement 'I hate the Moor' (1.3.385) is linked to the question of cuckoldry by the non-committal conjunction of enumeration: 'and'. Instead of offering a causal conjunction that might explain his hate (such as 'because' or 'as'), Iago simply adds the possibility of cuckoldry to his pre-existing hate in a reckoning against Othello. Leah Scragg contextualizes Iago's hostility through the tradition of morality and mystery plays, relating Iago to both the Vice figure of the former and the Devil, who appears in the latter (48).[103] Whereas the Vice lacks a concrete motive and may have served as a model for Iago's pronounced amorality, the Devil is driven by envy.[104] Like Milton's Satan, he envies 'those whose character or situation is in any way superior to his own' and suffers 'from a sense of injured merit' (Scragg 59).[105] His fall from heaven follows 'from a sense of being undervalued' (59). Scragg's characterization of the envious Devil helps to situate Iago in the context of an affective pathology of undervaluation and competition. As Korda points out, Othello's misestimation of Iago's worth figures as his first motive (134–135). Iago feels severely undervalued as 'his Moorship's Ancient' (1.1.32) and resents Cassio, who obtained the promotion that Iago feels should have been his:[106] 'and by the faith of man / I know my price, I am worth no worse a place' (1.1.9–10). The feeling that one has not received one's due, has not been 'priced' accurately, combines a sense of entitlement with begrudging envy, producing the affective pathology that Nietzsche famously called *ressentiment*.[107] Already Aristotle discussed envy as the emotion of those who feel they lack something ('begrudging or covetous envy', Ed Sanders 75).[108] In a tradition that stretches from Hesiod to Aristotle and the early modern age, envy characterizes a feeling experienced 'towards our equals' (*Rhet.* 1387b23), towards our 'fellow-competitors' (*Rhet.* II.10, 1388a9): 'those who follow the same ends as ourselves' (*Rhet.* II.10, 1388a12–13).[109] Iago, who begrudges Cassio's advancement,

---

[103] For an earlier discussion of Iago as 'descendant of the Vice', see Bernard Spivack, *Shakespeare and the Allegory of Evil*. See also Brennan, who described Iago as combining the roles of the 'commentator friend[]' and of the 'Vice-figure, a man who is an amoral rag-bag of confused motivations invested with a cynicism so profound that he must pervert or destroy any sign of virtue' (*Shakespeare's Dramatic Structures* 144). Belsey also compared Iago to the Vice who 'trod a fine line between putting on display the mechanics of temptation and ensnaring the audience itself in his own evil' ('Iago the Essayist' 159). Iago's 'I am not what I am' may also associate him with the Devil, as a direct inversion and negation of the biblical 'I am what I am' (Exodus 3:14).

[104] See also Lynn S. Meskill: 'Sixteenth-century mystery and miracle plays, in keeping with the theological tradition, would represent the devil's envy as the predominant motive for tempting Adam and Eve' (50). Korda also establishes a link between the perceived lack of motivation and envy in the early modern period. Quoting from George Whetstone's treatise on envy from 1586, she claims that envy is '"without any ground or reason"' (135).

[105] Charney also describes Iago as 'poisonously envious' and 'diabolic' (3).

[106] See also Kolb, who lists different reasons for 'Iago's self-assessment' (54).

[107] See section 10 of the First Essay of the *Genealogy of Morals* (22).

[108] In today's understanding, resentment is closely allied with envy. It is an element of what Ed Sanders calls malicious envy, a form of 'begrudging or covetous' envy, which will 'cause the patient to act to deprive the target of whatever has caused their envy' (18). Non-malicious envy, in contrast, 'will instead cause the patient to focus on his/her own shortcomings' (Sanders 18).

[109] See Meskill, who traces the genealogy of envy in chapter 2 of *Ben Jonson and Envy* 42–74.

fits this bill. While *phthonos* is clearly not exclusive to the early modern age, it may be particularly virulent in a socially mobile society. The mere possibility of social advancement may breed discontent with one's place, a sense of feeling undervalued, especially as one witnesses the rise of others with the same social aspirations.

Malicious envy turns Iago into an agent of rational irrationality who acts strategically, but is driven by passion rather than rational gain. His behaviour therefore remains opaque: it is not clear what he hopes to achieve for himself by destroying Othello and Desdemona. It is in seeking gain that economic agents become calculable; in Iago's case, that gain is obscured. Even 'the Turk'—throughout the play a symbol for all that is base and excessive—follows a calculus that renders him transparent. Upon receipt of contradictory messages concerning the Turkish fleet, the senators quickly come to an agreement about its real aim. In applying common economic logic—the principle of the greatest profit for the least expense—the senators deduce that the true destination must be Cyprus rather than Rhodes. Iago's profit is obscured by the inverse affective economy of envy: the envious man revels in another's losses even if he himself does not profit from them. George Webbe, in his *Arraignment of an Unruly Tongue* (first published in 1619), identifies two feathers that constitute the 'arrow' of envy, both of which are linked to the losses or successes of others: '1. Sadnesse at others prosperity. 2. Gladnesse at the aduersity of other men' (53; also qtd. in Orlin, *Private Matters* 198). In Aristotelian ethics, envy is an indication of the ethical status of a person's character. Where people of bad character feel *phthonos*, good people experience indignation or emulation (Ed Sanders 63–64). Iago's malicious and resentful envy characterizes him as a villain. It suits the role of the treacherous, competitive servant who seeks to dispossess his master. Iago's main instrument, rhetoric, is also typical of envy. Lynn S. Meskill highlights the function of the evil 'eye' in envy, but also of the 'tongue': 'Envy is located in the imbrication of eye and tongue, and it is this that constitutes its pervasive and unstoppable power' (65). In Iago's case, it is the tongue as the instrument of slander which wreaks the greatest damage.

Iago's envy may be a sign of the greater flexibility of social structures that creates competition between social climbers, allows servants to imagine themselves in their masters' shoes, and produces resentment through thwarted hopes. *Othello* enacts envy and jealousy as anarchic, destructive passions that threaten the rationality of social exchange. As is obvious in Iago's fate, the resentment of another's prosperity may actually hinder the rational pursuit of one's own prosperity. As envy is not focused on the desired object, but on the person who has it (Meskill 17), it cannot clear the path to wealth or social advancement. After all, the energy of envy is not expended on acquiring the object of desire, but on destroying the one who possesses it. Destruction becomes the desired object, substituting for rational self-interest. On the early modern stage, jealousy and envy are ways to explore the affective impact of market relations. In the case of envy, dispossession of others becomes an end in itself; in the case of jealousy, it is a fear so great that it clouds judgement. Jealousy and envy explore circulation as a process that does not end, but merely begins with the acquisition of a valuable object or place. In proto-commercial society, acquisition offers neither respite nor lasting satisfaction—anything gained may be taken away again, anything that is salvaged from exchange may re-enter circulation. This holds true not only for unfaithful wives, but for entire estates, as the redistribution of Othello's goods suggests.

Othello's fear of dispossession and Iago's resentment are thus tropes for the affective collateral damage of life in a socially mobile commercial society. Through his position within an affective economy of frustrated ambition and envy, Iago comes to embody the emotional disposition that accompanies new possibilities of social advancement. Here, as in other plays, the insubordinate servant signals the loosening of traditional ties of obligation and the sense of social disorder that afflicts a society in transformation and threatens the ethical basis of oeconomy. Together, the treacherous subordinate and the murderous householder point to the uneasy integration of oeconomy with a self-interested, mercantile agency that is bent on reaping profit through affective manipulation.

Conclusion

This chapter explored *The Alchemist*'s and *Othello*'s attention to the amoral and mercantile rationality of insubordinate servants. In both plays, the mercantile energy of trusted servants subverts the household order. While *Othello* ends with the destruction of the household, *The Alchemist* ultimately reinstates an orderly household, but it is changed enough to allow the housekeeper Jeremy at least some authority. Although Jeremy readily resumes his old role and asks for his master's forgiveness, he retains some of his newfound autonomy and power to shape the household's fate.

Whether through new alliances or as solitary individuals, enterprising subjects (in the Renaissance sense of those who are subjected to a master) benefit from the dispersal of agency in the household and seize opportunities to make a profit. Neither the tricksters nor Iago submit to social structures that would limit them, and their Machiavellian drive beyond inherited structures of power establishes them as agents rather than 'instruments', as Bacon would have it. Their attempts at emancipation from those structures are not heroic: as insubordinate servants, they are lowly characters with a social climber's mercenary drive. Yet their wilful disregard of established social hierarchies and their readiness to take their master's place signal a larger concern with socio-economic transformation and new possibilities of social advancement. In *Othello*, the military setting lessens the distance between master and servant: if Iago had become lieutenant, he might have replaced Othello directly. Iago's envy has a similar effect, especially as it might not only be directed against Cassio, but also against Othello himself, whom he wishes to deprive of his successes. As a passion that is directed at social equals, envy pulls Othello closer to Iago, diminishing the social distance between them.

The specific version of *Homo oeconomicus* which the plays examine, of man as a self-interested and calculating economic agent, is still a far cry from Adam Smith's conception of self-love as a force that works towards the good of all. In *Othello*, at least, Iago's private ends are dictated by envy and resentment; private interest is here a destructive force which wreaks havoc. In *The Alchemist*, the amoral pursuit of private interest threatens to produce an irresolvable entanglement, with numerous clients clamouring for the promised goods. At the same time, it appears as a pervasive, even normal impulse that renders people calculable: with the persistent sway of material profit and social advancement, the play recognizes a new ordering force. Whereas Iago appears as a singular villain whose evil plotting remains unintelligible to the other characters, Jonson's comedy examines greed and competitiveness as a pervasive condition and plotting as a communal enterprise that requires tactical alliances. Not only does the comedy feature tricksters in the plural, but the sheer number of business deals and clients offers a quasi-empirical basis for exploring means and motivations and establishes desire for gain as an anthropological constant.

As self-interested servants who broker exchanges in and out of the house, sell highly speculative products, and manipulate the perception of valuable objects, Iago and the tricksters are represented in ambiguous terms. While their successes can only ever be temporary, the ends of their plots do not spell the end of pragmatism and calculation on stage. Othello's assets are pragmatically redistributed even before his body has cooled, and Face is shrewd enough to change allegiances upon his master's return and to succeed with a new scheme. In their representations of insubordinate servants who embody entrepreneurial energy and agency, both plays suggest that the question of how to make one's fortune is a key one in a commercial society that allows for social mobility, and one that may destabilize and disrupt oeconomy. Face and Iago move in a world of contingencies which they seek to shape to their advantages. True to J. G. A. Pocock's description of the Machiavellian innovator, it is '[b]y the exercise of a partly nonmoral *virtù*' that the trickster or villain 'imposes form upon *fortuna*' (184).[110] Through these self-interested servants, Shakespeare and Jonson examine a form of prudence that is both entirely detached from ethics and highly effective. It upsets traditional positions of submission and authority and expectations of loyalty. In *Othello*, Iago is finally stopped by his wife's testimony. Although she does not share Desdemona's moral outlook, Emilia is the one truly loyal servant of the play and thus acts as a counterpart to Iago. Where he appears virtuous but is really deceitful, she appears to be lacking in virtue, but is really trustworthy.

---

[110] Pocock discusses *The Prince* as an extended meditation on the relation between *virtù* and fortune (156–182).

Even Iago and the tricksters cannot fully control the events their actions set in motion. As Pocock suggests in his discussion of *The Prince*, the self-authorizing force of the innovator who breaks with custom and moulds his own fortune risks letting loose 'sequences of contingency beyond [his] prediction or control' so that the very *virtù* that enables him to dominate *fortuna* also increases his risk of falling prey to it (167). Iago himself, for instance, asks Emilia to procure Desdemona's handkerchief—not realizing that his wife will later testify against him. And the tricksters' business is too flamboyant to remain concealed for long. Luckily, Face has a master who appreciates his 'wisdom of business' and ingenuity and is only too happy to profit from both. *Othello* pictures the instrumental use of business skills as villainous while *The Alchemist* represents it as object of satire, yet both plays highlight the entrepreneurial efficiency of 'wisdom of business', persuasive speech, theatrical self-display, and the manipulation of credit and desire. Their explorations of skills and strategies are part of a broader shift in interest towards the pragmatics of mercantile agency which theatre mediates, experiments with, and makes sense of.

My exploration of socio-economic agency within and without the household suggests a pragmatic scene of emergence of the subject in the early modern era which is inextricably entangled with mercantile agency and the drive towards social advancement. As the figure of the self-interested servant suggests, even within the household, which the organological metaphor imagines as a single body, individual agents may pursue diverging interests rather than act in concert. They act strategically and are always on the look-out for useful information and opportune moments. With Iago and the tricksters, the individual emerges as the scene of plotting in the service of private interest. Interestingly, *Othello* and *The Alchemist* do not posit this subjectivity as a universal model, but as an aberration. Neither the clients in *The Alchemist* nor Othello and Desdemona employ a hermeneutics of suspicion. All these characters are largely defenceless because they lack strategic acumen, suspicion, innovative force, and versatility. Othello and Desdemona are virtuous, the clients greedy, but all fall equal prey to those who have mastered 'wisdom of business'. Furthermore, both plays explore the tensions resulting from the subject's ambiguous position between self-reliant agency and subjection to pre-existing social and economic structures. In the context of a mercantile logic of exchange, the subject is ambiguously placed as agent and commodity, as the subject and object of acts of valuation. Pye makes an important point when he observes that the early modern subject is located at the point 'where economy establishes itself *as* a system' (*The Vanishing* 14), for it is precisely at this moment that the ambiguity between heightened individual possibilities and systematic restrictions may be most palpable, between a subject that may rise in the world and the limitations that are put in place by pre-existing structures of subjection. Perhaps relations of service are ideal sites both for imagining the urge to better one's station and for exploring the social implications and oeconomic impact of the primacy of exchange and the ubiquitous drive for profit.

4
Asynchronous Exchanges in *Volpone* and *Timon of Athens*

Introduction

The preceding chapters explored the household as a socio-economic space as well as its interfaces with political and mercantile contexts. This chapter moves away from a predominantly spatial perspective to interrogate the temporality of socio-economic exchange in Shakespeare's *Timon of Athens* and Jonson's *Volpone*. In socio-economic transactions, time is of the essence. Value accrues in time, just as losses accumulate over time; reputation is subject to the vagaries of the season. How to respond to contingent events and circumstances is a key question of economic success in a changeable world, even if the status of human agency remains uncertain within a cultural framework that accepts the idea of divine providence as easily as that of Fortune's fickle wheel. Francis Bacon emphasized the ability of the individual to shape their own life with his notions of 'wisedom of Businesse' and 'architecture of fortune' (*The Advancement of Learning* 157, 165). Human agency may be partial and limited by circumstances, hence the need to 'runne with the occasions' (Bacon, *The Advancement* 173), yet this does not diminish the interest of early modern plays and practical discourses in the possibilities and consequences of human action.

In a culture of credit and investment, the interval between an initial act of lending, borrowing, or investing and its recompense is particularly precarious because it leaves time enough for all kinds of complications. Craig Muldrew points out that asynchronous or dilated exchanges were the norm rather than the exception in the credit culture of early modern England. He notes that 'debt litigation' increased as 'chains of credit expanded' ('Hard Food for Midas' 83). The 'rising tide of legal cases involving debts and broken contracts' (Kerrigan 13) offers plenty of evidence for complications that ensue in and because of the time lag between an initial act and a reciprocal one. On the early modern stage, a play like *The Merchant of Venice* thrives on the incalculability of risks inherent to the time lag between a loan and its repayment. The uncertain future of dilated exchanges inscribes stories with an open-endedness that can mobilize suspense even when the story itself is familiar from myth or chronicles, as is the case with *Timon of Athens*.

This chapter discusses *Volpone* and *Timon of Athens*, two plays in which economic action transgresses the limits of oeconomy. In fact, the households they depict leave classical oeconomy far behind. From the standpoint of classical and early modern oeconomy, a household without a mistress was incapable of reproducing itself and thus seemed substantially lacking. In both plays, the absence of a wife and legitimate children means that the household is homo- rather than heterosocial, with the central relation being that of master and servant. In both plays, these homosocial households are wholly given to exchanges, forming part of an exclusively male network of gulls, false friends, and supplicants. In both plays, exchanges come in a dilated form, with a significant interval between a present payment or gift and a hoped-for or promised future recompense. Both plays explore the accrual and loss of wealth over time through the self-interested exploitation of this interval. And both plays use the gift as a model of dilated exchange to interrogate an economic calculus of obligation and delayed reciprocity that is symptomatic of the vagaries and opportunities of a culture of credit. Finally, both plays are deeply interested in the affective conditions of credit and investment: where *Volpone* traces the accumulation of self-aggrandizing pleasure together with the accrual of value, *Timon* stages disillusionment and bitterness as companions of misplaced trust and excessive expenditure. John Jowett describes their use of themes as inverted concerns: 'With *Timon of Athens*'s theme of expenditure and loss, and *Volpone*'s theme of acquisition and accumulation, it would seem that one play was written partly as a response to the other' ('Introduction' 7–8).[1]

Chapter 3 focused on the skills and strategies of entrepreneurial subordinates. This chapter recognizes the management of time as a crucial skill in a culture of credit and investment. The prudent man must manage an uncertain future by predicting the actions of others and by calculating the consequences of his own. J. K. Barret identifies the unpredictability of the future as a key concern of early modern literature.[2] In *Volpone* and *Timon of Athens*, economic success depends not just on rhetorical and performative skills and strategic acumen, but specifically on the ability of 'working time': of capitalizing on the uncertainty of the future and of rendering the interval between payment and recompense productive. As discussed in Chapter 1, Muldrew described the early modern credit economy as a moral economy that relied on trust (*The Economy of Obligation* 4). *Timon of Athens* and *Volpone* explore the vagaries and opportunities that the culture of credit presents, but with little optimism about trust as a socializing value. Instead, beyond their

---

[1] Jowett's introduction to the Oxford edition of *Timon of Athens* adds that 'the two plays depict city states and share strong elements of city comedy. In particular, they present extravagant and absurd pictures of the obsession with gold ... The trio of self-interested creditors in the middle scenes of *Timon of Athens* corresponds with the trio of avaricious would-be male heirs to Volpone' (7). Jowett suggests that *Timon of Athens* might even have been planned 'as a companion piece' (8).

[2] In *Untold Futures*, Barret claims more generally that in sixteenth- and seventeenth-century literature, 'the future rarely remains predictable' (3–4); instead, it is 'characterized by uncertainty and tentativeness' (5). I share in his interest in 'those moments in which English poets and playwrights imagine an earthly future shaped by the activity of human beings rather than classical precedent or divine providence' (8).

pessimistic portrayals of social relations, these plays express a new consciousness of time as the medium in which one's fortune may be built.[3]

Working time is an economic skill, but also a poetological requirement, as the organization of plot also involves the management of time. *Volpone* and *Timon of Athens* appear acutely conscious of this: they share not only a keen interest in the temporality of socio-economic action, but also a heightened awareness of the malleability of time in the progression of plot. Strategic delays and dilatory episodes prolong the performance, direct the audience's attention, and intensify (or amplify) its affective engagement. With a nod to Peter Brooks, we can understand plot as the 'organizing dynamic' of the interval between a primary complication and its ensuing resolution.[4] Were it not for the detailed performance of the interval between a tragic deed and the hero's death, or between the undertaking of an impossible venture and its ultimate failure, a play would be over as soon as it had begun.[5] The sense of a design, logic, or dynamic that shapes the plot-as-interval emerges in both plays through delay, repetition, and digression as means of temporal organization. Although primarily a rhetorical term, dilation in its Renaissance sense may help to specify the combination of delay and expansion, of 'false endings' and an iterative, episodic structure in both plays. According to Patricia Parker, "'[t]o dilate", in Renaissance English, meant not only to expand, disperse, or spread abroad, but also to put off, postpone, prolong, or play for time—meanings which still linger in the modern English "dilatory"' ('Dilation and Delay' 520). Although 'dilation' originally applied to prose narratives, the term can illuminate the mutual dependency of expansion and delay in *Volpone* and *Timon of Athens*: both plays employ delay as a plot device, and both plots branch out into an episodic, iterative structure that prolongs and fills the interval between an initial act and its final repercussions. The dilatory plot structure coincides in Jonson's *Volpone* and Shakespeare's *Timon of Athens* with a focus on dilated exchanges that play on gift, credit, and investment practices.

The first part of this chapter analyses Jonson's comedy. *Volpone* stages a ludicrous business venture in which a rich Venetian master pretends to be on his deathbed in order to collect gifts from legacy hunters. The chapter examines this

---

[3] In *The Machiavellian Moment*, J. G. A. Pocock described time in republican theory as the dimension 'of contingent events' (3). Time is also the dimension of socio-economic exchanges, and *their* contingencies provide the early modern stage with plenty of subject matter.

[4] Brooks defines plot as 'the principle of interconnectedness and intention which we cannot do without in moving through the discrete elements—incidents, episodes, actions—of a narrative' (5). Later he explains plot as 'an organizing dynamic' (7) and in terms of the 'logic and dynamic of narrative' (10). While Brooks focuses on fiction, his notion of plot is influenced by the Aristotelian concept of the tragic *mythos* and the idea of an organized whole.

[5] The need to fill in the interval between 'the command to revenge' and 'the satisfaction of the command' is at the heart of Margreta de Grazia's compelling account of Hamlet's delay in killing his murderous uncle Claudius: 'The extremes are set, and the middle—the meantime—is all that remains. That meantime takes the form not of a telic advance from start to finish, but rather of a filling up between those two endpoints' (196–197).

gift economy as a way to explore risks and opportunities in a culture of credit. It also discusses dilated exchange in the context of a shift in early modern English legal culture that draws attention to the intentionality and temporality of the promise. The chapter then delineates the interacting economies of wealth and pleasure by analysing the interval between an advance payment and its return as source of material and affective profit. The pleasure that accrues in the interval can be understood as a kind of delight in mastery that invites self-aggrandizement. Finally, the chapter discusses dilation as structuring principle of the comedy's plot.

Timon of Athens, a play that has given rise to much debate about authorship and genre,[6] offers a powerful exploration of the role of friendship in asynchronous exchanges and of the competing paradigms of credit and gift. Both the play's political angle and its consideration of debt have been analysed in some detail.[7] Yet the way the play negotiates different temporalities through the competing economies of credit and gift deserves further attention.[8] Hence, the second part of the chapter examines different modes of giving represented by Timon and his so-called friends: the free distribution of wealth versus acquisition. These conflicting modes imply different attitudes to the future as an object of anticipation and calculation, on the one hand, and, on the other, as a site of uncontrollable contingency. These different attitudes are dramatized through different configurations of delay: the measured and definite time of credit loans, and the vague and indeterminate time of counter-gifts. The chapter also reflects on delay and expansion as structuring principles of the tragedy's action.

Asynchronous Exchange and Accumulation in *Volpone*

Like *The Alchemist*, *Volpone* depicts a business venture that runs on nothing but empty promises and a skilled performance. In contrast to *The Alchemist*, this business is not enabled by the master's absence: in *Volpone*, the eponymous master himself capitalizes on the covetousness and naïvety of various 'clients' with the

---

[6] It is now widely accepted that *Timon of Athens* is the product of collaboration between Shakespeare and Middleton (Wells and Taylor 501; see also Brian Vickers, *Shakespeare, Co-Author: A Historical Study of Five Collaborative Plays* and Jowett's 'Introduction' to *Timon of Athens*). The play forms part of the tragedy section in the Folio, but it was published in a place that had been allotted to *Troilus and Cressida*, the publication of which was postponed '[o]wing to delays in securing copyright' (Wells and Taylor 501). It is 'the only play in the Tragedies section whose title does not name it as a tragedy' (501), and its position in the Folio is hardly conclusive as to its generic status. For a detailed discussion of its genre, see William Slights's essay 'Genera Mixta and Timon of Athens'.
[7] For a topical political analysis, see Coppélia Kahn, '"Magic of Bounty": Timon of Athens, Jacobean Patronage, and Maternal Power', Andrew Hadfield, 'Timon of Athens and Jacobean Politics', and David Bevington and David Smith, 'James I and Timon of Athens'. For the play's investment in debt, see Jowett, 'Middleton and Debt in Timon of Athens', and Amanda Bailey's illuminating chapter on *Timon* and the debt bond in her book *Of Bondage: Debt, Property, and Personhood in Early Modern England*.
[8] In this constellation, the gift highlights the ethical rather than the legal nature of obligation. See my article 'Gift, Credit and Obligation in *Timon of Athens*' 14.

help of his servant Mosca. The anomalous household set is completed by a dwarf, a eunuch, and a hermaphrodite, who entertain Volpone with interludes and song. Volpone happily admits that he has no social ties: 'I have no wife, no parent, child, ally' (Volp.1.1.73).[9] In Volpone's logic, there is no need for friends and family if one has gold to fill one's heart with joy. He addresses his gold treasure fondly: 'Thou being the best of things, and far transcending / All style of joy, in children, parent, friends, / Or any other waking dream on earth' (1.1.16–18). His sole ambition is to expand his treasure further. It is precisely because the household is not a 'proper' household, but lacks a wife and legitimate children, that it can so easily be turned into a profitable business. Volpone pretends to be on his deathbed so that the lack of an heir 'draws new clients, daily' (1.1.76) to his house, where they '[c]ontend in gifts' (1.1.84) for his affection:

> VOLPONE. I have no wife, no parent, child, ally,
> To give my substance to; but whom I make,
> Must be my heir; and this makes men observe me,
> This draws new clients, daily, to my house,
> Women, and men, of every sex, and age,
> That bring me presents, send me plate, coin, jewels,
> With hope, that when I die, which they expect
> Each greedy minute, it shall then return
> Tenfold upon them ...
>
> (1.1.73–81)

The usurious intent of the visitors who hope to inherit his fortune is marked by the tenfold increase in value that they aim for. As Robert N. Watson points out in his introduction, with the clients, Jonson 'leans heavily on the tradition of Aesopian beast-fables' ('Introduction' xi). *Nomen est omen*: Volpone is the fox, and Mosca the parasitical fly; together, they trick a number of bird-characters—'the vulture, the raven, the crow, the parrot and the hawk' (Barton 107)—into offering valuable gifts. Considering that in his *Apology for Poetry* (first published in 1595), Sir Philip Sidney used Aesop's fables as 'proof' to establish the poet as a 'right popular philosopher' (109), the use of an Aesopian pattern may be a way of laying claim to a moral and didactic purpose.[10] It is in line with this moral claim that in *Volpone*,

---

[9] Mosca later intimates that dwarf, eunuch, and hermaphrodite are but a few of Volpone's illegitimate children. As if to make the scandal of Volpone's excessive lust and misdirected procreative powers more graphic, Mosca explains that Volpone's numerous bastards were begotten 'on beggars, / Gypsies, and Jews, and blackmoors, when he was drunk' (1.5.44–45). This assembly of early modern outcasts is intended to underline Volpone's debauchery.

[10] Throughout his treatise, Sidney insists on the dual aim of poesy: 'Poesy therefore is an art of imitation, for so Aristotle termeth it in his word *mimesis*, that is to say, a representing, counterfeiting, or figuring forth—to speak metaphorically, a speaking picture—with this end, to teach and delight' (101).

in contrast to *The Alchemist*, poetic justice extends to the tricksters who are, in the end, heavily punished. Furthermore, the play includes two virtuous characters, as if to offset the vices of the others. Despite such efforts, it has been noted that the skill and attraction of the tricksters far exceeds any moralizing impetus.[11]

With the help of Mosca, Volpone capitalizes on the greed of the flock of bird-characters. Their strategic giving is self-interested and chrematistic: it is modelled on the logic of usury, in which an initial payment results in a profitable return. In return for precious gifts and other favours, Mosca assures each client that the dying Volpone prefers him—or, in the case of Lady Would-Be, her—over all others. By endlessly deferring his death, Volpone collects ever more gifts and grows ever richer, while Mosca prevents the blowing of Volpone's cover by managing the clients' expectations and by skilfully emplotting unforeseen events. A delay of death is usually a hoped-for delay, but in the context of the clients' covetous desire, it becomes an impediment to satisfaction: the clients expect Volpone's death 'each greedy minute' (1.1.80) and fear delay because it threatens to alter their fortunes. The tricksters, in contrast, profit from delay. Dilatory time invites further investments from the clients and extends a pleasurable plot.

The Temporality of the Gift

In *Volpone*, clients and tricksters alike seek to exploit the conventions and peculiar temporality of the gift. The gift shares the structural delay of a reciprocal action with credit. It is thus ideal for an exploration of the asynchronous temporality of profitable lending and investing. From the point of view of an emergent discourse of investing, the clients' gifts are profitable 'outlays or expenditures' (Forman 5) that promise to reap a profit. Yet the interval between giving and receiving challenges the calculations of practical reason, which anticipates future results in order to determine present investments. It also invites double-dealings by intentional actors. In *Volpone*, both parties seek to exploit the interval. The clients' calculus—giving in the present to reap future profit—exploits the conventions of gift-giving and allows for time in the interest of a surplus gain. Mosca's assurances of future wealth are tailored to meet the clients' hopes, but they can only be effective if the interval is continually elongated. Mosca's task is to manage the interval and its affective effects in order to ensure the flow of gifts. Although both parties integrate the interval between gift and recompense into an economic calculus, only the tricksters are—at least for a while—in control of time and timing. They delay Volpone's death and manage the clients' expectations. The clients, on the other

---

[11] See Jonas Barish about Jonson's 'rascals and manipulators' who 'are armed against our disapproval with a formidable weapon: the inventiveness of their talent, the gusto with which they exercise it. They command their own changes; they dictate their own motions; they keep the turning world turning' (146).

hand, are subjected to the vagaries of time: their fortune depends on a desired event that is beyond their immediate control. There is one exception, though: Corbaccio actually tries to seize control of Volpone's state of health by administering a poison to him. The murder is prevented by Mosca, but it shows that the clients are not hampered by moral concerns, but merely by a lack of discrimination and wit.

Volpone and Mosca's business scheme is a 'project' in the seventeenth-century sense of the word: a potentially dubious but innovative venture driven by the promise of profit and managed with wit and dexterity.[12] If projects were once connected with the ideas of the Commonwealthmen and thus with plans to address the needs of the poor (Thirsk, *Economic Policy* 18), controversial monopolies and patents turned projects into disreputable ventures:[13] 'The very name became a dirty word in the early seventeenth century, synonymous with rogue and speculator' (17).[14] Volpone and Mosca's business venture is the epitome of such a dubious project, a scam that invites speculation. With the ruse of the dying man without heir, the tricksters invite the clients to bet on a future that never comes; their investment proves lucrative only for the tricksters. At the same time as this 'project' proves profitable, 'projecting' also appears as a pleasurable activity. The pleasure of acquisition enacted in the play indicates a complex revaluation of entrepreneurship in a society that is increasingly shaped by commerce. Certainly, the tricksters' 'project' is amoral, but at least it speaks of an autonomous will to exercise one's skills. Its alternative is boredom and passive subjection to the vagaries of fortune.[15]

Volpone and Mosca's project generates instant gain at no expense as they reward gifts with false assurances that are of no consequence. The great risk the clients are willing to take in giving without certain return is commensurate with the great

---

[12] Joan Thirsk, who suggests that entrepreneurship fundamentally transformed the structure of economy in the early modern era (*Economic Policy* 2), describes the meaning of 'project' and 'projector' as follows: 'Everyone with a scheme, whether to make money, to employ the poor, or to explore the far corners of the earth had a "project"' (1).

[13] The Commonwealthmen 'were advocating the setting up of many new industries' in Britain (Thirsk, *Economic Policy* 18). According to Thirsk, Sir Thomas Smith's *The Discourse of the Commonweal* 'was in some sense a party programme' (16): it argued in favour of producing foreign wares at home to provide people with work. Thus the Commonwealthmen 'gained a reputation as friends and helpers of the poor' (18).

[14] This meaning lingers in the eighteenth century. Thirsk quotes Daniel Defoe to underscore this point: 'Projector, wrote Defoe, was a "despicable title". Such men always had "their mouths full of millions"' (17–18).

[15] In 'Jonson's Joyless Economy', Oliver Hennessey situates Volpone's pleasure economy within a changing socio-economic reality. Hennessey points out that for 'the moneyed classes of seventeenth-century Venice (as represented by an English playwright), the danger to subjective well-being is primarily one of boredom' (93). He argues that Volpone, although belonging to the ranks of the 'Venetian gentry' (98), is aligned with 'a non-normative mode of behaviour more associated with labor' and that he derives pleasure precisely from 'avoiding the hegemony of comfort' and the 'resultant ennui' of the elite (99). He claims that happiness in this play is associated with 'skilled labor' (100) and emphasizes the play's interest in 'alternative models of social organization—those based on orthodox feudalism, and those interested in self-ownership of labor and the acquisition of capital through production and economic activity' (100). See also page 101: 'What seems to be emerging is a model of well-being at work in the play which privileges the fiscal activity of entrepreneurs, projectors, and other forms of proto-capitalists over the feudal hoarders and mere displayers of wealth.'

extent of their desire. This desire translates mere hopes into near-certainties. As Mosca puts it: 'this hope / Is such a bait, it covers any hook' (1.4.134–135). Mosca acts as a 'third man' who manages exchanges on his master's behalf. Against the backdrop of the project as an innovative business with an uncertain outcome, we can appreciate his skill in baiting the clients as investors. His persuasive rhetoric of low risks and imminent recompense belies the uncertainty of future success. In his seductive rhetoric, every single gift is sure to decide the succession of Volpone's house for good, and Volpone is always already as good as dead. Mosca reassures clients, whets their appetites, and smoothes over the fact that the promised event is far from assured. He substitutes copious words for actual objects and deeds. Well versed in a Baconian version of practical wisdom, Mosca employs information strategically, by giving regular updates on Volpone's health and the status of his affection, and he uses a persuasive rhetoric that assures clients of Volpone's devotion and his own loyalty. In its attention to skills and strategies, and with a business venture that runs on naïve hopes, *Volpone* pre-empts key features of *The Alchemist*. Its setting has also structural similarities: an anomalous, purely homosocial household that fails the ideal of the Christian family and is invested in exchange rather than procreation.

Strategic Delay: The Temporality and Intentionality of the Promise

The tricksters' business model poses the problem of how to assure the clients of a future that is far from certain and even—as the audience knows—quite unlikely: Volpone is neither ill nor has he any intention of electing an heir. Mosca's work consists in lengthening the interval between the clients' gifts and the promised inheritance without letting the clients lose hope of recompense so that the gifts keep coming. As the future as the object of the clients' hopes is by definition uncertain, Mosca needs to rhetorically bridge the gap between a present act and its future response or result. The following section contextualizes the play's preoccupation with the futurity of recompense and Mosca's assurances of certain success with the help of an early modern legal problem: the rise of the action of *assumpsit*, which argued for a breach of contract on the grounds of a broken promise. As A. W. B. Simpson writes, 'the action of assumpsit' evolved in the 'sixteenth century' (68).[16]

[16] According to Simpson, 'An "assumpsit" is normally thought of as an undertaking, in the sense of an assurance, and for many purposes this is no doubt accurate enough to catch the sense of the word in the early cases' (215). While Simpson gives a highly differentiated account of differently nuanced meanings, for my purposes here it is enough to highlight the meaning of making oneself responsible or answerable for a certain act or outcome. As Simpson writes, the first uses of the action of assumpsit can be traced 'back into the 14th century', but 'it was not until the 16th century that it achieved any great prominence as a remedy for broken agreements, and not until the 17th century that it became the regular common law contractual action' (Abstract of 'Introduction', *A History of the Common Law of Contract*).

In contrast to the 'recuperatory action' of debt, it was 'an action for compensation for breach of promise' (68).

Before turning to the promise as a legal problem, however, I want to take a closer look at how Mosca's assurances work. It is conspicuous that many of his assurances actually deflect from the futurity of recompense by means of presentification. The encounter between Mosca and the first client provides a sufficient example. Mosca assures the lawyer Voltore: 'You are his heir, sir' (1.3.27). In answer to Voltore's anxious question, 'Am I inscribed his heir, for certain?' (1.3.33), Mosca ties his own fate to Voltore's to demonstrate his absolute loyalty and certainty of imminent success: 'All my hopes / Depend upon your worship: I am lost, / Except the rising sun do shine on me' (1.3.35–37). He claims to safeguard Voltore's prospects in the present in the hope that Voltore will take care of him in the future, and thus gives his own position credibility with the suggestion of a quid pro quo. In a textbook example of Thomas Wilson's ornamental figure of amplification, 'An Evident, or Plain, Setting-Forth of a Thing as Though It Were Presently Done' (203),[17] Mosca implies that he is already Voltore's servant and that Volpone's estate is also already as good as Voltore's:

> MOSCA.   Sir.
> I am a man that have not done your love
> All the worst offices: here I wear your keys,
> See all your coffers, and your caskets locked,
> Keep the poor inventory of your jewels,
> Your plate, and monies, am your steward, sir.
> Husband your goods here.
>
> (1.3.38–44)

This speech performs the symbolic transfer of Volpone's goods to Voltore. By combining the second-person possessive pronoun 'your' with the deictic anchor of a double 'here' plus present tense, Mosca transfers a possible future state into an actual present. In fact, he suggests that his undertaking has already proven successful, as the use of present perfect indicates: 'I am a man that have not done your love / All the worst offices: here I wear your keys'. Presentifying a desired future state has an amplifying effect. The inventory, here represented in Mosca's enumeration of goods, likewise whets Voltore's appetite. As with the tricksters in *The Alchemist*, Mosca's use of rhetorical amplification substitutes for the real acquisition of wealth. To fully assure Voltore, Mosca offers a hyperbolically sensory description of the recently signed testament: 'The wax is warm yet, and the ink scarce dry / Upon the parchment' (1.3.46–47). Offering a description of a desired state of affairs as if it was actually happening—had, in fact, just happened—works here to full effect:

---

[17] See Chapter 3, 145.

it renders Voltore's status as sole heir plausible, and deflects attention from the fact that Mosca's assurances can only be verified in the future.[18]

According to the play's argument, assuring the clients is one of Mosca's main duties: he 'receives / Presents of all, assures, deludes; then weaves / Other cross-plots' ('Argument'). No matter whether they imply a past or present event, Mosca's assurances are really implicit promises about future events—Volpone is not yet dead, and his goods are still his own, as Voltore will understand soon enough. Rhetorically speaking, however, Mosca's strategy makes perfect sense. Explicit promises about the future might counteract the effect of presentification and remind the gulls that nothing is certain until it is. In consequence, Mosca rarely uses the future tense to assure the clients of their future happiness. Mostly, he skilfully circumvents the futurity of the promise by intimating a present state, as discussed above. To give another example, he assures Corvino with the rhetorical question, 'Is not all, here, yours?' (1.5.77). By assuring the clients that Volpone's estate is already as good as theirs, Mosca obfuscates the interval between present gifts and future recompense. When he uses the future tense to outline his intention, he takes care to disarm any sense of uncertainty. He tells Corbaccio 'I / will so advise you, you shall have it all' (1.4.82–83), balancing the futurity of success with a determined 'shall'. Mosca himself takes here responsibility for Corbaccio's success; we might say that he has undertaken (*assumpsit*) to bring about this success through his advice.

Mosca's attempts to establish himself as the man who works tirelessly on each client's behalf, and his varied rhetorical assurances of imminent and certain success highlight the risks that dilated and future-orientated transactions imply: promises might be broken and expectations frustrated. The moral significance of the promise—already emphasized by Aristotle and Cicero—signals this very possibility. In the *Nicomachean Ethics*, being 'truthful both in life and in word' (*EN* IV.7, 1127a24–25) is the hallmark of the 'equitable' man (*EN* IV.7, 1127b4). Under the heading of 'keeping faith with compacts made', Cicero identifies fidelity to promises as a virtue in its own right (*Off*. 1.15). Around the turn of the seventeenth century, however, the promise to perform an action posed not only a moral but also a legal problem.[19] At the time, a protracted court case, *Slade vs. Morley*, raised the question of the relation between promise and contract and drew attention to 'issues of intentionality, temporality, and future fixity intrinsic to the commissive speech act' (Barrett 38). *Slade vs. Morley* was heard in different locations between

---

[18] Katharine Eisaman Maus makes a similar point about another client, Corvino. She argues that Mosca 'encourages the pathologically jealous Corvino to prostitute his wife to Volpone by emphasizing the certainty and immediacy of a return: "Why, 'tis directly taking a possession!" (2.6.85)' ('Idol and Gift in *Volpone*' 436).

[19] See Luke Wilson's introductory remarks on the rise of '[c]ontractualism and contract-related terms like *assumpsit* and *consideration*' and the 'extension of liability' around the turn of the seventeenth century (144).

1595 and 1602 and must have made a mark in public debate well before *Volpone* was first staged. The case drew attention to a series of issues relevant to a culture of frequently oral contract making, in which asynchronous exchanges relied fundamentally on promissory verbal obligations.[20] John Slade had sown rye and wheat, and Morley had bought it for the sum of sixteen pounds. Morley agreed 'to pay the sum at the Feast of St. John the Baptist next ensuing' (Sacks, 'The Promise' 31), but failed to deliver. The question at stake in the ensuing trial was whether the suit could be treated as an action on the case of *assumpsit* as well as an action for debt (32). An action for debt was problematic for the plaintiff because it allowed for the use of 'wager of law', a procedure which was common in debt cases and in which 'compurgators or oath helpers ... swore to their belief in the veracity of the oath-taker' (34), who could thereby deny the existence of a contract. An action on the case of *assumpsit* had the advantage of circumventing the 'wager of law'. Instead of aiming at retrieving the sum or objects that had been lent, it allowed for the suing for damages. Thus it placed emphasis 'on the breach of faith, or trust, involved rather than restitution of lost property, as was the case in suits of debt, and damages were awarded on the basis of this fact' (Muldrew, 'Interpreting the Market' 180). In essence, the question of which action was admissible in the case of a failed contract boiled down to the question of whether the 'making of a simple contract was simultaneously the making of a promise' (Sacks, 'The Promise' 33). Slade's lawyers saw 'the making of a contract as the equivalent of a speech act' (36), and hence perceived a contract as implied promise (37). In the end, the judges agreed. If there was sufficient consideration, i.e. a material benefit, the obligation that arose from a promise was enforceable under the Common Law.[21] *Slade vs. Morley* drew attention to the contractual issues that were at stake in dilated exchanges as well as to the future-orientation and intentionality of promises.[22]

In contrast to older conceptions of debt, the action of *assumpsit* emphasized the temporality of an executory contract. In his account of English contract law,

---

[20] Muldrew pointed out that the early modern culture of credit was to a large extent an oral culture: most credit was given on the basis of informal agreements ('Interpreting the Market' 174).

[21] Not every promise was legally actionable: the common law rejected 'promises that lacked a quid pro quo' (Sacks, 'The Promise' 38), such as, for instance, promises 'where only a charitable purpose could be discovered' (38) and which, therefore, lacked a material cause and hence 'consideration'. In the latter half of the sixteenth century, 'consideration', a notoriously difficult term, was linked with the 'quid pro quo' of contractual obligation (30). Sacks quotes from the 1624 edition of John and William Rastel's *Termes de la Ley*, which introduced consideration as legal term denoting 'the material cause of a contract without the which no contract can binde the party' (qtd. in Sacks, 'The Promise' 30). As J. H. Baker writes, 'This was the context in which discussion began as to what constituted a "good" consideration. Would a merely subjective motive (such as affection), or a "continuing" motive (such as kinship), give binding force to an undertaking; or must the plaintiff have done or promised something in return?' (342). By 1588, 'the courts had ruled out "love and affection" as consideration for an *assumpsit*' (J. H. Baker 344).

[22] The notion of assumpsit occurs explicitly in *The Alchemist* (Luke Wilson 156): in Act One, Scene Two, Face mock-forces Subtle to accept Dapper's case and forces the money on him. He is to take on Dapper's case 'Upon no terms, but an *assumpsit*' (*Alch.* 1.2.69). The assumpsit also influenced the contractual mode of the Induction in *Bartholomew Fair* (Luke Wilson 157).

Simpson juxtaposes a medieval understanding of debt as 'a consensual transaction' (79) with a more modern one, which centres on future performance. The older understanding of debt did not focus on a breach of promise and the damage this implied, but on a recuperatory action:

> In modern legal thought a contract is regarded primarily at least as an agreement (or a set of promises) binding the contracting party to do something in the future ... This was not at all the way in which a consensual debt transaction was looked upon in the old law; such transactions were thought of as giving, granting, or transferring a thing to the creditor. This 'thing', the debt, he could claim by writ of debt because the transaction had entitled him to it; the vice of the debtor who failed to pay up was not that he had failed to do something which he had said he was going to do, but rather that he was detaining or withholding something to which the creditor was entitled. He was guilty of misfeasance, not nonfeasance.
> (Simpson 79–80)

From this point of view, a debt contract regulated the spatial distribution of money or goods. Luke Wilson describes this as follows: 'In debt, contract is conceived as a relation between things and where they are located relative to where they ought to be located ... In debt, therefore, contract is conceived in atemporal terms' (153). In recognition of the temporality of promising, an action of *assumpsit* was not recuperatory, not directed at 'recover[ing] debt, but sought damages for breach of contract' (Barrett 40). It focused on the temporality of an executory contract, on the failure to do what one had promised to do. Wilson writes: 'The action of assumpsit distracts or distends the structure of the contract into a futurity that retroactively precipitates the promises, intentions, deceits, motives, and considerations according to which the action organizes itself' (153). The shift in legal action that the rise of the action of *assumpsit* implied is thus also a shift in attention to the futurity and intentionality of dilated exchanges. Mosca's assurances similarly draw attention to the risks that the futurity of recompense implies as soon as there is an interval that separates an initial payment and an act of recompense. The problem is not only that dilated exchanges open an interval that allows for all kinds of complications; it also provides a lucrative opportunity for deceitful agents and thus heightens the unpredictability of socio-economic exchanges. Volpone and Mosca's plot exemplifies the problematic status of the interval. At the same time, Mosca's repeated uses of presentification indicate that his clients are well aware of the uncertainty of the future, hence their eagerness to be reassured. And yet their greed is strong enough that they trust in the oral assurances of a subservient middleman whose function as a 'third man', to paraphrase Bacon, creates a triangle structure which complicates the quid pro quo of bilateral exchange. Clearly, both Mosca's intentionality and his authority to promise Volpone's estate are more than questionable. The clients' gullibility can only be explained by the strength of their acquisitive desire.

Delay as Pleasure Principle

Wealth is the aim of most transactions in *Volpone*. It constitutes a pervasive and powerful motivation, but the play establishes the pleasure that results from active deferral as a complementary and sometimes conflicting profit. The tricksters' delight stems not only from accruing wealth. It is also fed by the ongoing deferral of a resolution that would bring the tricksters' plot to a halt. Such a resolution—which could be either Volpone's actual death or the revelation of the scam—would end a lucrative series of gifts, but also put a stop to a thoroughly enjoyable 'sport', to use Iago's term. When it comes to pleasure derived from wit, no resolution is better than a happy resolution, as the 'false ending' proves, in which the tricksters are acquitted from any wrongdoing. After all, even a happy ending terminates the fun derived from a witty plot. The following section analyses the economy of pleasure that is maintained by the very deferral of satisfaction.

The play begins with Volpone's 'idolatrous worship of gold' (Ladegaard 65): 'Open the shrine, that I may see my saint' (1.1.2). The monologue establishes wealth as all-powerful motivation of human action, which makes 'men do all things':

> VOLPONE. Dear saint,
> Riches, the dumb god that giv'st all men tongues;
> That canst do nought, and yet mak'st men do all things;
> The price of souls; even hell, with thee to boot,
> Is made worth heaven! Thou art virtue, fame,
> Honour, and all things else! Who can get thee,
> He shall be noble, valiant, honest, wise—
>
> (1.1.21–27)

Christian writers had established covetousness as 'the root of all evil'; perversely, Volpone equates wealth with virtue. Within the world of the play, Volpone's description of the effect of 'riches' is entirely realistic. Mosca's swift ascent from servant to heir in the public eye is a case in point: his newly-acquired wealth substitutes for noble birth as the basis of social standing. Timon also addresses the levelling power of gold in his mock encomium in a passage that prompted Marx to state: 'Just as in money every qualitative difference between commodities is extinguished, so too for its part, as a radical leveller, it extinguishes all distinctions' (1: 229). Money acts as an equalizer. Similarly, Timon points out the transformative potential of gold in his speech: 'Thus much of this will make / Black white, foul fair, wrong right, / Base noble, old young, coward valiant' (*Tim.* 4.3.28–30).[23] This mutability corresponds with the alchemical trope in *The Alchemist*.

In the comedy, wealth as a singular motivation is counteracted by a different force. Right after his praise of gold, Volpone evokes an economy of pleasure in which delight stems not so much from the possession of wealth as from its clever pursuit: 'Yet, I glory / More in the cunning purchase of my wealth, / Than in the glad possession' (1.1.30–32). The term 'glory' transfers idolatrous admiration from the object (gold) to its 'cunning purchase'. Delay maintains not only an economy of wealth, but also of pleasure. In fact, delay itself heightens pleasure by postponing satisfaction. Withholding satisfaction from others, moreover, affords a pleasurable sense of control. Volpone and Mosca employ delay as a strategy for grooming and teasing the clients as a means to heighten their desire—hence the image of the cherry that knocks against the lips, only to be withdrawn in the next moment:

> VOLPONE. ... whilst some, covetous
> Above the rest, seek to engross me, whole,
> And counterwork, the one, unto the other,
> Contend in gifts, as they would seem, in love;
> All which I suffer, playing with their hopes,
> And am content to coin 'em into profit,
> And look upon their kindness, and take more,
> And look on that; still, bearing them in hand,
> Letting the cherry knock against their lips,
> And draw it by their mouths, and back again.
>
> (1.1.81–90)

For Volpone, delaying payback is not simply part of an economic calculus. It also proves inherently pleasurable: Volpone delights in withholding satisfaction, in teasing the clients with the cherry of his succession because he delights in a sense of control over others.[24] In contrast, Mosca—true to his role as servant—employs delay strategically for Volpone's enjoyment.[25] Volpone's affective investment is exemplified by the inventory of his estate after he has been proclaimed dead. In front of all the would-be heirs, Mosca takes stock of the estate, displaying all the goods in detail and number before resolving the question of succession. As noted earlier, Parker identifies the inventory as a paradigmatic figure of amplification

---

[23] As Jowett points out ('Introduction' 53), Marx quotes *Timon of Athens* in the *Ökonomisch-philosophische Manuskripte* (*Economic and Philosophical Manuscripts of 1844*). Marx includes the above passage from *Timon of Athens* and commends Shakespeare's understanding of the nature of money: 'Shakespeare schildert das Wesen des Geldes trefflich' (3.5.XLII).

[24] See also John Sweeney 224.

[25] Carol A. Carr discusses the differences between Mosca and Volpone: 'Mosca is detached and calculating with his eye ever on his advantage. Volpone, in contrast, is imaginatively involved in the moment and seeks, above all, pleasure' (146).

(*Literary Fat Ladies* 130).[26] Bacon explained this effect: 'So when a great moneyed man hath divided his chests and coines and bags, hee seemeth to himselfe richer then hee was, and therefore a way to amplifie any thing, is to breake it, and to make an anatomie of it in severall partes' (qtd. in Parker, *Literary Fat Ladies* 128).[27] As a rhetorical figure, *amplificatio* caters to acquisitive hunger. The inventory of goods heightens and intensifies affective reactions: hope and desire as well as disappointment and frustration. Stoically, Mosca resists the clients' questions until they have had the opportunity to peruse 'what they hope are now their treasures—until they read the will' (Redwine 310). Delaying the resolution of the question of succession until the very last moment, Mosca then informs the clients of his own newly-won status as heir. Their disappointment heightens Volpone's enjoyment; Volpone has watched the entire scene from a place of hiding, revelling not merely in this inventory of his wealth, but also, and perhaps even more so, in Mosca's humiliation of the bird-characters.

While Volpone enjoys teasing others by withholding satisfaction, he also enjoys deferral of his own satisfaction, at least if he is in control of the delay. Deferring ultimate victory or consummation for oneself can be as pleasurable as withholding satisfaction from others. Volpone's hot pursuit of entertainment through delay becomes obvious in the Celia scene, which lays bare both Volpone's compulsion to delay satisfaction and its vicissitudes. Here, desire has an overtly sexual nature: Volpone employs delay as an erotic strategy which, in the literature of Ovid, Dante, and Milton is associated with the female. Parker writes:

> In Ovid's *Ars Amatoria*, delay is the principal strategy of courtship, the postponing or putting off of consummation or coitus. Ovid's term for this erotic delay is *mora* (II.717–718; III.473–474; III.752). But in Andreas Capellanus's influential *De arte honeste amandi*, the Ovidian term is frequently replaced by *dilatio*: the deferral of consummation is thus its dilation, or delay, a specifically feminine plot in which holding a suitor at a distance creates both a space in between and an intervening time.
>
> ('Dilation and Delay' 528)[28]

---

[26] See Parker, *Literary Fat Ladies* 130–131. Parker uses dilation and amplification synonymously when she writes about 'amplification or dilation by division' (130). In 'Shakespeare and Rhetoric', Parker describes dilation and rhetorical amplification as interchangeable in Renaissance English (55). Like amplification, dilation leads to an intensification of affect.

[27] The quotation comes from the 1597 edition of Bacon's *Essays*: 'A Table of Coulers', 51.

[28] Barbour agrees that delay is feminized, but suggests that in terms of early modern beliefs about reproduction, a man had to 'mimic his wife's rhythms, linger wantonly, tease out her heat. Because a woman's arousal is indispensable to her fertility, a male erotics of delay, fusing erection and flirtation, is a social imperative, not an aberration' (1010).

Seemingly used as a strategy of seduction, in the Celia scene dilation serves to prolong and amplify Volpone's experience of power, pleasure, and sexual excitement. As Richmond Barbour points out, 'Volpone savors postponement' (1009): 'Reassuring himself of his vigor, he reaches a state of overdetermined excitation, a multiply libidinous meantime' (1010). Volpone 'entertains' Celia with compliments, songs, and sweet memories of his youthful erotic prowess. Crucially, expansion and delay are mutually dependent and reinforcing: delayed satisfaction opens up a space for expansive action, while such action itself takes up time and thus causes delay. Volpone's presentation of riches to Celia is superficially part of the wooing: 'See, behold, [*Shows the treasure*] / What thou art queen of' (3.7.187–188). In truth, however, showing off his possessions amplifies his own sense of his wealth. While superficially a compliment on *her* beauty, this performance unfolds or dilates to celebrate *his* skills, riches, and attractions, and to put off consummation of the sexual act. It is only when Celia refuses to play along and admire him that Volpone's self-satisfied mood changes:

> VOLPONE. I do degenerate, and abuse my nation,
>   To play with opportunity thus long:
>   I should have done the act, and then have parleyed.
>   Yield, or I'll force thee.
>
>   (3.7.262–265)

Celia's disinterest provokes a sharp decline in Volpone's pleasure; in consequence, he loses patience.

Volpone's focus on the pleasure of delay positions the expansion of wealth through dilated and asymmetrical exchange as a source of excitement and exhilaration. For creditors and debtors, but also for projectors who have invested in an uncertain venture, its success can be an existential matter: a question of losing one's estate (as in Middleton's *A Trick to Catch the Old One*) or even of life and death (as in *The Merchant of Venice*). Yet anxiety, fear, and regret are not the only emotions that attend high-risk enterprises.[29] As Volpone's and Mosca's performances of self-delight suggest, successful management of the interval creates pleasure and intensifies a sense of self.

Mastery and Self-Aggrandizement

Volpone's hypertrophic desire for continued pleasure through dilation also emerges in his inability to end the scam before things turn sour. After he and Mosca

---

[29] The anxiety that attaches to the interval is discussed at length in the first scene of *The Merchant of Venice*, where Salanio and Salarino discuss Antonio's seafaring venture as a possible source of his displeasure.

narrowly escape discovery in the first court scene, there is a pause in the action which is filled with Volpone's soliloquy. This is a rare pause in what 'has been an enormously *busy* play' (Greenblatt, 'The False Ending' 90).[30] Yet what should feel like a victory, the final conning of clients and judges in court, looks more like defeat. Stephen Greenblatt notes the peculiar 'deadness' (93) of Volpone's verse: 'Well, I am here; and all this brunt is past! / I ne'er was in dislike with my disguise, / Till this fled moment' (5.1.1–3). Volpone's disillusioned exclamation 'Well, I must be merry' (5.1.7) indicates a sense of emptiness—Volpone has lost his spirits:

> VOLPONE. Give me a bowl of lusty wine, to fright
> This humour from my heart—hum, hum, hum; (*He drinks*)
> 'Tis almost gone already: I shall conquer.
> Any device, now, of rare, ingenious knavery,
> That would possess me with a violent laughter,
> Would make me up, again! So, so, so, so. (*Drinks again*)
> This heat is life; 'tis blood, by this time! Mosca!
>
> (5.1.11–17)

These lines represent an attempt to sustain a sense of pleasure and, with it, of self-aggrandizement and substance to fill 'the void' that becomes tangible in this pause (Greenblatt, 'The False Ending' 93).[31] The cure for the deflation of Volpone's ego and pleasure are 'lusty wine' and a piece of 'ingenious knavery' that produces 'violent laughter'. These means would be enough to make Volpone 'up' again. This may be a sexual pun, but in any case, the sense of rising, together with 'violent laughter' with its influx of air, suggests another meaning of the word 'dilation': 'being "puffed up", or inflated' (Parker, 'Dilation and Delay' 526). The wine contributes to this meaning: as the pseudo-Aristotelian Problem XXX, 1 suggests, wine contributes warmth and air to the body and thus makes men cheerful and hopeful.[32] Allusions to airy inflation mark Volpone's substance as illusory: pleasure and excitement only puff him up, while the end of his witty plot deflates him.

With Volpone's refusal to accept the first court scene as an ending to his plot, the play separates pleasure from the acquisitive drive. In terms of dramatic tension and comedic effect, Volpone's alleged death achieves yet another turn of the screw. It is, however, uneconomic in that it cuts off the flow of gifts from the would-be

---

[30] Greenblatt points out that until the beginning of Act Five, 'The stage has been filled with frenetic activity' (90).

[31] Don E. Wayne also uses the term 'self-aggrandizement' to describe Jonson's characters. He ties it 'to the lust for gold' (105), whereas I see the pleasure of conning others as an additional and perhaps more important source.

[32] This problem is published in Raymond Klibansky, Erwin Panofsky, and Fritz Saxl's *Saturn and Melancholy*. It discusses melancholia and comments on wine in this context. It notes that 'all men are keen on drinking to the point of intoxication, for wine makes everybody hopeful' (27) and claims that 'both wine and bile contain air' (29).

heirs. At this point in the plot, the economies of wealth and pleasure part ways. It follows that pleasure, in *Volpone*, is not simply harnessed to the acquisition of wealth, but constitutes an independent object of desire. It is fed by wealth, but also nourished by inventive ideas and witty plots that confirm one's mastery over others. This hunger for outwitting others may be even greater than the appetite for wealth. Hence, despite the encomium to gold with which Volpone begins, wealth is neither the sole motivation nor the ultimate end of action in the play.

Volpone himself points out that he is more delighted with the 'cunning purchase' of gold than with the gold itself, and he takes pride in the fact that he gains '[n]o common way', uses 'no trade, no venture' (1.1.33) to increase his wealth. The term 'cunning' identifies the amoral exercise of wit and the duping of others as a source of pleasure. This pleasure is really delight in the self: Volpone is enchanted with his own ingenuity. Katharine Eisaman Maus describes 'Volpone's gold-worship' as 'idolatrous insofar as it is a self-delighted performance of mastery' ('Idol and Gift in *Volpone*' 441). His sense of mastery through the self-authorized and skilful use of wit accounts for Volpone's extreme enjoyment of the charade. In the first act, after the second visitor of the day has left, Volpone is half dead with suppressed laughter: 'O, I shall burst; / Let out my sides, let out my sides—' (1.4.132–133). The physical tension has a tropological correlate in the 'violent laughter' that Volpone desires in Act Five: Volpone's self-conceited delight in his own mastery inflates his ego, literally blowing him up to the point of bursting.[33] The pleasure of mastery feeds directly into self-aggrandizement.

The pleasures of wit and mastery are greater even than sexual delights. After the first court scene, Mosca 'expects to be congratulated on the "masterpiece" of misprision and misjustice that he, Mosca, has just directed in the fourth act' (Redwine 308). After some prompting ('You are not taken with it enough, methinks?' (5.2.9)), Volpone quickly reassures him:

> VOLPONE. O, more than if I had enjoyed the wench!
> The pleasure of all womankind's not like it.
>
> (5.2.10–11)

Here, mastery through wit constitutes a source of pleasure that far surpasses sexual excitement. As wealth fills the household's coffers by accumulation, mastery fills the self with assurance and delight. It provides the self with a growing sense of power and control. In contrast with this model of investing in the ego, sexuality affords only a comparatively uninteresting counter-model of frivolous spending and merely temporary delight. The play's investment in staging the pleasures of pursuit balances two temporal processes: the acquisition of material wealth and

---

[33] Greenblatt points out that 'The essential action of *Volpone* ... is the hero's attempt to "fill himself"', to puff himself up, not least by means of 'his endless accumulations of things' ('The False Ending' 96).

the acquisition of self-confidence and authority through the masterful exertion of wit.

The self-aggrandizing effects of wit and mastery are repeated and reflected in the role of Mosca. 'Mosca's directorial genius' (Redwine 304) drives the action: he controls and manages the different clients, persuades them of their imminent success, 'and sends them on their way full of deluded hopes' (Maus, 'Idol and Gift in *Volpone*' 435). No wonder that Mosca experiences the same self-satisfied thrill as Volpone and becomes dissatisfied with his role as underling. The beginning of Act Three sees Mosca delight in his performance: 'I fear I shall begin to grow in love / with my dear self' (3.1.1–2). As with Volpone, Mosca's self-delight is ultimately rooted in the experience of mastery, of his power to bring about profitable events at the expense of others. In the second court scene, the two inflated egos collide. The scene sees the fatal falling out of master and servant, when Mosca refuses to admit that his master is, in fact, alive and he himself no heir after all. In a whispered negotiation, Mosca asks for half of Volpone's wealth in exchange for his admission that Volpone lives—but Volpone declines the offer. A little later, Volpone relents, but now Mosca refuses to strike the deal. Once Mosca has the upper hand, he falls victim to the same delusion as Volpone. There is no stopping before he has won all: like Volpone, he also suffers now from 'self-aggrandizing impercipience' (Maus, *Ben Jonson* 115). Volpone then confesses the entire ruse and drags Mosca down with him.

Mosca overreaches here for the very same reason Volpone does earlier. His rational economic calculus is grounded in an irrational desire for mastery—even Mosca's coolly calculating mind is fettered by pride and ambition. Jakob Ladegaard is right in highlighting the irrationality of their actions, which sits ill with a notion 'of "rational self-interest" in the Adam Smithian sense' (67). Yet around 1600, there was no contradiction between self-interest and irrational behaviour. Calculation could be combined with the driving and excessive force of the passions to create the conflicted portrait of a skilled and egotistical overreacher.[34] Maus notes that, 'Jonson depicts egoism as a kind of perceptual handicap' (*Ben Jonson* 114), but we might also say that Jonson depicts the intoxicating effects of self-authorized agency and newly-acquired wealth that create hunger for more. The figure of the servant who comes to experience agency and self-reliance in socio-economic exchanges evokes Face in *The Alchemist* and Iago in *Othello*. Like Iago's, Mosca's and Volpone's sense of self-aggrandizement is linked to mastery over others. Their delight stems not just from self-empowerment through wit and wealth, but invokes the pleasure-and-pain economy of social competition. As James D. Redwine notes: '*Volpone* is almost a morality play on Pride' (302).

---

[34] Sweeney calls *Volpone* (and *Sejanus*) Jonson's 'first experiments with what one might call the theatre of self-interest' and explains this further: 'In *Volpone* characters seek other characters primarily to indulge the most primitive self-gratifying impulses, and the play defines its major characters not in relation to social values but in terms of what they want for themselves' (223).

Together with jealousy (the fear of dispossession) and envy (resenting others' successes), the affect of pride relates one's own position to socio-economic competitors. Glorying in one's achievements implies the happy recognition that others have less: pride establishes superiority. Middleton's *A Trick to Catch the Old One*, with its rivalry between two old usurers, is of course another prime example of economic competitiveness and its affective cost.

In this context, it is noteworthy that Anne Barton relates Mosca to Sejanus, the eponymous hero of Jonson's tragedy, calling him an earlier, more 'murderous version' (Barton 96) of Mosca. Like *Volpone*, *Sejanus* focuses on the relation between a master and servant who 'work together for a time with devastating efficiency and success, in a partnership which allows them a seemingly effortless control over other people, until it is destroyed by a mutual violation of trust' (Barton 105). Like Mosca at the beginning of Act Three, Sejanus 'hugs himself with self-satisfaction' in his soliloquy at the beginning of Act Five (97):

> SEJANUS. Great, and high,
>   The world knows only two, that's Rome, and I.
>   My roof receives me not; 'tis air I tread:
>   And, at each step, I feele my advancèd head
>   Knock out a star in heav'n!
>
>   (*Sej.* 5.1.5–9)

This striking metaphor of self-aggrandizement—'My roofe receives me not ... / I feele my advanced head / Knocke out a starre in heav'n'—suggests an ego that is not to be contained by common measures. It captures perfectly the megalomaniac delight and pride of Jonson's entrepreneurial 'over-reachers' (Barton 96).

At a superficial glance, the clients' desires appear clearly directed towards the acquisition of wealth, yet a closer look also reveals an ambition to succeed at the expense of others. The theme of pleasure in one's own cunning finds an echo in the clients. Thus, Corbaccio childishly insists that all Mosca's ideas are really his own 'invention' (1.4.119): 'This plot / Did I think on before' (1.4.108–109). Corvino, who thinks that Volpone is too far gone to notice him, delights in cursing the old man. Voltore is immensely pleased by Mosca's (fictitious) plot to have Corbaccio disinherit his son and to make sure that this added wealth benefits Voltore as sole heir. He even applauds Mosca's plan to pitch Bonario against his father Corbaccio in violent combat. Corvino succumbs to the temptation of forcefully shortening the dying man's last days, but he is coward enough to happily leave this task to Mosca. The unconscionable and avaricious gulls pride themselves on their wit. They relish in the destruction of their equals and overestimate their own agency. *Volpone* stages the accumulation of wealth not just to get rich and richer, but as means of increasing agency and a sense of authority that is based on mastering and managing others. Tricksters as well as clients exemplify this, but Mosca perhaps most radically—in the end, he breaks free from traditional social bonds and emerges for a moment as a self-made man. As the second half of the chapter will show, *Timon of Athens* does not share this interest in self-authorization and social advancement through cunning. Its servants are loyal and honest, while the greedy flatterers lack wit. In contrast to *Volpone*, Shakespeare's tragedy is decidedly less concerned with agency than with the moral implications of different economies of obligation.

Delay and Dilation: Principles of Credit and Plot

So far, our discussion has focused on dilation—or the management of the interval between gift and recompense—as a source of affective pleasure and material wealth. Yet the temporal dynamic of delay and expansion as the two faces of dilation also facilitates a deeper understanding of the play's peculiar plot structure. While dilation is a rhetorical term and may seem an unusual choice for describing the structure of a play, it captures perfectly the double thrust of the action: the forward movement prolonged by the repeated deferral of recognition or closure, and the branching out of the main plot into an expansive, episodic structure which also delays the progression of the main plot. The play's preoccupation with the management of the interval in dilated exchanges is thus also palpable in a plot dynamic that is organized around dilation. Inspired perhaps by the dramatic potential of the interval in credit relations, *Volpone*'s action is carefully managed to prolong the performance of the tricksters' plot and build suspense, as well as to nourish an increasingly ludicrous sense of comedy through dilatory episodes.

Volpone's expansive structure emerges in the basic constellation of tricksters versus clients that evolves in three similarly structured plot strands: 'the three intrigues instigated by Volpone and Mosca against, in turn, Voltore, the lawyer, the ageing Corbaccio and Corvino the merchant' (Pfister 213). These sequences 'follow a similar pattern' (214), repeating and varying the logic of self-interested gift-giving in exchange for Mosca's assurances of certain succession. These iterations serve to amplify comic effects and expose the pervasive dominance of greed. They also constitute a form of expansion and entanglement that delays progression towards the final catastrophe. At the same time as these iterations amplify the basic point—the pervasive presence of greed and stupidity—they also form an upward trajectory of rising tension and hilarity. The clients start out with gifts in the form of material objects, but then proceed to the more extreme gestures of disinheriting a first-born son and prostituting a beautiful wife.[35] When Volpone threatens

---

[35] Maus describes the progression of gifts from 'material objects' to 'morally compromising behaviour' ('Idol and Gift in *Volpone*' 435).

to rape the innocent Celia, the escalation of events threatens to transform comedy into tragedy.

Manfred Pfister calls the different sequences of client-trickster interaction 'functionally equally important strands of plot' (213). They may feel episodic in the first act, but they contribute considerably to the increasing complications of the action. The Would-Be episodes, in contrast, are only loosely plotted, being more properly episodic and digressive. The Would-Be subplot mirrors and emphasizes the more general obsession with plotting, wit, and social competition. In his *Discoveries* (1619), Jonson addresses the relation between plot and episodes. In an Aristotelian vein, he discusses 'the measure, and extent of a *Fable Dramaticke*' (103): what a complete action is and how the proper magnitude of an action may be determined. A complete action should allow for a reversal of fortune—'till either good fortune change into the worse, or the worse into the better'—and it should 'be let grow, till the necessity aske a Conclusion' (103). This necessity is defined by two elements: 'First, that it exceed not the compasse of one Day: Next, that there be place left for digression, and Art' (103). This is followed by an analogy that explains the nature of such 'digression': 'For the *Episodes*, and digressions in a Fable, are the same that houshold stuffe, and other furniture are in a house' (103). To describe episodes and digressions as household stuff and furniture gives them a peculiar status: they do not form a necessary part of the Fable (the 'house' itself), but they adorn it, amplify certain aspects, and, above all, fill time as the plot progresses, keeping the audience entertained. Iterative and digressive episodes dilate the interval between the tricksters' scam and its discovery.

In addition to these episodic elements, there is another device of delay: the so-called 'false ending' (Greenblatt, 'The False Ending' 90) of Act Four.[36] There are a few tricky moments even before Act Four that threaten to expose the ruse, yet the real crisis comes with the first court scene in Act Four, at the end of which the tricksters walk free, while Celia and Bonario—too virtuous even to become lovers by the end of the play—are imprisoned.[37] The false ending of Act Four prolongs and intensifies the audience's pleasure because it forebodes an even more outrageous twist of the plot after the *epitasis*, 'the complication of the plot, ending in a seeming but unsatisfactory resolution' (Redwine 303). It is in Act Five that the tricksters go finally too far with a fresh ploy ('the *catastasis*'), followed by 'the comic *catastrophe*', in which they are justly punished for their actions (303). Following the classical five-act structure, the play's delayed resolution at the end of Act Four may not seem exceptional, yet the marked pause or interval at the beginning

---

[36] As Sweeney points out, the play not only has a false ending, but also a 'false' or 'rather a second beginning' (227)—an initial delay of action by means of a theatrical interlude, which sees Volpone's household servants and perhaps illegitimate children perform a song and dance.

[37] Barton notes that 'Jonson has avoided throughout doing what would have seemed only natural to most other dramatists of the period: establishing any emotional bond between these two which, in time, might ripen into love' (118).

of Act Five emphasizes the function of delay as a plot device. When the delayed catastrophe finally comes, the tricksters dig their own graves. Their ending is not due to a whim of fortune, but a result of their own actions.

The first court scene delays discovery of the tricksters and recognition of Celia's and Bonario's virtuous characters to the very end of Act Five, but Act Five is itself a masterpiece of expansive action. It has twelve scenes in total: there is, first of all, Mosca's detailed inventory, which is followed by several scenes in which Volpone mocks the clients and their ambitions. Only in Scene Ten does the prolonged mockery finally come to a close when Voltore confesses his own misdeeds in the hope of dragging Mosca down with him. Yet, when Volpone in disguise reassures Voltore that he is not dead, adding 'you are still the man; your hopes the same; / And this was only a jest' (5.12.17–18), Voltore pretends to have been possessed by a demon and is pronounced an unreliable witness. Saved from discovery by others, Volpone and Mosca proceed to undo themselves. Volpone has been declared dead and Mosca his heir, and Volpone now requires Mosca to revoke this. Yet, perhaps rather predictably, Mosca, who appears in court as rich heir and gentleman and is universally admired by the judges, fails to cooperate. Seeing that he has lost all hope of recovering his place and fortune, Volpone confesses everything, and both receive their due punishment.

With the second court scene in Act Five, Jonson does indeed put a 'snaffle in their mouths, that cry out, We never punish vice in our interludes, etc.' ('The Epistle', in *Volpone* 169). In contrast to *The Alchemist*, *Volpone* metes out poetic justice at the end: all offending characters have to pay dearly for their greed. The harsh ending, combined with the high-spirited wit of the villains who take a fall, inscribe this comedy with a tragic touch.[38] It is almost as if, with the severe punishment at the end of *Volpone*, Jonson retroactively justifies his dilatory representation of the tricksters' rhetorical and performative skills, of their wit and inventiveness. Barbour perceives the relation between moral ending and delightful trickery in dynamic, even dialectical terms:

> With Jonson, durations and closures are dialectically intervolved, and it is a mistake to assume that he is more present in his endings than in his meantimes. That Volpone will be terribly punished, for example, suspends Jonson's working indignation and frees the playwright to inhabit his character's enthusiasms.
> (1006)

It is the moral ending that allows the free play of the interval—and the amoral interval that demands eventual closure.

---

[38] 'The great characters of Mosca and Volpone, even if they are vices and must have a fall, make the end potentially tragic, as if the ghost of the rejection of Falstaff has endured' (Hart 118). *The Alchemist*, in contrast, rewards both Face's wit and his master Lovewit. In light of 'its stunningly amoral (though not immoral) ending' (Bevington, 'The Major Comedies' 84), the law in *The Alchemist* 'proves to be superbly irrelevant' (81).

Despite the harsh punishment of the ending, *Volpone* is remarkable in its celebration of wit. The severity of the punishment is subverted by Volpone's final appeal to the audience:

> VOLPONE. The seasoning of a play is the applause.
> Now, though the fox be punished by the laws,
> He yet doth hope there is no suff'ring due
> For any fact which he hath done 'gainst you.
> If there be, censure him; here he doubtful stands.
> If not, fare jovially, and clap your hands.
>
> (Epilogue 1–6)

While 'Volpone cannot be forgiven within the play' (118), Barton argues, 'the Fox, like Face, can rely on the spectators to acquit him of any crime committed against the spirit of comedy, for having been predictable, unimaginative or tedious' (119).[39] The comedy effectively appeals to two paradigms of judging, one legal and moral, and the other poetic and dramatic. And yet, these two paradigms do not exist in separate spheres. The audience's admiration of the tricksters' wit does in fact have moral implications, and the scene of legal judgement and Volpone's appeal for applause in the epilogue are too close for comfort. As Jonathan Hart points out, 'Whatever the audience decides, there is a fascinating stress between the judgement of Volpone at the end of the comedy and his resurrection in this "epilogue"' (119). The play's use of rhetoric and performance in the service of wit and cunning implicates the audience, not least by inviting admiration of the tricksters as playmakers, an identification that is sealed by the epilogue's appeal. The tricksters' desire to prolong and heighten their own pleasure speaks to the audience's desire for the next hilarious plot twist, no matter how amoral. As Barbour puts it, Jonsonian theatre 'moves' in a 'provocative span of delay' (1018), which puts the audience into the morally compromising situation of desiring precisely this delay. Like the later *Alchemist*, *Volpone*'s set-up is metatheatrical: with its witty plot that is enacted predominantly in a single house and uses make-believe, role-playing, and rhetoric to generate money and pleasure, it references the enterprise of theatre. The self-conscious use of delay and dilation in structuring the plot mirrors the tricksters' management of time and forces the audience into an intermediate position. They share the tricksters' delight in a prolonged action and, due to dramatic irony, may identify with their experience of mastery.[40] At the same

---

[39] As instruments of exposition and poetic justice, the tricksters make it comparatively easy for the audience to dispense moral judgment and clap their hands in approval. Just as in *The Alchemist*, the tricksters operate by the 'rules of satirical exposure' (Bevington, 'The Major Comedies' 82), 'exposing and punishing folly' (83).

[40] Greenblatt emphasizes the audience's investment: 'And we, in the audience, participate in this flow, for we do not want Volpone to stop, any more than the crowd at a circus wants the tightrope walker to fall, though its enjoyment is predicated on that possibility' ('The False Ending' 91).

time, they, like the duped clients, pay money for witty make-believe by a 'directorial genius': Jonson, the playwright, who delights enough in his own plots and rhetoric to appear confidently as the author of plays that deserve to be read independently of any performance.[41] In the end, only their applause can properly end the interval that is the play.

Compared with the pleasures of delay, any ending may disappoint, but as a violation of the conventions of comedy, Jonson's ending proves particularly frustrating: with his harsh punishment of the tricksters and his refusal to provide the audience with a successful love story between Bonario and Celia, he lets satisfaction fall flat. However much the audience may feel that Volpone and Mosca are justly punished, the practical and theatrical skills, as well as the intellectual versatility Mosca and Volpone have demonstrated, are impressive enough to make sure that the audience has mixed feelings about the rather heavy-handed 'poetic justice' of the end.[42] On the one hand, the law lacks moral authority: with judges who would rather have 'compet[ed] for Mosca as a son-in-law' (Barton 117) than punish him, the ending is hardly 'the healthy reassertion of a temporarily violated social order' (117).[43] And, on the other, this end sits ill with the attraction of Jonson's trickster figures. Jonas Barish describes their self-reliance and agency in memorable words: 'They command their own changes; they dictate their own motions; they keep the turning world turning; and even as we recognize the subversive nature of their actions we find ourselves drawn to them in admiring fascination' (146). This is equally true for the tricksters in *The Alchemist*. The audience can hardly help but admire Face's entrepreneurial spirit and skills and his transformation from housekeeper into self-made businessman.[44] The tricksters' wit and efficiency and their desire to better their state against all social odds must have spoken to those men and women in the audience who were similarly striving to improve their fortunes in a society shaped by credit and commerce. The tricksters' aspirations may have been part not only of the satire, but also of the play's conscious appeal to its own time.

Volpone explores the crucial function of delay as a key factor of the tricksters' enterprise, but also uses delay self-consciously to engage the audience and to

---

[41] See Barish on how Jonson approaches his plays as literary entities (137) and positions himself as a proto-modern author who 'appeals to readers over the heads of playhouse audiences' in 'preface and dedication and apologetic epistle' (139). As is well known, 'For the 1616 folio he exercised an unprecedentedly close surveillance over the whole process' (140) of editing and publication. See also Barbara A. Mowat 217.

[42] Sweeney remarks on the ending: 'in relation to the rest of the play, it exists in a strangely diminished light'. He even claims: 'the rest of the play actively rejects the conclusion as the human body rejects foreign tissue' (221).

[43] In *Volpone*'s corrupt social world, the *Avocatori* 'resemble the gulls; they are easily manipulated and mercenary' (Hirsh 109).

[44] Anthony Ouellette also emphasizes the audience's affective involvement: Face 'control[s] much of the play's action, and with each successful orchestration of the play's characters and events, the spectators' admiration for and affiliation with him increases' (380).

manage and prolong the action. The temporality of accumulating capital at a time of increasingly global commerce and unprecedented trade is at the heart of the action, but the management of time emerges here also as a poetological concern and key skill in the enterprise of commercial theatre, in producing plays that sell. Like *The Alchemist*, *Volpone* enacts a fantasy of successfully working the future without investing anything of substantial value—only wit and a persuasive performance. At the same time, it *is* that enterprise: theatre sells nothing else.

Timon of Athens: Competing Paradigms of Exchange

Volpone examines the temporality and intentionality of credit and investment through a series of gifts and false assurances. Like *The Alchemist*, it combines this attention with an emphatic interest in the art of selling improbabilities. *Timon of Athens* shows less interest in the skill of working time than in competing models of socio-economic exchange and their respective time frames. It employs the gift to confront a moral and oral economy of giving based on friendship and need with strategic gifting as an investment practice and a credit economy that is based on debt bonds and definite terms. Gifting is in principle nobler than usurious credit practices, yet the play exposes the gift economy as highly vulnerable to calculating actors.

Like the clients in *Volpone*, the lords in *Timon of Athens* deploy gifts as part of an economic calculus. They know that Timon is always ready to oblige them with a richer counter gift, so they put their money and valuables to work as investments, which must generate a profitable return. In contrast to the greedy clients in *Volpone*, who are outsmarted by the tricksters, the lords' usurious strategy does not meet with any counter-plot: in *Timon of Athens*, there is no scheming intentionality on the other end of gift-exchange, no plot on Timon's part. Whereas Volpone and his 'clients' pursue the same acquisitive logic with varying degrees of skill and success, Timon follows an entirely different logic of socio-economic action: he acts as a feudal patron who distributes his wealth freely. If householders occupy a spectrum in how they relate to wealth, Timon and Volpone stand at its opposite ends: where Volpone is a money-grubber, Timon is a prodigal spender. His prodigality is exploited by acquisitive strategy to the point of 'destroying his domestic economy' (Greene 165). The confrontation of one set of values and practices with another suggests shifting paradigms of socio-economic action.[45] In *Timon of Athens*, feudal splendour and munificence are engulfed by strategic gifts and legally enforceable credit instruments.

---

[45] See also Richard Finkelstein: '*Timon of Athens* speaks to a Jacobean audience living in an age of transition economically, socially, and in the character of its ruler: from a medieval to an early modern market economy' (825).

John Kerrigan notes that 'Timon inhabits an Athens dominated by usury' (340). As early as the second act of the five-act play, Timon's excessive spending spree is cut short by the harsh reality of broken debt bonds. While usury establishes a specific moral environment in the play, Amanda Bailey argues that *Timon of Athens* explores 'not simply credit arrangements in general but the specific monetary instrument, the penal debt bond' (28).[46] The play refers to bonds repeatedly in both the stage directions and characters' speeches, and Timon's estate is identified as collateral ('his land's put to their books', *Tim.* 1.2.203). In the play, both gifts and lending on bonds are means to profit from Timon's prodigality. They ultimately 'eat up' his estate and thus, metaphorically speaking, Timon himself. Athens is quite as Curtilax, the sergeant in *The Roaring Girl*, describes the world in general: 'all that live in the world are but great fish and little fish, and feed upon one another, some eat whole men' (*Roaring Girl* 3.3.138–140). The cynic Apemantus makes sure that the audience cannot miss the consumptive, 'cannibalistic' relation between Timon and his 'friends': 'O you gods, what a number of men eats Timon and he sees 'em not!' (*Tim.* 1.2.39–40).[47] With Timon and his false friends, the play contrasts a feudal economy of liberal and even prodigal gift-exchange with the harsh reality of a credit economy, and enacts the head-on confrontation of a social system of feudal patronage with proto-capitalist accumulation. This contrast is rendered with a notable absence of nostalgia:[48] if commercialized society constitutes a harsh environment governed by greed, Timon's feudal world is not merely outdated, but unsustainable. It readily destroys itself through excessive spending. The clash between prodigal spending and the calculated accumulation of wealth is also the clash of different attitudes to the future: *Timon of Athens* contrasts the future of contractual bonds—a 'future which comes apace'—with the potentially indefinite delay of the reciprocal gift. It thus contrasts the future as an object of anticipation and calculation with the future as a site of contingency embodied by Fortune.

The Gift as Investment

Katherine Gillen describes the gifts that the lords give to Timon as part of an 'investment cycle' ('"That What He Speaks Is All in Debt"' 98), because any gift to him produces a surplus value in the form of a counter-gift. As investment principle,

---

[46] In a highly instructive reading, Bailey compares Timon to the early modern theatre entrepreneur Philip Henslowe (32), and analyses in detail how early modern theatre itself relied on credit relations.

[47] Bailey links Timon's speech about cutting up his body and sharing out its parts in Act Three, Scene Four to the legal framework of the bond which 'allowed the lender to claim property in the person of the borrower' (42) and suggests that Timon himself acts 'as a form of fungible property that his borrowers use and use up' (38).

[48] Verena Lobsien describes *Timon of Athens* as 'erstaunlich nostalgiefrei[]' (*Shakespeares Exzess* 182)—as surprisingly free of nostalgia.

the gift functions like a form of credit: the lords expect not only prompt 'recompense', but also a higher return. One of the lords compares this mysterious increase of wealth by means of gifts with the return that can be expected on loans:

> 2 LORD. ... no meed but he repays
> Sevenfold above itself, no gift to him
> But breeds the giver a return exceeding
> All use of quittance.
>
> (1.1.284–287)

As Kerrigan points out, this speech draws on the vocabulary of 'money markets', and the seven-fold increase is 'an extortionate rate of self-imposed interest' (340).[49] In *Volpone*, too, gifts represent usurious credit relations: the clients give richly in the hope of receiving an even richer inheritance. In *Timon of Athens*, the lords pursue a similar strategy: they present Timon with gifts and flattery in the hope of a higher return. As discussed in the first part of this chapter, in the exchange cycle of the gift, being the first to give constitutes a potentially profitable move because of the ethical precept of generous recompense (see Cicero, *Off.* 1.48). The lords and senators incorporate this precept into their economic calculus. They deploy gifts to Timon as a form of investment akin to lending money on interest: by knowing full well that Timon repays any gift seven-fold, they turn the cycle of gift exchange into an investment cycle that yields a profitable surplus. As if to emphasize the structural similarity with credit, lords and senators also make a contractual use of time through lending money on written bonds.

In gift theory, the gift establishes social relations by creating obligations. As Ken Jackson writes with reference to anthropologist Marcel Mauss, 'the human propensity to give and to reciprocate helps to form and maintain any social system' (38). The reciprocity of gifting is characterized by asynchronicity, with a greater or lesser delay between gift and counter-gift:

> [I]n every possible form of society it is in the nature of a gift to impose an obligatory time limit. By their very definition, a meal shared in common, a distribution of *kava*, or a talisman that one takes away, cannot be reciprocated immediately. Time is needed in order to perform any counter-service.
>
> (Mauss 45–46)

Mauss identifies deferred reciprocity as the constitutive feature of the gift. His anthropological study offers one way to approach the social practice of the gift and the imperative of reciprocity, but, as suggested earlier in this chapter, Aristotle had already reflected on reciprocity as a form of justice. Cicero, too, discussed

---

[49] In his Essay XLI, 'Of Usurie', Bacon suggests five per cent as a general rate of interest ('*Five in the Hundred*') and a slightly higher one for merchants (127–128).

the obligations that arise from gifts: 'There are two kinds of generosity: the first bestows a kindness, and the second repays it. It is up to ourselves whether we bestow a favour or not, but the failure to repay one is not an option for a good man, so long as he can reciprocate without injustice to anyone' (*Off.* 1.48). The difference between bestowing and repaying poses the problem of reciprocity in terms of temporal order. Cicero is acutely aware of the possibility of unseemly delay in reciprocating a favour. He emphasizes the pressing nature of this obligation: 'If we are in receipt of favours which cause us not to bestow kindness but to reciprocate it, we must take particular pains, for no obligation is more pressing than the return of a favour' (*Off.* 1.47–48). 'Pressing' has ethical as well as temporal implications—reciprocation must take priority over other obligations. The precept of a greater return was also inherited wisdom in the early modern age. Paraphrasing Hesiod, Cicero wrote: '[W]e must if possible repay in greater measure what we have received for our benefit' (*Off.* 1.48).

Considering the imperative of reciprocity, for the gift to succeed as a calculable investment strategy, it needs as its counterpart an exaggerated form of generosity: prodigality. Timon observes this principle dutifully. He reciprocates every single gift 'in greater measure'. Where his own gifts are concerned, he either refuses to be recompensed altogether or accepts flattery, mere words, in return. Timon rewards material gifts and lavish praise by others in equal terms. The admiring exclamation of one of the lords—'O, he's the very soul of bounty' (1.2.213)— earns the rich reward of 'a bay courser' (2.1.215). In contrast, Timon's own gifts prove far from profitable: the second lord offers in return for a jewel only 'more than common thanks' (1.2.212), a phrase which ironically observes the 'greater measure' in rhetorical terms. By creating occasions for a counter-gift or reward, the lords tilt the balance of exchange in their favour without any resistance on Timon's part. Jackson describes the cycle of gift-giving as a 'circular economy of exchange that almost always annuls the gift' (42), yet the gift exchange examined in the play is hardly a 'cycle', but rather an asymmetrical flow. Timon, as Michael Chorost explains, 'creates a *linear* gift economy in which the *net* flow of gifts goes in one direction, from himself to his courtiers' (351). The play thus exposes circular exchange as something that benefits all parties equally as a fantasy.[50] The zero-sum hypothesis of commerce quoted in an earlier chapter appears far more accurate: 'One man's loss is another man's gain'.

Timon's investment in unilateral and lavish giving has prompted very different readings: critics tend to either condemn Timon's refusal of reciprocity as motivated by power, vainglory, or egotism,[51] or they see it as an attempt to escape an

---

[50] Critics tend to use the notion of 'circular economy' (e.g., Grav 145), but, in the case of *Timon of Athens*, this is fairly euphemistic.

[51] Terry Eagleton notes that Timon's 'grotesque generosity to his friends is a subtle form of egotism' (84). See also Gillen, '"That What He Speaks Is All in Debt"'; Bailey, *Of Bondage: Debt, Property, and*

omnipresent exchange paradigm.⁵² According to Chorost, who is deeply critical of Timon's largesse, Timon's reduction of reciprocity to a merely 'theoretical possibility' (350) creates a permanent moral imbalance.⁵³ By rendering reciprocity defunct, he disables the delay that constitutes gift exchange and establishes lasting obligations. In this perspective, Timon's unilateral gift is paramount to a debt that can never be discharged, but keeps his friends bound forever.⁵⁴ Yet even critics who emphasize Timon's moral tyranny perceive in his behaviour and rhetoric an ambiguity which invites 'a dual view of Timon that is both admiring and critical' (Bevington and Smith 72). Chorost himself suggests that 'Timon's rhetoric supports the idea of a different kind of gift economy, one where goods and money move circularly within a community to foster mutual ties of obligation' (350). While Chorost dismisses this as mere rhetoric, Jackson takes Timon's attempt to move beyond an economy of exchange seriously. In his article on *Timon of Athens*, he discusses Timon not as a feudal patron who instrumentalizes favours to solidify his superior position and morally bind others, but as someone who attempts to transcend the economy of exchange: 'Timon still believes in something like magical bounty, the existence of something not generated by an economy of exchange' (48). Jackson makes this point repeatedly: Timon 'gives truly, absolutely, without exchange' (50), 'Timon seeks to give' (51). Yet Jackson also perceives Timon's role as problematic: 'In that Timon's giving in some way precipitates his fall, the tendency to find some fault in it remains strong even for those, like myself, predisposed to admire that giving' (50).

Both Chorost and Jackson realize the possibility of an alternative reading. They react to an insurmountable ambiguity, but one which is, I believe, far less problematic than one might think. The character dramatizes precisely the thin line between generosity and prodigality, selfless help and vainglory. Timon is both admirably liberal *and* excessive, just as his attitude to friendship is both naïve and noble.⁵⁵ In terms of the moral economy of tragedy, it is crucial that although Timon is unwise, he is also generous, and hence not a bad man. As Timon himself puts it, once he

---

Personhood in Early Modern England; Bevington and Smith, 'James I and *Timon of Athens*'; Chorost, 'Biological Finance in Shakespeare's *Timon of Athens*'.

⁵² Jackson notes that 'while Timon seeks the gift, he finds, for the most part, exchange' (48).

⁵³ As Chorost writes, 'he wants only the theoretical possibility of reciprocation, since the real thing would diminish the accumulated sense of obligation built up in his courtiers' (350). Timon's spending practice is not only excessive, it can also be perceived as 'aggressive' gesture (Gillen, '"That What He Speaks Is All in Debt"' 97). As Gillen writes, 'Timon relies on an unbalanced cycle of gift-giving to bind others to him in relationships of service and obligation' ('"That What He Speaks Is All in Debt"' 97). She sees his rejection of reciprocity as attempt to keep 'his fellow Athenians in his debt' (97).

⁵⁴ See also Bailey 39: 'The play certainly supports the notion that by making his recipients endlessly grateful, Timon subordinates them'.

⁵⁵ Richard Finkelstein also points out that criticism of Timon often 'falls into two camps ... either blaming the central character for his dissolute nature or seeing him as seduced and abused by a corrupt society' (803). He argues quite simply that 'Timon seems sometimes right and sometimes wrong in his assumptions and goals' (804) and explains Timon's ambiguity with the play's uses of different and sometimes contradictory ideas on friendship as they emerge in Cicero's, Seneca's, and Plutarch's discourses.

realizes that he has lost his estate: 'No villainous bounty yet hath passed my heart— / Unwisely, not ignobly, have I given' (2.2.173-174). Timon's magnanimity is, as Clifford Davidson suggests, 'at once a great virtue and a great fault' (187). The real conflict of the play lies not within his role—a feudal lord may be generous as well as patronizing, excessive, and proud—but between the spending practices of the aristocrat and the acquisitive desire and proto-bourgeois strategies for accumulation practiced by the lords and senators. Timon's practices can still be contained within an ethical framework, but the pervasive presence of self-interested, calculating, and unashamedly selfish agents in the play shifts that very frame and renders it defunct: the structuring force of gain puts the model of aristocratic virtues and faults under pressure.

The Moral Economy of the Gift

Timon's prodigal spending practices contrast with the accumulative strategies of his social equals, who exploit the principle of reciprocity in the interest of gain. In the *De Amicitia*, Cicero emphasizes that true friendship need not 'keep an exact balance of credits and debits' (*Amic.* 16.58) and that the beginnings of friendship do 'not spring from the hope of gain' (*Amic.* 9.30-31).[56] Timon's friends, however, are motivated by acquisitive desire in their demonstrations of love. Their presents to Timon are at odds with the authoritative ethical standpoint as defined by Cicero in the *De Officiis*:

> In both granting a kindness and returning a favour, our greatest obligation, all else being equal, is to lend help above all to the person in greatest need. But many do just the opposite. They look to the interests particularly of the man from whom they have the greatest expectations, even if he has no need of their assistance.
> (1.49)

The calculated gifts to Timon fit neatly into the category of selfish giving to 'the man from whom they [the givers] have the greatest expectations' (*Off.* 1.49-50), a characterization which also applies to the gulls in Jonson's comedy. Mutual help based on need is exemplified through Timon's servants' performance of mutual support in Act Four, Scene Two, when they share out the remaining money in a scene that signifies a lasting bond of loyalty and fellowship. Although it is true that, within the world of the play, this practice appears somewhat outdated, this ethos of mutual support might have been recognized as a desirable and perhaps even familiar feature of life by an early modern audience.[57] As argued in Chapter 1,

---

[56] See also Clifford Davidson, who paraphrases Cicero: 'There can be nothing calculating about true friendship, no cool weighing of profit and loss' (186).

[57] In Richard Finkelstein's terms, 'the Flavian way represents the past' (823).

helping family members, friends, or neighbours in need was a daily practice in the early modern culture of credit.[58] The scene certainly highlights the moral scandal of the failure of Timon's 'friends' to help him at a time of need.

From a Senecan point of view, Timon's false friends violate a key precept that resonates with Cicero's critique of self-interested giving and reminds us once more of the legacy hunters in *Volpone*: 'let us make our benefits not investments, but gifts' (*Ben.* 1.1.9).[59] Shakespeare's play is certainly in dialogue with Cicero and Seneca (and possibly Plutarch).[60] Rather than attempting a detailed exegesis of these influences, I want to use Cicero's *De Officiis* and *De Amicitia* and Seneca's *De Beneficiis* to illuminate the moral implications of gifts and friendship. The question of how to reckon with the future provides the horizon for this discussion of the gift and the expectations and hopes that attach to friendship. With its different attitudes to the gift and its juxtaposition of gift and credit relations, *Timon of Athens* examines different configurations of the interval between giving and recompense: the definite and legally enforceable interval in credit relations as exemplified by bills and bonds; an indeterminate interval in gift exchange that is nonetheless pressing from the point of view of the beneficiary; and an indefinite delay that is conditional on need from the point of view of the benefactor.

The nature of Timon's gifts is harder to understand than the gift-as-investment that his 'friends' practice. Does Timon, too, expect something in return? Jackson opposes two types of gifts, which he derives from his reading of Derrida: a 'true' gift (49) versus a gift which instigates a cycle of successive giving. Yet while Jackson seeks to align Timon with the 'true' gift, Timon's gift-giving escapes this binarism. His gifts are not linked to the hope for prompt or higher 'repayment', but they do come with certain expectations: both of gratitude and of a reciprocal readiness to help a friend in need. Timon's refusal to accept Ventidius's repayment may help to render the precise nature of Timon's expectations intelligible. In the very first scene of the play, Timon frees Ventidius from debtor's prison. In the second scene, Ventidius offers prompt repayment 'in greater measure' (Cicero, *Off.* 1.48):

> VENTIDIUS. Most honoured Timon,
> It hath pleased the gods to remember
> My father's age and call him to long peace.
> He is gone happy and has left me rich.

---

[58] As Keith Wrightson explains, 'Doubtless the interest on small sums was in the form of the "social interest" of goodwill and the tacit assumption of reciprocal aid in time of need, something on which no cash value could be placed' (*English Society 1580–1680* 53).

[59] Apart from a few exceptions, I quote from John W. Basore's translation of Seneca's *De Beneficiis*. Quotations from Golding's early modern translation are clearly marked with the translator's name in brackets.

[60] For a detailed discussion of Cicero's, Seneca's, and Plutarch's discourses of friendship and how they relate to *Timon of Athens*, see Richard Finkelstein, 'Amicitia and Beneficia in *Timon of Athens*'. John M. Wallace concentrates in his article '*Timon of Athens* and the Three Graces' on the play's involvement with Seneca.

> Then, as in grateful virtue I am bound
> To your free heart, I do return those talents,
> Doubled with thanks and service, from whose help
> I derived liberty.
>
> (1.2.1–8)

Clearly, Ventidius observes here all the relevant advice from Cicero about the 'pressing' need of reciprocation. Yet Timon refuses to be recompensed:

> TIMON. O, by no means,
> Honest Ventidius, you mistake my love:
> I gave it freely ever, and there's none
> Can truly say he gives if he receives.
> If our betters play at that game, we must not dare
> To imitate them; faults that are rich are fair.
>
> (1.2.8–13)

This can be interpreted as desire to bestow a 'true gift' or as a refusal of reciprocity motivated by the desire to display social status and power. Both these readings, however, presume that Timon rejects reciprocity. Yet perhaps Timon rejects only automatic repayment and the 'language of commercial exchange' (Bevington and Smith 74), not reciprocity as such.[61]

As becomes clearer in Timon's speech in the same scene, Timon resists the transformation of his gift into a business-like exchange that would devalue his generous act, but hopes for reciprocal favours from his friends, should he ever need them, in an indeterminate future:

> TIMON. O no doubt, my good friends, but the gods themselves have provided that I shall have much help from you—how had you been my friends else? Why have you that charitable title from thousands, did not you chiefly belong to my heart? ... O you gods, think I, what need we have any friends, if we should ne'er have need of 'em? They were the most needless creatures living should we ne'er have use for 'em, and would most resemble sweet instruments hung up in cases that keeps their sounds to themselves. Why, I have often wished myself poorer that I might come nearer to you. We are born to do benefits, and what better or properer can we call our own than the riches of our friends? O, what a precious comfort 'tis to have so many like brothers commanding one another's fortunes.
>
> (1.2.87–103)

---

[61] Peter Grav points out that '[t]he language of the play is relentlessly commercial' (133).

For Timon, friendship promises support in times of need; its true value emerges in times of adversity. Modern critics sometimes perceive Timon's definition of friendship as instrumental, yet the question of whether friendship is an affective or an economic matter misses the point: it is part of the early modern understanding of friends that they are close to each other's hearts and therefore ready to help each other in need.

Considering early modern ethics, Timon can hardly be blamed for his rejection of automatic recompense. Laurie McKee argues that early modern writers insisted that 'gifts must be given gratuitously and without thought of return' (4). She corroborates this with a quotation from Arthur Golding's translation of Seneca (from 1578): 'No man keepes a register of his benefites ... A good man neuer thinketh upon the good tournes he hath doon ... For otherwyse they passe intoo *the* nature of dettes' (*Ben.* A2v; also qtd. in McKee 4). Here, the thin line between a gift and a debt becomes obvious. After all, both create obligations. Seneca states explicitly that the giver should bestow a gift as a 'free-gift' and compares the 'reckening of benefites' as if they were 'expenses' with nothing less than 'vyle Usurie' (Golding, *Ben.* A2v).[62] This account of how to bestow benefits upon others condemns the behaviour of Timon's friends, but not Timon himself.

From a Senecan standpoint, Timon errs rather in his careless giving.[63] While Seneca insists that the benefactor should not expect anything in return and should only have the beneficiary's interests at heart, his treatise offers advice on giving benefits in ways that facilitate gratitude. As John M. Wallace summarizes Seneca, benefits should be freely given, but 'nicely calculated to insure grateful recipients' (352).[64] Timon fails miserably in identifying worthy recipients, a failure that Seneca describes as the first cause of the common vice of ingratitude: 'we do not pick out those who are worthy of receiving our gifts' (*Ben.* 1.1.2). If we bestow benefits indifferently—'without any discrimination' (*Ben.* 1.1.2)—we must not expect recompense: 'For it follows that, if they are ill placed, they are ill acknowledged, and, when we complain of their not being returned, it is too late; for they were lost at the time they were given' (*Ben.* 1.1.1–2).

Timon is similarly wanting in his excessive disappointment at the ingratitude of his 'friends'. Seneca comments drily: 'A man is not revealed as ungrateful without bringing shame on us, since, in fact, to complain of the loss of a benefit is proof

---

[62] In John W. Basore's translation, the passage runs as follows: 'In benefits the book-keeping is simple—so much is paid out; if anything comes back, it is gain, if nothing comes back, there is no loss. I made the gift for the sake of giving. No one enters his benefactions in his account-book, or like a greedy tax-collector calls for payment upon a set day, at a set hour. The good man never thinks of them unless he is reminded of them by having them returned; otherwise, they transform themselves into a loan. To regard a benefit as an amount advanced is putting it out at shameful interest. No matter what the issue of former benefits has been, still persist in conferring them upon others' (*Ben.* 2.2.3–4).

[63] As well as, perhaps, in his emphatic display of wealth: Seneca chastises the 'pryde of greate prosperitie' which prompts a man to 'too ouerdoo all thinges' (Golding, *Ben.* D4v).

[64] The implications of this are highly political, for 'If generosity was the heart of the society Seneca envisaged, then reciprocity was its pulse' (Wallace 352).

that it was not well bestowed' (*Ben.* 7.29.1–2). And Wallace paraphrases Seneca as follows: 'We had the fruit of our benefit when we gave it, and the experience of ingratitude will make us not slower in giving but more careful (7.32.1)' (353).[65] Timon, however, refuses to learn his lesson and do better. The *De Amicitia* suggests why such a stoic attitude might be hard to maintain. Here, friendship has such significance that its failure is likely to have severe implications. As Cicero writes, friendship 'lessens the burden of adversity by dividing and sharing it' (*Amic.* 6.22), and thus 'projects the bright ray of hope into the future, and does not suffer the spirit to grow faint or to fall' (*Amic.* 7.23). It follows that the loss of friendship may result in an utter loss of hope and trust in the future—hence Timon's extreme bitterness and misanthropy.

That Timon's friends are blinded to the moral dimension of the gift by their focus on its material value becomes clearer when we consider that for Seneca, as his early modern translator writes, material gifts are but 'badges of benefites' (Golding, *Ben.* B1r)—signs of benefit, not the thing itself:

> The benifite it selfe may bee carried in hart, but it cannot be touched with hand. There is greate difference betweene the matter of a benefite, and the benefite it selfe. Therefore, neither Gold, nor Siluer, nor any of the thinges that wee receiue of our neighbours, is a benefite: but the good will of the giuer.
>
> (Golding, *Ben.* B1r)[66]

In his speech, Timon approaches borrowing from friends as a matter of affection, just as Golding's translation of Seneca describes the benefit as an immaterial gesture that comes from the heart: 'If I would broach the vessels of my love / And try the argument of hearts by borrowing, / Men and men's fortunes could I frankly use' (2.2.177–179). Timon's friends, on the other hand, are among those people who value only what can be seen and possessed. They confuse the transitory sign of a benefit with the benefit itself and neglect what is 'deere and precious': 'the good turne [which] endureth still' (Golding, *Ben.* B1r). For Timon, in contrast, the material benefits are secondary: Timon's celebratory speech about friendship emphasizes the immaterial bond of which benefits are but a sign.[67] The gulls in *Volpone* are also effectively characterized through a distinction between material

---

[65] According to Richard Finkelstein, 'Seneca argues that the wise man should be immune to hurt from disappointment' (811). He quotes Seneca: 'If a man is ungrateful, he has done, not me, but himself, an injury' (*Ben.* 7.32.1, qtd. in Finkelstein 811).

[66] Interestingly, Basore's translation has not the heart, but the mind as the site where the benefit is felt (the Latin states 'res animo geritur'): 'But these things are the marks of services rendered, not the services themselves. A benefit cannot possibly be touched by the hand; its province is the mind. There is a great difference between the matter of a benefit and the benefit itself; and so it is neither gold nor silver nor any of the gifts which are held to be most valuable that constitutes a benefit, but merely the goodwill of him who bestows it' (*Ben.* 1.5.2).

[67] See also Richard Finkelstein: 'Like Cicero and Plutarch, he imagines a friendship anterior to materiality' (816).

sign and immaterial benefit: their gifts are intended to appear as signs of love, but are really empty signifiers.

Timon's gifts to his friends assume a certain bond that lasts well into an otherwise uncertain future. Rather than rejecting reciprocity altogether, his use of recompense is contingent on a potential reversal of fortune. Bailey describes debt as a social relation that 'suspends equality between two parties who cannot walk away from one another so long as they desire restitution' (47), but this applies just as well to the binding nature of the gift. If reciprocity in classical and early modern thought constitutes a social adhesive, the deferral of recompense to an indeterminate future based on trust is not a bad thing: it prolongs social contact and solidifies social relations through creating obligations.

In the moral economy of the play, it is clearly wrong that the legal obligation of the bond should trump ethical obligations. The subplot involving Alcibiades articulates this theme most fully.[68] Alcibiades appears in front of the Senate to defend a friend and fellow soldier who has trespassed against the law. He reminds the senators that 'pity is the virtue of the law' (3.6.8) and implores them to be so generous as to forgive his friend's fault: 'O my lords, / As you are great, be pitifully good' (3.6.51–52). The subplot thus pitches virtue against legal right and reinforces the question the play as a whole poses of the binding power of reciprocity. Alcibiades reminds the Senate of his friend's faithful service to Athens: 'Why, I say, my lords, he's done fair service / And slain in fight many of your enemies' (3.6.63–64). Alcibiades is the type of friend Timon lacks. Alcibiades pawns his own merits and honour to compensate for his friend's fault and to vouch for his moral recovery:

> ALCIBIADES. And for I know your reverend ages love
>   Security, I'll pawn my victories, all
>   My honour, to you upon his good returns.
>
> (3.6.80–82)

This is not accidentally phrased in economic terms. It exemplifies an act of friendship which Timon needs but does not get: Timon lacks a friend who vouches for him, who is willing to pawn his fortune and risk his future to underwrite Timon's credit. The Alcibiades plot also demonstrates that the failure of reciprocity has not only economic implications, but social and political ones as well.[69] Ignoring

---

[68] According to Grav, 'the purpose of this scene is to establish a story of ingratitude and alienation parallel to *Timon*'s central plot' (140). Terry Eagleton reads the subplot slightly differently: 'The Senate are as formalistic in their insistence that Alcibiades' friend must die as Timon is in his whimsical patronage; the law, as we have seen already, is coolly indifferent to particular individuals, and thus ironically apes Timon's supposed generosity' (84–85).

[69] Richard Finkelstein points out that 'for Cicero, friendship is a crucial building block for republican governments' (805). The social benefits of friendship and the destructive implications of its lack as formulated in the *De Amicitia* are considerable: 'But if you should take the bond of goodwill out of the universe no house or city could stand, nor would even the tillage of the fields abide. If that statement

the ethical obligation of reciprocity dissolves social ties and may result in social conflict and even civil war.

Futurity and the Failure of the Promise

In relation to his broken bonds, Timon's ethics are clearly questionable. Already Cicero pointed out that acting honourably requires 'keeping faith with compacts made' (*Off.* 1.15). Timon's disregard of the definite interval in credit relations sits ill with an earlier scene in which Timon stakes his honour explicitly on keeping his promise. He tells the Old Athenian: 'My hand to thee, mine honour on my promise' (1.1.152). Timon's readiness to honour gifts or award benefits and his failure to even *remember* his credit obligations, as if such things were beneath him, creates a strange divide. Surely, a debt is also an obligation that must be honoured. In the logic of the legal action of *assumpsit*, a contract of debt is also a promise, a promise to repay a certain sum in the future. To account for Timon's disregard of his debts, I want to take a closer look at different models of debt and Timon's reaction to the temporality of the bond.

Beleaguered by his creditors' servants, who eagerly wave their notes at him, Timon turns to his steward, apparently completely surprised by this turn of events:

> TIMON. How goes the world, that I am thus encountered
> With clamorous demands of broken bonds
> And the detention of long-since-due debts
> Against my honour?
>
> (2.2.38–41)

Timon's 'How goes the world' betrays his lack of any sense of agency in the matter; it is as if he had no part in what is happening. The phrasing suggests an impersonal course of events reminiscent of Hamlet's famous realization that, 'The Time is out of joint' (*Ham.* 1.5.186). It also implies a momentous change or shift that affects 'the world' as such. Timon's use of 'encountered' suggests the surprising suddenness of this confrontation. Yet how can he be surprised if the debts are 'long-since-due'? This phrase expresses more than that the date of payment is long past; it also conveys Timon's exasperation and sense of being offended at the creditors' insistence on the payback date. As he himself hands out gifts without any expectation as to a set return date, he cannot understand the scandal of a broken deadline. Timon is clearly not attuned to the credit economy, with its definite and enforceable use of time. In his understanding of debt, time hardly matters, and he seems to have little conception of the consequences of non-payment. His model of debt seems

---

is not clear, then you may understand how great is the power of friendship and of concord from a consideration of the results of enmity and disagreement. For what house is so strong, or what state so enduring that it cannot be utterly overthrown by animosities and division?' (7.23).

primarily spatial, which means that the clamouring insistence on broken terms may appear to him almost beside the point. From Timon's perspective, there is no harm done because the money is not lost. It is just not in the right place. From the point of view of debt before the rise of the *assumpsit*, Timon's failure to repay his debts means simply that he is holding on too long to what belongs to someone else. In Timon's view, this is hardly a problem, as he foresees no trouble in rectifying the situation. If he is obliged to return money that he was granted, his 'friends' will feel the same way and give him what they themselves had received. In Timon's model, the amount of value that circulates remains essentially the same, it is simply dispersed according to need and can be retrieved; his friends' interest, in contrast, is to increase their portion of money permanently. Timon is easy prey because he fails to see a difference between the obligation imposed by the gift and that of the written bond, which has a clear timeframe and is legally enforceable. From the point of view of the *assumpsit*, which approaches a contract as a promise, however, the matter looks quite different: Timon failed to deliver on what he said he would do and must pay damages for nonfeasance. In Timon's model of obligation, time is of little consequence, yet for his usurious creditors and false friends, broken bonds are a chance for profit: their loans and gifts to Timon function as capital that generates a surplus.

That Timon's understanding of debt is outdated becomes clear when Flavius discusses his refusal to acknowledge his debts early on in an aside:

> FLAVIUS. What will this come to?
>   He commands us to provide and give great gifts,
>   And all out of an empty coffer;
>   ...
>   His promises fly so beyond his state
>   That what he speaks is all in debt—he owes
>   For every word. He is so kind that he now
>   Pays interest for't; his land's put to their books.
>   (1.2.194–203)

Flavius's initial question points straight to the future, underlining its urgency: 'What will this come to?' The gifts which surpass Timon's means are financed with credit and lead him further into debt, so that Timon effectively '[p]ays interest' for his kindness. That '[h]is promises fly so beyond his state / That what he speaks is all in debt' suggests that Timon lacks the power to turn promises into facts: already in Act Two, his coffers are empty, and he is unable to honour his promissory notes and bonds. Flavius is well attuned to the measurable future of investments and debts. Whereas Mosca in *Volpone* spurs his master on in his limitless greed and relentless plotting, Flavius attempts to hold his master back, to prevent him from going any farther. Seeing that his steward understands the temporal regime of credit and the bond, Timon's largesse appears all the more outdated. His understanding of exchange belongs to a world that is gone. Following Don E. Wayne, Luke Wilson associates the changing conception of debt with a more general social shift from status to contract: 'Where social relations had once been understood as depending on who you were (your status), they were increasingly determined by what you did, that is, by the legal relationships you voluntarily entered into' (144).[70] If Timon's status-conscious generosity constitutes a counter-model to the future-orientation of debt bonds and promissory notes, it is no longer viable in Athens's usurious society: 'Timon maintains a façade of inherited wealth on the shifting sands of usury' (Kerrigan 341). Flavius's personification of the future— 'the future comes apace' (2.2.148)—exemplifies the temporality of a contractual credit culture: the unstoppable and continuous progression of time towards a definite moment. Credit practices with interest and penalties instal a temporal regime in which time is money.

Flavius accuses Timon of promising carelessly what he cannot guarantee. Cicero had already identified the peculiar temporality of the promise, which references a future fact:

> The foundation of justice is good faith, in other words truthfully abiding by our words and agreements. So though some may find this rather difficult to accept, let us steel ourselves to imitate the Stoics in their zealous pursuit of etymologies, and accept that good faith (*fides*) is so called because what is promised becomes fact (*fiat*).
>
> (*Off.* 1.23)

The futurity of the promise requires trust, 'good faith'. Yet trust can fail in two ways: a promise may be thwarted by circumstances, or it may be insincere.[71] It is in relation to those two kinds of failures that Timon's use of words differs from that of his flatterers, and also from the tricksters in *Volpone*: Timon is imprudent and lacks the means to pay up, but he means what he says. His 'friends' are more alike to Jonson's tricksters; their promises are tactical and insincere. They are counterfeits that have no real value. This emerges in the first scene of Act Five, which harkens back to the very first scene of the play. In this scene, Poet and Painter discuss the status of promising and the relation between promises and performances:

> POET. What have you now to present unto him?
> PAINTER. Nothing at this time but my visitation; only I will
> promise him an excellent piece.

---

[70] Wayne borrows the 'distinction between *status* and *contract* societies' from Henry Sumner Maine (104, n.4). He sees two opposing principles at work in *Bartholomew Fair*: 'on the one hand, the traditional moral doctrine of social obligation according to status, and, on the other, the more modern principles of rational self-interest and voluntary contractual obligation' (104).

[71] In speech act theory, the 'serious' utterance of a promise that implies the intention to perform the promised object is a condition of a successful promise (Searle 407).

> POET. I must serve him so too, tell him of an intent that's coming toward him.
> PAINTER. Good as the best. Promising is the very air o' th' times; it opens the eyes of expectation. Performance is ever the duller for his act and, but in the plainer and simpler kind of people, the deed of saying is quite out of use. To promise is most courtly and fashionable; performance is a kind of will or testament which argues a great sickness in his judgement that makes it.
>
> (5.1.17–28)

Promises emerge here as the paradigmatic speech act 'o' th' times'. They are as pervasive and insubstantial as air. By 'open[ing] the eyes of expectation', promising invites an advance payment. This emphasis on expectation sounds very much like Mosca's characterization of the 'hope [that is] such a bait, it covers any hook' (*Volp.* 1.4.134–135). It is indicative of the state of moral corruption of Athenian society that to deliver on a promise is seen as ill-judged and out of fashion. This, again, evokes Jonson's Venice: nothing is exchanged here *but* signs—empty promises on the one hand, and, on the other, valuables that signify affection but really mean nothing.

The exaggerated use of promises applies to everyone in Athens, *including* Timon, but two aspects allow us to differentiate between Timon and those who profit from him. First, Timon's promises are sincere even when spoken in debt; those of his 'friends' and fellow citizens, however, are part of an economic calculus, to be honoured only if doing so proves profitable. Second, if Timon himself does not see his broken bonds as broken promises, the moral scandal of a failure to deliver mainly exists in the eyes of his usurious creditors, who try to capitalize on his failure. Yet, ultimately, the unfounded words of both Timon and his flatterers reveal the problematic role of speech in an oral culture of credit, in which the question of what a promise was worth could be existential.

Friendship and Fortune

Timon of Athens examines different forms of dilated exchange and pitches the calculability of contractual credit instruments and strategic investments against Timon's sense of an uncertain future in which one can only bank on the help of one's friends. The question of what the future brings is linked to the status of Fortune and whether and how it can be shaped to one's advantage, as Bacon's 'architecture of fortune' suggests. In a play that represents a diverse array of forms of dilated exchanges and awarenesses of the future, the allegory of Fortune in the opening scene is highly interesting. It foreshadows Timon's downfall and the refusal of his 'friends' to help him up again, posing the question of how to brace oneself for and deal with future adversity.

The Poet, who seeks Timon's patronage, pictures Fortune and those who try to win her favour. He describes a vision of a society in which all men seek to better and raise their states. The upward climb is symbolized by the 'high and pleasant hill' upon which Fortune sits enthroned:

> POET. Sir, I have upon a high and pleasant hill
> Feigned Fortune to be throned. The base o' th' mount
> Is ranked with all deserts, all kind of natures
> That labour on the bosom of this sphere
> To propagate their states.
>
> (1.1.65–69)

Lewis Walker notes that the allegory accords Timon no power to act whatsoever ('Fortune and Friendship' 577), but it does include him amongst those who seek to 'propagate their states'. The only difference between him and the others seems to be that Fortune singles him out as her special favourite:

> POET. Amongst them all
> Whose eyes are on this sovereign Lady fixed,
> One do I personate of Lord Timon's frame,
> Whom Fortune with her ivory hand wafts to her,
> Whose present grace to present slaves and servants
> Translates his rivals.
>
> (1.1.69–74)

Fortune operates according to its own temporal logic of sudden shifts and unexpected changes, and her fickle favouritism makes 'rivals' out of equals.[72] The double use of 'present' intimates the swift changes of fortune—presently graced favourites may shortly be 'slaves and servants'.[73] The Poet describes Fortune's changeability in the following:

> POET. When Fortune in her shift and change of mood
> Spurns down her late beloved, all his dependants,
> Which laboured after him to the mountain's top
> Even on their knees and hands, let him slip down,
> Not one accompanying his declining foot.
>
> (1.1.86–90)

---

[72] A. D. Nuttall even identifies 'an obscure competitive anxiety' behind Timon's intense generosity (68).
[73] See the editor's note to the Arden edition: 'The wit of the phrase depends on the pun on present as "in the present" and "in the immediate future"' (167).

Far from actively *making* his fortune, Timon enjoys it while it lasts, only to collapse when his luck runs out. For Ruth Levitsky, who reads Timon against the morality tradition, 'the question of how a man ought to react to conditions of both prosperity and adversity' (107) is precisely the point of the play:[74]

> The hero's fall from prosperity may result from his own imprudence, from the fickleness of those who should befriend and counsel him, or from the caprices of fortune. That a man should bear these losses manfully, however, is a part of both the Morality and the classical tradition.
>
> (108)

What is at stake in the play, according to Levitsky, is fortitude, which many Roman writers considered the greatest virtue of all: 'From Seneca, Cicero, Plutarch, Marcus Aurelius, and Epictetus—not to mention such Renaissance humanists as Erasmus and Elyot—Shakespeare would have learned that fortitude, rather than temperance, was often considered the crowning virtue' (110).

In *The Machiavellian Moment*, J. G. A Pocock discusses the relation between fortune and virtue or *virtus*.[75] He explains that virtue or virtus and the unpredictability of fortune 'were regularly paired as opposites' (37).[76] If the beginning of the play leads us to believe that Timon has *virtus*—'the quality of personality that commanded good fortune' and 'the quality that dealt effectively and nobly with whatever fortune might send' (37)—this impression is revealed to be illusory. Timon does nothing to preserve his good fortune other than shift responsibility for his future well-being onto his friends. With his misanthropic rage, he evidences none of 'the heroic fortitude that withstood ill fortune' and could shape 'circumstances to the actor's advantage' (37). In terms of the necessity of adapting to changing circumstances and emplotting unforeseen events as discussed in Chapter 3, Timon lacks not just fortitude, but versatility, strategic acumen, and temporal awareness in a contingent world peopled by self-interested actors.

In the allegory, it is Fortune who casts Timon down—in the play, it is the harsh reality of the credit economy, in which the failure of credit renders payback urgent. It is also, however, Timon's own imprudence. Bacon suggests in his Essay XL, 'Of Fortune', that 'the Folly of one Man is the *Fortune* of Another' and adds: 'For no Man prospers so suddenly, as by Others Errours' (122). Timon is brought down

---

[74] See also Walker's essay 'Timon of Athens and the Morality Tradition' for a reading of the play in this context.

[75] Pocock focuses on Boethius's *De Consolatione*: 'Boethius, whose thought is so strikingly Platonic and neo-Platonist as to render the quality, if not the fact, of his Christianity debatable, opposes *virtus* to *fortuna* in a way which both brings out the diverse Roman, Platonic, and Christian connotations of *virtus* and transmits the use of *fortuna* and the *virtus-fortuna* polarity to subsequent centuries of Augustinian Christianity' (37–38). Fortune's symbol 'is the wheel, by which men are raised to power and fame and then suddenly cast down by changes they cannot predict or control' (38).

[76] Levitsky also discusses 'the long enmity between Virtue and Fortune' (108) in *Liberality and Prodigality*, a play from the morality tradition.

not by blind Fortune, but through his own actions—and by men who make *their* fortune by profiting from *his*. Just like the others, Poet and Painter play their part in bleeding Timon dry—they are as calculating as the gulls in *Volpone*. This state of moral corruption turns the Poet's sombre warning into a hypocritical and generic act which reproduces mere 'sententious truisms' (Bevington and Smith 73).[77] Timon's reversal of fortune is not merely a turn of the wheel—it is facilitated by his own behaviour and that of his friends and flatterers. In his essay, Bacon comments on the relation between Fortune and human agency. He argues that a man's fortune is related to how he comports himself and his affairs—to his 'Vertues, or rather Faculties and Customes' ('Of Fortune' 123): 'chiefly', Bacon writes, the Mould of a Mans *Fortune*, is in his owne hands' (122). At the same time, men who are too sure of themselves and pride themselves on their 'Wisedom, and Policie' often 'end *Infortunate*' (124). Bacon refers here explicitly to '*Timotheus* the Athenian' (124).

In Shakespeare's play, Timon expresses his readiness to rely on his friends should his fortune turn: 'O no doubt my good friends, but the gods themselves have provided that I shall have much help from you—how had you been my friends else?' Timon's phrase 'We are born to do benefits' echoes Cicero's statement in *De Officiis* that 'men have been begotten for men's sake to be of service to each other' (*Off.* 1.22). As Cicero puts it, 'love is further strengthened by the receiving of a kindly service, by the evidence of another's care for us, and by closer familiarity' (*Amic.* 9.29),[78] but it is important that 'friendship springs rather from nature than from need' (*Amic.* 8.27). Cicero writes: 'It is not the case, therefore, that friendship attends upon advantage, but, on the contrary, that advantage attends upon friendship' (*Amic.* 14.51).[79] This is also Timon's understanding of friendship: friends constitute, so to speak, an insurance policy against the inconstancy of fortune—this is why they are such 'a precious comfort' (*Tim.* 1.2.102). The two Antonios in *The Merchant of Venice* and *Twelfth Night* help to illustrate this point. They help their friends in moments of crisis, and the homoerotic touch to these friendships accentuates their attachment and keen sense of obligation. In these plays, the risk of unilateral attachment by one party and exploitation of this attachment by the other is hinted at, but proves void.

---

[77] Gail Kern Paster points out that the Poet's 'hope of material gain from the man he claims to be instructing undercuts the moral validity his work might otherwise have had' (*The Idea of the City* 92–93). Gillen's account of Poet and Painter, in contrast, seems somewhat too optimistic: 'Despite their reliance on Timon's patronage, the Poet and the Painter reject mercenary art in favour of the Renaissance ideal that art should teach as well as delight, in this case providing Timon with valuable information regarding his precarious condition' ('"That What He Speaks Is All in Debt"' 101).

[78] See also Walker on the relation between need and friendship in Cicero's *De Amicitia* ('Fortune and Friendship' 589).

[79] Elsewhere, Cicero explains that it is not to be sought for advantage even though it may come with great advantages (*Amic.* 9.30–31).

The problem with being favoured by fortune is that wealth acts as 'intermediary', as 'a sort of broker between friends' (Walker, 'Fortune and Friendship' 588). The social relations which it institutes alter with *fortuna*'s alterations. A heightened sense of the fickleness of fortune is endemic to the favouritism of patronage systems; sudden reversals of fortune are not per se a proto-capitalist experience. Yet the play's concern with credit, trust, and reciprocity as well as social rivalry gives the allegory of fortune an additional layer of meaning. It associates the play's prominent placing of fickle Fortune and social rivalry with new financial opportunities and increased social mobility.[80] Timon's complete lack of Baconian suspicion and of a temporal consciousness, as well as his failure to adapt and to seize a chance that presents itself, pose the question of the skills needed to make one's fortune—even if only *ex negativo*. Bacon finds it hard enough to name these skills in his essay 'Of Fortune'. Lacking English terms, he draws on Latin, Spanish, Italian, and French to develop his idea. He emphasizes versatility ('*Versatile Ingenium*') and claims that it is advantageous 'to have a *Little* of the *Foole*; and not *Too Much* of the *Honest*' ('Of Fortune' 123). Framed with these recommendations, the trickster figures of the early modern stage with their crazy schemes and disregard for honesty appear in an ambiguous light. Amoral, yes, but also enterprising and resourceful, they fit the bill of men who command good fortune, even if they overshoot in their pursuit of gain and lack the self-control needed to keep their own passions at bay. Timon, on the other hand, lacks an awareness that the future can be shaped—and by other means than placing trust in unreliable and false friends. He is too inflexible to retain his good fortune in a changing world, and certainly not calculating enough to be successful in a credit economy. Whether he is too honest or too much of a fool is in the end irrelevant—for Bacon, it may amount to the same thing.

Exploring the Interval: Delay and Dilation as Plot Devices

The future-orientation of credit and gift implies an interval that poses risks—especially in interactions with self-interested agents. Timon's false friends capitalize on his rich gifts. They exploit his obsession with imminent and generous recompense. Without a time limit and with only a moral obligation to reciprocate, the interval between their gifts and a reciprocal action can be infinitely extended so that the 'debt' is never paid. While these false friends make the most of asynchronous exchanges, Timon's failure in calculating time results in bankruptcy. Delayed recompense creates conflict and generates tension. At the same time, delay and dilation function as poetological principles in the organization of the plot. In

---

[80] Derek Cohen highlights how 'the individual's social locus' in the play is 'fixed and unfixed in relation to' wealth as an 'external measurable phenomen[on]' (149).

his discussion of Jonson's work and the rise of the action of *assumpsit*, Luke Wilson extends the temporal structure of the executory contract to the performance of a play. Executory means that a contract is 'not completed at the time of the bargain but only upon mutual performance' (153) Referring to the prologue of *Bartholomew Fair*, Wilson argues: 'To make a contractual agreement and its attendant mutual promises the founding act of a theatrical performance is to construct the space of that performance—the "space of two hours and a half and somewhat more"—as a specifically contractual interval' (159). I am interested in the management of this interval and its conscious dilation for the sake of a successful performance. As in *Volpone*, dilation prolongs the performance, creates suspense, and amplifies affective engagement.

The development of the plot in *Timon of Athens* is straightforward enough, yet its linear progression is delayed by a marked caesura between Acts Three and Four, by the Alcibiades subplot, and by a repetitive episodic structure. As a fake promise of restitution, the banquet delays Timon's inevitable expulsion from the city to make room for a scene of symbolic revenge. With its sense of finality, the mock banquet is comparable to the 'false ending' in *Volpone*. It marks a break, a 'narrative schism' (Bailey 28): afterwards, Timon leaves town, disillusioned and angry, and moves to the woods. The philanthropist turns into a misanthrope. In the woods, the chance for a reversal of the action offers itself: digging for roots, Timon finds a gold treasure. Even though he refuses to 'runne with the occasions' (Bacon, *Advancement* 173) and to enjoy the turning of his fortune, the gold find affords a new impulse for the plot. It prolongs the action and delays Timon's inevitable death in the woods with a dilatory stream of visitors eager to profit from the newly found riches.[81] The mock banquet and the discovery of the gold delay the progression of the tragic plot, which moves haltingly towards Timon's death. At the same time, the repetitive and episodic quality of individual acts constitute a dilatory structure worth considering in some detail.

The first half of the play, up to the end of Act Three, can be divided into three sequences or intervals between an action and its consequence or recompense. The first sequence extends from Timon's excessive gifts to his broken bonds. It begins with Act One, which sees a series of flatterers and friends 'taste Lord Timon's bounty' (1.1.281). In various episodic scenes, Timon extends favours and gifts to all and is universally admired. His incessant and repetitive gifts force the progression of time: Timon's generosity ends abruptly as future turns into present and his credit runs out. Act Two sees creditors and their servants approach Timon with demands for payback. The sequence ends in Scene Two of Act Two when Flavius finally succeeds in making Timon understand that he has forfeited his estate:

---

[81] Grav also notes this repetitive structure and its effect: 'The repetitive nature of the delegations that Shakespeare depicts arriving thereafter melds thieves, artists and politicians, all bound by the cult of self-interest, into one' (154).

"Tis all engaged, some forfeited and gone, / And what remains will hardly stop the mouth / Of present dues; the future comes apace' (2.2.146–148). Yet as quickly as Timon realizes that all is lost, he gathers new hope on the grounds of friendship and admonishes his steward: 'Why dost thou weep? Canst thou the conscience lack / To think I shall lack friends? Secure thy heart' (2.2.175–176). With his tears and, later, with his selfless giving, Flavius provides a striking contrast to Mosca and his cool, self-interested calculations.

Thus the second sequence stretches from Timon reaching out to his friends until the end of Act Three, Scene Four, when—having received no help whatsoever—Timon counts out his body parts in reaction to the bills that are presented to him: 'Cut my heart in sums ... Tell out my blood ... Five thousand drops pays that' (3.4.90–94).[82] This sequence is as iterative as the first: a repetitive structure makes the same point in different variations. Timon's servants fan out to implore his friends for cash, but they are universally refused. Despite superficial differences, their refusal is so uniform that Flavius states: 'They answer in a joint and corporate voice' (2.2.204). The repetition of uniform excuses amplifies the inevitability of Timon's downfall. If reciprocity binds the members of a community together, it seems that greed restructures social ties to the point where 'the community of friends' becomes 'an illusion', 'a fiction generated by the corrosive fascination of wealth' (Pierce 82).

It is at the precise moment when Timon's expectations of reciprocal help are disappointed that '[t]he theme of revenge emerges' (Bailey 43). The third sequence involves, for once, a well-planned action on Timon's part. The episode is intersected by the Alcibiades subplot, which acts as a device of delay between Timon's invitation to the lords and his exposure of their greed. Timon takes control of events and their timing when he invites his 'friends' to a feast. Having raised their expectations, he frustrates them with a banquet of pots filled with lukewarm water and pelts them with stones and invectives. This revenge is as symbolic as social credit: without actual money to implement his revenge, Timon reverts to a symbolic gesture. The mock banquet scene cuts the play in half, staging the transformation from philanthropic to misanthropic Timon.

The enigmatic gold treasure of Act Four has an important structural function, because it allows the plot to turn back onto itself and to begin once more the cycle of supplication, flattery, and gift-giving. In structural terms, it is a potential fresh start, though not for Timon. Timon is as excessive in his misanthropy as he was in his liberality: 'the snarling misanthropy which then overtakes him is merely an

---

[82] The metaphor of a body that is cut up in payment of the debt becomes intelligible when we consider Bailey's book chapter on *Timon of Athens*. She explains here that the debtor's body served as 'collateral' or 'forfeit' for the debt in a penal debt bond: 'the law allowed an unsatisfied creditor rights in his debtor's person, which as collateral was considered a form of property like the original loan. This meant that while a creditor could not use or destroy his debtor, for instance by forcing him to perform labor or by murdering him, he could detain his debtor indefinitely' (30).

inverted image of his erstwhile beneficence' (Eagleton 84). He spends as freely as before, but with the destructive intention of spreading murder, corruption, and war: his bounty has become 'villainous'. The Athenians also remain true to themselves: once more, they seek his affection for love of gold.

As an instance of fortune, the gold disrupts the temporal order of definite and measurable periods. It turns the political order upside down as Timon gives most of it to Alcibiades to finance an army. Once more he gives unilaterally, but with a destructive intention. Alcibiades's sudden wealth exposes the crucial difference between the two characters. In his excessive desire for revenge, Timon uses the gold against mankind, whereas Alcibiades finally leaves the path of revenge in favour of justice: 'Alcibiades miraculously transforms insatiable, self-consuming revenge from a mode of intemperance into a means of restitution' (Bailey 46). As wealth gave Timon the power to determine what is valuable, so the gold now gives Alcibiades the power to determine what is just. Although Alcibiades may serve as a counter-model to Timon's excessive thirst for revenge, his power to define justice is disquieting. In the first part of the play, Timon determines the value of things.[83] In the second part, Alcibiades evolves into the arbiter of justice. Determining value and determining virtue emerge as similar operations. Even if Alcibiades proves a more acute observer of virtue than Timon, the play ties justice to the determining power of money, which finances military force.

Conclusion

The asymmetrical economies that Jonson and Shakespeare imagine in their plays operate with the temporal logic of credit and investment, with the accumulation of value and the accrual of losses in and through time. Overindulgence in credit transactions eats up Timon's estate and brings about the end of Volpone's household. In both cases, their departure from the normative heterosocial household accentuates the household's complete immersion in exchange networks. Instead of forming contrasting spheres, household and market collapse into one. This is not to say that heterosocial households are exempt from exchange networks. As we saw in the preceding chapters, women channel consumptive desires both as objects and subjects and thus integrate oeconomic and commercial concerns. Yet the almost complete absence of women in *Volpone* and *Timon of Athens* reduces the household or estate to a site of avaricious intent.

In both plays, gulls and false friends try their hands at advancing valuables in the hope of a profitable return. This is the principle of capital. As Marx says, capital

---

[83] As Bailey writes, 'Timon is recognized as the sole dispenser and arbiter of value' (39), and Richard Finkelstein suggests that Timon 'seems the noncontingent determinant of worth and goodness' (824).

is money 'not spent, it is merely advanced' (1: 249), that is, invested in the expectation of a greater return. In the interval between lending or investing money and its return, value can generate a surplus. Marx explains that 'the valorization [or expansion, A. E.] of value takes place only within this constantly renewed movement' (1: 253). The term 'movement' indicates the temporality of advance and return. Yet Marx's account of capital circulation implies more than just an interval, namely the transformation of money into commodities and finally back into money ('M—C—M', 1: 251).[84] Valerie Forman's work suggests, however, that an awareness of this transformation predates Marx significantly. Thomas Mun had already shifted 'attention from the store of treasure to the flow of money and goods' and taken an interest in 'productive transformations' as a source of profit (4). In the logic of investing that emerges in the early modern period, '[t]he transformative powers of wares and money make loss the source of future accumulation' (5). The plays, however, have no interest in 'productive transformations': in *Volpone*, the clients' expenditures are simply losses with no return, a case of misguided speculation, whereas in *Timon of Athens*, the return on the individual gifts is prompt and almost magical. Significantly, the false friends are only interested in exchange and not use value; their expectation of a seven-fold increase marks value as quantitative. With the surplus in value which they gain merely through advancing gifts, their transactions resemble Marx's representation of 'interest-bearing capital' (1: 256), in which 'the circulation M—C—M presents itself in abridged form, in its final result and without any intermediate stage ... as M—M' (1: 256–257). The early modern model for this quantitative and quasi-magical expansion of value is usury, a form of credit in which money appeared to breed money without any labour or risk. In *Timon of Athens*, those who are suspicious of Athens's ethical state—Apemantus, misanthropic Timon, and Alcibiades—invoke and denounce usury explicitly. While Timon's false friends advance valuables rather than money, they, too, interpret their actions in usurious terms as 'breeding' an excessive return (*Tim.* 1.1.286–287). With its focus on usury, the play strips down the process of capital circulation to its bare bones, highlighting the seemingly inexplicable and effortless, even magical, quality with which the value of capital expands.

While *Volpone* focuses on the entrepreneurial potential and pleasure of deferred recompense, *Timon of Athens* concentrates on the social implications of a failure of reciprocity. Dilated exchanges nominally imply a merely temporary asymmetry, yet they carry the risk of a permanent imbalance. Both plays should be seen in the context of an early modern culture of credit, in which oral promises played a major role and in which legal discourses drew attention to the temporality and intentionality of dilated exchanges. In that context, the plays explore desire for gain and opportunities of 'cheating and fraud' (Muldrew, 'Interpreting the Market' 174). Both portray a commercial society that encourages the desire to succeed

---

[84] See chapter 4 in Marx's *Capital*, Volume 1: 'The General Formula for Capital' (247–257).

at the expense of others. Their attention to promises, hopes, and failed obligations implies a heightened interest in the role of the future and in working time as a crucial skill in building one's fortune. In both plays, the vagaries of the interval in dilated exchanges are key concerns of the plot, yet the conscious management of the interval between giving and getting also emerges in the organization of the action. Their linear progression is halted by delays, and both plots branch out into iterative structures and digressive episodes. This dilation (as I have called it, with a view to the double function of postponing closure and filling in the interval) prolongs the plays and amplifies their comic and tragic effects. In *Volpone*, iteration enhances the comic effects of gulling, and in *Timon of Athens* it renders the repeated refusals of Timon's friends more painful. Delay and dilation represent forms of poetological engagement with temporality and the interval between giving and getting that acquires urgency in a contractual culture of credit and investment.

Instances of delayed reciprocity allow for an exploration of different attitudes towards time: management or even mastery of time versus temporal subjection. Whereas tricksters and usurers use time by putting their money to work, Volpone's clients and Timon are subjected to temporal developments that they cannot control (due to the uncertain event of death or the inescapable temporality of the bond). Despite different degrees of temporal control, the Venice of *Volpone* is almost universally characterized by commercialization, acquisitive desire, and more or less successful attempts at calculation. *Timon of Athens* contrasts calculation with a contingency of fortune that Timon hopes to counterbalance with the certainty of friendship. The play juxtaposes different temporalities: a definite time frame versus arbitrary twists of fortune and indefinite obligations. In the confrontation of gift and proto-capitalist credit economies, Timon's inability to reckon with concrete future risks ensures that his economic success is notably short-lived. He is a willing victim, as excessive in giving as in borrowing, yet he deserves our sympathy because he falls prey to the greater evil of accumulation and gain. With its juxtaposition of the calculable future of proto-bourgeois accumulation and the contingency of fortune in a feudal society, *Timon of Athens* also juxtaposes an economic existence that relies on the immutability of status with contractual relations and a future-orientated intentionality. As a side effect of this comparison, the play dramatizes *ex negativo*, namely through Timon's lack of attention to the terms of bills and bonds, temporal consciousness as an emerging requirement of commercial society. In fact, Timon's endless raging in the second, 'misanthropic' half of the play still testifies to his scorn for a definite and limited timeframe, which proves as ineffective as his former disregard for terms.

Volpone examines the pleasures of projecting and of temporal control and its implications for a heightened sense of self-awareness and -confidence. *Timon of Athens*, in contrast, is more interested in a failing ethics of reciprocity and its social significance. With notions of 'need' and the 'human bond', it suggests an alternative logic to the paradigm of profitable exchange, as well as to feudal patronage. An early modern audience may have recognized some of its own experiences in the play's performance of mutual support in the scene with Flavius and his fellow servants in which Flavius shares his remaining money: 'Good fellows all / The latest of my wealth I'll share amongst you' (4.2.22–23).[85] In the early modern culture of credit, the significance of prompt and informal help was crucial for community life and individual survival. If there is a positive model of sharing in this play, it is to be found in the servants' quarters. In the governing ranks, any hope for reformation and restitution of an ethical frame remains more than doubtful.

The concern with futurity in both plays goes hand in hand with the performance of a credit culture which is grounded in insubstantiality. Economies of empty promises comment on the insubstantiality and instability of value in a system in which there is not enough bullion to cover all debts. Oral promises, promissory notes, bills of exchange, and debt bonds are forms of currency without substance—mere signs. Empty assurances and the delay of payback in *Timon of Athens* and *Volpone* are ways to represent and work through the peculiar nature of a credit-based economy, in which, as Muldrew argues, commercial exchange in local and daily interactions relied fundamentally on trust (*The Economy of Obligation* 4). The lack of substance becomes palpable in Volpone and Mosca's plot, in which wealth increases without any real material investment, and it emerges when Timon's bonds are overdue. The plays extend the threat of insubstantiality to the self and its social relations: Timon's friendships lack substance, while accumulation and wit in *Volpone* succeed only temporarily in giving substance and weight to an otherwise insubstantial self. In a commercial society that runs on credit and in which the market determines value through exchange, a crisis of value and substance extends easily to the social sphere. At the same time, *Volpone* acknowledges that persuasive fictions generate real credit.

---

[85] As Grav points out, 'the steward's sharing of his savings with his fellows lacks any motive of self-interest' (150).

Conclusion

Focusing on the household as the key unit of economic thought, the preceding chapters discussed the ambiguous status of private interest and the plays' keen attention to a skills-orientated and time-sensitive form of prudence. They analysed relations within the household and examined the exchanges that integrate it into a network of relations and obligations. Theatre's interest in households that are in disarray or simply transformed into businesses suggests that the values of classical and Christian oeconomy are under stress in a world increasingly determined by commercial interests and transactions. Navigating this world requires a form of practical wisdom that is as pragmatic as the political wisdom that Machiavelli discusses in *The Prince*. It implies the strategic acquisition of intelligence and a healthy dose of suspicion, the ability to dissimulate one's true intentions, as well as versatility and a persuasive rhetoric. Finally, it entails the ability to manage events in time and to consider future effects. Command of these skills is instrumental in facilitating the acquisition of wealth and the pleasurable experience of self-aggrandizement.

With its spirited and highly skilled trickster figures, dexterous villains, and social climbers, the theatre around 1600 experiments with the revaluation of profit and the instrumental turn of prudence that is also underway in oeconomic and theological discourses of the time. As suggested in the Introduction, early modern oeconomies betray an interest in how to increase the profitability of agricultural estates, while Christian sermons and treatises laud thrift and diligence as prerequisites for improvement. At the same time, mercantile handbooks offer practical expertise for the sake of profitable commerce. Yet the pervasive interest in profitability that is tangible in these writings is usually balanced by a firm defence of inherited values: by an insistence on an ethics of moderation and the common good, a reluctance to validate purchases on credit, and the classical identification of oeconomy with questions of production and use rather than exchange. If oeconomies and mercantile texts hint at a loosening of the ethical ties of prudence, they do so in subtle ways: by paying detailed attention to practicalities and with hair-splitting and casuistic arguments about the difference between legitimate and illegitimate practices that only highlight the difficulty of categorical distinction.

The early modern stage does not share prescriptive literature's preoccupation with an ideal that combines classical with Christian values. Moreover, it has no need to balance conflicting demands. If oeconomies and mercantile tracts suggest that it is possible to improve one's personal finances *and* work towards the common good, drama derives dramatic interest and tension from staging conflicting aims without necessarily offering the comfort of a common good. It puts a spotlight on individuals who pursue their own interests at the expense of others and scrutinizes the instrumental form that practical reason assumes in the process. Early modern plays portray households that are immersed in the market and social relations inflected by mercantile tactics and aims. Their detailed attention to the practicalities of economic success suggests a heightened awareness of commerce as a force that shapes social life. Tellingly, most dramatic characters are preoccupied with how to get what they want rather than how to be good and do the right thing. As this cross-generic study suggests, what people want is less varied than one might think: the plays discussed here highlight acquisitive desire as an omnipresent motive, even if they do not suggest that it is an exclusive one. Acquisitive appetite joins forces and occasionally competes with desire for social advancement and self-aggrandizement. Those aims *can* exist in harmony and help to satisfy each other. The accumulation of wealth feeds a sense of potency and self-satisfaction and opens up new avenues of social advancement. At the same time, social advancement offers new possibilities for enriching and valourizing the self. On occasion, however, these aims drift apart, leading to conflicts of interests, as when Volpone is willing to forego the chance at wangling more gifts off the gulls for a climactic bit of conning. In *Volpone*, as in the other plays, private interest comes with a calculating angle, but it is also an excessive and irrational force that drives individuals to go too far in pursuit of their aims. It is at once the new normal, an omnipresent and even prudent motive that renders agents calculable, and a kind of self-defeating madness that leads to irrational action. The fates of Face in *The Alchemist* and of the Touchwoods, Allwits, and Kixes in *A Chaste Maid* suggest that a versatile and pragmatic approach to wealth may lead to better results than Volpone's obsession with wealth and self or Othello's hypertrophic investment in exclusive possession. Instead of being driven by an all-powerful acquisitive urge, these characters are versatile enough to make compromises and to come up with pragmatic solutions in contingent circumstances.

The following discussion briefly reviews key insights of the preceding analyses through the lens of genre. This book's cross-generic approach was designed to demonstrate theatre's pervasive concern with socio-economic relations and exchanges, but it may also help to initiate a broader discussion of how different dramatic genres approach and mediate them. Genre adapts inherited forms to the representation of changing social frameworks, but it also comes with its own concerns and priorities. Different dramatic forms highlight different aspects. The discussion below looks at how comedies and tragedies represent the household in relation to the larger community as well as to ethics, politics, and commerce. It also reviews how they explore desire for wealth and social advancement and how they conceive of time as the dimension of contingent events and the future.

Oeconomy and Commerce

The ideal household is omnipresent in the homiletic literature of the sixteenth and seventeenth centuries, but a rare thing on the early modern stage. Around 1600, early modern playwrights portray households that are disorderly, deficient, and inextricably caught up in processes of commercialization. If Hesiod's classical household required the triad of house, wife, and ox, there is nary a classical homestead to be found on the London stages. At the centre of the plays are urban and noble households, not agricultural estates. Yet it is not just the missing ox that signals the stage households' deviation from the ideal, but also their disorderly state or even complete absence of marital relations. In the homiletic and practical literature, husband and wife are the governing 'society' of the household, with the wife acting as 'fellow helper'. They must work as one to ensure the wellbeing of the household, which effectively means that the wife must subject herself in all matters to her husband's will. Yet Volpone and Timon have no wives at all. Othello has one, but thinks he has lost her, only to then destroy her with his own hands. Macbeth has a wife, but she does not obey him, nor does she bear him any children. The Kixes in *A Chaste Maid* are equally childless, while Touchwood has a wife and numerous children, but no money to maintain a house. The same is true for Allwit, whose house is kept by Sir Walter. The household in *The Alchemist* lacks not only a wife, but also (at least temporarily) a master. None of these households are complete, and none are fit for reproduction within economically sound and morally legitimate bounds. They bear little resemblance to the self-sufficient and orderly houses of the prescriptive literature. Obsessed with their own interests, invested in dilated exchanges, and without a clear internal hierarchy, these households contribute little to the social order. In Xenophon's classical discourse, the household creates strong and competent citizens; in early modern discourse, the benefit of well-run households lies in their establishment of discipline and a binary order of authority and subjection. The households of the early modern stage achieve neither. Instead, the households of tragedy disrupt the socio-political order, while the households of comedy engage with a new, commercial order that is maintained by fervent exchange.

Genre plays an important part in determining how households are positioned in relation to the greater community. Aristotle's *Poetics* had demanded that tragedy should portray noble characters; early modern writers from Stephen Gosson to Sir Philip Sidney (see Munro 87–88) reiterate this demand. Admittedly, clear-cut generic types are rare on the early modern stage.[1] Both comedies and tragedies are

---

[1] Not even the simple requirement of tragedy dealing with noble characters holds in all cases: it is subverted by domestic tragedies such as *Arden of Faversham* and *A Woman Killed with Kindness* (Munro 97). *Arden of Faversham* introduces its tragic hero as a gentleman and his wife, Alice, as a woman of gentle birth. Yet Mosbie, the villain, is an upstart, who acts as steward, and the real, historical Arden was, in fact, a self-made man. *A Warning for Fair Women* involves common characters

varied enough to ensure that there are multiple exceptions to any apparent rule.[2] Yet with characters 'drawn from history or legend' (Reiss 1301), Shakespeare's tragedies follow the well-established pattern of tragedy recounting 'the falls of princes' (Hunter, 'Elizabethan Theatrical Genres' 250). In the tragedies discussed in this book, the households at the centre of the action belong to the governing class and communicate with other governing bodies: with the king and thanes in *Macbeth*, the Venetian senate in *Othello*, and the Athenian lords and senators in *Timon of Athens*. The pronounced political angle of oeconomy in the tragedies is part and parcel of tragedy's investment in noble characters whose actions are either directly political or have political implications. Lady Macbeth's ambitions are directed at acquiring political power, Othello's mad jealousy threatens his ability to govern Cyprus, and Timon loses political influence along with his land. Thus in all three tragedies discussed in this book, the failure of oeconomy has political repercussions (see also Richardson, 'Tragedy, Family and Household' 24). Whether through Macbeth as potential heir to the throne, the noble warrior and governor of Cyprus Othello, or Lord Timon, whom the Athenian nobles admire as *primus inter pares*, the plays stage a failure of order that is simultaneously oeconomic *and* political. Tragedies like *Macbeth*, *Othello*, and *Timon of Athens*—not to mention *Hamlet* and *King Lear*—relate the destabilization of the political order to households in disarray.

The tragedies also pose ethical problems. Even in Aristotle's *Poetics*, the emphasis on 'noble' action is ambiguous enough to encompass both the characters' social status and the moral dimension of their actions.[3] Othello and Macbeth submit to violent passions such as jealousy and ambition, and Timon indulges in prodigal spending. In all three tragedies, these passions lead to the downfall of their houses. The tragedies thus not only represent households in disarray, but also highlight the corruption of oeconomy's ethical framework. No longer governed by a clear moral code that orientates the household towards sufficiency, a merely modest surplus, and order, the households of tragedy disintegrate, consumed by prodigal

---

and 'depends for its effect on its local familiarity' (Hunter 'Elizabethan Theatrical Genres' 251). With its interest in common people and the household, and with its investment in local settings, domestic tragedy 'subverts neoclassical assumptions' (250) and offers plenty of points of contact with city comedy.

[2] Jill Levenson makes this point for comedy: 'English Renaissance critics sporadically devised generic norms for comedy according to structure, content, and moral import', but '[m]ost dramatists regularly ignored those norms, as they ignored the norms for tragedy, producing a genre irrepressible in its creative innovation and variety' (263). This variety is hardly surprising, as the influences on English comedy were wide-ranging: from the New Comedies of Plautus and Terence to the Old Comedy of Aristophanes. Both were mediated through Italian drama, both academic and popular.

[3] George K. Hunter suggests that 'The Aristotelian comment that Englishmen found most germane to their own priorities was that which distinguished tragedy from comedy in terms of noble [*spoudaios*] versus ignoble [*phaulos*] actions. The definition of these terms is, of course, capable of endless reinterpretation. Is the distinction a moral one (good versus bad), or do the words have a social meaning? Renaissance commentators had few doubts; the idea that tragedy was separated from comedy by the gulf between rulers and ruled was a standard assumption' ('Elizabethan Theatrical Genres' 253).

spending, hypertrophic desire, and outbreaks of violent passion. As the analyses of *Macbeth*, *Othello*, and *Timon of Athens* suggest, the classical continuity of ethics, oeconomy, and politics is destabilized on all levels by a commercial dynamic that redefines individual values and aims, alters the functions of the household, prioritizes exchange, and drives contractual credit. *Timon of Athens* portrays the destruction of social bonds in what the play depicts as shift towards a contractual society. That play is more explicitly concerned with usurious relations and economic failure than any of the other tragedies. Yet as Chapter 3 suggests, *Othello* is also intensely preoccupied with the commercialization of social relations: with a shift in evaluation that prioritizes exchange value, with a mercantile form of practical wisdom, and with social and spatial mobility in a world of global trade. *Macbeth* is more interested in the nexus between oeconomy and politics than in commerce, and yet the force that disrupts the household and the political order is the familiar excessive desire for more—for an increase in power that continues to accumulate in the future and comes, as Malcolm suggests, with unlimited possibilities of enrichment. Where the household takes centre stage, Shakespeare's focus on noble figures has the distinctive effect of highlighting the nexus of ethics, oeconomy, and politics: not to demonstrate a positive continuity, but to show its disintegration.

Households in the comedies are also a far cry from the ideal, yet they have a different social status and are part of a different and far more urban society. City comedy does not principally depict the nobility, but rather Londoners of all sorts, including 'characters of low station and commonplace behaviour' (Hunter, 'Elizabethan Theatrical Genres' 250): merchants, grocers, goldsmiths, and their apprentices, along with prostitutes, tricksters, and gentlemen. Consequently, the comedies' interest lies not in the interface of oeconomy and politics, but of household and market. Rather than serving as a disciplinary school for a hierarchically ordered society, the households of city comedy participate in a restructuring of social life. They are not models of government, but nodal points in a network of exchange relations. The tragedies depict households that stand apart from the community, separated by the crime of murder, the scandal of foreignness, and the drama of broken bonds. In the city comedies, by contrast, households are not isolated from a political community; they are immersed in and integrated into a market community. The commodification of household relations is frequently symbolized through sexual affairs. In the tragedies, the impact of commercialization on *oikos* and *polis* is subtler, but their relation is nonetheless shaped by the persistent interference of a chrematistic logic, which is orientated towards private gain and social advancement and threatens the order of household and commonwealth.

The households of the London comedies embrace exchange joyfully, as, for instance, in *A Chaste Maid*. Here, households freely trade sexual favours and money, barter away children, and beget new ones. In *Volpone* and *The Alchemist*, householders and their servants replace oeconomic considerations and ambitions with mercantile ones. The entanglements of all households in *A Chaste Maid* creates an open market structure that is contrary to the notion of the *oikos* as a distinct and self-contained unit. In *Volpone* and *The Alchemist*, the household is still a circumscribed space and distinct social entity, but it has lost its original function of producing and using goods and exists mainly for the purpose of acquisition. The reorientation of the household towards exchange signals a shift in socio-economic structures. In the city comedies, oeconomy adapts to commercial society. In the tragedies, in contrast, households die clinging to an outdated understanding of the household as distinct and detached from the sphere of circulation. The eponymous heroes of *Othello*, *Timon of Athens*, and *Macbeth* fail not because they are too invested in exchange, but because they are unable to face and accept its ubiquity. Timon resists exchange entirely and is blind to his friends' use of gifts as capital. The Macbeths isolate themselves and shut down the give-and-take of profitable exchange, putting an end to all forms of sociability. Othello is haunted by the phantasm of a circulating wife. He is also unable to understand his own position in exchange relations and lacks the strategic frame of mind that might enable him to remain in Venice's favour.

The household's integration and even active participation in a market of paid labour, dilated exchanges, and fluctuating credit is perhaps most obvious when wives and daughters are treated as sexual commodities, but it also emerges in the figure of the servant who acts as mercantile broker. The almost complete absence of production and reproduction, and their replacement with unilateral spending or acquisition, is staged through the homosocial households of *Volpone* and *Timon of Athens*. Together, tragedies and comedies suggest an omnipresent and persistent concern with private interests; specifically, with material profit and social advancement. The tragedies represent this shift in a critical vein that highlights its ethical and political problems, but they do not end with a promise of renewal. The ubiquitous influence of commercial practices and modes of evaluation is permanent and continues to shape social and political structures and individual aims. The city comedies depict even more clearly a commercial reality that is shaped by the profit impulse: here, acquisitive desire is a uniform motive that renders others calculable. Together, the comedies and tragedies suggest that acquisitive desire is a social constant. A model of oeconomy that is opposed to commerce no longer appears viable in early capitalist society: it neither provides adequate orientation for the individual household, nor is it a functional model for the commonwealth. Instead, the relation between oeconomy and commerce must be reconceived to accommodate the commercial interests of both agricultural estates and city households. Mercantilist and bullionist authors merge oeconomic and commercial concerns in their principle of a balance of trade. The advice to be first and foremost a seller, not a buyer, aligns the state with the commercial interests of the individual household and thus newly invigorates the analogy between household and commonwealth.

In their own ways, the plays discussed here explore the interfaces between household and market and examine how they shape the community. Theatre thus contributes to the ongoing renegotiation of the relation between oeconomy and commerce.

The Discontents of Social Mobility

Oeconomic disorder concerns the vertical axis of social hierarchies. In the plays discussed, traditional positions of authority and subjection in household and commonwealth are precarious or even reversed. Wives talk back to their husbands, servants manipulate their masters, and noblemen and commoners alike desire to move up in the world. The insubordinate servants of *Volpone*, *The Alchemist*, and *Othello* in particular draw attention to shifting positions in a socially mobile society and to the fantasies and desires that accompany greater possibilities of social advancement. The passions that the plays explore are also linked to this dynamic. The Macbeths' limitless ambition for kingship drives them to murder. Iago's malicious envy suggests that the sheer possibility of climbing the social ladder may provoke resentment, especially when one is overtaken by former social equals. The tricksters enjoy not just indulging an acquisitive desire, but the feeling of pride that results from their mastery over others. Othello's jealousy reminds the audience that what is won may also be lost. As the plays suggest, the new mobility of early modern society comes with its own affective burden and social pathology of ambition, envy, jealousy, and pride.

A desire for climbing the social ladder goes hand in hand with the sense that one's rightful place is elsewhere, namely higher up. Iago's envy and the ambition of the Macbeths signal a disparity between what one is and what one feels one should be. Mosca's proud refusal to take off the robes he has borrowed from Volpone equally demonstrates his sense that he deserves a higher station. The Yellowhammers are bent on climbing the social ladder; they attempt to secure their entry into the ranks of the gentry through their children's marriages. The desire for social advancement or an exalted position points to a gap between accustomed social structures and positions on the one hand and individual desires and trajectories on the other. Timon is perhaps a special case because, at least in the beginning, he feels no disparity between who he is and wants to be. Yet he is only content because he fails to realize that his status is already in decline. Othello is similarly happy with his place, until Iago convinces him that he does not have what he has—a virtuous wife—and that he is not what he is—a loved husband, a prudent general, and a benevolent governor—but something that only 'a will most rank' and 'unnatural' would want.

How the conflict between individual desires and social possibilities is represented correlates with genre conventions. Garrett A. Sullivan describes a specifically tragic subjectivity that is created by the very society with which it is at odds:

> [T]ragic subjectivity arises out of a character's non-identicality to his or her social position; it depends upon the inadequacy of that position, and of the social order as a whole, to accommodate a given character's desires. Of course, society has also contributed to the creation of those desires. Tragic subjectivity is born of the ways in which society fails the subject it helps to create.
>
> (75)

The notion of non-identicality helps to relate individual characters' desires to their status. Macbeth's reaching for the crown, Timon's insistent performance of unmatched generosity even when he has nothing left to give, and Othello's desire for appreciation, belonging, and inalienable property challenge existing structures. Yet to suggest an opposition between stable structures and mobile subjects would be misleading. The problem lies not just with individuals who are dissatisfied with their positions, but with a social order that is itself in motion. In *Timon of Athens*, the brittleness of the socio-political order is obvious; friendships collapse in the aftermath of Timon's bankruptcy, and the government succumbs all too easily to Alcibiades's accession. Perhaps Timon's exaggerated and incongruous generosity is an attempt to stabilize shifting social structures and his own position within them. Othello's self-division into hero and racialized villain symbolizes unstable frames of inclusion and exclusion, cooperation and competition, in a world of transnational exchange. The scene at the Duke's court in Act One suggests a lack of consensus on fundamental social questions—and the answers to those questions are clearly shaped by circumstance and political exigencies. Othello's excessive jealousy signals his desire for possession and belonging in a world in which he remains a foreigner. The self-authorization and ambition of the Macbeths is triggered by the promise of a political change that is already underway, as the prophecy of the weird sisters implies. Macbeth's easy usurpation of the throne and Malcolm's introduction of a peerage system point to political structures in flux, whose very instability fuels the ambition of the Macbeths. In the tragedies, socio-political structures appear to be as fragile and uncertain as the social positions of the protagonists. Yet, in the end, flux does not equal flexibility: the confrontation between the desires of individual characters and shifting social structures leads to frustration and violent destruction.

The comedies, in contrast, do not portray non-identicality as an essential conflict. Here, the social order is corrupt anyway, and individual characters are flexible enough to adapt to changing circumstances. If one avenue to socio-economic success is barred, people make concessions, work around the obstacle, or simply resign themselves to the limits of their agency and eke out an existence by other means. *The Alchemist* is a case in point: Jeremy slips back into his role as servant, while Dol and Subtle run away to try their luck elsewhere. *A Chaste Maid* offers plenty of evidence for the beneficial effects of versatility and adaptation, not just with Allwit and Touchwood, but even with the Yellowhammers, who resign themselves to seeing their ambitions thwarted. Where excessive pride and ambition outweigh versatility, however, the punishment can be drastic—as is the case with Mosca and Volpone. In a world of shifting social structures, *versatile ingenium* becomes key to success. *Volpone*'s heavy-handed justice at the end frustrates generic expectations of reconciliation, but it suggests that some characters' tragic endings may be related to the fact that they are too set in their desires, virtues, and vices to move with the times or, as Francis Bacon might say, to 'runne with the occasions' (*The Advancement of Learning* 173).

The diverging interests of masters and servants not only exemplify a general awareness of social mobility, they also demonstrate the ex-centric force that comes to bear on the household in a market society. The division of labour and the delegation of responsibilities for the sake of profitability as well as new opportunities for social advancement create individual subject positions with diverging interests within the house, rather than preserving the fiction of an undivided household whose interests are identical to the householder's. They suggest that the interface of household and market does not simply connect individual households with the larger community, but shapes duties, interests, and identities within the house.

The 'Architecture of Fortune' and the Future

In all the plays discussed here, the drama revolves around individual characters who seek to become architects of their fortune. They regard the future as malleable and receptive to their desires and hopes. Bacon's notion of the 'Architecture of fortune' (*The Advancement* 165) retains the temporal character of Fortuna's wheel, but substitutes the cyclical image with a sense of progressive growth. If one's fortune can be built like a house—in individual steps according to a plan—it is possible to strategically increase one's wealth and reputation over time. A prerequisite for success and a crucial part of 'wisedom of Businesse' (Bacon, *The Advancement* 157) is, therefore, the ability to keep one eye on the future, to act strategically, and to manage or 'emplot' unforeseen events when they occur. Along with versatility, an ability to reckon with the future is a distinctive quality of the protagonists of comedy as opposed to tragedy.

In the comedies, the tricksters engage playfully in economies of insubstantiality that thrive on empty promises. They try to shape their own future by exploiting the future-orientated temporal structure of credit and thus actively use time to build their fortune. The open-ended future of credit operations moves questions of temporal management centre-stage. When there is nothing to be given in return, when delivery is deferred into a future that never comes, the delay of compensation is a continual challenge and existential need that demands special skills. Yet delay is not the only temporal challenge and concern. The tricksters have another crucial skill: they recognize and are capable of seizing profitable opportunities when they present themselves. In Bacon's terms, they eagerly take hold of the forelock of Occasion before she turns away again to present her 'Bald Noddle' ('Of Delayes' 68).[4] With this skill, the tricksters are not just able to adapt to contingent events, but manage to turn those events into profitable opportunities. Be it an absent master or a lost handkerchief, versatile characters are able to turn such events to their advantage. Significantly, they also have an intellectual grasp of what makes an 'occasion' and what it means in an economic context. They use this knowledge to create the illusion of opportunities for others and thus tempt gullible clients into spending their wealth on projects that have no substance. Seizing and creating (illusory) opportunities is to engage with temporal events and to change their course rather than passively wait for a bit of luck. Predictably, this activity means that the tricksters have a strong tendency to overreach, not just because of their excessive desire for material goods and social success, but also because creating opportunities means triggering a new series of events that produces its own circumstances that then need to be managed in turn. In both *Volpone* and *The Alchemist*, there comes a point when the tricksters are caught in a spider's web of their own creation.

When considering the gullible clients and the tragic heroes, however, it is clear that submitting to contingent events and subjecting oneself to an uncontrollable future is hardly a viable alternative. On the early modern stage, characters who are unable to foresee the future consequences of their actions frequently lose out. While the protagonists of the comedies actively manage time and thus take their future in hand, Macbeth and Timon are unable to even consider the future, much less integrate it into an oeconomic calculus. Macbeth accepts only the part of the prophecy that predicts his ascent to power, but not the part that claims that his house will be unable to retain it. In their desire to seize the throne in the present, the Macbeths neglect to consider the future of their childless house beyond the act of murder. Timon is ignorant of the future of broken bonds that 'comes apace' (*Tim.* 2.2.148). Instead, he trusts blindly in his friends as a provision against inconstant Fortuna. Othello leaves the interpretation of Desdemona's love-choice and the fashioning of the future entirely to Iago. Of course, the question of how to approach the future involves more than personality. As the fated world of tragedy has little space for human agency and the future of tragic heroes is already plotted, the tragic characters act out a generic condition: there is no open future in tragedy, no fortune that could be built.

---

[4] Bacon, Essay XXI, 'Of Delayes': '*Occasion ... turneth a Bald Noddle, after she hath presented her locks in Front, and no hold taken*' (68). See also Chapter 3, 141.

Theatre's peculiar take on the 'architecture of fortune' emphasizes the theatricality of socio-economic behaviour. As suggested in the individual chapters, the city comedies in particular associate mercantile with theatrical skills: with role-playing, disguise, dissimulation, rhetoric, and plotting. With Lady Macbeth as hostess, the false friends in *Timon of Athens*, and Iago as confidant in *Othello*, the tragedies employ theatrical forms of self-display such as flattery and dissimulation. They, too, examine in detail what it means to play a social role. Across genres, Lady Macbeth's ritualized hospitality, the conspicuous consumption performed by Mrs Allwit's lying-in, the display of marriageable Moll in the goldsmith's shop, and the artificial posturing of her educated brother offer examples for stylized and highly theatrical forms of socio-economic behaviour. As William Scott's *Essay of Drapery* from 1635 and Bacon's notion of 'wisdom of business' suggest, how to present oneself is as important at home and in business as it is in court politics. Captain Face's ability to don one face and discard another serves mercantile interests just as much as Volpone's performance of impending death. Iago's and Mosca's performances are tied to strategic self-display in a culture of credit that allows for a certain degree of social mobility: one's performance might enhance or diminish one's creditworthiness and pave or obstruct the road to social advancement. With its doubling of socio-economic practices for an observing audience, theatre is singularly suited to exposing the theatricality of social roles.

Yet theatre's detailed attention to role-playing and persuasive fictions may signal more than an increasing awareness of questions of conduct and social roles in matters of business. It is also self-reflexive and metatheatrical. It provides evidence for Paul Yachnin's hypothesis that drama is not just 'a mirror of the culture' but 'depicts the world in ways refracted by the interests of the playing companies and the playwrights' (xiii). In his article 'Poetaster, the Author and Cultural Production', Alan Sinfield (following Bourdieu) argues similarly. He describes 'ideological production as *doubly determined*', suggesting 'that we should expect texts to be responsive not only to the interests they (ostensibly) serve, but also to the interests of those who produce them ... This is likely to occur when, as in early modern England, the idea of the writer is, itself, provisional and riven by unstable boundaries' (85). In the frequent combination of commercial interests with theatrical displays, the drama of the time reflects not least on its own condition as a medium that makes money with all that which is, in other business transactions, ethically dubious: free invention, persuasive rhetoric, and simulation. With the creation and orchestration of believable plots, the tricksters and Iago perform the creative and constructive work of the playwright and actors who will reap a material and affective profit for making the possible (or even impossible) plausible.[5] This profit is contingent, however, as the Epilogue to *Volpone* suggests, on

---

[5] See Aristotle's famous comment in the *Poetics*: 'For the purposes of poetry a convincing impossibility is preferable to an unconvincing possibility' (*Poet.* 1461b11–12).

whether the play pleases its audience—and *this* will be decided by the applause at the end of the performance, and hence in an uncertain future.

To conclude, early modern theatre's preoccupation with households in disarray, with 'wisdom of business', private interests, and asymmetrical exchanges indicates shifting logics of socio-economic action. It offers evidence for the revaluation of gain as a pervasive motive and for the rebirth of prudence as a form of practical expertise in the service of profit. Additionally, the plays give insight into the affective dimensions of entrepreneurial action and social competition, the theatricality of self-display, and the efficiency of calculating agents who are determined to build their fortunes and rise in the world. They point to a mercantile agency and emerging subjectivity that signals the transformation of inherited social structures and frameworks of interpretation. While theatre is not a mirror of socio-economic structures and realities, it clearly engages with social changes and the fantasies, fears, and desires that they provoke. As my brief discussion of genre and metatheatricality suggests, early modern drama draws on traditions of its own and brings its own interests and concerns to bear on the representation and exploration of socio-economic changes. At the same time, the socio-economic transformations of early modern society have a poetological force that comes to full fruition in an urban theatre that is shaped by global commerce and caters to the interests of diverse audiences, including the middling sort. The keen attention to the dramatic possibilities of the interval of credit and the use of delay and dilation to shape dramatic plots; entrepreneurial characters who drive the action as they seek to acquire wealth, status, and self-satisfaction; and households that become sites of plotting in the service of diverging private interests offer ways and tropes to explore and address life in this commercial environment.

Works Cited

Plays

Fletcher, John. *The Tamer Tamed. Women on the Early Modern Stage*, edited by Emma Smith. Bloomsbury Publishing, 2014. New Mermaids Anthologies.

Heywood, Thomas. *A Woman Killed With Kindness. Women on the Early Modern Stage*, edited by Emma Smith. Bloomsbury Publishing, 2014. New Mermaids Anthologies.

Jonson, Ben. *The Alchemist*, edited by Elizabeth Cook, Bloomsbury Publishing, 2016. New Mermaids.

Jonson, Ben. *Volpone*, edited by Robert N. Watson. Bloomsbury Publishing, 2015. New Mermaids.

Jonson, Ben. *Epicoene. Four Plays*, edited by Robert N. Watson, Bloomsbury Publishing, 2014. New Mermaids Anthologies.

Jonson, Ben. *Sejanus His Fall. Six Elizabethan & Jacobean Tragedies*, with an introduction by Brian Gibbons. Bloomsbury Publishing, 1984. New Mermaids.

Middleton, Thomas. *A Chaste Maid in Cheapside*, edited by Alan Brissenden. Bloomsbury Publishing, 2015. New Mermaids.

Middleton, Thomas. *Women Beware Women. Four Plays*, edited by William C. Carroll. Bloomsbury Publishing, 2014. New Mermaids Anthologies.

Middleton, Thomas. *A Trick to Catch the Old One. Five Plays*, edited by Brian Loughrey and Neil Taylor. Penguin Books, 2006.

Shakespeare, William. *The Merchant of Venice*, edited by John Drakakis. Bloomsbury Publishing, 2014. The Arden Shakespeare Third Series.

Shakespeare, William. *Othello*, revised 2nd edition, edited by E.A.J. Honigmann and with a new introduction by Ayanna Thompson. Bloomsbury Publishing, 2016. The Arden Shakespeare Third Series.

Shakespeare, William. *Timon of Athens*, edited by Anthony B. Dawson, and Gretchen E. Minton. Bloomsbury Publishing, 2008. The Arden Shakespeare Third Series.

Shakespeare, William. *Hamlet*, edited by Ann Thompson and Neil Taylor. Bloomsbury Publishing, 2006. The Arden Shakespeare Third Series.

Shakespeare, William. *King Richard II*, edited by Charles R. Forker. Bloomsbury Publishing, 2002. The Arden Shakespeare Third Series.

Shakespeare, William. *King Lear*, edited by Richard A. Foakes. Bloomsbury Publishing, 1997. The Arden Shakespeare Third Series.

Shakespeare, William. *Macbeth*, edited by Kenneth Muir. Bloomsbury Publishing, 1984. The Arden Shakespeare Second Series.

Classical and Early Modern Sources

Anonymous. *The Husband's Instructions to His Family; Or, Household Observations Fit to be Observed by Vvife, Children, and Servants*. London, 1685. Early English Books Online.

Anonymous. *Tell-Trothes New-Yeares Gift Beeing Robin Good-Fellowes Newes Out of those Countries, Where Inhabites neither Charity nor Honesty. With His Owne Inuectiue Against Ielosy*. London, 1593. Early English Books Online.
Anonymous. *A Glasse for Housholders Wherin Thei Maye Se, Bothe Howe to Rule Theim Selfes [and] Ordre their Housholde Verye Godly and Fruytfull*. London, 1542. Early English Books Online.
Aquinas, St. Thomas. 'Summa Theologiae'. *Injustice*, vol. 38 (2a2ae 63-79), Cambridge University Press, 2006.
Aristotle. *The Complete Works of Aristotle*, vol. 2, edited by Jonathan Barnes. Princeton University Press, 1985.
Bacon, Francis. *The Advancement of Learning, The Oxford Francis Bacon*, vol. 4, edited by Michael Kiernan. Clarendon Press, 2003 [1605].
Bacon, Francis. *The Essayes or Counsels, Civill and Morall. The Oxford Francis Bacon*, vol. 15, edited by Michael Kiernan. Oxford University Press, 1985.
Bacon, Francis. *Essayes. Religious Meditations. Places of Perswasion & Disswasion. Seene and Allowed*. London, 1597. Early English Books Online.
Bourne, Immanuel. *The Godly Mans Guide with a Direction for all, especially, Merchants and Tradsmen, Shewing how they may so Buy, and Sell, and Get Gaine, that they may Gaine Heauen: Preached in a Sermon at Paules Crosse, the 22. of August, 1619, being the Sunday before Saint Bartholomew Day/by Immanuel Bourne*. London, 1620. Early English Books Online.
Brathwaite, Richard. *The English Gentleman Containing Sundry Excellent Rules Or Exquisite Observations, Tending to Direction of Every Gentleman, of Selecter Ranke and Qualitie; how to Demeane or Accommodate Himselfe in the Manage of Publike or Private Affaires. By Richard Brathwait Esq*. London, 1630. Early English Books Online.
Browne, John. *The Marchants Avizo Very Necessarie for their Sonnes and Seruants, when they First Send them Beyond the Seas, as to Spaine and Portingale Or Other countreyes. Made by their Hartie Wellwiller in Christ. I.B. marchant*. London, 1589. Early English Books Online.
Burton, Robert. *The Anatomy of Melancholy*, vols. 1-6, edited by Thomas C. Faulkner et al. Clarendon Press, 1989 [1621].
Cicero, Marcus Tullius. *On Obligations [De Officiis]*, translated and with an introduction and notes by P. G. Walsh. Oxford University Press, 2000.
Cicero, Marcus Tullius. *On Old Age. On Friendship. On Divination [De senectute; De amicitia; De divinatione]*. Translated by William Armistead Falconer. Harvard University Press, 1923.
Cleaver, Robert. *A Godlie Forme of Householde Gouernment for the Ordering of Priuate Families, According to the Direction of Gods Word*. London, 1598. Early English Books Online.
Defoe, Daniel. *The Complete English Tradesman*. 1725. Eighteenth Century Collections Online.
Defoe, Daniel. 'Review of the State of the British Nation', 11 June 1709, vol. 6, no. 30. *Defoe's Review in 22 Facsimile Books*, Facsimile Book 14, reproduced from the original editions, with an introduction and bibliographical notes by Arthur Wellesley Secord. Columbia University Press, 1938.
Elyot, Sir Thomas. *The Boke, Named the Gouernor Deuised by Sir Thomas Elyot Knight*. London, 1580 [1531]. Early English Books Online.
Estienne, Charles, et al. *Maison Rustique, Or the Countrie Farme*, printed by Edm. Bollifant for Bonham Norton. London, 1600. Early English Books Online.

Fenner, Dudley. *The Artes of Logike and Rethorike [Sic] Plainelie Set Foorth in the Englishe Tounge, Easie to be Learned and Practised: Togeather with Examples for the Practise of the Same, for Methode in the Gouernment of the Familie, Prescribed in the Word of God, and for the Whole in the Resolution Or Opening of Certaine Partes of Scripture, According to the Same*. Middelburg, 1584. Early English Books Online.

Fitzherbert, John. *Fitzharberts Booke of Husbandrie Deuided into Foure Seuerall Bookes, very Necessary and Profitable for all Sorts of People. and Now Newlie Corrected, Amended, and Reduced, into a More Pleasing Forme of English then before*. London, 1598 [1523]. Early English Books Online.

Gataker, Thomas. *A Good Vvife Gods Gift and, a Vvife Indeed. Tvvo Mariage Sermons. By Thomas Gataker B. of D. and Pastor of Rotherhith*. London, 1623. Early English Books Online.

Gouge, William. *Of Domesticall Duties Eight Treatises. I. an Exposition of that Part of Scripture Out of which Domesticall Duties are Raised ... VIII. Duties of Masters. By William Gouge*. London, 1622. Early English Books Online.

Harrison, William. *The Description of England*, edited by Georges Edelen. Folger Shakespeare Library, 1968.

James I. *Basilikon Doron Devided into Three Bookes*. Edinburgh, 1599. Early English Books Online.

Jonson, Ben. *Discoveries*, reprinted edition, 1641. John Lane and Dutton Company, 1923.

Leigh, Edward. *A Systeme Or Body of Divinity Consisting of Ten Books: Wherein the Fundamentals and Main Grounds of Religion are Opened, the Contrary Errours Refuted, most of the Controversies between Us, the Papists, Arminians, and Socinians Discussed and Handled, several Scriptures Explained and Vindicated from Corrupt Glosses: A Work Seasonable for these Times, Wherein so Many Articles of our Faith are Questioned, and so Many Gross Errours Daily Published*. London, 1654. Early English Books Online.

Machiavelli, Niccolò. *Art of War*, translated, edited, and with a commentary by Christopher Lynch. University of Chicago Press, 2003 [1521].

Machiavelli, Niccolò. *The Prince*, translated and with an introduction by Harvey C. Mansfield. University of Chicago Press, 1998 [1532].

Malynes, Gerard. *The Center of the Circle of Commerce. Or, A Refutation of a Treatise, Intituled the Circle of Commerce, Or the Ballance of Trade, Lately Published by E. M. by Gerard Malynes Merchant*. London, 1623. Early English Books Online.

Malynes, Gerard. *Consuetudo, Vel Lex Mercatoria, Or the Ancient Law-Merchant Diuided into Three Parts: According to the Essentiall Parts of Trafficke. Necessarie for all Statesmen, Iudges, Magistrates, Temporall and Ciuile Lawyers, Mint-Men, Merchants, Marriners, and all Others Negotiating in all Places of the World. By Gerard Malynes Merchant*. London, 1622. Early English Books Online.

Malynes, Gerard. *The Maintenance of Free Trade According to the Three Essentiall Parts of Traffique; Namely, Commodities, Moneys and Exchange of Moneys, by Bills of Exchanges for Other Countries, Or, An answer to a Treatise of Free Trade, Or the Meanes to make Trade Flourish, Lately Published ... By Gerard Malynes Merchant*. London, 1622. Early English Books Online.

Malynes, Gerard. *Englands Vievv, in the Vnmasking of Two Paradoxes with a Replication Vnto the Answer of Maister Iohn Bodine. By Gerrard De Malynes Merchant*. London, 1603. Early English Books Online.

Malynes, Gerard. *A Treatise of the Canker of Englands Common Wealth Deuided into Three Parts: Wherein the Author Imitating the Rule of Good Phisitions, First, Declareth the*

Disease. Secondarily, Sheweth the Efficient Cause Thereof. Lastly, a Remedy for the Same. By Gerrard De Malynes Merchant. London, 1601. Early English Books Online.

Misselden, Edward. *The Circle of Commerce. Or the Ballance of Trade in Defence of Free Trade: Opposed to Malynes Little Fish and His Great Whale, and Poized Against them in the Scale. Wherein also, Exchanges in Generall are Considered: And Therein the Whole Trade of this Kingdome with Forraine Countries, is Digested into a Ballance of Trade, for the Benefite of the Publique. Necessary for the Present and Future Times. By E. M. Merchant.* London, 1623. Early English Books Online.

Misselden, Edward. *Free trade, Or, the Meanes to make Trade Florish. Wherein, the Causes of the Decay of Trade in this Kingdome are Discouered and the Remedies also to Remooue the Same are Represented.* London, 1622. Early English Books Online.

Mun, Thomas. *England's Treasure by Forraign Trade, Or, the Ballance of our Forraign Trade is the Rule of our Treasure Written by Thomas Mun; and Now Published for the Common Good by His Son John Mun.* London, 1664. Early English Books Online.

Mun, Thomas. *A Discourse of Trade, from England Vnto the East-Indies Answering to Diuerse Obiections which are Vsually made Against the Same. By T. M.* London, 1621. Early English Books Online.

Nichols, Josias, 1555. *An Order of Houshold Instruction by which Euery Master of a Familie, may Easily and in Short Space, make His Whole Houshold to Vnderstand the Principall and Chiefe Points of Christian Religion, without the Knowledge Whereof, no Man can be Saued.* London, 1595. Early English Books Online.

Nowell, Alexander. *A catechism written in Latin by Alexander Nowell, Dean of St. Paul's: Together with the same catechism translated into English by Thomas Norton. Appended is a sermon preached by Dean Nowell before Queen Elizabeth at the opening of the Parliament which met January 11, 1563.* Edited for The Parker Society by G. E. Corrie, D. D., master of Jesus College, Cambridge. Cambridge, 1853 [1570].

Peacham, Henry. *The Garden of Eloquence Conteining the most Excellent Ornaments, Exornations, Lightes, Flowers, and Formes of Speech, Commonly Called the Figures of Rhetorike. By which the Singular Partes of Mans Mind, are most Aptly Expressed, and the Sundrie Affections of His Heart most Effectuallie Vttered. Manifested, and Furnished Vvith Varietie of Fit Examples, Gathered out of the most Eloquent Orators, and Best Approued Authors, and Chieflie Out of the Holie Scriptures. Profitable and Necessarie, as Wel for Priuate Speech, as for Publicke Orations. Corrected and Augmented by the First Author. H. P.* London, 1593 [1577]. Early English Books Online.

Perkins, William. *Christian Oeconomie: Or, A Short Survey of the Right Manner of Erecting and Ordering a Familie According to the Scriptures. First Written in Latine by the Author M. W. Perkins, and Now Set Forth in the Vulgar Tongue, for More Common Vse and Benefit, by Tho. Pickering Bachelar of Diuinitie.* London, 1609. Early English Books Online.

Perkins, William. *The Whole Treatise of the Cases of Conscience Distinguished into Three Bookes: The First Whereof is Revised and Corrected in Sundrie Places, and the Other Two Annexed. Taught and Deliuered by M. W. Perkins in his Holy-Day Lectures, Carefully Examined by His Owne Briefes, and Now Published Together for the Common Good, by T. Pickering Bachelour of Diuinitie.* Cambridge, 1606. Early English Books Online.

Perkins, William. *A Treatise of the Vocations, Or, Callings of Men, with the Sorts and Kinds of them, and the Right Vse Thereof. Written by Mr. W. Perkins.* London, 1603. Early English Books Online.

Scott, William. *An Essay of Drapery: Or, The Compleate Citizen Trading Iustly. Pleasingly. Profitably. By William Scott.* London, 1635. Early English Books Online.

Seneca. *Moral Essays, Volume III:* De Beneficiis, translated by John W. Basore. Loeb Classical Library 310. Harvard University Press, 1935.

Seneca. *The Vvoorke of the Excellent Philosopher Lucius Annaeus Seneca Concerning Benefyting that is Too Say the Dooing, Receyuing, and Requyting of Good Turnes. Translated Out of Latin by Arthur Golding.* London, 1578. Early English Books Online.

Sidney, Sir Philip. *An Apology for Poetry or The Defence of Poesy,* edited by Geoffrey Shepherd. Manchester University Press, 1973.

Smith, Adam. *An Inquiry into the Nature and Causes of the Wealth of Nations. Vol. 1–2. The Glasgow Edition of the Works and Correspondence of Adam Smith.* William B. Todd, textual editor. R. H. Campbell and Andrew S. Skinner, general editors. Oxford University Press, 1976 [reprinted 2004].

Smith, Henry. *A Preparatiue to Mariage the Summe Whereof was Spoken at a Contract, and Inlarged After. Whereunto is Annexed a Treatise of the Lords Supper, and another of Vsurie. By Henrie Smith.* London, 1591. Early English Books Online.

Smith, Thomas Sir. *A Discourse of the Commonweal of This Realm of England,* edited by Mary Dewar. University Press of Virginia, 1969.

Stow, John. *The Annales, Or a Generall Chronicle of England, Begun First by Maister Iohn Stow, and After Him Continued and Augmented with Matters Forreyne, and Domestique, Auncient and Moderne, Vnto the Ende of This Present Yeere 1614. By Edmond Howes, Gentleman.* London, 1615. Early English Books Online.

Tasso, Torquato. *The Housholders Philosophie VVherein is Perfectly and Profitably Described, the True Oeconomia and Forme of Housekeeping, with a Table Added Thereunto of all the Notable Thinges Therein Contained. First Written in Italian by that Excellent Orator and Poet Signior Torquato Tasso, and Now Translated by T.K. Whereunto is Anexed a Dairie Booke for all Good Huswiues.* London, 1588. Early English Books Online.

Tilney, Edmund. *A Briefe and Pleasant Discourse of Duties in Mariage, Called the Flower of Friendship.* London, 1568. Early English Books Online.

Topsell, Edward. *The House-Holder: Or, Perfect Man in the Commendation of Wisedome. Diligence. Knowledge. Frugality, and Liberall House-Keeping. And the Discomme[n]dation of Folly, Naturall & Spirituall. Negligence. Ignorance. Unthriftinesse, and Illiberal House-Keeping. Preached in Three Sermons Lately at Hartfield in Sussex, by Ed: Topsell.* London, 1609. Early English Books Online.

Treswell, Ralph. *A Publication of Surueying and Measuring of Mannors, Lands, and Lordships: And Arts Mathematicall, Geometrie, Astrologie, Geomancie, and the Art of Dialling.* London, 1616. Early English Books Online.

Tusser, Thomas. *Fiue Hundreth Pointes of Good Husbandrie, as Well for the Champion or Open Countrie, as also for the Woodland Or Seuerall, Mixed in Euerie Month with Huswiferie, Ouer and Besides the Booke of Huswiferie. ... Newlie Set Foorth by Thomas Tusser Gentleman.* London, 1590 [1573]. Early English Books Online.

Udall, Nicholas. *Respublica: An Interlude for Christmas 1553. Published for the Early English Text Society by Geoffrey Cumberledge.* Oxford University Press, 1952.

Webbe, George. *The Araignement of an Vnruly Tongue Wherein the Faults of an Euill Tongue are Opened, the Danger Discouered, the Remedies Prescribed, for the Taming of a Bad Tongue, the Right Ordering of the Tongue, and the Pacifying of a Troubled Minde Against the Wrongs of an Euill Tongue. by George Web, Preacher of Gods Word at Stepleashton in Wiltshire.* 1619. Early English Books Online.

Whately, William. 'A Bride-Bush (1623)'. *Two Early Modern Marriage Sermons: Henry Smith's A Preparative to Marriage (1591) and William Whately's A Bride Bush (1623),* edited by Robert Matz. Routledge, 2016. https://doi.org/10.4324/9781315235486.

Wheeler, John. *A Treatise of Commerce· VVherin are Shevved the Commodities Arising by a Wel Ordered, and Ruled Trade, such as that of the Societie of Merchantes Adventurers is Proved to Bee, Written Principallie for the Better Information of those Who Doubt of the Necessarienes of the Said Societie in the State of the Realme of England, by Iohn Wheeler, Secretarie to the Said Societie.* Middleburg, 1601. Early English Books Online.

Wilkinson, Robert. *The Merchant Royall A Sermon Preached at White-Hall before the Kings Maiestie, at the Nuptials of the Right Honourable the Lord Hay and His Lady, Vpon the Twelfe Day Last, being Ianuar. 6, 1607.* London, 1607. Early English Books Online.

Wilson, Thomas. *The Art of Rhetoric (1560).* Edited with Notes and Commentary by Peter E. Medine. Pennsylvania State University Press, 1994 [1553].

Xenophon. *Oeconomicus: A Social and Historical Commentary,* translated by Sarah B. Pomeroy. Clarendon Press, 1994.

Xenophon. *Xenophons Treatise of Housholde.* London, 1532. Early English Books Online.

Other Sources

Aaron, Melissa D. *Global Economics: A History of the Theater Business, the Chamberlain's/King's Men, and Their Plays, 1599–1642.* University of Delaware Press, 2005.

Adelman, Janet. 'Iago's Alter Ego: Race as Projection in Othello'. *Shakespeare Quarterly,* vol. 48, no. 2, 1997, pp. 125–144.

Agnew, Jean-Christophe. *Worlds Apart: The Market and the Theater in Anglo-American Thought, 1550–1750.* Cambridge University Press, 1988.

Akhimie, Patricia. *Shakespeare and the Cultivation of Difference: Race and Conduct in the Early Modern World.* New York, Routledge, 2018.

Altieri, Joanne. 'Against Moralizing Jacobean Comedy: Middleton's "Chaste Maid"'. *Criticism,* vol. 30, no. 2, 1988, pp. 171–187.

Alwes, Derek B. 'The Secular Morality of Middleton's City Comedies'. *Comparative Drama,* vol. 42, no. 2, 2008, pp. 101–119.

Amussen, S. D. 'Gender, Family and the Social Order, 1560–1725'. *Order and Disorder in Early Modern England,* edited by Anthony Fletcher, and John Stevenson. Cambridge University Press, 1985.

Anglin, Sallie. 'Subject Formation in *A Chaste Maid in Cheapside*'. *Rocky Mountain Review,* vol. 66, no. 1, 2012, pp. 11–31.

Appleby, Joyce Oldham. *Economic Thought and Ideology in Seventeenth-Century England.* Princeton University Press, 1978.

Archer, Ian. 'Material Londoners?'. *Material London, ca. 1600,* edited by Lena Cowen Orlin. University of Pennsylvania Press, 2000, pp. 174–193.

Armitage, David, Conal Condren, and Andrew Fitzmaurice, editors. *Shakespeare and Early Modern Political Thought.* Cambridge University Press, 2009.

Bailey, Amanda. *Of Bondage: Debt, Property, and Personhood in Early Modern England.* University of Pennsylvania Press, 2013.

Baker, David J. *On Demand: Writing for the Market in Early Modern England.* Stanford University Press, 2010.

Baker, J. H. 'Origins of the "Doctrine" of Consideration, 1535–1585'. *On the Laws and Customs of England: Essays in Honor of Samuel E. Thorne,* edited by Morris S. Arnold, et al. University of North Carolina Press, 1981, pp. 336–358.

Balizet, Ariane M. *Blood and Home in Early Modern Drama: Domestic Identity on the Renaissance Stage*. Routledge, 2014.
Barbour, Richmond. '"When I Acted Young Antinous": Boy Actors and the Erotics of Jonsonian Theater'. *PMLA*, vol. 110, no. 5, 1995, pp. 1006–1022.
Barish, Jonas A. *The Antitheatrical Prejudice*. University of California Press, 1981.
Barret, J. K. *Untold Futures: Time and Literary Culture in Renaissance England*. Cornell University Press, 2016.
Barry, Jonathan, and Christopher Brooks, editors. *The Middling Sort of People: Culture, Society, and Politics in England, 1550–1800*. Macmillan, 1994.
Barton, Anne. *Ben Jonson, Dramatist*. Cambridge University Press, 1984.
Beckerman, Bernard. *Shakespeare at the Globe, 1599–1609*. Macmillan, 1962.
Beever, Allan. *Forgotten Justice: Forms of Justice in the History of Legal and Political Theory*. Oxford University Press, 2013.
Beier, Benjamin V. 'The Art of Persuasion and Shakespeare's Two Iagos'. *Studies in Philology*, vol. 111, no. 1, Winter 2014, pp. 34–64. Project MUSE, 10.1353/sip.2014.0002.
Belsey, Catherine. 'Iago the Essayist'. *Shakespeare in Theory and Practice*. Edinburgh University Press, 2008, pp. 157–171.
Belsey, Catherine. *Shakespeare and the Loss of Eden: The Construction of Family Values in Early Modern Culture*. Macmillan, 1999.
Bentley, Eric. *The Life of the Drama*. Atheneum, 1965.
Berry, Christopher J. *The Idea of Luxury: A Conceptual and Historical Investigation*. Cambridge University Press, 1994.
Bevington, David. 'The Major Comedies'. *The Cambridge Companion to Ben Jonson*, edited by Richard Harp, and Stanley Stewart. Cambridge University Press, 2000, pp. 72–89.
Bevington, David, and David L. Smith. 'James I and *Timon of Athens*'. *Comparative Drama*, vol. 33, no. 1, 1999, pp. 56–87.
Bicks, Caroline. *Midwiving Subjects in Shakespeare's England*. Ashgate, 2003.
Bradley, Andrew Cecil. *Shakespearean Tragedy: Lectures on Hamlet, Othello, King Lear, Macbeth*. Macmillan, 1992.
Brennan, Anthony. *Shakespeare's Dramatic Structures*. Routledge, 2005.
Brennan, Anthony. *Onstage and Offstage Worlds in Shakespeare's Plays*. Routledge, 1989.
Brenner, Robert. *Merchants and Revolution: Commercial Change, Political Conflict, and London's Overseas Traders, 1550–1653*. Princeton University Press, 1993.
Bristol, Michael D. *Big-Time Shakespeare*. Routledge, 1996.
Brooks, Christopher. 'Apprenticeship, Social Mobility and the Middling Sort, 1500–1800'. *The Middling Sort of People: Culture, Society and Politics in England, 1550–1800*, edited by Jonathan Barry and Christopher Brooks. Macmillan, 1994, pp. 52–83.
Brooks, Peter. *Reading for the Plot: Design and Intention in Narrative*. Alfred A. Knopf, 1984.
Brückner, Martin, and Kristen Poole. 'The Plot Thickens: Surveying Manuals, Drama, and the Materiality of Narrative Form in Early Modern England'. *ELH*, vol. 69, no. 3, Autumn 2002, pp. 617–648. Project MUSE, 10.1353/elh.2002.0021.
Bruster, Douglas. *Drama and the Market in the Age of Shakespeare*. Cambridge University Press, 1992.
Bullough, Geoffrey, editor. *Narrative and Dramatic Sources of Shakespeare, vol. VII*. Columbia University Press, 1973.
Burke, Kenneth. 'Othello: An Essay to Illustrate a Method'. *The Hudson Review*, vol. 4, no. 2, Summer 1951, pp. 165–203. JSTOR, 10.2307/3856783.

Burnett, Mark Thornton. *Masters and Servants in English Renaissance Drama and Culture: Authority and Obedience*. St. Martin's Press, 1997.
Capp, Bernard. *When Gossips Meet: Women, Family, and Neighbourhood in Early Modern England*. Oxford University Press, 2003.
Carr, Carol A. 'Volpone and Mosca: Two Styles of Roguery'. *College Literature*, vol. 8, no. 2, 1981, pp. 144–157.
Carroll, William C. 'Spectacle, Representation and Lineage in Macbeth 4.1'. *Shakespeare Survey*, vol. 67, edited by Peter Holland. Cambridge Core, 2014, pp. 345–371.
Carruthers, Bruce G. *City of Capital: Politics and Markets in the English Financial Revolution*. Princeton University Press, 1996.
Cavaillé, Jean-Pierre. *Dis/Simulations: Jules-César Vanini, François La Mothe Le Vayer, Gabriel Naudé, Louis Machon et Torquato Accetto; Religion, Morale et Politique Au XVIIe Siècle*. Champion, 2002.
Chamberlain, Stephanie. 'Fantasizing Infanticide: Lady Macbeth and the Murdering Mother in Early Modern England'. *College Literature*, vol. 32, no. 3, Summer 2005, pp. 72–91. Project MUSE, 10.1353/lit.2005.0038.
Charney, Maurice. *Shakespeare's Villains*. Fairleigh Dickinson University Press, 2012.
Chatterji, Ruby. 'Theme, Imagery, and Unity in "A Chaste Maid in Cheapside"'. *Renaissance Drama*, vol. 8, 1965, pp. 105–126.
Chorost, Michael. 'Biological Finance in Shakespeare's *Timon of Athens*'. *English Literary Renaissance*, vol. 21, no. 3, 1991, pp. 349–370.
Christofides, R. M. 'Iago and Equivocation: The Seduction and Damnation of Othello'. *Early Modern Literary Studies*, vol. 15, no. 1, 2010.
Clay, C. G. A. *Economic Expansion and Social Change: England 1500–1700: Industry, Trade and Government*, vol. 2. Cambridge University Press, 1984.
Cohen, Derek. 'The Politics of Wealth: *Timon of Athens*'. *Neophilologus*, vol. 77, no. 1, 1993, pp. 149–160.
Cook, Elizabeth. 'Introduction'. *The Alchemist*, by Ben Jonson, Bloomsbury Publishing, 2016, pp. 1–22.
Cooper, John. *Reason and Emotion: Essays on Ancient Moral Psychology and Ethical Theory*. Princeton University Press, 1999.
Coral, Jordi. 'Anxious Householders: Theft and Anti-Usury Discourse in Shakespeare's Venetian Plays'. *The Seventeenth Century*, vol. 30, no. 3, 2015, pp. 285–300.
Cressy, David. *Literacy and the Social Order: Reading and Writing in Tudor and Stuart England*. Cambridge University Press, 1980.
Cummings, Brian. *The Literary Culture of the Reformation*. Oxford University Press, 2002.
Cummings, Brian, and Freya Sierhuis, editors. *Passions and Subjectivity in Early Modern Culture*. Ashgate, 2013.
Curtis, Mark Hubert. *Oxford and Cambridge in Transition, 1558–1642. An Essay on Changing Relations between the English Universities and English Society*. Clarendon Press, 1959.
Damlos-Kinzel, Christiane. *Von der Ökonomik zur politischen Ökonomie: Ökonomischer Diskurs und dramatische Praxis in England vom 16. bis zum 18. Jahrhundert*. Königshausen & Neumann, 2003.
Davetian, Benet. *Civility: A Cultural History*. University of Toronto Press, 2009.
Davidson, Clifford. '"Timon of Athens": The Iconography of False Friendship'. *Huntington Library Quarterly*, vol. 43, no. 3, 1980, pp. 181–200.

Davis, Dorothy. *Fairs, Shops, and Supermarkets. A History of English Shopping*. University of Toronto Press, 1966.
Deng, Stephen. *Coinage and State Formation in Early Modern English Literature*. Palgrave Macmillan, 2011.
Deng, Stephen. 'Healing Angels and 'Golden Blood': Money and Mystical Kingship in Macbeth'. *Macbeth: New Critical Essays*, edited by Nick Moschovakis. Routledge, 2008, pp. 163–181.
De Quincey, Thomas. 'On the Knocking at the Gate in Macbeth' [1823]. *The Collected Writings of Thomas De Quincey*, vol. 10, edited by David Masson. Adam and Charles Black, 1890.
Dessen, Alan C. *Recovering Shakespeare's Theatrical Vocabulary*. Cambridge University Press, 1995.
Dessen, Alan C. *Elizabethan Stage Conventions and Modern Interpreters*. Cambridge University Press, 1985.
Dionne, Craig, and Steve Mentz, editors. *Rogues and Early Modern English Culture*. University of Michigan Press, 2004.
Dolan, Frances E. 'Afterword'. *Staged Normality in Shakespeare's England*, edited by Rory Loughnane, and Edel Semple. Palgrave Shakespeare Studies. Palgrave Macmillan, 2019, pp. 277–286.
Dolan, Frances E. 'Household Chastisements: Gender, Authority, and "Domestic Violence"'. *Renaissance Culture and the Everyday*, edited by Patricia Fumerton and Simon Hunt. University of Pennsylvania Press, 2014, pp. 204–225.
Dolan, Frances E. 'Afterword'. *Dangerous Familiars: Representations of Domestic Crime in England, 1550–1700*. Cornell University Press, 1994.
Donaldson, Ian. *Ben Jonson: A Life*. Oxford University Press, 2011.
Donaldson, Ian. *Jonson's Magic Houses: Essays in Interpretation*. Oxford University Press, 1997.
Dowd, Michelle M. *Women's Work in Early Modern English Literature and Culture*. Palgrave Macmillan, 2009.
Drakakis, John. 'Introduction'. *Macbeth: A Critical Reader*, edited by John Drakakis and Dale Townshend. Bloomsbury Publishing, 2013, pp. 1–17.
Eagleton, Terry. *William Shakespeare*. Blackwell, 1986.
Earle, Peter. 'The Middling Sort in London'. *The Middling Sort of People: Culture, Society and Politics in England, 1550–1800*, edited by Jonathan Barry and C. W. Brooks. Macmillan, 1994, pp. 141–158.
Eklund, Hillary. *Literature and Moral Economy in the Early Modern Atlantic*. Ashgate, 2015.
Enderwitz, Anne. '"So good that he is good for nothing". Francis Bacon's Umwertung der Werte'. *Der Essay als 'neue' Form*, edited by Andreas Mahler, *Wolfenbütteler Abhandlungen zur Renaissanceforschung*, vol. 38. Harrassowitz-Verlag, 2020, pp. 157–170.
Enderwitz, Anne. 'Ökonomie und politisches Kalkül: Macbeth und die Reformation'. *Shakespeare und die Reformation*, vol. 154, edited by Sabine Schülting, *Shakespeare Jahrbuch*, Kamp, 2018, pp. 106–125.
Enderwitz, Anne. 'Eifersucht und Oeconomia im englischen Theater der Frühen Neuzeit'. *Das Haus schreiben: Bewegungen ökonomischen Wissens im Theater der Frühen Neuzeit*, edited by Christina Schaefer and Simon Zeisberg, Harrassowitz-Verlag, 2018, pp. 209–227.
Enderwitz, Anne. 'Humanistische Bildung und Ökonomisches Kalkül in Middletons *A Chaste Maid in Cheapside*'. *Zeitsprünge*, vol. 21, no. 3/4, edited by Judith Frömmer and André Otto. Klostermann, 2017, pp. 239–258.

Enderwitz, Anne. 'Gift, Credit and Obligation in *Timon of Athens*'. *Shakespeare Seminar Online*, vol. 11, 2013, edited by Felix Sprang and Christina Wald, http://shakespeare-gesellschaft.de/en/publications/seminar/ausgabe-11-2013.html.

Engle, Lars. '"Thrift Is Blessing": Exchange and Explanation in *The Merchant of Venice*'. *Shakespeare Quarterly*, vol. 37, no. 1, Spring 1986, pp. 20–37. JSTOR, 10.2307/2870189.

Evans, Jennifer. *Aphrodisiacs, Fertility and Medicine in Early Modern England*. Woodbridge Royal Historical Society, 2014.

Farber, Lianna. *An Anatomy of Trade in Medieval Writing: Value, Consent, and Community*. Cornell University Press, 2006.

Finkelstein, Andrea. *Harmony and the Balance: An Intellectual History of Seventeenth-Century English Economic Thought*. University of Michigan Press, 2000.

Finkelstein, Richard. '*Amicitia* and *Beneficia* in *Timon of Athens*'. *Studies in Philology*, vol. 117, no. 4, 2020, pp. 801–825.

Finlay, Roger. *Population and Metropolis: The Demography of London, 1580–1650*. Cambridge University Press, 1981.

Fischer-Lichte, Erika. *Semiotik des Theaters: Das System der theatralischen Zeichen*, vol. 1. Gunter Narr, 1983.

Fissell, Mary. 'Gender and Generation: Representing Reproduction in Early Modern England'. *Gender & History*, vol. 7, no. 3, 1995, pp. 433–456.

Fitzpatrick, Tim. *Playwright, Space, and Place in Early Modern Performance: Shakespeare and Company*. Ashgate, 2011.

Fletcher, Anthony. *Gender, Sex, and Subordination in England, 1500–1800*. Yale University Press, 1995.

Folbre, Nancy. *Greed, Lust & Gender: A History of Economic Ideas*. Oxford University Press, 2009.

Force, Pierre. *Self-Interest before Adam Smith: A Genealogy of Economic Science*. Cambridge University Press, 2003.

Forman, Valerie. *Tragicomic Redemptions Global Economics and the Early Modern English Stage*. University of Pennsylvania Press, 2008.

Fossheim, Hallvard. 'Justice in the Nicomachean Ethics Book V'. *Aristotle's Nicomachean Ethics: A Critical Guide*, edited by Jon Miller. Cambridge University Press, 2011, pp. 254–275.

Foucault, Michel. 'Governmentality'. *The Foucault Effect: Studies in Governmental Nationality: With Two Lectures by and an Interview with Michel Foucault*, edited by Graham Burchell, Colin Gordon, and Peter M. Miller. Harvester Wheatsheaf, 1991, pp. 87–104.

Foucault, Michel. *The History of Sexuality: The Use of Pleasure*, vol. 2, translated by Robert Hurley. Vintage Books, 1990.

Foucault, Michel, and Jay Miskowiec. 'Of Other Spaces'. *Diacritics*, vol. 16, no. 1, 1986, pp. 22–27.

Freud, Sigmund. *The Standard Edition of the Complete Psychological Works of Sigmund Freud. 1917–1919: An Infantile Neurosis and Other Works*, vol. 17, edited by James Strachey. Hogarth Press, 1973.

Fumerton, Patricia. *Cultural Aesthetics: Renaissance Literature and the Practice of Social Ornament*. University of Chicago Press, 1991.

Fumerton, Patricia, and Simon Hunt. *Renaissance Culture and the Everyday*. University of Pennsylvania Press, 2014.

Genster, Julia. 'Lieutenancy, Standing In, and *Othello*'. *ELH*, vol. 57, no. 4, 1990, pp. 785–809.

Gibbons, Brian. *Jacobean City Comedy: A Study of Satiric Plays by Jonson, Marston and Middleton*. Harvard University Press, 1968.

Gibson, Gail McMurray. 'Scene and Obscene: Seeing and Performing Late Medieval Childbirth'. *Journal of Medieval and Early Modern Studies*, vol. 29, no. 1, 1999, pp. 10–11.

Gillen, Katherine. *Chaste Value: Economic Crisis, Female Chastity and the Production of Social Difference on Shakespeare's Stage*. Edinburgh University Press, 2017.

Gillen, Katherine. '"That What He Speaks Is All in Debt": Credit, Representation and Theatrical Critique in "Timon of Athens"'. *Shakespeare Jahrbuch*, vol. 150. Kamp, 2014, pp. 94–109.

Goldberg, Jonathan. 'Speculations: Macbeth and Source'. *Shakespeare Reproduced: The Text in History and Ideology*, edited by Jean E. Howard. Methuen, 1987, pp. 242–264.

Grady, Hugh. 'Iago and the Dialectic of Enlightenment: Reason, Will, and Desire in "Othello"'. *Criticism*, vol. 37, no. 4, 1995, pp. 537–558.

Grav, Peter F. *Shakespeare and the Economic Imperative: 'what's Aught but as 'tis Valued?'*. Routledge, 2008.

Grazia, Margreta de. *Hamlet Without Hamlet*. Cambridge University Press, 2007.

Green, Ian. *Humanism and Protestantism in Early Modern English Education*. Ashgate, 2009.

Greenblatt, Stephen J. *Shakespearean Negotiations: The Circulation of Social Energy in Renaissance England*. Clarendon Press, 2001.

Greenblatt, Stephen J. 'The False Ending in "Volpone"'. *The Journal of English and Germanic Philology*, vol. 75, no. 1/2, 1976, pp. 90–104.

Greene, Jody. '"You Must Eat Men': The Sodomitic Economy of Renaissance Patronage'. *GLQ: A Journal of Lesbian and Gay Studies*, vol. 1, no. 2, 1994, pp. 163–197.

Gurr, Andrew. *The Shakespearean Stage 1574–1642*. Cambridge University Press, 2009.

Gurr, Andrew. *Playgoing in Shakespeare's London*. Cambridge University Press, 2000.

Habib, Imtiaz. 'The Black Alien in Othello: Beyond the European Immigrant'. *Shakespeare and Immigration*, edited by Ruben Espinosa and David Ruiter. Routledge, 2014, pp. 135–158.

Hackett, Helen. *Early Modern Exchanges: Dialogues between Nations and Cultures, 1550–1750*. Ashgate, 2015.

Hadfield, Andrew. 'Timon of Athens and Jacobean Politics'. *Shakespeare Survey*, vol. 56, 2003, pp. 215–226.

Hankins, James, editor. *The Cambridge Companion to Renaissance Philosophy*. Cambridge University Press, 2007, pp. 97–112.

Hanson, Elizabeth. 'Normal School: Merry Wives and the Future of a Feeling'. *Staged Normality in Shakespeare's England*, edited by Rory Loughnane and Edel Semple. Palgrave Macmillan, 2019, 69–87.

Hanson, Elizabeth. *Discovering the Subject in Renaissance England*. Cambridge University Press, 1998.

Harding, Vanessa. 'Cheapside: Commerce and Commemoration'. *The Huntington Library Quarterly*, vol. 71, no. 1, 2008, pp. 77–96.

Harding, Vanessa. 'London, Change and Exchange'. *The Culture of Capital: Property, Cities, and Knowledge in Early Modern England*, edited by Henry S. Turner. Routledge, 2002, pp. 129–138.

Harris, Jonathan Gil. *Sick Economies: Drama, Mercantilism, and Disease in Shakespeare's England*. University of Pennsylvania Press, 2004.

Hart, Jonathan. 'The Ends of Renaissance Comedy'. *Reading the Renaissance: Culture, Poetics, and Drama*, edited by Hart. Garland, 1996, pp. 91–127.

Hawkes, David. *The Culture of Usury in Renaissance England*. Palgrave Macmillan, 2010.
Haynes, Jonathan. 'Representing the Underworld: "The Alchemist"'. *Studies in Philology*, vol. 86, no. 1, 1989, pp. 18–41.
Heilman, Robert B. 'The Economics of Iago and Others'. *PMLA*, vol. 68, no. 3, 1953, pp. 555–571. JSTOR, 10.2307/459870.
Heinemann, Margot. 'Political Drama'. *The Cambridge Companion to English Renaissance Drama*, edited by A. R. Braunmuller, and Michael Hattaway. Cambridge University Press, 1990, pp. 161–205.
Henderson, Diana E. 'The Theater and Domestic Culture'. *A New History of Early English Drama*, edited by John D. Cox and David Scott Kastan. Columbia University Press, 1997, pp. 173–194.
Hennessey, Oliver. 'Jonson's Joyless Economy'. *English Literary Renaissance*, vol. 38, no. 1, 2008, pp. 83–105.
Herzog, Don. *Household Politics: Conflict in Early Modern England*. Yale University Press, 2013.
Hill, Christopher. 'Protestantism and the Rise of Capitalism'. *Essays in the Economic and Social History of Tudor and Stuart England in Honour of R. H. Tawney*, edited by Richard Henry and Frederick Jack. Cambridge University Press, 1961, pp. 15–39.
Hill, Janet. *Stages and Playgoers: From Guild Plays to Shakespeare*. McGill-Queen's University Press, 2002.
Hirschman, Albert O. *The Passions and the Interests: Political Arguments for Capitalism before its Triumph*. Princeton University Press, 2013.
Hirsh, James E. *New Perspectives on Ben Jonson*. Fairleigh Dickinson University Press and Associated University Press, 1997.
Hobbes, Thomas. *Leviathan: Authoritative Text: Backgrounds, Interpretations*. W. W. Norton & Company, 1997.
Hopkins, Lisa. 'Household Words: Macbeth and the Failure of Spectacle'. *Shakespeare and Language*, edited by Catherine Alexander. Cambridge University Press, 2004, pp. 251–265.
Howard, Jean E. 'Afterword: Accommodating Change'. *Global Traffic: Discourses and Practices of Trade in English Literature and Culture from 1550 to 1700*, edited by Barbara Sebek, and Stephen Deng. Palgrave Macmillan, 2008, pp. 265–271.
Howard, Jean E. *Theater of a City: The Places of London Comedy, 1598–1642*. University of Pennsylvania Press, 2007.
Howard, Jean E. 'Women, Foreigners, and the Regulation of Urban Space'. *Material London, ca. 1600*, edited by Lena Cowen Orlin. University of Pennsylvania Press, 2000, pp. 150–167.
Howard, Jean E. 'Cross-Dressing, the Theater, and Gender Struggle in Early Modern England'. *Crossing the Stage: Controversies on Cross-Dressing*, edited by Lesley Feris. Routledge, 1993, pp. 20–46.
Howard, Jean E. 'The New Historicism in Renaissance Studies'. *English Literary Renaissance*, vol. 16, no. 1, 1986, pp. 13–43. Wiley Online Library, 10.1111/j.1475-6757.1986.tb00896.x.
Howell, Wilbur Samuel. *Logic and Rhetoric in England, 1500–1700*. Princeton University Press, 1956.
Hunter, George K. 'Elizabethan Theatrical Genres and Literary Theory'. *The Cambridge History of Literary Criticism*, vol. 3, edited by Glyn P. Norton. Cambridge University Press, 2006, pp. 248–258.

Hunter, George K. 'Flatcaps and Bluecoats: Visual Signals on the Elizabethan Stage'. *Essays and Studies* 33, 1980, pp. 16–47.

Hurka, Thomas. 'Aristotle on Virtue: Wrong, Wrong, and Wrong'. *Aristotelian Ethics in Contemporary Perspective*, edited by Julia Peters. Routledge, 2013, pp. 9–26.

Hutson, Lorna. *The Usurer's Daughter: Male Friendship and Fictions of Women in Sixteenth-Century England*. Routledge, 1994.

Inbody, Megan Marie. *Town/Gown Relations: The Forms and Functions of Female Gossip Communities and Networks in Early Modern Comedy*. Michigan State University, PhD Dissertation, 2012. *MSU Libraries Digital Repository* https://d.lib.msu.edu/etd/2015/datastream/OBJ/View/.

Ingram, Jill Phillips. *Idioms of Self-Interest: Credit, Identity, and Property in English Renaissance Literature*. Routledge, 2006.

Jackson, Ken. '"One Wish" or the Possibility of the Impossible: Derrida, the Gift, and God in *Timon of Athens*'. *Shakespeare Quarterly*, vol. 52, no. 1, 2001, pp. 34–66.

Jackson, MacDonald P. *Determining the Shakespeare Canon: Arden of Faversham and A Lover's Complaint*. Oxford University Press, 2014.

Jacobsen, Ken. 'Iago's Art of War: The "Machiavellian Moment" in *Othello*'. *Modern Philology*, vol. 106, no. 3, 2009, pp. 497–529.

Jenstad, Janelle Day. 'Lying-in Like a Countess: The Lisle Letters, the Cecil Family, and *A Chaste Maid in Cheapside*'. *Journal of Medieval and Early Modern Studies*, vol. 34, no. 2, Spring 2004, pp. 373–403.

Jewell, Helen M. *Education in Early Modern England*. Macmillan, 1998.

Jordan, Constance. 'The Household and the State: Transformations in the Representation of an Analogy from Aristotle to James I'. *Modern Language Quarterly*, vol. 54, no. 3, 1993, pp. 307–326. https://doi.org/10.1215/00267929-54-3-307.

Jowett, John, editor. 'Introduction'. *The Life of Timon of Athens*. Oxford University Press, 2004, pp. 1–153.

Jowett, John. 'Middleton and Debt in Timon of Athens'. *Money and the Age of Shakespeare: Essays in New Economic Criticism*, edited by Linda Woodbridge. Palgrave Macmillan, 2003, pp. 219–235.

Kahn, Coppélia. '"Magic of Bounty": "Timon of Athens," Jacobean Patronage, and Maternal Power'. *Shakespeare Quarterly*, vol. 38, no. 1, 1987, pp. 34–57.

Kahn, Victoria. *Machiavellian Rhetoric: from the Counter-Reformation to Milton*. Princeton University Press, 1994.

Kahn, Victoria, and Lorna Hutson, editors. *Rhetoric and Law in Early Modern Europe*. Yale University Press, 2001.

Kearney, Hugh F. *Scholars and Gentlemen: Universities and Society in Pre-industrial Britain, 1500–1700*. Faber, 1970.

Keene, Derek. 'Material London in Time and Space'. *Material London, ca. 1600*, edited by Lena Cowen Orlin. University of Pennsylvania Press, 2000, pp. 55–74.

Keene, Derek. 'Shops and Shopping in Medieval London'. *Medieval Art, Architecture and Archaeology in London, The British Archaeological Association*, 1990, pp. 29–46.

Keller, Eve. *Generating Bodies and Gendered Selves: The Rhetoric of Reproduction in Early Modern England*. University of Washington Press, 2007.

Keller, J. Gregory. 'The Moral Thinking of Macbeth'. *Philosophy and Literature*, vol. 29, no. 1, 2005, pp. 41–56.

Kernan, Alvin B. *Shakespeare, the King's Playwright: Theater in the Stuart Court, 1603–1613*. Yale University Press, 1995.

Kernan, Alvin B. 'Base Metal into Gold (1959)'. *Jonson 'Every Man in His Humour' and 'The Alchemist': A Casebook*, edited by R. V. Holdsworth. Palgrave Macmillan, 1978, pp. 164–177.
Kerridge, Eric. *Usury, Interest and the Reformation*. Ashgate, 2002.
Kerridge, Eric. *Trade and Banking in Early Modern England*. Manchester University Press, 1988.
Kerrigan, John. *Shakespeare's Binding Language*. Oxford University Press, 2016.
Kiernan, Michael, editor. *The Oxford Francis Bacon*, vol. 4: *The Advancement of Learning*. Oxford University Press, 2000.
Kinney, Arthur F. *Lies like Truth: Shakespeare, Macbeth, and the Cultural Moment*. Wayne State University Press, 2001.
Kitch, Aaron. *Political Economy and the States of Literature in Early Modern England*. Routledge, 2016.
Klibansky, Raymond, Erwin Panofsky, and Fritz Saxl. *Saturn and Melancholy*. Kraus Reprint, 1979.
Kliman, Bernice W. *Macbeth*. Manchester University Press, 2004.
Knapp, Peggy. 'The Work of Alchemy'. *Journal of Medieval and Early Modern Studies*, vol. 30, no. 3, 2000, pp. 575–599.
Knapp, Peggy. 'Ben Jonson and the Publicke Riot: Ben Jonson's Comedies'. *Staging the Renaissance*, edited by David Kastan and Peter Stallybrass. Routledge, 1991, pp. 164–180.
Kohn, Meir G. 'Bills of Exchange and the Money Market to 1600'. *Dartmouth College Department of Economics Working Paper* no. 99-04, 1999. SSRN, http://dx.doi.org/10.2139/ssrn.151849.
Kolb, Laura. *Fictions of Credit in the Age of Shakespeare*. Oxford University Press, 2021.
Korda, Natasha. *Shakespeare's Domestic Economies: Gender and Property in Early Modern England*. University of Pennsylvania Press, 2002.
Kraye, Jill. 'The Revival of Hellenistic Philosophies'. *The Cambridge Companion to Renaissance Philosophy*, edited by James Henkins. Cambridge University Press, 2007, pp. 97–112.
Kraye, Jill. 'The Tripartite Division of Moral Philosophy'. *The Cambridge History of Renaissance Philosophy*, edited by C. B. Schmitt and Quentin Skinner. Cambridge University Press, 1996, pp. 303–386.
Ladegaard, Jakob. 'Luxurious Laughter. Wasteful Economy in Ben Jonson's Comedy *Volpone, or the Fox* (1606)'. *European Review*, vol. 24, no. 1, 2016, pp. 63–71.
Lammers, Lukas. *Shakespearean Temporalities: History on the Early Modern Stage*. Routledge, 2018.
Landreth, David. *The Face of Mammon: The Matter of Money in English Renaissance Literature*. Oxford University Press, 2012.
Laslett, Peter. *The World We Have Lost*. Routledge, 2000.
Latour, Bruno. *Pandora's Hope: Essays on the Reality of Science Studies*. Harvard University Press, 1999.
Lefebvre, Henri. *The Production of Space*, translated by Donald Nicholson-Smith. Blackwell, 1991.
Leggatt, Alexander. *Introduction to English Renaissance Comedy*. Manchester University Press, 1999.
Leinwand, Theodore B. *Theatre, Finance and Society in Early Modern England*. Cambridge University Press, 1999.
Leinwand, Theodore B. 'Shakespeare and the Middling Sort'. *Shakespeare Quarterly*, vol. 44, no. 3, Autumn 1993, pp. 284–303. JSTOR, 10.2307/2871420.

Leinwand, Theodore B. *The City Staged: Jacobean Comedy, 1603–1613*. University of Wisconsin Press, 1986.

Lemon, Rebecca. 'Sovereignty and Treason in Macbeth'. *Macbeth: New Critical Essays*, edited by Nick Moschovakis. Routledge, 2008, pp. 73–87.

Levenson, Jill. 'Comedy'. *The Cambridge Companion to English Renaissance Drama*, edited by A. R. Braunmuller and Michael Hattaway. Cambridge University Press, 1990, pp. 263–300.

Levin, Harry. 'Two Scenes from Macbeth'. *Shakespeare's Craft: Eight Lectures*, edited by Philip H. Highfill, Jr. Southern Illinois University Press, 1982.

Levin, Richard. 'The Four Plots of a Chaste Maid in Cheapside'. *Review of English Studies*, vol. 16, no. 61, 1965, pp. 14–24.

Levitsky, Ruth. '*Timon*: Shakespeare's Magnyfycence and an Embryonic Lear'. *Shakespeare Studies*, vol. 11, 1978, pp. 107–121.

Liebler, Naomi Conn. *Shakespeare's Festive Tragedy: The Ritual Foundations of Genre*. Routledge, 1995.

Lines, David A. 'Humanistic and Scholastic Ethics'. *The Cambridge Companion to Renaissance Philosophy*, edited by James Hankins. Cambridge University Press, 2007, pp. 304–318.

Lobsien, Verena. *Shakespeares Exzess: Sympathie und Ökonomie*. Berlin University Press, 2015.

Lobsien, Verena. *Transparency and Dissimulation Configurations of Neoplatonism in Early Modern English Literature*. De Gruyter, 2010.

Logan, Sandra. 'Domestic Disturbance and the Disordered State in Shakespeare's Othello'. *Textual Practice*, vol. 18, no. 3, 2004, pp. 351–375.

Lupton, Julia Reinhard. 'Macbeth's Martlets: Shakespearean Phenomenologies of Hospitality'. *Criticism*, vol. 54, no. 3, Summer 2012, pp. 365–376. Project MUSE, 10.1353/crt.2012.0020.

Magnus, Laury. 'Performance History'. *Macbeth: A Critical Reader*, edited by John Drakakis and Dale Townshend. Bloomsbury Publishing, 2013, pp. 55–94.

Magnusson, Lars. *Mercantilism: The Shaping of an Economic Language*. Routledge, 1994.

Mahler, Andreas. 'Topologie'. *Handbuch Literatur & Raum*, edited by Andreas Mahler and Jörg Dünne. De Gruyter, 2015, pp. 27–29.

Mahler, Andreas. 'Welt Modell Theater—Sujetbildung und Sujetwandel im englischen Drama der frühen Neuzeit'. *Poetica*, vol. 30, no. 1–2, 1998, pp. 1–45.

Marchitello, Howard. 'Speed and the Problem of Real Time in Macbeth'. *Shakespeare Quarterly*, vol. 64, no. 4, Winter 2013, pp. 425–448.

Marotti, Arthur F. 'Fertility and Comic Form in "A Chaste Maid in Cheapside"'. *Comparative Drama*, vol. 3, no. 1, 1969, pp. 65–74.

Marx, Karl. *Ökonomisch-philosophische Manuskripte*. Felix Meiner Verlag, 2005.

Marx, Karl. *Capital*, translated by Ben Fowkes. Penguin Books, 1990.

Maus, Katharine Eisaman. 'Idol and Gift in Volpone'. *English Literary Renaissance*, vol. 35, no. 3, 2005, pp. 429–453.

Maus, Katharine Eisaman. Introduction to *The Alchemist*. *English Renaissance Drama: A Norton Anthology*, edited by David Bevington, Lars Engle, Katharine Eisaman Maus, and Eric Rasmussen. W. W. Norton & Company, 2002, pp. 861–867.

Maus, Katharine Eisaman. *Ben Jonson and the Roman Frame of Mind*. Princeton University Press, 1984.

Mauss, Marcel. *The Gift: The Form and Reason for Exchange in Archaic Societies*, edited by Mauss with a foreword by Mary Douglas. Routledge Classics, 2002.

Mckee, Laurie. 'Giving and Serving in *Timon of Athens*'. *Early Modern Literary Studies*, vol. 16, no. 3, 2013, pp. 1–22.
McRae, Andrew. *God Speed the Plough*. Cambridge University Press, 1996.
McRae, Andrew. 'Husbandry Manuals and the Language of Agrarian Improvement'. *Culture and Cultivation in Early Modern England: Writing and the Land*, edited by Michael Leslie and Timothy Raylor. Leicester University Press, 1992, pp. 35–62.
Meikle, Scott. 'Aristotle and Exchange Value'. *A Companion to Aristotle's 'Politics'*, edited by David Keyt. Blackwell, 1991, pp. 156–181.
Mendelson, Sara Heller, and Patricia Crawford. *Women in Early Modern England: 1550–1720*. Clarendon Press, 1998.
Mentz, Stephen R. 'The Fiend Gives Friendly Counsel: Launcelot Gobbo and Polyglot Economics in *The Merchant of Venice*'. *Money and the Age of Shakespeare: Essays in New Economic Criticism*, edited by Linda Woodbridge. Palgrave Macmillan, 2003, pp. 177–187.
Meskill, Lynn S. *Ben Jonson and Envy*. Cambridge University Press, 2009.
Miller, Shannon. 'Consuming Mothers/Consuming Merchants: The Carnavalesque Economy of Jacobean City Comedy'. *Modern Language Studies*, vol. 26, no. 2/3, Spring–Summer 1996, pp. 73–97.
Morrison, Kathryn A. *English Shops and Shopping: An Architectural History*. Yale University Press, 2003.
Moschovakis, Nick, editor. *Macbeth: New Critical Essays*. Routledge, 2008.
Mowat, Barbara A. 'The Theatre and Literary Culture'. *A New History of Early English Drama*, edited by John D. Cox and David Scott Kastan. Columbia University Press, 1997, pp. 213–230.
Muir, Kenneth. 'Introduction'. *Macbeth*, by William Shakespeare. Bloomsbury Publishing, 1984, pp. xiii–lxv.
Muldrew, Craig. '"Hard Food for Midas": Cash and its Social Value in Early Modern England'. *Past & Present*, vol. 170, no. 1, 2001, pp. 78–120.
Muldrew, Craig. *The Economy of Obligation: The Culture of Credit and Social Relations in Early Modern England*. St. Martin's Press, 1998.
Muldrew, Craig. 'Interpreting the Market: The Ethics of Credit and Community Relations in Early Modern England'. *Social History*, vol. 18, no. 2, 1993, pp. 163–183.
Mullaney, Steven. *The Place of the Stage: License, Play, and Power in Renaissance England*. University of Michigan Press, 1997.
Mullaney, Steven. 'Lying like Truth: Riddle, Representation and Treason in Renaissance England'. *ELH*, vol. 47, no. 1, Spring 1980, pp. 32–47.
Munro, Lucy. 'Tragic Forms'. *The Cambridge Companion to English Renaissance Tragedy*, edited by Emma Smith and Garrett A. Sullivan. Cambridge University Press, 2010, pp. 86–101.
Neill, Michael, editor. *The Oxford Shakespeare: Othello: The Moor of Venice*. Oxford University Press, 2006.
Neill, Michael. *Putting History to the Question*. Columbia University Press, 2000.
Neill, Michael. 'Servant Obedience and Master Sins: Shakespeare and the Bond of Service'. *Proceedings of the British Academy*, 101, 1999, pp. 131–171.
Netzloff, Mark. 'The Lead Casket: Capital, Mercantilism and *The Merchant of Venice*'. *Money and the Age of Shakespeare: Essays in New Economic Criticism*, edited by Linda Woodbridge. Palgrave Macmillan, 2003, pp. 159–176.

Newbold, W. Webster. 'Traditional, Practical, Entertaining: Two Early English Letter Writing Manuals'. *Rhetorica*, vol. 26, no. 3, Summer 2008, pp. 267–300. JSTOR, 10.1525/rh.2008.26.3.267.

Newman, Karen. *Essaying Shakespeare*. University of Minnesota Press, 2009.

Newman, Karen. '"Goldsmith's ware": Equivalence in *A Chaste Maid in Cheapside*'. *Huntington Library Quarterly*, vol. 71, no. 1, University of Pennsylvania Press, March 2008, pp. 97–113. JSTOR, 10.1525/hlq.2008.71.1.97.

Newman, Karen. *Fashioning Femininity and English Renaissance Drama*. University of Chicago Press, 1991.

Newman, Karen. 'City Talk: Women and Commodification in Jonson's Epicoene'. *ELH*, vol. 56, no. 3, Autumn 1989, pp. 503–518. JSTOR, 10.2307/2873195.

Newman, Karen. 'Portia's Ring: Unruly Women and Structures of Exchange in *The Merchant of Venice*'. *Shakespeare Quarterly*, vol. 38, no. 1, Spring 1987, pp. 19–33. JSTOR, 10.2307/2870399.

Nicholson, Catherine. '*Othello* and the Geography of Persuasion'. *English Literary Renaissance*, vol. 40, no. 1, Winter 2010, pp. 56–87. Wiley Online Library, 10.1111/j.1475-6757.2009.01061.x.

Nielsen, Donald A. '*The Protestant Ethic and the "Spirit" of Capitalism* as Grand Narrative: Max Weber's Philosophy of History'. *The Protestant Ethic Turns 100: Essays on the Centenary of the Weber Thesis*, edited by William H. Swatos and Lutz Kaelber. Paradigm Publishers, 2005, pp. 53–75.

Nietzsche, Friedrich. *On the Genealogy of Morals: A Polemic. By Way of Clarification and Supplement to My Last Book Beyond Good and Evil*, translated by Douglas Smith. Oxford University Press, 1996.

Norbrook, David. 'Macbeth and the Politics of Historiography'. *Politics of Discourse: The Literature and History of Seventeenth-Century England*, edited by Kevin Sharpe and Steven N. Zwicker. University of California Press, 1987, pp. 78–116.

Nuttall, Anthony D. *Timon of Athens*. Harvester Wheatsheaf, 1989.

Oresme, Nicholas. *The De Moneta of Nicholas Oresme and English Mint Documents*, translated and with an introduction and notes by Charles Johnson. Nelson, 1956.

Orlin, Lena Cowen. 'Introduction'. *Othello: The State of Play*, edited by Lena Cowen Orlin. Bloomsbury Arden Shakespeare, 2014, pp. 1–16.

Orlin, Lena Cowen. *Locating Privacy in Tudor London*. Oxford University Press, 2007.

Orlin, Lena Cowen, editor. *Material London, ca. 1600*. University of Pennsylvania Press, 2000.

Orlin, Lena Cowen. 'Desdemona's Disposition'. *Shakespearean Tragedy and Gender*, edited by Shirley Nelson Garner and Madelon Gohlke Sprengnether. University of Indiana Press, 1996, pp. 171–192.

Orlin, Lena Cowen. *Elizabethan Households: An Anthology*. Folger Shakespeare Library, 1995.

Orlin, Lena Cowen. *Private Matters and Public Culture in Post-Reformation England*. Cornell University Press, 1994.

Orrell, John. *The Quest for Shakespeare's Globe*. Cambridge University Press, 1983.

Ouellette, Anthony. '"The Alchemist" and the Emerging Adult Playhouse'. *Studies in English Literature, 1500–1900*, vol. 45, no. 2, 2005, pp. 375–399.

Oxford English Dictionary: OED Online. Oxford University Press, 2022.

Parker, Patricia. 'Cassio, Cash, and the "Infidel 0": Arithmetic, Double-entry Bookkeeping, and *Othello*'s Unfaithful Accounts'. *A Companion to the Global Renaissance: English Literature and Culture in the Era of Expansion*, edited by Jyotsna G. Singh. John Wiley & Sons, 2009, pp. 223-241.

Parker, Patricia. *Literary Fat Ladies: Rhetoric, Gender, Property*. Methuen, 1987.

Parker, Patricia. 'Shakespeare and Rhetoric: "Dilation" and "Delation" in Othello'. *Shakespeare and the Question of Theory*, edited by Patricia Parker and Geoffrey H. Hartman. Methuen, 1985, pp. 54-74.

Parker, Patricia. 'Dilation and Delay: Renaissance Matrices'. *Poetics Today*, vol. 5, no. 3, 1984, pp. 519-535.

Partridge, Edward B. 'The Imagery of *The Alchemist* (1958)'. *Jonson 'Every Man in His Humour' and 'The Alchemist': A Casebook*, edited by R. V. Holdsworth. Macmillan, 1978, pp. 156-164.

Paster, Gail Kern. *The Body Embarrassed: Drama and the Disciplines of Shame in Early Modern England*. Cornell University Press, 1993.

Paster, Gail Kern. *The Idea of the City in the Age of Shakespeare*. University of Georgia Press, 1985.

Patterson, William Brown. *William Perkins and the Making of a Protestant England*. Oxford University Press, 2014.

Paul, Henry N. *The Royal Play of Macbeth: When, Why, and How It Was Written by Shakespeare*. Macmillan, 1950.

Pepys, Samuel. *The Diary of Samuel Pepys: A New and Complete Transcription*, vol. 7. Bell, 1972.

Pfister, Manfred. *The Theory and Analysis of Drama*. Cambridge University Press, 2000.

Pierce, Robert B. 'Tragedy and "Timon of Athens"'. *Comparative Drama*, vol. 36, no. 1/2, 2002, pp. 75-90.

Pocock, J. G. A. *The Machiavellian Moment: Florentine Political Thought and the Atlantic Republican Tradition*, edited and with a new afterword by the author. Princeton University Press, 2003.

Polansky, Ronald. 'Giving Justice Its Due'. *The Cambridge Companion to Aristotle's Nicomachean Ethics*, edited by Ronald Polansky. Cambridge University Press, 2014, pp. 151-179.

Pollock, Linda. 'Childbearing and Female Bonding in Early Modern England'. *Social History*, vol. 22, no. 3, 1997, pp. 286-306.

Poovey, Mary. *A History of the Modern Fact: Problems of Knowledge in the Sciences of Wealth and Society*. University of Chicago Press, 1998.

Pye, Christopher. *The Storm at Sea: Political Aesthetics in the Time of Shakespeare*. Fordham University Press, 2015.

Pye, Christopher. *The Vanishing: Shakespeare, the Subject, and Early Modern Culture*. Duke University Press, 2000.

Pye, Christopher. 'The Theater, the Market, and the Subject of History'. *ELH*, vol. 61, no. 3, 1994, pp. 501-522.

Rappaport, Steve. *Worlds within Worlds: Structures of Life in Sixteenth-Century London*. Cambridge University Press, 1989.

Ratcliffe, Susan. *Oxford Treasury of Sayings and Quotations*. Oxford University Press, 2011.

Reddaway, T. F. 'Elizabethan London—Goldsmith's Row in Cheapside, 1558-1645'. *The Guildhall Miscellany*, vol. 2, 1963, pp. 181-206.

Redwine, James D. 'Volpone's "Sport" and the Structure of Jonson's *Volpone*'. *Studies in English Literature, 1500-1900*, vol. 34, no. 2, 1994, pp. 301-321.

Reiss, Timothy J. 'Tragedy'. *The New Princeton Encyclopedia of Poetry and Poetics*, vol. 3, edited by Alex Preminger. Princeton University Press, 1993, pp. 1296–1302.

Reynolds, Paige Martin. 'Sin, Sacredness, and Childbirth in Early Modern Drama'. *Medieval and Renaissance Drama in England*, vol. 28, 2015, pp. 30–48.

Richards, Jennifer. *Rhetoric and Courtliness in Early Modern Literature*. Cambridge University Press, 2003.

Richardson, Catherine. *Domestic Life and Domestic Tragedy in Early Modern England: The Material Life of the Household*. Manchester University Press, 2013.

Richardson, Catherine. 'Domestic Life in Jacobean London'. *Thomas Middleton in Context*, edited by Suzanne Gossett. Cambridge University Press, 2011, pp. 52–60.

Richardson, Catherine. *Household Servants in Early Modern England*. Manchester University Press, 2010.

Richardson, Catherine. 'Tragedy, Family and Household'. *The Cambridge Companion to English Renaissance Tragedy*, edited by Emma Smith and Garrett A. Sullivan. Cambridge University Press, 2010, pp. 17–29.

Richardson, Catherine. 'Early Modern Plays and Domestic Spaces'. *Home Cultures*, vol. 2, no. 3, 2005, pp. 269–284.

Riggs, David. *Ben Jonson: A Life*. Harvard University Press, 1989.

Robinson, Benedict S. *Islam and Early Modern English Literature: The Politics of Romance from Spenser to Milton*. Palgrave Macmillan, 2007.

Ross, Cheryl Lynn. 'The Plague of *The Alchemist*'. *Renaissance Quarterly*, vol. 41, no. 3, 1988, pp. 439–458.

Rossini, Manuela. 'The Gendered Spatiology of Middleton's *A Chaste Maid in Cheapside*'. *SPELL: Swiss Papers in English Language and Literature*, vol. 17, 2005, pp. 85–97.

Rust, Jennifer R. 'Forms of Governmentality in *The Alchemist*'. *SEL Studies in English Literature 1500–1900*, vol. 58, no. 1, Winter 2018, pp. 95–121.

Ryan, Kiernan. *Shakespeare*. Palgrave Macmillan, 2002.

Ryner, Bradley David. *Performing Economic Thought: English Drama and Mercantile Writing, 1600–1642*. Edinburgh University Press, 2014.

Sacks, David Harris. 'The Promise and the Contract in Early Modern England: Slade's Case in Perspective'. *Rhetoric and Law in Early Modern Europe*, edited by Victoria Kahn and Lorna Hutson. Yale University Press, 2001, pp. 28–53.

Sacks, David Harris. 'London's Dominion'. *Material London, ca. 1600*, edited by Lena Cowen Orlin. University of Pennsylvania Press, 2000, pp. 20–54.

Sanders, Ed. *Envy and Jealousy in Classical Athens: A Socio-Psychological Approach*. Oxford University Press, 2014.

Sanders, Julie. *The Cambridge Introduction to Early Modern Drama, 1576–1642*. Cambridge University Press, 2014.

Saunders, Ann. *The Royal Exchange*. Guardian Royal Exchange, 1991.

Schmitt, Charles B. 'Aristotle's Ethics in the Sixteenth Century: Some Preliminary Considerations'. *The Aristotelian Tradition and Renaissance Universities*, edited by Charles B. Schmitt. Variorum Rpt., 1984, pp. 87–112.

Schmitt, Charles B. 'Philosophy and Science in Sixteenth-Century Universities: Some Preliminary Comments'. *Studies in Renaissance Philosophy and Science*, edited by Charles B. Schmitt, Variorum Rpt., 1981, pp. 485–530.

Schülting, Sabine. 'What Is't You Lack? Material Culture in Thomas Middleton's *A Chaste Maid in Cheapside*'. *Literaria Pragensia*, vol. 24, no. 47, 2014, pp. 97–111.

Scodel, Joshua. *Excess and the Mean in Early Modern English Literature*. Princeton University Press, 2002.

Scragg, Leah. 'Iago—Vice or Devil?'. *Aspects of Othello: Articles Reprinted from Shakespeare Survey*, edited by Kenneth Muir and Philip Edwards. Cambridge University Press, 1977, pp. 48–60.

Searle, John R. 'Austin on Locutionary and Illocutionary Acts'. *The Philosophical Review*, vol. 77, no. 4, 1968, pp. 405–424.

Sebek, Barbara, and Stephen Deng, editors. *Global Traffic: Discourses and Practices of Trade in English Literature and Culture from 1550 to 1700*. Palgrave Macmillan, 2008.

Shanahan, John. 'Ben Jonson's "Alchemist" and Early Modern Laboratory Space'. *Journal for Early Modern Cultural Studies*, vol. 8, no. 1, 2008, pp. 35–66.

Sharpe, Kevin. 'Virtues, Passions & Politics in Early Modern England'. *History of Political Thought*, vol. 32, no. 5, 2011, pp. 773–798.

Shell, Marc. *The Economy of Literature*. Johns Hopkins University Press, 1993.

Shepard, Alexandra. *Accounting for Oneself: Worth, Status, and the Social Order in Early Modern England*. Oxford University Press, 2015.

Sherman, Sandra. *Finance and Fictionality in the Early Eighteenth Century: Accounting for Defoe*. Cambridge University Press, 1996.

Siemon, James. 'Making Ambition Virtue? *Othello*, Small Wars, and Martial Profession'. *Othello: State of Play*, edited by Lena Cowen Orlin. Bloomsbury Arden Shakespeare, 2014, pp. 177–202. Bloomsbury Collections, 10.5040/9781472577955.ch-007.

Simpson, Alfred William Brian. *A History of the Common Law of Contract: The Rise of the Action of Assumpsit*. Clarendon, 1987.

Sinfield, Alan. 'Poetaster, the Author, and the Perils of Cultural Production'. *Material London, ca. 1600*, edited by Lena Cowen Orlin. University of Pennsylvania Press, 2000, pp. 75–89.

Slights, William. '*Genera Mixta* and *Timon of Athens*'. *Studies in Philology*, vol. 74, no. 1, 1977, pp. 39–62.

Smallwood, R.L. '"Here in the Firars:" Immediacy and Theatricality in The Alchemist'. *The Review of English Studies*, vol. 32, no. 126, 1981, pp. 142–160.

Smith, Adam. *An Inquiry into the Nature and Causes of the Wealth of Nations. The Glasgow Edition of the Works and Correspondence of Adam Smith*, vol. 1, edited by W. B. Todd. Clarendon Press, 2004.

Smith, Emma, and Garrett A. Sullivan, editors. *The Cambridge Companion to English Renaissance Tragedy*. Cambridge University Press, 2010.

Snyder, Jon R. *Dissimulation and the Culture of Secrecy in Early Modern Europe*. University of California Press, 2009.

Solomon, Julie. *Objectivity in the Making: Francis Bacon and the Politics of Inquiry*. Johns Hopkins University Press, 1998.

Sorensen, Gert. 'The Reception of the Political Aristotle'. *Renaissance Readings of the Corpus Aristotelicum: Proceedings of the Conference Held in Copenhagen 23–25 April 1998*, edited by Marianne Pade. Museum Tusculanum Press, University of Copenhagen, 2001, pp. 9–25.

Spencer, Eric. 'Taking Excess, Exceeding Account: Aristotle Meets *The Merchant of Venice*'. *Money and the Age of Shakespeare: Essays in New Economic Criticism*, edited by Linda Woodbridge. Palgrave Macmillan, 2003, pp. 143–158.

Spivack, Bernard. *Shakespeare and the Allegory of Evil: The History of a Metaphor in Relation to His Major Villains*. Columbia University Press, 1958.

Stallybrass, Peter. 'Patriarchal Territories: The Body Enclosed'. *Rewriting the Renaissance*, edited by Margaret Ferguson, Maureen Quilligan, and Nancy Vickers. University of Chicago Press, 1986, pp. 123–142.

Stanivukovic, Goran V., editor. *Remapping the Mediterranean World in Early Modern English Writings*. Palgrave Macmillan, 2007.

Stern, Tiffany. *Documents of Performance in Early Modern England*. Cambridge University Press, 2009.

Stern, Tom. *Philosophy and Theatre: An Introduction*. Routledge, 2013.

Stevenson, Laura Caroline. *Praise and Paradox: Merchants and Craftsmen in Elizabethan Popular Literature*. Cambridge University Press, 1984.

Stewart, Alan. '"Come from Turkie": Mediterranean Trade in Late Elizabethan London'. *Remapping the Mediterranean World in Early Modern English Writings*, edited by Goran V. Stanivukovic. Palgrave Macmillan, 2007, pp. 157–177.

Stone, Lawrence. *The Family, Sex and Marriage in England: 1500–1800*. Weidenfeld and Nicolson, 1977.

Sullivan, Garrett A. 'Tragic Subjectivities'. *The Cambridge Companion to English Renaissance Tragedy*, edited by Garrett A. Sullivan and Emma Smith. Cambridge University Press, 2010, pp. 73–85.

Sweeney, John. '*Volpone* and the Theater of Self-Interest'. *English Literary Renaissance*, vol. 12, no. 2, 1982, pp. 220–241.

Tawney, R. H. *Religion and the Rise of Capitalism: A Historical Study, with a Prefatory Note by Charles Gore*. Penguin, 1984.

Tawney, R. H. 'The Rise of the Gentry, 1558–1640'. *The Economic History Review*, vol. 11, no. 1, 1941, pp. 1–38.

Thirsk, Joan. 'Making a Fresh Start: Sixteenth-Century Agriculture and the Classical Inspiration'. *Culture and Cultivation in Early Modern England: Writing and the Land*, edited by Michael Leslie and Timothy Raylor. Leicester University Press, 1992, pp. 15–34.

Thirsk, Joan. *Economic Policy and Projects*. Clarendon Press, 1978.

Thirsk, Joan, editor. *The Agrarian History of England and Wales, Vol IV: 1500–1640*. Cambridge University Press, 1967.

Tilmouth, Christopher. *Passion's Triumph Over Reason: A History of the Moral Imagination from Spenser to Rochester*. Oxford University Press, 2010.

Tribble, Evelyn. 'Skill'. *Oxford Twenty-First Century Approaches to Literature: Early Modern Theatricality*, edited by Henry S. Turner. Oxford University Press, 2013, pp. 173–188.

Turner, Henry S. *The Corporate Commonwealth: Pluralism and Political Fictions in England, 1516–1651*. Chicago University Press, 2016.

Turner, Henry S. *The English Renaissance Stage: Geometry, Poetics and the Practical Spatial Arts*. Oxford University Press, 2006.

Twyning, John. *London Dispossessed: Literature and Social Space in the Early Modern City*. Macmillan, 1998.

University of Oxford. *Statutes of the University of Oxford Codified in the Year 1636 under the Authority of Archbishop Laud, Chancellor of the University*, edited by J. Griffiths, with an introduction on the history of the Laudian Code by C. L. Shadwell et al. Clarendon Press, 1888.

Vickers, Brian. *Shakespeare, Co-Author: A Study of Five Collaborative Plays*. Oxford University Press, 2004.

Vickers, Brian. 'Francis Bacon and the Progress of Knowledge'. *Journal of the History of Ideas*, vol. 53, no. 3, 1992, pp. 495–518.

Vickers, Brian. '"The Power of Persuasion": Images of the Orator, Elyot to Shakespeare'. *Renaissance Eloquence. Studies in the Theory and Practice of Renaissance Rhetoric*, edited by J. J. Murphy. University of California Press, 1983, pp. 411–435.

Vitkus, Daniel J. '"The Common Market of All the World": English Theatre, the Global System, and the Ottoman Empire in the Early Modern Period'. *Global Traffic: Discourses and Practices of Trade in English Literature and Culture from 1550 to 1700*, edited by Barbara Sebek and Stephen Deng. Palgrave Macmillan, 2008, pp. 19–37.

Vitkus, Daniel J. *Turning Turk: English Theater and the Multicultural Mediterranean, 1570–1630*. Palgrave Macmillan, 2008.

Vogl, Joseph. *Kalkül und Leidenschaft: Poetik des ökonomischen Menschen*. Sequenzia, 2002.

Walker, Lewis. '*Timon of Athens* and the Morality Tradition'. *Shakespeare Studies*, vol. 12, 1979, pp. 159–177.

Walker, Lewis. 'Fortune and Friendship in *Timon of Athens*'. *Texas Studies in Literature and Language*, vol. 18, no. 4, 1977, pp. 577–600.

Wall, Wendy. *Staging Domesticity: Household Work and English Identity in Early Modern Drama*. Cambridge University Press, 2002.

Wallace, John M. '*Timon of Athens* and the Three Graces: Shakespeare's Senecan Study'. *Modern Philology*, vol. 38, no. 4, 1986, pp. 349–363.

Walsh, P. G. 'Introduction'. *On Obligations [De Officiis]*, edited by Marcus Tullius Cicero. Oxford University Press, 2000, pp. ix–xlvii.

Warley, Christopher. 'Reforming the Reformers: Robert Crowley and Nicholas Udall'. *The Oxford Handbook of Tudor Literature: 1485–1602*, edited by Mike Pincombe and Cathy Shrank. Oxford University Press, 2012, pp. 273–290.

Warren, Christopher N. *Literature and the Law of Nations, 1580–1680*. Oxford University Press, 2015.

Watson, Robert N. 'Introduction'. *Volpone*, by Ben Jonson. Bloomsbury Academic, 2003, pp. vii–xxxiii.

Wayne, Don E. 'Drama and Society in the Age of Jonson: An Alternative View'. *Renaissance Drama*, vol. 13, 1982, pp. 103–129.

Weber, Max. *The Protestant Ethic and the Spirit of Capitalism*. Taylor & Francis Group, 2001.

Weil, Judith. *Service and Dependency in Shakespeare's Plays*. Cambridge University Press, 2005.

Weimann, Robert. *Authority and Representation in Early Modern Discourse*, edited by David Hillman. Johns Hopkins University Press, 1996.

Weimann, Robert. *Shakespeare und die Macht der Mimesis: Autorität und Repräsentation im elisabethanischen Theater*. Aufbau, 1988.

Weimann, Robert. 'History and the Issue of Authority in Representation: The Elizabethan Theater and the Reformation'. *New Literary History*, vol. 17, no. 3, Spring 1986, pp. 449–476. JSTOR, 10.2307/468823.

Wells, Stanley, and Gary Taylor, editors. *William Shakespeare: A Textual Companion. With John Jowett and William Montgomery*. Clarendon Press, 1987.

Wells, Susan. 'Jacobean City Comedy and the Ideology of the City'. *ELH*, vol. 48, no. 1, pp. 37–60.

Werner, Sarah. *Studying Early Printed Books, 1450–1800: A Practical Guide*. Wiley Blackwell, 2019.

Whipday, Emma. 'Everyday Murder and Household Work in Shakespeare's Domestic Tragedies'. *Staged Normality in Shakespeare's England*, edited by Rory Loughnane, and Edel Semple. Palgrave Macmillan, 2019, pp. 215–236.

Wilson, Adrian. *The Making of Man-Midwifery: Childbirth in England, 1660–1770*. University College London Press, 1995.

Wilson, Luke. 'Ben Jonson and the Law of Contract'. *Rhetoric and Law in Early Modern Europe*, edited by Victoria Kahn and Lorna Hutson. Yale University Press, 2001, pp. 143–165.
Wood, Diana. *Medieval Economic Thought*. Cambridge University Press, 2002.
Woodbridge, Linda, editor. *Money and the Age of Shakespeare: Essays in New Economic Criticism*. Palgrave Macmillan, 2003.
Wright, Louis B. *Middle-Class Culture in Elizabethan England*. Methuen & Co. Limited, 1964.
Wrightson, Keith. *English Society 1580–1680*. Routledge, 1995.
Wrightson, Keith. '"Sorts of People" in Tudor and Stuart England'. *The Middling Sort of People: Culture, Society and Politics in England, 1550–1800*, edited by Jonathan Barry and C. W. Brooks. Palgrave Macmillan, 1994, pp. 28–51.
Young, Charles M. 'Aristotle's Justice'. *The Blackwell Guide to Aristotle's Nicomachean Ethics*, edited by Richard Kraut. Blackwell, 2006, pp. 179–197.

Index

For the benefit of digital users, indexed terms that span two pages (e.g., 52–53) may, on occasion, appear on only one of those pages.

A

Agnew, Jean-Christophe, 3–5, 8–9, 11
Alchemist, The (Jonson)
   accumulation in, 136, 144, 145–146, 149, 150
   acquisitive desire in, 143–146, 148–149, 174
   alchemical trope in, 147–151
   dissimulation in, 140–142, 147–148
   domestic authority in, 132–133, 150–151
   emplotment in, 139–142
   female agency in, 133–135
   fortune in, 128, 137–139, 148, 150, 175
   insubstantiality of value in, 76–77
   knowledge and distrust in, 136–138
   master-servant relationship in, 128, 135, 149–151
   mercantile agency in, 128, 131–132, 135–136, 150
   mercantile transformation of the household in, 132–133, 140–141, 149–151
   persuasion in, 140–147
   private interest in, 136, 148, 151, 174, 175
   prudence in, 128, 131, 133, 136, 140–142
   res publica in, 133–134
   rhetorical amplification in, 143–146, 160–161
   service in, 131, 149–151, 175
   tricksters in, 128, 132–135, 137–138, 141–148, 153–154, 160–161, 163, 173–175
   versatility in, 138–142
Aquinas, Thomas, 26–27, 48
   Summa Theologiae, 63–64, 115 n.70
Arden of Faversham, The (anon.), 129–130, 163–164
Aristotle
   on acquisition of wealth, 9, 57–59
   on chrematistics, 9, 35–36, 57–73
   Economics, 34, 133–134
   on household government, 42
   on household management, 9, 34–36, 57–58
   on injustice, 114
   on jealousy and envy, 169–172
   on money, 58, 164–166
   Nicomachean Ethics, 28–30, 34–35, 59–60, 185–186
   on the passions, 30
   on persuasion, 143–144
   Poetics, 7–8, 228–230
   Politics, 9, 28–29, 34, 35–36, 57
   practical philosophy of, 28–29
   on prudence, 16–17, 35
   on reciprocity, 59–60
   Rhetoric, 143–144
   theory of conception, 110–111
   virtue ethics, 30, 34–35, 48, 56–57
assumpsit, action of, 183–188, 212–213, 219–220
audiences
   engagement of, 3–4, 100–101, 103–104 n.56, 107–108, 131, 151–152 n.48, 178, 197–198, 236
   historical, 2–4, 91, 98–100, 111–112, 114, 123–124, 128–129, 138–139 n.29, 141–142, 148, 157–159, 201 n.45, 206–207, 224–225, 237

B

Bacon, Francis
   The Advancement of Learning, 1 n.1, 16–19, 95–96, 135 n.22, 138–139, 143
   on architecture of fortune, 95–96, 176, 215, 234–236
   on business negotiations, 17–19, 130–131, 136–137
   on civil knowledge, 17–19, 107
   on dissimulation, 141–142
   Essay IV, 'Of Simulation and Dissimulation,' 17 n.45
   Essay XIII, 'Of Goodnesse And Goodnesse of Nature,' 17 n.44
   Essay XXI, 'Of Delayes,' 140–141, 234–235 n.4
   Essay XL, 'Of Fortune,' 17 n.45, 135 n.22, 217–219
   Essay XLI, 'Of Usurie,' 76, 203 n.49
   Essay XLVII, 'Of Negociating,' 130–131
   and hermeneutics of suspicion, 137–138
   on rhetoric, 147
   on versatility, 138–139, 219
   wisdom of behaviour, 107

wisdom of business, 1, 16, 95–96, 106–107, 128, 136–137, 176, 234, 236
bill of exchange, 49 n.45., 49–51 n.48., 51, 54–55, 73–75
bodies *see also* women
　female bodies, 21–22, 44–47, 88–89, 93–94, 112–119
　as metaphor for the household, 44–45, 109, 111–112, 129–130
bonds *see also* Timon of Athens
　advent of, 51
　in commerce, 73–74
　forfeiture in, 76
　penal sum in, 75–76
　playhouses financed on, 2–3, 53–54 n.59
　and time, 75–76, 201, 202, 207, 224
Bourne, Immanuel, 36, 62, 65
Browne, John, 11, 26–27, 47–48, 54–55, 69, 100–101
Buchanan, George, 101–102
bullionist and mercantilist writers, 11, 24, 25–26, 47–48, 69, 162–163, 231–232
Burbage, James, 51–52
Burton, Robert, 12, 56, 170 n.102

C
Cecil, Robert, 51–52
Chaste Maid in Cheapside, A (Middleton)
　chrematistic logic in, 80–83, 94–96, 98
　conspicuous consumption in, 86–89
　fortune in, 96, 97
　household space in, 81–89, 84–87, 94–96, 123–125
　lying-in in, 86–89
　marriage in, 84–85, 89–96
　mercantile transformation of the household in, 82–83, 85–89, 94–96, 123–125
　practical rationality in, 82, 96
　pregnancy in, 92–93
　private interest in, 82, 95, 127
　sexuality in, 82–83, 85–89
　social advancement in, 53–54, 79–81, 87–91, 94–96, 125
　zero-sum hypothesis in, 21–22, 96–98
chrematistics *see* Aristotle; *Chaste Maid, A*; commerce; exchange; *Macbeth*; profit; wealth acquisition
Cicero
　on ambition, 114
　cardinal virtues in, 29–30 n.11, 48
　De Amicitia, 206–207, 209–210, 211–212 n.69
　De Officiis, 29–30, 32 n.16, 60–61, 114, 206, 218
　in early modern England, 29–30, 56–57 n.68

on friendship, 206, 209–210
on gifts, 203–204, 207
as mediator of Aristotle, 28
on promising, 185–186, 212, 214
and prudence, 16–17, 115
on reciprocity, 60–61, 203–204, 207–208
and virtue ethics 34, 64–65
city comedies *see also Alchemist, The*; *Chaste Maid in Cheapside, A*; *Volpone*
　exchange in, 230–231
　as genre, 5, 20, 230–232
　juxtaposition with tragedies, 20–22, 230–232
　New Comedy, 20 n.51, 84, 150, 228–229 n.2
　oeconomy in, 21–22, 27–28, 230–232
　as social critique and accommodation, 5
　and socio-economic transformation, 20, 80, 125, 230–231
　trickster figure in *see also Alchemist, The*, 16, 20–21, 219, 226, 230, 232, 234–237
civil knowledge *see* Bacon, Francis
Cleaver, Robert, 10–11, 39, 40, 42, 43 n.33, 44, 46–47, 64–65 n.79, 100–101, 111–112
coins
　in bullionist and mercantilist writings, 69–70, 71 n.88, 162–163
　in culture of credit, 73–75
　devaluation of, 69–70, 165–166
　and female value, 89–90, 163–170
　genealogy of money, 58, 165–166 n.87
　value of, 162–165
commerce *see also* exchange; profit; wealth acquisition
　circulation, 6–7, 84, 95–96, 163–170, 172–173, 222–223
　in culture of credit, 73–77
　financial instruments and, 51
　London as a centre of, 49–53
　persuasion in, 146–147
　as retail trade, 48, 57–59, 63–69
common good
　ethical priority of, 9, 15, 18–19, 26, 48, 77
　merchants and the, 53–57, 64, 72–73, 77
　in tension with private interest, 1–2, 9–10, 18–19, 55–56, 67–68, 72–73, 78, 82–83, 98–101, 114–115, 123, 126, 226–227
consumption
　conspicuous consumption, 51–52, 86–89, 144, 236
　excessive consumption, 77, 146
　at London's exchanges, 51–52
　women and, 46–47, 51–52, 87–89, 163
credit
　culture of credit, 73–77, 114, 176, 177–178, 185–186 n.20, 206–207, 215, 223–225

and gift *see Timon of Athens*
insubstantiality of value in, 51, 76–77, 225
social credit, 17–18 n.46, 132, 143–144, 153–154, 156–159, 162–163, 166–168, 221
temporality of *see Timon of Athens*

D
Defoe, Daniel, 51, 65–66
De Quincey, Thomas, 107–108
dissimulation *see also* Macbeth; Othello
ethical ambiguity of, 68–69, 159–160
as mercantile skill, 64, 68–69, 159
and prudence, 140–142
versus simulation, 64
as social strategy, 11–12, 14–15

E
East India Company, 49–51
education
classical authors in, 28–29 n.6, 29–30 n.11, 56–57 n.68
the family as a school, 38, 41 n.29
social advancement through, 89–91
of women, 31–32, 47, 89–90
efficiency
in business, 4–5, 100–101
in early modern drama, 1, 4, 16, 78, 200, 237
in *Macbeth*, 80, 82, 98–103, 113–115, 124, 127
in oeconomic and mercantile works, 7–8, 14–15, 100–101, 147
Elyot, Sir Thomas, 139–140, 217
emotions
acquisitive desire, 12–13, 59, 143–146, 149, 153–154, 174
in classical writings, 30, 45 n.35, 143–144
cultivating the passions, 30, 116–117, 123
gender and passion, 45, 46 n.39, 46–47, 88–90, 111–113
Iago's manipulations of affect and social credit, 132, 153–154, 162–163
jealousy and envy *see* Aristotle; Othello
the passions as destructive force, 126–127, 172–173, 194–195, 229–230, 232
the passions as motivating force, 80, 116–117, 123–174
pleasure of delay, 188–191
principle of countervailing passions, 30 n.15, 116–117
entrepreneurial characters, 1, 4, 21, 78, 80–81, 100–103, 126–127, 131–132, 136, 147–148, 174, 200, 237
entrepreneurship, 182
ethics

ethical exchange, 60
oeconomy and, 9–10, 79–82, 88–89, 93–96, 98, 100, 123
continuity with oeconomy and politics, 28–29, 38, 229–230
practical wisdom and, 16–18, 35
private interest and, 11–12, 23, 25–26
prudence and, 5, 9–10, 16–17, 34–35
virtue ethics *see* Aristotle; Cicero
exchange *see also* credit; gifts
asychronous, 20–21, 23, 176–179, 181–182, 185–186, 203, 219–220
in the city comedies, 230–231
in culture of credit, 73–77, 176, 223–225
exchange networks, 84, 96, 124–125, 169–170, 222, 230
justice in, 59–61
promise and oral contracts in, 185–188
reciprocity and, 59–61, 66–67, 96–98, 119–122, 203–204
sexuality as an object of, 82–83, 85–87, 89–91, 93–96

F
family
disciplinary function of, 37–42
patriarchal authority in, 37–38, 42–44, 45–47, 99–100, 105, 111–112, 115, 154, 157, 232
women's role in, 42–47, 105, 111–112
Fenner, Dudley, 40, 42, 85
Fitzherbert, John, 10–11, 13–14, 27, 37, 44
Fletcher, John, 46
fortune, *see Timon of Athens*; virtue
Foucault, Michel, 28, 32, 33, 38, 82 n.6

G
gender *see also* Macbeth; marriage; oeconomy; women
and division of labour, 10–11, 25–26, 31–32, 43, 47, 111–112, 155
patriarchal authority, 28 n.5, 37–38, 42–45, 99–100, 111–112, 163, 168, 232
in Xenophon's *Oeconomicus*, 28
gifts *see also* exchange; *Timon of Athens*; *Volpone*
interval between gift and repayment, 20–21, 176–177, 181–185, 196, 203–204, 207, 219–220
as investment, 202–206
moral economy of, 206–212
reciprocity of, 202–206, 208–212, 221, 224
Glasse for Housholders, A (anon.), 43
Globe, 2–3
Gurr, Andrew, 2–3

H

Hesiod, 34, 133–134, 170–172, 203–204, 228
Hervet, Gentian, 10–11, 31–32
Hirschman, Albert O., 12–13, 30 n.15, 114, 116–117
Holinshed, Raphael, 101–102
household *see also* gender; marriage; oeconomy; politics
   as body, 44–45, 129–130
   ancient Greek *oikos*, 9, 28, 31–36
   early modern *oikos*, 36–37
household management *see* oeconomy
Howard, Jean, 2–5, 49–51
husbandry manuals, 1–2, 7–8, 10–11, 13–14, 27–28, 36–37, 77–78, 226
Hutson, Lorna, 31–32, 111–112, 136, 139–140

I

interest *see also* private interest
   revaluation of, 12–16
   usury and, 75–76, 203, 222–223

J

James I, 53–54, 80–81, 102 n.49, 123
joint-stock companies, 24–25, 49–51
Jonson, Ben *see also* Alchemist, The (Jonson); *Volpone* (Jonson)
   Epicoene, 46
   Sejanus, 194–195 n.34, 195

K

Kahn, Victoria, 1 n.1., 11–12, 16–17
knowledge
   civil knowledge, 17–19, 106–107
   prudence and, 136–138
   wisdom of business and, 136–137

L

Latour, Bruno, 3–4, 8 n.25
Leigh, Edward, 128–129, 130–131 n.9
Levant Company, 49–51
luxury goods
   balance of trade and, 71
   excessive desire for, 27–28, 46, 51–52, 88–89 n. 22
   global commerce and, 25–26
   in London, 51–52, 79–80, 83–84

M

Macbeth (Shakespeare)
   accumulation in, 98–99, 121–122, 123
   ambition in, 102–103, 104, 109, 113–114, 116–117, 123, 126
   avarice in, 117–119, 123, 126
   bodily transformation in, 22, 109
   chrematistic logic in, 80–81, 100, 123–124, 126
   dissimulation in, 118–120, 122, 126–127
   dissolution of ethical oeconomy in, 79–81, 88–89, 100–101, 113, 123–124, 126, 229–230
   domestic disorder in, 80–82, 109–112, 228–230
   domestic space in, 81–82, 98–99, 101, 103–108, 124
   female agency in, 21, 80–81, 100, 101–103, 104–107, 109–112, 126–127
   fortune in, 101, 115, 116, 124, 126–7
   future in, 115, 123, 127
   hospitality in, 99, 105–107
   the knocking at the gate in, 107–108, 124
   marriage in, 99–103, 110–112, 116–117, 121, 125
   motivation in, 80, 100–102, 113–114, 116–119
   patrilineal transmission in, 110–111
   political implications of oeconomy in, 80, 82–83, 98–100, 103–105, 107–108, 111–112, 123
   political readings of, 80–81
   practical rationality in, 82, 113–115, 116–117, 118–119
   private interest in, 80, 82–83, 98, 100–101, 106, 113–114, 121–122, 123–124, 126
   reciprocity in, 119–122
Machiavelli, Niccolo
   on dissimulation, 140
   and ethics, 4, 14–15
   La Mandragola, 92
   Machiavellian rhetoric, 11–12
   Machiavellian turn in business matters, 4, 19, 131–132, 173–174
   The Prince, 16–17, 136, 175, 226
   prudence in, 16–17, 136, 139–140
   on versatility, 139
   on *virtù*, 1, 16–17, 19, 174
Malynes, Gerard de, 11, 37–38, 47–48, 69–73
marriage *see also* gender; *Macbeth*; oeconomy; women
   chastity and, 47, 90, 156 n.60, 157 n.61, 162–164, 167
   household management and, 27–28, 31–32, 42–44, 92–93, 111–112, 129–130
   as partnership, 31, 42–44, 105, 129–130, 133–135
   profitable marriage in *A Chaste Maid*, 85–86, 88–93
   in Xenophon's *Oeconomicus*, 31–32, 43–44

INDEX   265

marriage sermons, 27–28, 43–46, 49
Marx, Karl, 59–60 n.73, 188–189, 222–223
Mauss, Marcel, 203–204
mercantile writings *see also* bullionist and mercantilist writers
  audiences for, 49
  balance of trade in, 11, 15–16, 37–38, 70–72, 77, 78, 231–232
  common good in, 55–57, 72–73
  ethics in, 47–49, 61–69
  exchange and reciprocity in, 65–67
  legitimizing trade and profit in, 1, 12, 24, 48–49, 61–66, 66–69, 100–101
  merchant's role in, 53–56, 62, 65–66, 100–101
  national economy in, 48–49, 69, 70–71
  practical knowledge in, 16, 54–55, 61–62, 68–69, 77–78
  value of currency in, 69–71, 73–74
Middleton, Thomas *see also Chaste Maid in Cheapside, A* (Middleton), 76
  A Trick to Catch the Old One, 60–61, 76, 191, 194–195
  Women Beware Women, 46
Milles, Thomas, 11, 47–48, 69, 71
Misselden, Edward, 11, 15–16, 47–48, 69–72, 74–75
More, Sir Thomas, 53–54
Muldrew, Craig, 73–76, 165–166 n.86., 176–178, 185–186, 223–225
Mun, Thomas, 11, 15–16, 47–48, 69–71, 222–223

N
New Exchange, 51–52

O
Oeconomicus (Xenophon), 10, 28, 31–34, 43
oeconomy/oeconomics *see also* household; marriage; women; Xenophon
  agrarian, 1–2, 10–11, 33, 36–37
  Aristotelian, 9, 30, 34
  commerce and, 8, 22–23, 25–26, 51–52, 77, 79–80, 98–99, 105, 107–108, 159, 228
  division of labour in, 10–11, 25–26, 31–32, 43, 123–124, 155, 234
  early modern, 27, 228
  ethics in, 9–12, 14–15, 30, 35–37, 79–80, 226
  etymology of, 1–2, 9, 24
  family and, 37
  husbandry manuals, 7–8, 10–14, 27, 36–37, 77–78
  and lineage, 87, 93
  marital harmony in, 43–44, 129–130

  politics and, 32–34, 38–42, 105–108, 123, 228–229
  prescriptive nature of, 6
  prudence in, 16, 18–19
  and Reformation, 10–11, 24, 27, 31, 42, 111–112
  socio-economic problems in, 27–28
  in theatre, 1–2, 6–8, 12, 27–28, 79–80, 226–228
  thrift in, 9–11, 13–14, 25–26 n.2, 31, 36, 44, 78, 130–131 n.9
  translations of, 10–11, 31–34
  wealth acquisition and, 35–36, 41–42, 48–49, 57–58
  in Xenophon's *Oeconomicus*, 31
oikos see household; oeconomy
Othello (Shakespeare)
  dissimulation in, 159–162
  female agency in, 156–158
  female virtue and value in, 153–154, 156–158, 162–169
  fortune in, 155, 174, 175
  Iago as self-interested servant, 130–132, 151–156, 174–175
  Iago's manipulations of affect and social credit, 132, 153–156, 162–163
  intrinsic vs extrinsic value in, 132, 162–168
  jealousy and envy in, 132, 161–162, 169–173, 173–174
  mercantile agency in, 153–155
  merging of the military and the domestic in, 131, 142, 151–152
  Othello's military value, 168–169
  persuasion in, 159–162
  practical rationality in, 151, 153
  private interest in, 174–175
  redistribution of wealth in, 152–153, 174
  rhetorical amplification, 160
  social mobility in, 158–159, 169, 171–173
  transnational travel and, 155–159, 161–162
  Vice figure in, 131 n.12, 171
Ovid, 190

P
Parker, Patricia, 142 n.36, 154–155, 160–161, 178, 189–190
passions *see* emotions
Peacham, Henry, 143–145, 161–162
Perkins, William, 10–11, 26–27, 39, 42–43, 48, 61–62, 64–66, 69, 99–101, 105
Plato, 30
Pocock, J. G. A., 1, 7–8, 115, 174–175, 176–177 n.3, 217
political economy, 8 n.25, 11 n.32, 15–16, 24

politics *see also* oeconomy
  household and, 32–34, 37–42, 80, 82–83, 103–108, 111–112, 123, 230
  political discourse in *The Alchemist*, 133–134
practical wisdom *see* prudence
private interest *see also* common good; interest; prudence
  in early modern writings, 26, 69–70, 72–73
  ethics and, 11–12, 23, 25–26
  as excessive and rational, 12–15
  practical wisdom in service of, 9–10, 15–16, 18–19
  revaluation of, 1, 4, 12–13, 15–16, 18–19
  self-interested servants, 128
  on the stage, 1, 4–5, 8, 12–13, 35, 78, 82–83, 94, 114–117, 122, 123, 126–127, 135–136, 148, 174–175, 226–227, 234, 237
profit *see also* wealth acquisition
  in agriculture, 10–11, 13–14, 36–37
  in husbandry manuals, 1–2, 14–15, 36–37
  legitimate profit, 10–11 n.30, 13–16, 36, 66–69
  in mercantile writings, 1–2, 12, 14–15, 24, 48–49, 61–62, 66–69, 100–101
projects, 27–28, 182
Protestant writings *see also* Cleaver, Robert; Perkins, William, 11, 14–15, 36, 44, 61–62, 71, 99–101, 116–117
prudence *see also* Aristotle
  in advice literature, 15–16
  aspects of, 115, 136, 142
  Bacon's wisdom of business, 16
  ethics and, 5, 9–10, 16–18, 34–35
  military prudence, 136–142
  as profitable and pragmatic faculty, 1–2, 5, 9–10, 15–16, 18–19, 131–132, 136
  in servants, 130–131
  temporality of, 115
  transformation of, 16, 147–148

R
rhetoric
  amplification, 143–147, 160–161, 184–185, 189–190
  commonplaces, 137–138, 147, 161–162
  dilation *see also Volpone*, 178, 189–190 n.26, 196
  Iago's rhetorical skills, 159–162
  Machiavellian rhetoric, 11–14
  in the marketplace, 146–147, 159
  persuasion, 140, 143, 146–148, 182–186
Royal Exchange, 25–26, 51–52

S
Scott, William, 11, 26–27, 47–48, 66, 69, 100–101, 236
self-interest *see* private interest
Seneca, 207, 209–211
servants *see also The Alchemist*; *Othello*; *Volpone*
  early modern meaning of service, 128–129
  figure of insubordinate servant, 129–130
  as intermediaries, 130–131
  master-servant relationships, 128–133, 135–136, 141–142, 149–152, 154–156, 158–159, 170–177, 195, 213–214, 232, 234
  prudent servants, 130–131
  self-interested servants, 128, 130–131, 135–136, 153, 155
Shakespeare, William *see also Macbeth*; *Othello*; *Timon of Athens*; tragedies, 2–3 n.6
  comedies, 5 n.18, 20–21, 218
  Hamlet, 178 n.5, 212–213, 228–229
  Merchant of Venice, The, 20–22 n.54., 176, 191 n.29, 218
  Twelfth Night, 218
Sidney, Sir Philip, 138–139 n.29, 180–181, 203, 228–229
Smith, Adam, 4, 8 n.25, 12–13, 15–16, 24–25, 30 n.15, 116–117, 174, 194–195
social mobility
  affective framework of, 6–7, 132
  discontents of, 232
  drama and, 6–7, 20, 24–25, 148 n.43, 219
  servants and, 128–130, 150, 158–159, 174, 234
  transnational travel and, 155
socio-economic praxis, 1–2, 10–11, 24–26
Stow, John, 51–52, 165–166
Stubbes, Philip, 3
sufficiency
  in business, 59, 61, 64–65, 138–139
  dissolution of idea, 9–10
  in oeconomy, 8–10, 37, 48–49, 57, 100, 126, 229–230

T
Tamer Tamed, The (Fletcher), 46
Tawney, R. H., 13–14 n.37, 14–15, 79–80 n.1
theatre *see also* audiences
  commercial, 2–3, 23, 24–25, 51–52, 200–201
  and the culture of credit, 53–54 n.59
  explorations of economic practices and values, 1–4, 6, 16, 23, 26, 79–80

the household in, 1–2, 27–28, 79–80, 226, 228, 237
popular appeal of, 3–4
contrast with prescriptive literature, 6, 79–80, 123–124, 226–228
props and scenery in, 103–106, 124
socio-cultural function of, 3–5
Tilney, Edmund, 156–158, 169–170
time *see also* assumpsit; gift; credit
  dilated exchange, 176–179, 185–188, 215, 222–224, 228, 231–232
  dilation, 178
  dilatory plot structures, 178–179, 181, 196–201, 219–222, 223–224, 237
  working time in credit culture, 178, 223–224
Timon of Athens
  bonds in, 202, 203, 207, 212–215, 220, 224–225, 235
  credit and gift in, 179, 201–202, 203, 207, 212–215, 219–220, 222–225
  dilatory plot structure in, 178, 219–220, 223–224
  false friends in, 206–207, 214–215, 217–219, 221
  fortune in, 215–219, 222
  friendship and gift in, 206–212, 220–221
  futurity of recompense in, 202, 212–215, 220–221
  gift as investment in, 201–202, 206–207
  gift as model of dilated exchange in, 20, 176–177, 201, 203–204, 222–223
  gold in, 188–189, 220, 221–222
  the household in, 176–177, 201, 222
  imprudence in, 214, 217
  insubstantiality of credit in, 76–77, 225
  prodigal spending versus acquisition in, 179, 201, 204, 206
  promising in, 212–215, 223–225
  reciprocity in, 204–205, 208, 211–212, 221, 223–225
  self-interest in, 206, 207, 217, 219, 220 n.81, 221, 225 n.85
  temporality of credit in, 176–179, 201–202, 203, 212, 213–214
  Timon's gift-giving, 207–212, 220–221
  zero-sum logic in, 204
  virtus vs fortune in, 217
  wealth acquisition in, 176–177, 179, 201
tragedies *see also* Macbeth; Othello; *Timon of Athens*
  ambiguity of, 21
  contrasted with city comedies, 20–21, 228–235
  economic criticism of, 20–22

ethical problems in, 229–230
the household in, 27–28, 228–231
individual desires and social possibilities, 232–233
trading companies, 2–3, 49 n.45, 49–51 n.49, 52–53 n.59
Tusser, Thomas, 10–11, 27, 32, 36, 37, 43–44, 73–74, 130–131 n.9

U
usury *see* interest

V
value
  accrual of, 176–177, 202–203, 222–223
  Aristotle on monetary value, 58–59, 60, 164–165
  of chastity, 85–86, 89–90, 163–164
  circulation of, 163–167, 222–223
  of currency in mercantile writings, 11, 70–71, 73–74
  debasement of, 162–169, 165–167
  exchange value, 88–89, 162–163, 166–169, 229–230
  fair exchange of, 59–61, 63–64, 66
  of female virtue, 89–90, 153–158, 162–169
  of information, 138
  instability of, 26–27, 51, 76–78, 225
  intrinsic vs extrinsic, 74–75, 132, 157, 162–169
  and personal worth, 162–169, 172
  of reputation, 75, 156–157, 166–167
virtue *see also* prudence
  fortitude, 29–30 n.11, 115 n.71, 217
  fortune and, 115 n.71, 174–175, 216–218
  justice, 34, 48, 59–61, 63–67, 114, 203–204, 222
  moderation, 1–2, 9, 36, 37, 45–47, 54–55, 78, 79–80, 85–86, 100, 102, 126–127, 226
  temperance, 34–35, 46–48, 59, 117–118
  thrift, 9–11, 13–14 n.39, 25–26 n.2, 31, 32 n.16, 36, 44, 78, 130 n.9, 226
  virtù, 1, 16–17, 19, 113, 126–127, 174–175
  virtue ethics, 30, 34–36, 48
Volpone (Jonson)
  accumulation in, 176–177, 193, 195, 201
  economies of wealth and pleasure in, 178–179, 192–193, 195–196
  dilated exchange in, 176–179, 183–188, 189–190
  dilatory plot structure of, 178–179, 196–201, 223–224
  fortune in, 177–178, 181–182, 197–198, 200, 223

futurity of recompense in, 183–188
gift economy in, 178–179, 181–183, 222–223
the household in, 176–177, 179–180, 183, 222
insubstantiality of credit relations, 76–77, 176, 222, 225, 234–235
pleasure of delay in, 188–191, 223–224
promising in, 181–183, 183–188
prudence in, 183
rhetoric, 183–186, 184–186, 189–190, 198, 199–200
rhetorical amplification in, 184, 189–190
self-aggrandizement in, 177, 179, 191–196, 199, 226
self-interest in, 177, 181, 194, 196
temporality of the gift in, 181–183
wit in, 193–195, 198–200
wealth acquisition in, 79–80, 176–177, 182, 184–185, 192–196, 201

W

wealth acquisition *see also Alchemist, The*; *Chaste Maid in Cheapside, A*; commerce; oeconomy; private interest; profit; *Timon of Athens*; *Volpone*
acquisitive desire, 12–13, 16, 78, 88–89, 143–146, 148–149, 153–154, 174, 187–190, 192–193, 205–206, 224, 227, 231–232
Christian ethics and, 48–49, 62–65, 188–189
covetousness, 48, 58–59, 64, 65, 67–68, 117–118, 170, 179–180, 188–189
household management and, 35–37, 41–42, 48–49, 57–59

rhetorical amplification and, 143–146, 184–185, 189–190
social advancement and, 2–3, 36, 79–80, 132, 226–227
sufficiency and, 9, 37, 48–49, 59, 64–65, 126
Weber, Max, 14–15 n.40.
Weber-Tawney thesis, 14–15
Wheeler, John, 11, 47–48, 55–56, 69–72, 146–147
Wilkinson, Robert, 25–26 n.2, 42 n.32, 43–46, 54–55 n.64, 55–56 n.65
Wilson, Thomas, 143–145, 146 n.77, 184
women *see also Alchemist, The*; exchange; gender; *Macbeth*; marriage; oeconomy; *Othello*
chastity of, 46–47, 89–90, 162–164, 167
consumption and, 46–47, 51–52, 77, 78, 86–89, 163
education of, 31–32, 47, 89–90
female bodies, 44–47, 88–89, 93–95, 109–112
gossip and gossiping, 46–47, 86–89 n.23
as housewives, 31–32, 42–47, 104–105, 156–158
lying-in, 86–89, 236
public display of, 85–86
reversal of gender roles, 109, 111–112, 125, 133–135

X

Xenophon, 10–11, 28, 30, 31–34, 39, 43–44, 83, 228